Paternalism

The University of Minnesota Press
gratefully acknowledges assistance provided
by the McKnight Foundation
for publication of this book.

PATERNALISM

Rolf Sartorius
Editor

University of Minnesota Press □ Minneapolis

Library of Congress Cataloging in Publication Data

Main entry under title:
Paternalism.
  Bibliography: p.
  Includes index.
  1. Paternalism—Addresses, essays, lectures.
2. Individualism—Addresses, essays, lectures.
3. Liberty—Addresses, essays, lectures. I. Sartorius,
Rolf E.
JC571.P3 1983   320.5'12   83-1089
ISBN 0-8166-1172-6
ISBN 0-8166-1174-2 (pbk.)

The University of Minnesota is an equal-opportunity educator and employer.

Preface

The papers contained in this volume were all authored by scholars who were among the twenty-two participants in a conference on paternalism that it was my pleasure to direct at Lutsen, Minnesota, during a four-day period in September, 1980. The papers contained in Part I had been previously published; those contained in Part II were prepared for the conference.

I would like to thank Richard Wasserstrom for so expertly moderating the sessions at which the papers were discussed.

The conference was made possible by the generous support of the Liberty Fund, Inc., of Indianapolis, Indiana, whose Executive Director, Kenneth Templeton, Jr., provided me with invaluable advice and assistance in all stages of its planning.

Finally, I would like to thank the management and the staff of the Lutsen Resort for the organizational assistance and excellent services that they provided.

R. S.

Contents

Introduction

Rolf Sartorius

Originally published in 1859, John Stuart Mill's essay *On Liberty* is devoted to the defense of

one very simple principle, as entitled to govern absolutely the dealings of society with the individual in the way of compulsion and control . . . . That principle is, that the sole end for which mankind are warranted, individually or collectively, in interfering with the liberty of action of any one of their number, is self-protection. That the only purpose for which power can be rightfully exercised over any member of a civilized community, against his will, is to prevent harm to others. His own good, either physical or moral, is not a sufficient warrant.[1]

Over a hundred years of continuous controversy have established at least one thing beyond any doubt: The anti-paternalist principle that Mill so passionately defended in *On Liberty* is anything but "simple." There are difficulties in interpreting the principle, in reconciling it with Mill's general utilitarian position, and in defending it under any particular interpretation. The essays collected in this volume well represent the shape that philosophical discussions of paternalism have taken in the past decade or so. As they clarify, so do they perplex. The issues are numerous and complex, and debate is sure to continue to surround them as long as some people believe that they are justified in interfering with others' liberty in the name of promoting their (the paternalized's) own welfare. Rather than attempt to summarize the contributions to this volume, I shall, by way of introduction, simply seek to highlight the basic questions that they address and in turn challenge others to try to answer.

What is it that we are talking about? The range of examples of what would ordinarily be taken to constitute forms of intervention, the primary or at least a chief putative justification for which is paternalistic, is vast. It includes entire systems of human relationships as traditionally conceived, for example, the parent-child relationship. It characterizes the physician-patient relationship to a considerable degree. It lies at the foundation of controversial bodies of regulatory law, as in occupational health and safety regulations. It is a driving force behind extensive legal practices that are seriously invasive of individual liberty, as with involuntary commitment of the mentally ill on the grounds of danger to self. According to Herbert Morris's account, we must recognize paternalistic justifications for punishment as well. By way of specific examples of controversial prohibitions of the criminal law, we are reminded of Mill's perceptive comment that either the individual's physical or moral good may be put forward as a warrant for paternalistic intervention. Consider laws prohibiting prostitution (taken by many to be a form of mutual noncoercive exploitation, as discussed in Feinberg's "Noncoercive Exploitation"), laws prohibiting gambling (which some states profitably monopolize), laws concerning drug use (which turned a whole generation of American youth into criminals), and laws regulating pornography (which, as with other of these examples, may represent legal moralism working in tandem with legal paternalism).

Is there one definition of paternalism capable of including such a great diversity of cases? Gerald Dworkin's "Second Thoughts" on this question, prompted in part by cases discussed in Allen Buchanan's "Medical Paternalism," suggest that there may be difficulties in providing one. As suggested by the theme of one of Wikler's papers, when does persuasion (attempts at which Mill believed permissible) leave off and coercion begin? And just what constitutes interference with individual liberty? If A withholds information from B that, if B had it, would cause B to choose differently than B will without it, has A interfered with B's liberty? Indeed, as suggested by Buchanan's discussion of the *severely* retarded in his "The Limits of Proxy Decision-Making," it may be that some of the prime candidates for paternalistic treatment can't even be described as having a "liberty of action" to be interfered with. That there may be room for controversy as to which individuals are capable of truly voluntary and rational choice is a separate point well made in Wikler's discussion of the *mildly* retarded.

Virtually everyone would agree that there are instances in which paternalism is justified and instances in which it is not. Even Mill recognized children and "the uncivilized" as proper objects of paternalistic intervention. When disagreement arises over particular cases, it may be understood as being rooted in one (or more) of the following sources.

As the exchange between Dahl and Brock makes clear, different theories may incorporate quite different conceptions of the individual's good, this in turn generating different accounts of when freedom of choice has genuine value (however, its value is to be represented by the principles that different theories might contain).

Different theories of the individual, as opposed to theories of an individual's good, may generate very different results when attached to a principle like Mill's. Donald Regan's essay, which begins with arguments that would support an anti-paternalistic position, develops a view of personal identity that suggests that for certain moral purposes different stages of the same self may be treated as different persons, thus providing a foundation for claiming that, in preventing an individual from harming a later self, one is merely (as Mill would permit) preventing harm to another. Thus does moral philosophy lead to metaphysics.

Disagreements of principle are perhaps the most significant source of controversy. As a matter of principle, as a question of what it would be permissible for an ideal moral agent acting with perfect knowledge to do, the act-utilitarian— who would evaluate the rightness or wrongness of particular acts on the basis of the consequences for the general welfare of performing them—has no basis whatsoever for objecting to paternalism. As James Fitzjames Stephen put it in his attack upon Mill one hundred years ago:

> If . . . the object aimed at is good, if the compulsion employed is such as to attain it, and if the good obtained overbalances the inconvenience of the compulsion itself, I do not understand how, upon utilitarian principles, the complusion can be bad.[2]

As a matter of principle, it is only a libertarian such as Robert Nozick, adopting the view that coercion may only be permissibly employed to prevent people from violating the rights of others,[3] who is in a position to defend an absolute prohibition on paternalistic intervention of the sort that Mill so boldly proclaimed. Intermediate principles are adopted by Feinberg and Dworkin in their original contributions, both agreeing that paternalism is normally objectionable because it violates an independent moral right that people have to be free to act as they choose (as long as they're not harming others), unless they are not capable of acting in a fully voluntary (Feinberg) or rational (Dworkin) manner.

To be sharply distinguished from disagreements over matters of principle are disagreements over what might be called matters of policy. Given a principle that would permit paternalistic intervention only under certain conditions, one might argue that an attempt to implement the principle as a matter of policy—due to human fallibility in the real world of practice—would lead to the principle being more often violated than not. When this is the case, there is a good argument against specific forms of paternalism. In my own contribution to this volume, I contend that what Mill described as the ''strongest of all the arguments against the interference of the public with purely personal conduct'' is of just this sort, and that is applies in particular with great force against present policies concerning involuntary civil commitment on paternalistic grounds. For a utilitarian, the policy argument will be put in terms of the consequences for the paternalized in terms of their general well-being or happiness. For a rights-based theorist, such as Feinberg or Dworkin, the policy argument will be cast in terms of unjustifiable violations of an individual right to liberty of action. Although they will thus rely on different principles, both will be policy arguments of the same (consequentialist) form.

Policy arguments against specific forms of paternalism are available to both rights-based theorists and utilitarians, and the latter are by virtue of their underlying moral principle committed to following where they lead. Rights-based theorists, I suggest, should appeal to them only with extreme caution. For, although they may lead to desired results as applied to some paternalistic practices, they may, as must utilitarian policy arguments, lead to quite unhappy results when applied to other practices. Such policy arguments are consequentialist in character and, as with their utilitarian kin, look only to the maximization of some value in the aggregate—in this case, genuine freedom, let us say. But being totally oblivious to distributional considerations, except insofar as they are causally relevant, such a "utilitarianism of rights" (as Nozick has called it[4]) is subject to essentially the same objection that has motivated many to move away from utilitarianism to rights-based theories in the first place: it may permit (indeed, require) the sacrifice of some in the name of the promotion of the welfare of the many. Paternalistic practices may succeed in preventing the majority of those who come within their clutches from irrationally or involuntarily harming themselves; their rights, on an account like Feinberg's or Dworkin's, are surely not violated. But what of those who will inevitably be *mistakenly* identified as proper candidates for paternalistic treatment? Their rights will have been violated. And, unless one adopts the view that proper candidates for paternalistic treatment have a right (a "welfare right"?) to be paternalized, this implies an important asymmetry. With respect to virtually all paternalistic policies that are of interest, adopting them is virtually certain to require violating the rights of some, whereas failure to adopt them can be argued to violate the rights of none. If, as many recent writers have urged, rights are to be taken seriously,[5] and if taking them seriously requires treating them as side constraints on the morally permissible use of coercion against others,[6] recognition of a right to liberty of action may require the rejection of virtually all the coercive forms of paternalism that our society has adopted. Indeed, if proper candidates for paternalistic treatment can claim no right to it, paternalistic public policies financed through coercive taxation may be condemned on independent grounds. That (as Douglas's essay suggests) paternalistic practices may fit in more comfortably with the underlying political morality of societies quite different from our own is more, rather than less, reason to subject them to close moral scrutiny. Although it is likely that each of the different contributions to this volume will do different things for different readers, I hope that in combination they will for each reader both encourage and inform the kind of rethinking of paternalism that I believe is called for by the recent philosophical and political concern with basic moral rights.

Notes

1. John Stuart Mill, *On Liberty* (Indianapolis, IN: Bobbs-Merrill, Inc., 1956), p.13.
2. James Fitzjames Stephen, *Liberty, Equality, Fraternity,* originally published 1882, reprinted in part in *Limits of Liberty,* ed. P. Radcliff (Belmont, CA: Wadsworth Publishing Co., 1966). Quotation from p.51 of the latter.
3. Robert Nozick, *Anarchy, State and Utopia* (New York: Basic Books, Inc., 1974), p.14.
4. *Ibid.,* p. 28.
5. See Ronald Dworkin, *Taking Rights Seriously* (Cambridge, MA: Harvard University Press, 1977).
6. Nozick, *Anarchy, State and Utopia,* Ch. 3.

Part I

Chapter 1

Legal Paternalism

Joel Feinberg

The principle of legal paternalism justifies state coercion to protect individuals from self-inflicted harm or, in its extreme version, to guide them, whether they like it or not, toward their own good. Parents can be expected to justify their interference in the lives of their children (e.g., telling them what they must eat and when they must sleep) on the ground that "We know best." Legal paternalism seems to imply that since the state often can know the interests of individual citizens better than the citizens know them themselves, it stands as a permanent guardian of those interests *in loco parentis*. Put in this blunt way, paternalism seems a preposterous doctrine. If adults are treated as children they will come in time to be like children. Deprived of the right to choose for themselves, they will soon lose the power of rational judgment and decision. Even children, after a certain point, had better not be treated as children; otherwise they will never acquire the outlook and capability of responsible adults.

Yet if we reject paternalism entirely, and deny that a person's own good is *ever* a valid ground for coercion, we seem to fly in the face of both common sense and our long established customs and laws. In the criminal law, for example, a prospective victim's freely granted consent is no defense to the charge of mayhem or homicide. The state simply refuses to permit people to agree to their own disablement or killing. The law of contracts, similarly, refuses to recognize as valid contracts to sell oneself into slavery, or to become a mistress, or to enter a bigamous marriage. Any ordinary citizen is legally justified in using reasonable

Joel Feinberg, "Legal Paternalism," *Canadian Journal of Philosophy* 1, no. 1, pp. 106-24. Copyright © 1971 by the Canadian Association for Publishing in Philosophy. Reprinted with permission. Also, presented as the Phi Beta Kappa lecture at Franklin and Marshall College, 1970; to the Pacific Division of the American Philosophical Association, April 1970; to the Summer Workshop at the Catholic University of America, June, 1970; and to "Philosopher's Holiday" at Vassar College, November 1970.

force to prevent another's self-mutilation or suicide. No one is allowed to purchase certain drugs, even for therapeutic purposes, without a physician's prescription ("Doctor knows best"). The use of other drugs, such as heroin, merely for pleasure is permitted under no circumstances whatever. It is hard to find any plausible rationale for such restrictions apart from the arguments that beatings, mutilations, and death, concubinage, slavery, and bigamy are always bad for a person, whether he or she knows it or not, and that antibiotics are too dangerous for any non-expert, and heroin for anyone at all, to take on his or her own initiative.

The trick to stopping short once we undertake this path, unless we wish to ban whiskey, cigarettes, and fried foods, which tend to be bad for people too, whether they know it or not. The problem is to reconcile somehow our general repugnance for paternalism with the apparent necessity, or at least the reasonableness, of some paternalistic regulations. My method of dealing with this problem will not be particularly ideological. Rather, I shall try to organize our elementary intuitions by finding a principle that will render them consistent. Let us begin, then, by rejecting the views both that the protection of people from themselves is *always* a valid ground for interference in their affairs, and that it is *never* a valid ground. It follows that it is a valid ground only under certain conditions, and we must now try to state those conditions.[1]

I

It will be useful to make some preliminary distinctions. The first distinction is between harms or likely harms that are produced directly by people upon themselves and those produced by the actions of another person to which the first party has consented. Committing suicide would be an example of self-inflicted harm; arranging for a person to put one out of one's misery would be an example of a harm inflicted by the action of another to which one has consented. There is a venerable legal maxim traceable to Roman Law, *"Volenti non fit injuria,"* that is sometimes translated misleadingly as: "To one who consents no harm is done." I suppose that the notion of consent applies, strictly speaking, only to the actions of another person that affect oneself. If so, then, consent to one's *own* actions is a kind of metaphor. Indeed, to say that I consented to my own actions seems just a colorful way of saying that I acted voluntarily. My involuntary actions, after all, are, from the moral point of view, no different from the actions of someone else to which I have not had an opportunity to consent. In any case, it seems plainly false to say that people cannot be *harmed* by actions, whether their own or those of another, to which they have consented. People who quite voluntarily eat an amount that is in fact too much cause themselves to suffer from indigestion; and women who consent to advances sometimes become pregnant.

One way of interpreting the *Volenti* maxim is to take it as a kind of presumptive principle. People do not generally consent to what they believe will be, on balance, harmful to themselves and, by and large, individuals are in a better position to appraise risks to themselves than are outsiders. Given these data, and considering convenience in the administration of the law, the *Volenti* maxim might be understood to say that for the purposes of the law (whatever the actual facts might be) nothing is to count as harm to a given person that he or she has freely consented to. If this presumption is held to be conclusive, then the *Volenti* maxim becomes a kind of "legal fiction" when applied to cases of undeniable harm resulting from behavior to which the harmed one freely consented. A much more likely interpretation, however, takes the *Volenti* maxim to say nothing at all, literal or fictional, about *harms*. Rather, it is about what used to be called injuries, that is, injustices or wrongs. To one who freely consents to a thing no *wrong* is done, no matter how harmful to him the consequences may be. "He cannot waive his right," says Salmond, "and then complain of its infringement."[2] If the *Volenti* maxim is simply an expression of Salmond's insight, it is not a presumptive or fictional principle about harms, but rather an absolute principle about wrongs.

The *Volenti* maxim (or something very like it) plays a key role in the argument for John Stuart Mill's doctrine about liberty. Characteristically, Mill seems to employ the maxim in both of its interpretations, as it suits his purposes, without noticing the distinction between them. On the one hand, Mill's argument purports to be an elaborate application of the calculus of harms and benefits to the problem of political liberty. The state can rightly restrain those who wish to harm others. Why then can it not restrain those who wish to harm themselves? After all, a harm is a harm whatever its cause and if our sole concern is to minimize harms all round, why should we distinguish between origins of harm? One way Mill answers this question is to employ the *Volenti* maxim in its first interpretation. For the purposes of his argument, he will presume conclusively that "to one who consents no *harm* is done." Self-inflicted or consented-to harm simply is not to count as harm at all; and the reasons for this are that the coercion required to prevent such harm is itself a harm of such gravity that it is likely in the overwhelming proportion of cases to outweigh any good it can produce for the one coerced; moreover, individuals themselves, in the overwhelming proportion of cases, can know their own true interests better than any outsiders can, so that outside coercion is almost certain to be self-defeating.

But as Gerald Dworkin has pointed out,[3] arguments of this merely statistical kind create at best a strong but rebuttable presumption against coercion of people in their own interests. Yet Mill purports to be arguing for an absolute prohibition. Absolute prohibitions are hard to defend on purely utilitarian grounds, so Mill, when his confidence wanes, tends to move to the second interpretation of the *Volenti* maxim. People can be harmed by what they consent to, but they cannot be wronged; and Mill's "harm principle," reinterpreted accordingly, is designed to protect people only from wrongful invasions of their interest. Moreover, when the state intervenes on any other ground, its own intervention is a wrongful invasion. What justifies the absolute prohibition of interference in primarily self-regarding affairs is *not* that such interference is self-defeating and likely (merely likely) to cause more harm than it prevents, but rather that it would itself be an injustice, a wrong, a violation of the private sanctuary which is every person's self; and this is so whatever the calculus of harms and benefits might show.[4]

The second distinction is between those cases in which people directly produce harm to themselves, where the harm is the certain upshot of their conduct and its desired end, on the one hand, and those cases in which people simply create a *risk* of harm to themselves in the course of activities directed toward other ends. The woman who knowingly swallows a lethal dose of arsenic will certainly die, and death must be imputed to her as her goal in acting. A man is offended by the sight of his left hand, so he grasps an ax in his right hand and chops off his left hand. He does not thereby "endanger" his interest in the physical integrity of his limbs or "risk" the loss of his hand. He brings about the loss directly and deliberately. On the other hand, to smoke cigarettes or to drive at excessive speeds is not to harm oneself directly, but rather to increase beyond a normal level the probability that harm to oneself will result.

The third distinction is between reasonable and unreasonable risks. There is no form of activity (or inactivity either for that matter) that does not involve some risks. On some occasions we have a choice between more and less risky actions and prudence dictates that we take the less dangerous course; but what is called "prudence" is not always reasonable. Sometimes it is more reasonable to assume a great risk for a great gain than to play it safe and forfeit a unique opportunity. Thus it is not necessarily more reasonable for a coronary patient to increase life expectancy by living a life of quiet inactivity than to continue working hard at a career in the hope of achieving something important even at the risk of a sudden fatal heart attack at any moment. There is no simple mathematical formula to guide one in making such decisions or in judging them "reasonable" or "unreasonable." On the other hand, there are other decisions that are manifestly unreasonable. It is unreasonable to drive at sixty miles an hour through a twenty-mile-an-hour zone in order to arrive at a party on time, but may be reasonable to drive fifty miles an hour to get a seriously ill person to the hospital. It is foolish to resist an armed robber in an effort to protect one's wallet, but it may be worth a desperate lunge to protect one's very life, or the life of a loved one.

In all these cases a number of distinct considerations are involved.[5] If there is time to deliberate one should consider: (1) the degree of probability that harm to oneself will result from a given course of action; (2) the seriousness of the harm being risked, i.e., the value or importance of that which is exposed to the risk; (3) the degree of probability that the goal inclining one to shoulder the risk will in fact result from the course of action; (4) the value or importance of achieving that goal, that is, just how worthwhile it is to one (this is the intimately personal factor, requiring a decision about one's own preferences, that makes the reasonableness of a risk-assessment on the whole so difficult for the *outsider* to make); and (5) the necessity of the risk, that is, the availability or absence of alternative, less risky, means to the desired goal. Certain judgments about the reasonableness of risk-assumptions are quite uncontroversial. We can say, for example, that the *greater* the probability of harm to self (1) and the magnitude of the harm risked (2), the *less* reasonable the risk; and the *greater* the probability the desired goal will result (3), the importance of the goal to the doer (4), and the necessity of the means (5), the *more* reasonable the risk. But in a given difficult case, even where questions of probability are meaningful and beyond dispute, and where all the relevant facts are known, the risk-decision may defy objective assessment because of its component personal value judgments. In any case, if the state is to be given the right to prevent individuals from risking harm to themselves (and only themselves) this must be not only on the ground that the prohibited action is highly risky, but also on the ground that, in respect to its objectively assessable components, it is manifestly unreasonable. There are, sometimes, very good reasons for regarding even a person's judgment of personal worthwhileness (consideration 4) to be "manifestly unreasonable," but it remains to be seen whether (or when) that kind of unreasonableness can be sufficient grounds for interference.

The fourth and final distinction is between fully voluntary and not fully voluntary assumptions of a risk. One assumes a risk in a fully voluntary way when one shoulders it while fully informed of all relevant facts and contingencies, with one's eyes wide open, so to speak, and in the absence of all coercive pressure. There must be calmness and deliberateness, no distracting or unsettling emotions, no neurotic compulsion, no misunderstanding. To whatever extent there is compulsion, misinformation, excitement or impetuousness, clouded judgment (as from alcohol), or immature or defective faculties of reasoning, to that extent the choice falls short of perfect voluntariness. Voluntariness then is a matter of degree. One's "choice" is *completely involuntary* when it is no choice at all, properly speaking—when one lacks all muscular control of one's movements; or when one is knocked down, or pushed, or sent reeling by a blow, or a wind, or an explosion; or when through ignorance one chooses something other than what one means to choose, as when one thinks the arsenic powder is table salt, and thus chooses to sprinkle it on one's scrambled eggs. Most harmful choices, like most choices generally, fall somewhere between the extremes of perfect voluntariness and complete involuntariness.

The terms voluntary and involuntary have a variety of disparate but overlapping uses in philosophy, law, and ordinary life, and some of them are not altogether clear. I should point out here that my usage does not correspond with that of Aristotle, who allowed that infants, animals, drunkards, and people in a towering rage might yet act voluntarily if only they are undeceived and not overwhelmed by external physical force. What I call a voluntary assumption of risk corresponds more closely to what Aristotle called "deliberate choice." Implusive and emotional actions, and those of animals and infants are voluntary in Aristotle's sense, but they are not *chosen*. Chosen actions are those that are decided upon by *deliberation,* and that is a process that requires time, information, a clear head, and highly developed rational faculties. When I use such phrases as "voluntary act," "free and genuine consent," and so on, I refer to acts that are more than "voluntary" in the Aristotelian sense, acts that Aristotle himself would call "deliberately chosen." Such acts not only have their origin "in the agent," they also represent the agent faithfully in some important way: they express his or her settled values and preferences. In the fullest sense, therefore, they are actions for which the agent can take responsibility.

II

The central thesis of John Stuart Mill and other individualists about paternalism is that the fully voluntary choice or consent of a mature and rational human being concerning matters that affect only the individual's own interests is such a precious· thing that no one else (and certainly not the state) has a right to interfere with it simply for the person's "own good." No doubt this thesis was also meant to apply to almost-but-not-quite fully voluntary choices as well, and probably also even to some substantially nonvoluntary ones (e.g., a neurotic person's choice of a wife who will satisfy his neurotic needs but only at the price of great unhappiness, eventual divorce, and exacerbated guilt); but it is not probable that the individualist thesis was meant to apply to choices near the bottom of the scale of voluntariness, and Mill himself left no doubt that he did *not* intend it to apply to completely involuntary "choices." Nor should we *expect* anti-paternalistic individualism to deny people protection from their own nonvoluntary choices, for insofar as the choices are not voluntary they are just as alien to the individual as the choices of someone else.

Thus Mill would permit the state to protect people from their own ignorance at least in circumstances that create a strong presumption that their uninformed or misinformed choice would not correspond to their eventual one.

> If either a public officer or anyone else saw a person attempting to cross a bridge which had been ascertained to be unsafe, and there were no time to warn him of his danger, they might seize him and turn him back, without any real infringement of his liberty; for liberty consists in doing what one desires, and he does not desire to fall into the river.[6]

Of course, for all the public officer may know, the man on the bridge does desire to fall into the river, or to take the risk of falling for other purposes. If the person is then fully warned of the danger and wishes to proceed anyway, then, Mill argues, that is his business alone; but because most people do *not* wish to run such risks, there was a solid presumption, in advance of checking, that this person did not wish to run the risk either. Hence the officer was justified, Mill would argue, in his original interference.

On other occasions a person may need to be protected not from ignorance but from some other condition that may render an informed choice substantially less than voluntary. The individual may be "a child, or delirious, or in some state of excitement or absorption incompatible with the full use of the reflecting faculty."[7] Mill would not permit any such person to cross an objectively unsafe bridge. On the other hand, there is no reason why a child, or an excited person, or a drunkard, or a mentally ill person should not be allowed to proceed home across a perfectly safe thoroughfare. Even substantially nonvoluntary choices deserve protection unless there is good reason to judge them dangerous.

It may be the case, for all we can know, that the behavior of a drunk or an emotionally upset person would be exactly the same even if the individual were sober and calm. But when the behavior seems patently self-damaging and is of a sort that most calm and normal persons would not engage in, then there are strong grounds, if only a statistical sort, for inferring that it would not be the same; and these grounds, on Mill's principle, would justify interference. It may be that there is no action of which it can be said, "No mentally competent adult in a calm, attentive mood, fully informed, etc., would ever choose (or consent to) *that*." Nevertheless, there are actions that create a powerful *presumption* that any given actor, if he were in his right mind, would not choose them. The point of calling this hypothesis a "presumption" is to require that it be completely overridden before giving legal permission to a person who has already been interfered with to go on as before. For example, if a police officer (or anyone else) sees John Doe about to chop off his hand with an ax, the person is perfectly justified in using force to prevent him, because of the presumption that no one could voluntarily choose to do such a thing. The presumption, however, should always be taken as rebuttable in principle; and now it will be up to Doe to prove before an official tribunal that he is calm, competent, and free, and that he still wishes to chop off his hand. Perhaps this is too great a burden to expect Doe himself to "prove," but the tribunal should require that the presumption against voluntariness be overturned by evidence from some source or other. The existence of the presumption should require that an objective determination be made, whether by the usual adversary procedures of law courts, or simply by a collective investigation by the tribunal into the available facts. The greater the presumption to be overridden, the more elaborate and fastidious should be the legal paraphernalia required, and the stricter the standards of evidence. (The law of wills might prove a model for this.) The point of the procedure would not be to evaluate the wisdom or worthiness of a person's choice, but rather to determine whether the choice really is his.

This seems to lead us to a form of paternalism that is so weak and innocuous that it could be accepted even by Mill, namely, that the state has the right to prevent self-regarding harmful conduct when but only when it is substantially nonvoluntary or when temporary intervention is necessary to establish whether it is voluntary or not. A strong presumption that no normal person would voluntarily choose or consent to the kind of conduct in question should be a proper ground for detaining the person until the voluntary character of the choice can be established. We can use the phrase "the standard of voluntariness" as a label for the considerations that mediate the application of the principle that a person may properly be protected from his own folly. (Still another ground for forcible delay and inquiry that is perfectly compatible with Mill's individualism is the possibility that important third-party interests might be involved. Perhaps a man's wife and family should be heard before he is permitted to commit suicide—or even to chop off his hand.)

III

Working out the details of the voluntariness standard is far too difficult to undertake here, but some of the complexities can be illustrated by a consideration of some typical hard cases. Consider first of all the problem of harmful drugs. Suppose Mary Roe requests a prescription of drug X from Dr. Doe, and the following discussion ensues:

> Dr. Doe: I cannot prescribe drug X to you because it will do you physical harm.
>
> Mary Roe: But you are mistaken. It will not cause me physical harm.

In a case like this, the state, of course, backs the doctor. The state deems medical questions to be technical matters subject to expert opinions. This means that non-expert laypeople are not the best judge of their own medical interests. If a layperson disagrees with a physician on a question of medical fact the layperson can be presumed wrong, and if she nevertheless chooses to act on her factually mistaken belief, her action will be substantially less than fully voluntary in the sense explained above. That is to say that the action of *ingesting a substance which will in fact harm her* is not the action she voluntarily chooses. Hence the state intervenes to protect her not from her own free and voluntary choices, but from her own ignorance.

Suppose however that the exchange goes as follows:

> Dr. Doe: I cannot prescribe drug X to you because it will do you physical harm.
>
> Mary Roe: Exactly. That's just what I want. I want to harm myself.

In this case Roe *is* properly apprised of the facts. She suffers from no delusions or misconceptions. Yet her choice is so odd that there exists a reasonable presumption that she has been deprived somehow of the "full use of [her] reflecting faculty." It is because we know that the overwhelming majority of choices to inflict injury for its own sake on oneself are not fully voluntary that we are entitled to presume that the present choice too is not fully voluntary. If no further evidence of derangement, illness, severe depression, or unsettling excitation can be discovered, however, and the patient can convince an objective panel that the choice is voluntary (unlikely event!) and further if there are no third-party interests, for example, those of spouse or family, that require protection, then our "voluntariness standard" would permit no further state constraint.

Now consider the third possibility:

> Dr. Doe: I cannot prescribe drug X to you because it is very likely to do you physical harm.
>
> Mary Roe: I don't care if it causes me physical harm. I'll get a lot of pleasure first, so much pleasure in fact, that it is well worth running the risk of physical harm. If I must pay a price for my pleasure I am willing to do so.

This is perhaps the most troublesome case. Roe's choice is not patently irrational on its face. A well though-out philosophical hedonism may be one of her profoundest convictions. She may have made a fundamental decision of principle commiting herself to the intensely pleasurable, even if brief, life. If no third-party interests are directly involved, the state can hardly be permitted to declare these philosophical convictions unsound or "sick" and prevent her from practicing them without assuming powers that it will inevitably misuse disastrously.

On the other hand, this example may be very little different from the preceding one, depending, of course, on what the exact facts are. If the drug is known to give only an hour's mild euphoria and then to cause an immediate violently painful death, the risks incurred appear so unreasonable as to create a powerful presumption of nonvoluntariness. The desire to commit suicide must always be presumed to be both nonvoluntary and harmful to others until shown otherwise. (Of course, in some cases it *can* be shown otherwise.) On the other hand, drug X may be harmful in the way nicotine is now known to be harmful; twenty or thirty years of heavy use may create a grave risk of lung cancer or heart disease. Using the drug merely for pleasure, when the risks are of this kind may be to run unreasonable risks, but that is not strong evidence of nonvoluntariness. Many perfectly normal, rational persons voluntarily choose to run precisely these risks for whatever pleasures they find in smoking.[8] The way the state can assure itself that such practices are truly voluntary is to confront smokers continually with the ugly medical facts so that there is no escaping the knowledge of exactly what the medical risks to health are. Constant reminders of the hazards should be at every hand and with no softening of the gory details. The state might even be justified in using its taxing, regulatory, and persuasive powers to make smoking (and similar drug usage) more difficult or less attractive; but to prohibit it outright for everyone would be to tell voluntary risk-takers that even their informed judgments of what is worthwhile are less reasonable than those of the state, and that, therefore, they may not act on them. This is paternalism of the strong kind, unmediated by the voluntariness standard. As a principle of public policy, it has an acrid moral flavor, and creates serious risks of governmental tyranny.

IV

Another class of difficult cases are those involving contracts in which one party agrees to restrict his own liberty in some respect. The most extreme case is that in which one party freely sells himself into slavery to another, perhaps in exchange for some benefit that is to be consumed before the period of slavery begins or perhaps for some reward to be bestowed upon some third party. Our point of departure will be Mill's classic treatment of the subject:

> In this and most other civilized countries . . . . an engagement by which a person should sell himself, or allow himself to be sold, as a slave, would be null and void; neither enforced by law nor by opinion. The ground for *thus limiting his power of voluntarily disposing of his own lot in life* [italics mine] is apparent, and is very clearly seen in this extreme case. The reason for not interfering, unless for the sake of others, with a person's voluntary acts is consideration for his liberty. His voluntary choice is evidence that what he so

chooses is desirable, or at the least endurable, to him, and his good is on the whole best provided for by allowing him to take his own means of pursuing it. But by selling himself for a slave, he abdicates his liberty; he forgoes any future use of it beyond the single act. He therefore defeats, in his own case, the very purpose which is the justification of allowing him to dispose of himself. He is no longer free; but is thenceforth in a position which has no longer the presumption in its favor, that would be afforded by his voluntarily remaining in it. The principle of freedom cannot require that he should be free not to be free.[9]

It seems plain to me that Mill, in this one extreme case, has been driven to embrace the principle of paternalism. The "harm-to-others principle," as mediated by the *Volenti* maxim[10] would permit competent, fully informed adults, who are capable of rational reflection and free of undue pressure, to be themselves the judge of their own interests, no matter how queer or perverse their judgments may seem to others. There is, of course, always the presumption, and a very strong one indeed, that those who elect to "sell" themselves into slavery are either incompetent, unfree, or misinformed. Hence the state should require very strong evidence of voluntariness—elaborate tests, swearings, psychiatric testifying, waiting periods, public witnessing, and the like—before validating such contracts. Similar forms of official "making sure" are involved in marriages and wills, and slavery is an even more serious thing, not to be rashly undertaken. Undoubtedly, very few slavery contracts would survive such procedures, perhaps even none at all. It may be literally true that "no one in his right mind would sell himself into slavery," but if this is a truth it is not an a priori one but rather one that must be tested anew in each case by the application of independent, noncircular criteria of mental illness.

The supposition is at least possible, therefore, that every now and then a normal person in full possession of her or his faculties would voluntarily consent to permanent slavery. We can imagine any number of intelligible (if not attractive) motives for doing such a thing. A person might agree to become a slave in exchange for a million dollars to be delivered in advance to a loved one or to a worthy cause, or out of a religious conviction requiring a life of humility or penitence, or in payment for the prior enjoyment of some supreme benefit, as in the *Faust* legend. Mill, in the passage quoted earlier, would disallow such a contract no matter how certain it is that the agreement is fully voluntary, apparently on the ground that the permanent and irrevocable loss of freedom is such a great evil, and slavery so harmful a condition, that no one ought ever to be allowed to choose it, even voluntarily. Any person who thinks to gain, in the end, from such an agreement, Mill implies, is simply wrong whatever the reasons, and the individual can be known a priori to be wrong. Mill's earlier argument, if I understand it correctly, implies that people should be permitted to mutilate their bodies, take harmful drugs, or commit suicide, provided that the decision to do these things is voluntary and no other person will be directly and seriously harmed. But voluntarily acceding to slavery is too much for Mill to stomach. Here is an evil of another order, he seems to say; so the "harm to others" principle and the *Volenti* maxim come to their limiting point here, and paternalism in the strong sense (unmediated by the voluntariness test) must be invoked, if only for this one kind of case.

There are, of course, other ways of justifying the refusal to enforce slavery contracts. Some of these are derived from principles not acknowledged in Mill's moral philosophy but which at least have the merit of being non-paternalistic. One might argue that what is odious in "harsh and unconscionable" contracts, even when they are voluntary on both sides, is not that people should suffer the harm they freely risk, but rather that another party should "exploit" or take advantage of them. What is to be prevented, according to this line argument, is one person exploiting the weakness, foolishness, or recklessness of another. If a weak, foolish, or reckless person freely chooses or risks self-harm, that is all right, but that is no reason why another should be a party to it, or be permitted to benefit at the first person's expense. (This principle, however, can only apply to extreme cases, else it will ban all competition.) Applied to voluntary slavery, the principle of non-exploitation might say that it isn't aimed at preventing one person from being a slave so much as preventing the other from being a slave-owner. The basic principle of argument here is a form of legal moralism. To own another human being, as one might own a table or a horse, is to be in a relation to that person that is inherently immoral, and therefore properly forbidden by law. That, of course, is a line of argument that would be uncongenial to Mill, as would also be the Kantian argument that there is something in every human being that is not his or hers to alienate or dispose of: the "humanity" that we are enjoined to "respect, whether in our own person or that of another."

There are still other ways of arguing against the recognition of slavery contracts, however, that are neither paternalistic (in the strong sense) nor inconsistent with Mill's primary principles. One might argue, for example, that weakening respect for human dignity (which is weak enough to begin with) can lead in the long run to harm of the most serious kind to nonconsenting parties. Or one might use a variant of the "public charge" argument commonly used in the nineteenth century against permitting even those without dependents to assume the risk of penury, illness, and starvation. We could let people gamble recklessly with their lives, and then adopt inflexibly unsympathetic attitudes toward the losers. "They made their beds," we might say in the manner of some proper Victorians, "now let them sleep in them." But this would be to render the whole national character cold and hard. It would encourage a general insensitivity and impose an unfair economic penalty on those who possess the socially useful virtue of benevolence. Realistically, we just can't let people wither and die right in front of our eyes; and if we intervene to help, as we inevitably must, it will cost us a lot of money. There are certain risks then of an *apparently* self-regarding kind that people cannot be permitted to run, if only for the sake of others who must either pay the bill or turn their backs on intolerable misery. This kind of argument, which can be applied equally well to the slavery case, is at least not *very* paternalistic.

Finally, a non-paternalistic opponent of voluntary slavery might argue (and this is the argument to which I wish to give the most emphasis) that while exclusively self-regarding and fully voluntary slavery contracts are unobjectionable in principle, the legal machinery for testing voluntariness would be so cumbersome and expensive as to be impractical. Such procedures, after all, would have to be paid for out of tax revenues, the payment of which is mandatory for taxpayers. (And psychiatric consultant fees, among other things, are very high.) Even expensive legal machinery might be so fallible that there could be no sure way of determining voluntariness, so that some mentally ill people, for example, might become enslaved. Given the uncertain quality of evidence on these matters, and the enormous general presumption of nonvoluntariness, the state might be justified simply in *presuming nonvoluntariness conclusively in every case as the least risky course.* Some rational bargain-makers might be unfairly restrained under this policy, but under the alternative policy, perhaps even more people would become unjustly (mistakenly) enslaved, so that the evil prevented by the absolute prohibition would be greater than the occasional evil permitted. The principles involved in this argument are of two kinds: (1) It is better that one hundred people be wrongly denied permission to be enslaved than that one be wrongly permitted, and (2) If we allow the institution of voluntary slavery at all, then no matter how stringent our tests of voluntariness are, it is likely that a good many persons *will* be wrongly permitted.

V

Mill's argument that leads to a strong paternalistic conclusion in this one case (slavery) employs only calculations of harms and benefits and the presumptive interpretation of *Volenti non fit injuria.* The notion of the inviolable sovereignty of individual persons over their own lives does not appear in the argument. Liberty, he seems to tell us, is one good or benefit (though an extremely important one) among many, and its loss is one evil or harm (though an extremely serious one) among many types of harm. Since the aim of the law is to prevent harms of all kinds and from all sources, the law must take a very negative attitude toward forfeitures of liberty. Still, by and large, legal paternalism is an unacceptable policy because, in attempting to impose upon people an external conception of their own good, it is very likely to be self-defeating. "His voluntary choice is *evidence* [italics mine] that what he so chooses is desirable, or at least endurable to him, and his good is *on the whole* [italics mine] best provided for by allowing him to take his own means of pursuing it."

On the whole, then, the harm of coercion will outweigh any good it can produce for the person coerced. But when the person chooses slavery, the scales are clearly and necessarily tipped the other way, and the normal case against intervention is defeated. The ultimate appeal in this argument of Mill's is to the prevention of personal harms, so that permitting people to sell their freedom voluntarily would be to permit them to be "free not to be free," that is, free to inflict an *undeniable* harm upon themselves, and this (Mill would say) is as paradoxical as permitting a legislature to vote by a majority to abolish majority rule. If, on the other hand, our ultimate principle expresses respect for a person's voluntary choice *as such*, even when it is the choice of a loss of freedom, we can remain adamantly opposed to paternalism even in the most extreme cases of self-harm, for we shall be committed to the view that there is something even more important than the avoidance of harm. The principle that shuts and locks the door leading to strong paternalism is that every human being has a right to "voluntarily dispose of his or her own lot in life" whatever the effect on the net balance of benefits (including "freedom") and harms.

What does Mill say about less extreme cases of contracting away liberty? His next sentence (but one) is revealing: "These reasons, the force of which is so conspicuous in this particular case [slavery], are evidently of far wider application, yet a limit is everywhere set to them by the necessities of life, which continually require, not indeed that we should resign our freedom, but that we should consent to this and the other limitation of it."[11] Mill seems to say here that the same reasons that justify preventing the total and irrevocable relinquishment of freedom also militate against agreements to relinquish lesser amounts for lesser periods, but that unfortunately such agreements are sometimes rendered necessary by practical considerations. I would prefer to argue in the very opposite way, from the obvious permissibility of limited resignations of freedom to the permissibility in principle of even extreme forfeitures, except that in the case of slavery the "necessities of life"—administrative complications in determining voluntariness, high expenses, and so on—forbid it.

Many perfectly reasonable employment contracts involve an agreement by the employees virtually to abandon their liberty to do as they please for a daily period, and even to do (within obvious limits) whatever their boss tells them, in exchange for a salary that the employer, in turn, is not at liberty to withhold. Sometimes, of course, the terms of such agreements are quite unfavorable to one of the parties, but when the agreements have been fairly bargained, with no undue pressure or deception (i.e., when they are fully voluntary), the courts enforce them even though lopsided in their distribution of benefits. Employment contracts, of course, are relatively easily broken; in that respect they are altogether different from slavery contracts. Perhaps better examples for our purposes are contractual forfeitures of some extensive liberty for long periods of time or even forever. Certain contracts "in restraint of trade" are good examples. Consider contracts for the sale of the "good will" of a business.

> Manifestly, the buyer of a shop or of a practice will not be satisfied with what he buys unless he can persuade the seller to contract that he will not immediately set up a competing business next door and draw back most of his old clients or customers. Hence the buyer will usually request the seller to agree not to enter into competition with him. . . . Clauses of this kind are [also] often found in written contracts of employment, the employer

requiring his employee to agree that he will not work for a competing employer after he leaves his present work.[12]

There are limits, both spatial and temporal, to the amount of liberty the courts will permit to be relinquished in such contracts. In general, it is considered reasonable for a seller to agree not to reopen a business in the same neighborhood or even the same city for several years, but not reasonable to agree not to re-enter the trade in a distant city, or for a period of fifty years. The courts insist that the agreed-to self restraint be no wider "than is reasonably necessary to protect the buyer's purchase;"[13] but where the buyer's interests are very large the restraints may cover a great deal of space and time:

> For instance, in the leading case on the subject, a company which bought an armaments business for the colossal sum of £287,000 was held justified in taking a contract from the seller that he would not enter into competition with this business anywhere in the world for a period of twenty-five years. In view of the fact that the business was world-wide in its operations, and that its customers were mainly governments, any attempt by the seller to re-enter the armament business anywhere in the world might easily have affected the value of the buyer's purchase.[14]

The courts then do permit people to contract away extensive liberties for extensive periods of time in exchange for other benefits in reasonable bargains. Persons are even permitted to forfeit their future liberties in exchange for cash. Sometimes such transactions are perfectly reasonable, promoting the interests of both parties. Hence there would appear to be no good reason why they should be prohibited. Selling oneself into slavery is forfeiting *all* one's liberty for the rest of one's life in exchange for some prized benefit, and thus is only the extreme case of contracting away liberty, but not altogether different in principle. Mill's argument that liberty is not the sort of good that by its very nature can properly be traded does not seem a convincing way of arguing against voluntary slavery.

On the other hand, a court does permit the seller of a business to forfeit freely any more liberty than is reasonable or necessary, and reserves to *itself* the right to determine the question of reasonableness. This restrictive policy *could* be an expression of paternalism designed to protect contractors from their own foolishness; but in fact it is based on an entirely different ground—the public interest in maintaining a competitive system of free trade. The consumer's interest in having prices determined by a competitive marketplace rather than by uncontrolled monopolies requires that the state make it difficult for wealthy business people to buy off their competitors. Reasonable contracts "in restraint of trade" are a limited class of exceptions to a general policy designed to protect the economic interests of third parties (consumers) rather than the expression of an independent paternalistic policy of protecting free bargainers from their own mistakes.

There is still a final class of cases that deserves mention. These too are instances of persons voluntarily relinquishing liberties for other benefits; but they occur under such circumstances that prohibitions against them could not be plausibly justified except on paternalistic grounds, and usually not even on those grounds. I have in mind examples of persons who voluntarily "put themselves under the protection of rules" that deprive them and others of liberties, when those liberties are unrewarding and burdensome. Suppose all upperclass undergraduates are given the option by their college to live either in private apartment buildings entirely unrestricted or else in college dormitories subject to the usual curfew and parietal rules. If one chooses the latter, he or she must be in after a certain hour, be quiet after a certain time, and so on, subject to certain sanctions. In "exchange" for these forfeitures, of course, one is assured that the other students too must be predictable in their habits, orderly, and quiet. The net gain for one's interests as a student over the "freer" private life could be considerable. Moreover, the curfew rule can be a great convenience for a girl who wishes to date boys often, but who also wishes: (a) to get enough sleep for good health, (b) to remain efficient in her work, and (c) to be free of tension and quarrels when on dates over the question of when it is time to return home. If the rule requires a return at a certain time then neither the girl nor the boy has any choice in the matter, and what a boon that can be! To invoke these considerations is *not* to resort to paternalism unless they are employed in support of a prohibition. It is paternalism to *forbid* students to live in a private apartment "for their own good" or "their own safety." It is not paternalism to *permit* them to live under the governance of coercive rules when they freely choose to do so, and the other alternative is kept open to them. In fact it would be paternalism to deny people the liberty of trading liberties for other benefits when they voluntarily choose to do so.

VI

In summary: There are weak and strong versions of legal paternalism. The weak version is hardly an independent principle and can be entirely acceptable to the philosopher who, like Mill, is committed only to the "harm to others" principle as mediated by the *Volenti* maxim, where the latter is more than a mere presumption derived from generalizations about the causes of harm. According to the strong version of legal paternalism, the state is justified in protecting people against their will, from the harmful consequences even of their fully voluntary choices and undertakings. Strong paternalism is a departure from the "harm to others" principle and the strictly interpreted *Volenti* maxim that Mill should not, or need not, have taken in his discussion of contractual forfeitures of liberty. According to the weaker version of legal paternalism, people can rightly be prevented from harming themselves (when other interests are not directly involved) only if their intended action is substantially nonvoluntary or can be presumed to be so in the absence of evidence to the contrary. The "harm to others" principle, after all, permits us to protect individuals from the choices of other people; weak paternalism would permit us to protect people from "nonvoluntary choices," which, being the choices of no one at all, are no less foreign to them.

18   JOEL FEINBERG

Notes

1. The discussion that follows has two important unstated and undefended presuppositions. The first is that in some societies and at some times, a line can be drawn (as Mill claimed it could be in Victorian England) between other-regarding behavior and behavior that is primarily and directly self-regarding and only indirectly and remotely, therefore trivially, other-regarding. If this assumption is false, there is no interesting problem concerning legal paternalism since all paternalistic restrictions could be defended as necessary to protect persons other than those restricted, and hence would not be wholly paternalistic. The second presupposition is that the spontaneous repugnance toward paternalism (which I assume the reader shares with me) is well-grounded and supportable.

2. See Glanville Williams, ed., *Salmond on Jurisprudence*, 11th ed. (London: Sweet & Maxwell, 1957), p. 531.

3. See his excellent article, "Paternalism," in *Morality and the Law*, ed. R.A. Wasserstrom (Belmont, CA: Wadsworth Publishing Co., 1971).

4. Mill's rhetoric often supports this second interpretation of his argument. He is especially fond of such political metaphors as independence, legitimate rule, dominion, and sovereignty. The state must respect the status of the individual as an independent entity whose "*sovereignty* over himself" (in Mill's phrase), like Britain's over its territory, is absolute. In self-regarding affairs, a person's individuality ought to "*reign* uncontrolled from the outside" (another phrase of Mill's). Interference in those affairs, whether successful or self-defeating, is a violation of *legitimate boundaries,* like trespass in law, or aggression between states. Even self-mutilation and suicide are permissible if the individual truly chooses them, and other interests are not directly affected. Individual persons have an absolute right to choose for themselves, to be wrong, to go to hell on their own, and it is nobody else's proper *business* or *office* to interfere. Individuals *own* (not merely possess) their lives; they have *title* to them. They alone are *arbiters* of their own lives and deaths. See how legalistic and un-utilitarian these terms are! The great wonder is that Mill could claim to have foregone any benefit in argument from the notion of an abstract right. Mill's intentions aside, however, I can not conceal my own preference for this second interpretation of his argument.

5. The distinctions in this paragraph are borrowed from: Henry T. Terry, "Negligence," *Harvard Law Review* 29, 1915.

6. John Stuart Mill, *On Liberty* (New York: Liberal Arts Press, 1956), p. 117.

7. *Ibid.*

8. Perfectly rational individuals can have "unreasonable desires" as judged by other perfectly rational individuals, just as perfectly rational people (e.g., great philosophers) can hold "unreasonable beliefs" or doctrines as judged by other perfectly rational people. Particular unreasonableness, then, can hardly be strong evidence of general irrationality.

9. Mill, *On Liberty,* p. 125.

10. That is, the principle that prevention of harm to others is the sole ground for legal coercion, and that what is freely consented to is not to count as harm. These are Mill's primary normative principles in *On Liberty.*

11. Mill, *On Liberty*, p. 125.

12. P.S. Atiyah, *An Introduction to the Law of Contracts* (Oxford: Clarendon Press, 1961), p.176.

13. *Ibid.*, pp. 176-77.

14. *Ibid.*, p.177.

Chapter 2

Paternalism

Gerald Dworkin

> Neither one person, nor any number of persons, is warranted in saying to another human creature of ripe years, that he shall not do with his life for his own benefit what he chooses to do with it.

> John Stuart Mill

> I do not want to go along with a volunteer basis. I think a fellow should be compelled to become better and not let him use his discretion whether he wants to get smarter, more healthy or more honest.

> General Hershey

I take as my starting point the "one very simple principle" proclaimed by Mill in *On Liberty*: "That principle is, that the sole end for which mankind are warranted, individually or collectively, in interfering with the liberty of action of any of their number, is self-protection. That the only purpose for which power can be rightfully exercised over any member of a civilized community, against his will, is to prevent harm to others. . . . He cannot rightfully be compelled to do or forbear because it will be better for him to do so, because it will make him happier, because, in the opinion of others, to do so would be wise, or even right."[1]

This principle is neither "one" nor "very simple." It is at least two principles: one asserting that self-protection or the prevention of harm to others is sometimes a sufficient warrant, and the other claiming that the individual's own good is *never* a sufficient warrant for the exercise of compulsion either by the society as a whole or by its individual members. I assume that no one, with the possible exception of extreme pacifists or anarchists, questions the correctness of the first half of the principle. This essay is an examination of the negative claim embodied in Mill's principle—the objection to paternalistic interferences with a person's liberty.

Gerald Dworkin, "Paternalism," *The Monist* 56, no. 1 (1972), pp. 64-84. Reprinted with the permission of the author and the publisher.

I

By paternalism I shall understand roughly the interference with a person's liberty of action justified by reasons referring exclusively to the welfare, good, happiness, needs, interests, or values of the person being coerced. One is always well-advised to illustrate one's definitions by examples, but it is not easy to find "pure" examples of paternalistic interferences. Almost any piece of legislation is justified by several different reasons, and even if historically a piece of legislation can be shown to have been introduced for purely paternalistic motives, it may be that advocates of the legislation with an anti-paternalistic outlook can find sufficient reasons justifying the legislation without appealing to the reasons that were originally adduced to support it. Thus, for example, it may be that the original legislation requiring motorcyclists to wear safety helmets was introduced for purely paternalistic reasons. But the Rhode Island Supreme Court recently upheld such legislation on the grounds that it was "not persuaded that the legislature is powerless to prohibit individuals from pursuing a course of conduct which could conceivably result in their becoming public charges," thus clearly introducing reasons of a quite different kind. I regard this decision as being based on reasoning of a very dubious nature, but it illustrates the kind of problem one has in finding examples. The following is a list of the kinds of interferences I have in mind as being paternalistic.

1. Laws requiring motorcyclists to wear safety helmets when operating their machines.
2. Laws forbidding persons from swimming at a public beach when lifeguards are not on duty.
3. Laws making suicide a criminal offense.
4. Laws making it illegal for women and children to work at certain types of jobs.
5. Laws regulating certain kinds of sexual conduct, e.g., homosexuality among consenting adults in private.
6. Laws regulating the use of certain drugs that may have harmful consequences to the user, but do not lead to anti-social conduct.
7. Laws requiring a license to engage in certain professions with those not receiving a license subject to fine or jail sentence if they do engage in the practice.
8. Laws compelling people to spend a specified fraction of their income on the purchase of retirement annuities (Social Security).
9. Laws forbidding various forms of gambling (often justified on the grounds that the poor are more likely to throw away their money on such activities than the rich who can afford to).
10. Laws regulating the maximum rates of interest for loans.
11. Laws against duelling.

In addition to laws that attach criminal or civil penalties to certain kinds of action, there are laws, rules, regulations, and decrees that make it either difficult or impossible for people to carry out their plans and that are also justified on paternalistic grounds. Example of this are:

1. Laws regulating the types of contracts that will be upheld as valid by the courts, e.g., no one may make a valid contract for perpetual involuntary servitude (an example of Mill's to which I shall return).
2. Not allowing as a defense to a charge of murder or assault the consent of the victim.
3. Requiring members of certain religious sects to have compulsory blood transfusions. This is made possible by not allowing the patient to have recourse to civil suits for assault and battery and by means of injunctions.
4. Civil commitment procedures when these are specifically justified on the basis of preventing the persons being committed from harming themselves. (The D.C. Hospitalization of the Mentally Ill Act provides for involuntary hospitalization of a person who "is mentally ill, and because of that illness, is likely to injure *himself* or others if allowed to remain at liberty." The term injure in this context applies to unintentional as well as to intentional injuries.)
5. Putting fluorides in the community water supply.

All my examples are of existing restrictions on the liberty of individuals. Obviously one can think of interferences that have not yet been imposed. Thus one might ban the sale of cigarettes, or require that people wear safety-belts in automobiles (as opposed to merely having them installed), enforcing this by not allowing motorists to sue for injuries, even when caused by other drivers, if the motorist was not wearing a seat-belt at the time of the accident.

I shall not be concerned with activities that though defended on paternalistic grounds, are not interferences with the liberty of persons, e.g., the giving of subsidies in kind rather than in cash on the grounds that the recipients would not spend the money on the goods that they really need, or not including a $1000 deductible provision in a basic-protection automobile-insurance plan on the ground that the people who would elect it could least afford it. Nor shall I be concerned with measures such as truth-in-advertising acts and the Pure Food and Drug legislation, which are often attacked as paternalistic but which should not be considered so. In these cases all that is provided—it is true, by the use of compulsion—is information which it is presumed that rational persons are interested in having in order to make wise decisions. There is no interference with the liberty of consumers unless one wants to stretch a point beyond good sense and say that their liberty to apply for a loan without knowing the true rate of interest is diminished. It is true that sometimes there is sentiment for going further than providing information, for example, when laws against usurious interest are passed, preventing those who might wish to contract loans at high rates of interest from doing so, and these measures may correctly be considered paternalistic.

II

Bearing these examples in mind, let me return to a characterization of paternalism. I said earlier that I meant by the term, roughly, interference with people's liberty for their own good. But, as some of the examples show, the class of persons whose good is involved is not always identical with the class of persons whose freedom is restricted. Thus, in the case of professional licensing, it is the practitioner who is directly interfered with, and it is the would-be patient whose interests are presumably being served. Not allowing the consent of the victim to be a defense to certain types of crime primarily affects the would-be aggressor, but it is the interests of the willing victim that we are trying to protect. Sometimes a person may fall into both classes, as would be the case if we banned the manufacture and sale of cigarettes and a given manufacturer happened to be a smoker as well.

Thus we may first divide paternalistic interferences into ''pure'' and ''impure'' cases. In ''pure'' paternalism, the class of persons whose freedom is restricted is identical with the class of persons whose benefit is intended to be promoted by such restrictions. Examples: the making of suicide a crime, requiring passengers in automobiles to wear seat-belts, requiring a Jehovah's Witness to receive a blood transfusion. In the case of ''impure'' paternalism, in trying to protect the welfare of a class of persons we find that the only way to do so will involve restricting the freedom of other persons besides those who are benefited. It might be thought that there are no cases of ''impure'' paternalism, since any such case could always be justified on nonpaternalistic grounds, i.e., in terms of preventing harm to others. Thus we might ban cigarette manufacturers from continuing to manufacture their product on the grounds that we are preventing them from causing illness to others in the same way that we prevent other manufacturers from releasing pollutants into the atmosphere, thereby causing danger to members of the community. The difference is, however, that in the former but not the latter case the harm is of such a nature that it could be avoided by those individuals affected, if they so chose. The incurring of the harm requires the active cooperation of the victim. It would be a mistake in theory and hypocritical in practice to assert that our interference in such cases is just like our interference in standard cases of protecting others from harm. At the very least, people interfered with in this way can reply that no one is complaining about their activities. It may be that impure paternalism requires arguments or reasons of a stronger kind in order to be justified, since there are persons who are losing a portion of their liberty and they do not even have the solace of having it done ''in their own interest.'' Of course, in some sense, if paternalistic justifications are ever correct, we are protecting others, we are preventing some from injuring others, but it is important to see the differences between this and the standard case.

Paternalism, then, will always involve limitations on the liberty of some individuals in their own interest, but it may also extend to interferences with the liberty of parties whose interests are not in question.

III

By way of some more preliminary analysis, I want to distinguish paternalistic interferences with liberty from a related type with which it is often confused. Consider, for example, legislation that forbids employees to work more than, say forty hours per week. It is sometimes argued that such legislation is paternalistic, for if employees desired such a restriction on their hours of work they could agree among themselves to impose it voluntarily. But because they do not, society imposes its own conception of their best interests upon them by the use of coercion. Hence, this is paternalism.

It may be that some legislation of this nature is, in fact, paternalistically motivated. I am not denying that. All I want to point out is that there is another possible way of justifying such measures that is not paternalistic in nature. It is not paternalistic because, as Mill puts it in a similar context, such measures are "required not to overrule the judgment of individuals respecting their own interest, but to give effect to that judgment: they being unable to give effect to it except by concert, which concert again cannot be effectual unless it receives validity and sanction from the law."[2]

The line of reasoning here is a familiar one, first found in Hobbes and developed with great sophistication by contemporary economists in the last decade or so. There are restrictions that are in the interests of a class of persons taken collectively, but are such that the immediate interest of each individual is furthered by violating the rule when others adhere to it. In such cases, the individuals involved may need the use of compulsion to give effect to their collective judgment of their own interest by guaranteeing each individual compliance by the others. In these cases, compulsion is not used to achieve some benefit that is not recognized to be a benefit by those concerned, but rather because it is the only feasible means of achieving some benefit which *is* recognized as such by all concerned. This way of viewing matters provides us with another characterization of paternalism in general. Paternalism might be thought of as the use of coercion to achieve a good that is not recognized as such by those persons for whom the good is intended. Again, while this formulation captures the heart of the matter—it is surely what Mill is objecting to in *On Liberty*—the matter is not always quite like that. For example, when we force motorcyclists to wear helmets we are trying to promote a good—the protection of the person from injury—which is surely recognized by most of the individuals concerned. It is not that cyclists don't value their bodily integrity; rather, as a supporter of such legislation would put it, they either place, perhaps irrationally, another value or good (freedom from wearing a helmet) above that of physical well-being or, perhaps, while recognizing the danger in the abstract, either they do not fully appreciate it or they underestimate the likelihood of its occurring. Now we are approaching the question of possible justifications of paternalistic measures, and the rest of this essay will be devoted to that question.

IV

For dialectical purposes, I shall begin by discussing Mill's objections to paternalism, and then go on to discuss more positive proposals.

A feature that initially strikes one is the absolute nature of Mill's prohibitions against paternalism. It is so unlike the carefully qualified admonitions of Mill and his fellow Utilitarians on other moral issues. He speaks of self-protection as the *sole* end warranting coercion, of the individuals' own goals as *never* being a sufficient warrant. Contrast this with his discussion of the prohibition against lying in *Utiliterianism*.

> Yet that even this rule, sacred as it is, admits of possible exception, is acknowledged by all moralists, the chief of which is where the with-holding of some fact . . . would save an individual . . . from great and unmerited evil.[3]

The same tentativeness is present when he deals with justice.

> It is confessedly unjust to break faith with any one: to violate an engagement, either express or implied, or disappoint expectations raised by our own conduct, at least if we have raised these expectations knowingly and voluntarily. Like all the other obligations of justice already spoken of, this one is not regarded as absolute, but as capable of being overruled by a stronger obligation of justice on the other side.[4]

This anomaly calls for some explanation. The structure of Mill's argument is as follows:

1. Since restraint is an evil, the burden of proof is on those who propose such restraint.
2. Since the conduct that is being considered is purely self-regarding, the normal appeal to the protection of the interests of others is not available.
3. Therefore, we have to consider whether reasons involving reference to the individuals' own good, happiness, welfare, or interests are sufficient to overcome the burden of justification.
4. Either we cannot advance the interests of the individual by compulsion, or the attempt to do so involves evil that out-weighs the good done.
5. Hence, the promotion of the individual's own interests does not provide a sufficient warrant for the use of compulsion.

Clearly the operative premise here is 4. It is bolstered by claims about the status of individuals as judges and appraisers of their own welfare, interests, needs, etc.

> With respect to his own feelings and circumstances, the most ordinary man or woman has means of knowledge immeasurably surpassing those that can be possessed by any one else.[5]

> He is the man most interested in his own well-being: the interest which any other person, except in cases of strong personal attachment, can have in it, is trifling, compared to that which he himself has.[6]

These claims are used to support the following generalizations concerning the utility of compulsion for paternalistic purposes.

The interferences of society to overrule his judgment and purposes in what only regards himself must be grounded on general presumptions; which may be altogether wrong, and even if right, are as likely as not to be misapplied to individual cases.[7]

But the strongest of all arguments against the interference of the public with purely personal conduct is that when it does interfere, the odds are that it interferes wrongly and in the wrong place.[8]

All errors which the individual is likely to commit against advice and warning are far outweighed by the evil of allowing others to constrain him to what they deem his good.[9]

Performing the utilitarian calculation by balancing the advantages and disadvantages, we find that:

Mankind are greater gainers by suffering each other to live as seems good to themselves, than by compelling each other to live as seems good to the rest.[10]

From which follows the operative premise 4.

This classical case of a utilitarian argument with all the premises spelled out is not the only line of reasoning present in Mill's discussion. There are asides, and more than asides, that look quite different, and I shall deal with them later. But this is clearly the main channel of Mill's thought, and it is one that has been subjected to vigorous attack from the moment it appeared—most often by fellow Utilitarians. The link that they have usually seized on is, as Fitzjames Stephen put it, the absence of proof that the "mass of adults are so well acquainted with their own interests and so much disposed to pursue them that no compulsion or restraint put upon them by any others for the purpose of promoting their interest can really promote them."[11] Even so sympathetic a critic as Hart is forced to the conclusion that:

In Chapter 5 of his essay Mill carried his protests against paternalism to lengths that may now appear to us as fantastic. . . . No doubt if we no longer sympathize with this criticism this is due, in part, to a general decline in the belief that individuals know their own interest best.[12]

Mill endows the average individual with "too much of the psychology of a middle-aged man whose desires are relatively fixed, not liable to be artificially stimulated by external influences; who knows what he wants and what gives him satisfaction of happiness; and who pursues these things when he can."[13]

It is interesting to note that Mill himself was aware of some of the limitations on the doctrine that individuals are the best judges of their own interests. In his discussion of government intervention in general (even when the intervention does not interfere with liberty, but provides alternative institutions to those of the market), he makes claims that are parallel to those just discussed, e.g.:

People understand their own business and their own interests better, and care for them more, than the government does, or can be expected to do.[14]

He goes on to an intelligent discussion of the "very large and conspicuous exceptions" to the maxim that:

Most persons take a juster and more intelligent view of their own interest, and of the means of promoting it than can either be prescribed to them by a general enactment of the legislature, or pointed out in the particular case by a public functionary.[15]

Thus, there are things

of which the utility does not consist in ministering to inclinations, nor in serving the daily uses of life, and the want of which is least felt where the need is greatest. This is peculiarly true of those things which are chiefly useful as tending to raise the character of human beings. The uncultivated cannot be competent judges of cultivation. Those who most need to be made wiser and better, usually desire it least, and, if they desired it, would be incapable of finding the way to it by their own lights.

. . . . A second exception to the doctrine that individuals are the best judges of their own interest, is when an individual attempts to decide irrevocably now what will be best for his interest at some future and distant time. The presumption in favor of individual judgment is only legitimate, where the judgment is grounded on actual, and especially on present, personal experience; not where it is formed antecedently to experience, and not suffered to be reversed even after experience has condemned it.[16]

The upshot of these exceptions is that Mill does not declare that there should never be government interference with the economy but rather that

in every instance, the burden of making out a strong case should be thrown not on those who resist but on those who recommend government interference. Letting alone, in short, should be the general practice: every departure from it, unless required by some great good, is a certain evil.[17]

In short, we get a presumption, not an absolute prohibition. The question is: Why doesn't the argument against paternalism go the same way?

I suggest that the answer lies in seeing that, in addition to a purely utilitarian argument, Mill uses another as well. As a Utilitarian, Mill has to show, in Fitzjames Stephen's words, that:

Self-protection apart, no good object can be attained by any compulsion which is not in itself a greater evil than the absence of the object which the compulsion obtains.[18]

It is impossible to show this, one reason being that it isn't true. Preventing people from selling themselves into slavery (a paternalistic measure which Mill himself accepts as legitimate), or from taking heroin, or from driving a car without wearing seat-belts may constitute a lesser evil than allowing them to do any of these things. A consistent Utilitarian can only argue against paternalism on the grounds that it (as a matter of fact) does not maximize the good. It is always a contingent question that may be refuted by the evidence. But there is also a noncontingent argument that runs through *On Liberty*. When Mill states that "there is a part of the life of every person who has come to years of discretion, within which the individuality of that person ought to reign uncontrolled either by any other person or by the public collectively" he is saying something about what it means to be a person, an autonomous agent. It is because coercing individuals for their own good denies their status as independent entities that Mill objects to it so strongly and in such absolute terms. To be able to choose is a good that is independent of the wisdom of what is chosen. A person's "mode of laying out his existence is the best, not because it is the best in itself, but because it is his own mode."[19]

> It is the privilege and proper condition of a human being, arrived at the maturity of his faculties, to use and interpret experience in his own way.[20]

As further evidence of this line of reasoning in Mill, consider the one exception to his prohibition against paternalism.

> In this and most civilised countries, for example, an engagement by which a person should sell himself, or allow himself to be sold, as a slave, would be null and void; neither enforced by law nor by opinion. The ground for thus limiting his power of voluntarily disposing of his own lot in life, is apparent, and is very clearly seen in this extreme case. The reason for not interfering, unless for the sake of others, with a person's voluntary acts, is consideration for his liberty. His voluntary choice is evidence that what he so chooses is desirable, or at least endurable, to him, and his good is on the whole best provided for by allowing him to take his own means of pursuing it. But by selling himself for a slave, he abdicates his liberty; he foregoes any future use of it beyond that single act.
>
> He therefore defeats, in his own case, the very purpose which is the justification of allowing him to dispose of himself. He is no longer free; but is thenceforth in a position which has no longer the presumption in its favour, that would be afforded by his voluntarily remaining in it. The principle of freedom cannot require that he should be free not to be free. It is not freedom to be allowed to alienate his freedom.[21]

Leaving aside the fudging on the meaning of freedom in the last line, it is clear that part of this argument is incorrect. While it is true that *future* choices of slaves are not reasons for thinking that what they choose then is desirable for them, what is at issue is limiting their immediate choice; and since this choice is made freely, individuals may be correct in thinking their interests are best provided for by entering such a contract. But the main consideration for not allowing such a contract is the need to preserve the liberty of the person to make future choices. This gives us a principle—a very narrow one—by which to justify some paternalistic interferences. Paternalism is justified only to preserve a wider range of freedom for the individual in question. How far this principle could be extended, and whether it can justify all the cases in which we are inclined upon reflection to think paternalistic measures are justified, remains to be discussed. What I have tried to show so far is that there are two strains of argument in Mill—one a straightforward Utilitarian mode of reasoning and one which relies not on the goods to which free choice leads, but on the absolute value of the choice itself. The first cannot establish any absolute prohibition, but at most a presumption and indeed a fairly weak one given some fairly plausible assumptions about human psychology; the second, while a stronger line of argument, seems to me to allow on its own grounds a wider range of paternalism than might be suspected. I turn now to a consideration of these matters.

V

We might begin looking for principles governing the acceptable use of paternalistic power in cases in which it is generally agreed that it is legitimate. Even Mill intends his principles to be applicable only to mature individuals, not to those in what he calls "non-age." What justifies us in interfering with children is the fact that they lack some of the emotional and cognitive capacities required in order to make fully rational decisions. It is an empirical question to just what extent children have an adequate conception of their own present and future interests, but there is not much doubt that there are many deficiencies. For example, it is very difficult for children to defer gratification for any considerable period of time. Given these deficiencies and given the very real and permanent dangers that may befall children, it becomes not only permissible but even a duty of parents to restrict children's freedom in various ways. There is, however, an important moral limitation on the exercise of such parental power that is provided by the notion of children eventually coming to see the correctness of the parents' interventions. Parental paternalism may be thought of as a wager by parents on children's subsequent recognition of the wisdom of the restrictions. There is an emphasis on what could be called future-oriented consent—on what chldren will come to welcome, rather than on what they do welcome.

The essence of this idea has been incorporated by idealist philosophers into various types of "real-will" theory, as applied to fully adult persons. Extensions of paternalism are argued for by claiming that, in various respects, chronologically mature individuals share the same deficiencies in knowledge, capacity to think rationally, and the ability to carry out decisions that children possess. In interfering with such people, we are in effect doing what they would do if they were fully rational. Hence, we are not really opposing their will, hence we are not really interfering with their freedom. The dangers of this move have been sufficiently exposed by Berlin in his Two Concepts of Liberty. I see no gain in theoretical clarity, nor in practical advantage, in trying to pass over the real nature of the interferences with liberty that we impose on others. Still, the basic notion of consent is important, and seems to me the only acceptable way of trying to delimit an area of justified paternalism.

Let me start by considering a case in which the consent is not hypothetical in nature. Under certain conditions, it is rational for individuals to agree that others should force them to act in ways that, at the time of action, the individuals may not see as desirable. If, for example, certain individuals know that they are subject to breaking their resolves when temptation is present, they may ask friends to refuse to entertain their requests at some later stage.

A classical example is given in the Odyssey when Odysseus commands his men to tie him to the mast and to refuse all future orders to set him free, because he knows the power of the Sirens to enchant men with their songs. In this case, we are on relatively sound ground in later refusing Odysseus' request to be set free. He may even claim to have changed his mind, but since it is just such changes that he wished to guard against, we are entitled to ignore them.

A process analogous to this may take place on a social rather than on an individual basis. An electorate may mandate its representatives to pass legislation that when it comes time to ''pay the price,'' may be unpalatable. I may believe that a tax increase is necessary to halt inflation, although I may resent the lower paycheck each month. However, in both this case and that of Odysseus, the measure to be enforced is specifically requested by the party involved, and at some point there is genuine consent and agreement on the part of those persons whose liberty is infringed. Such is not the case for the paternalistic measures we have been speaking about. What must be involved here is not consent to specific measures, but rather consent to a system of government, run by elected representatives, with an understanding that they may act to safeguard our interests in certain limited ways.

I suggest that since we are all aware of our irrational propensities—deficiencies in cognitive and emotional capacities and avoidable and unavoidable ignorance—it is rational and prudent for us to take out ''social insurance policies.'' We may argue for and against proposed paternalistic measures in terms of what fully rational individuals would accept as forms of protection. Since the initial agreement is not about specific measures, we are clearly dealing with a more-or-less blank check and, therefore, there have to be carefully defined limits. What I am looking for are certain conditons that make it plausible to suppose that rational people could reach agreement to limit their liberty even when other people's interests are not affected.

Of course, as in any kind of agreement schema, there are great difficulties in deciding what rational individuals would or would not accept. Particularly in the sensitive areas of personal liberty, there is always a danger of the dispute over agreement and rationality being a disguised version of evaluative and normative disagreement.

Let me suggest situations in which it seems plausible to suppose that fully rational individuals would agree to having paternalistic restrictions imposed upon them. It is reasonable to suppose that there are "goods" such as health that any person would want to have in order to pursue his or her own good—no matter how that good is conceived. This is an argument that is used in connection with compulsory education for children, but it seems to me that it can be extended to other goods that have this character. One could agree that the attainment of such goods should be promoted even when not recognized as a good, at the moment, by the individuals concerned.

An immediate difficulty with this approach stems from the fact that people are always faced with competing goods, and that there may be reasons that even a value such as health—or indeed life—may be overridden by competing values. An example of this is the problem with Jehovah's Witnesses and blood transfusions. It may be more important for them to reject "impure substances" than to go on living. The difficult problem that must be faced is whether one can give sense to the notion of a person irrationally attaching weights to competing values.

Consider those individuals who know the statistical data on the probability of being injured when not wearing seat-belts in an automobile and who know the types and gravity of the various injuries. They insist that the inconvenience attached to fastening the belt every time they get in and out of the car outweighs for them the possible risks to themselves. In this case, I am inclined to think that such a weighing is irrational. Given these individuals' life-plans, which we are assuming are those of the average person, their interest and commitments already under-taken, I think it is safe to predict that we can find inconsistencies in their calculations at some point. I am assuming that these are not people who, for some conscious or unconscious reasons, are trying to injure themselves, nor are they people who just like to "live dangerously." I am assuming that they are like us in all the relevant respects, but just put an enormously high negative value on inconvenience—one which does not seem comprehensible or reasonable.

It is always possible, of course, to assimilate these people to creatures like myself. I, also, neglect to fasten my seat-belt, and I concede such behavior is not rational, but not because I weigh the inconvenience differently from those who fasten the belts. It is just that having made roughly the same calculation as everybody else, I ignore it in my actions. (Note: This is a much better case of weakness of the will than those usually given in ethics texts.) A plausible explanation for this deplorable habit is that, although I know in some intellectual sense what the probabilities and risks are, I do not fully appreciate them in an emotionally genuine manner.

We have two distinct types of situation in which people act in a nonrational fashion. In one case they attach incorrect weights to some of their values; in the other, they neglect to act in accordance with their actual preferences and desires. Clearly there is stonger and more persuasive argument for paternalism in the latter situation. Here we are really not—by assumption—imposing a good on another person. But why may we not extend our interference to what we might call evaluative delusions? After all, in the case of cognitive delusions, we are often prepared to act against the expressed will of the person involved. If an individual believes that upon jumping out the window he or she will float upwards—Robert Nozick's example—would we not detain the person, forcibly if necessary? The reply will be that this individual doesn't wish to be injured, and if we could convince the person that he or she is mistaken as to the consequences of this action, the person would no longer wish to perform the action. But part of what is involved in claiming that people who don't fasten their seat-belts are attaching an irrational weight to the inconvenience of fastening them is that if they were to be involved in an accident and severely injured, they would look back and admit that the inconvenience wasn't as bad as all that. So there is a sense in which if I could convince a person of the consequences of an action the individual also would not wish to continue that course of action. Now the notion of consequences being used here is covering a lot of ground. In one case, it's being used to indicate what will or can happen as a result of a course of action; in the other, it's making a prediction about the future evaluation of the consequences—in the first sense—of a course of action. Whatever the difference between facts and values—whether it be hard and fast or soft and slow—we are genuinely more reluctant to consent to interferences when evaluative differences are the issue. Let me now consider another factor that comes into play in some of these situations, a factor that may make an important difference in our willingness to consent to paternalistic restrictions.

Some of the decisions we make are of such a character that they produce changes that are in one or another way irreversible. Situations are created in which it is difficult or impossible to return to anything like the initial stage at which the decision was made. In particular, some of these changes will make it impossible to continue to make reasoned choices in the future. I am thinking specifically of decisions that involve taking physically or psychologically addictive drugs and decisions that are destructive of one's mental and physical capacities.

I suggest we think of the imposition of paternalistic interferences in situations of this kind as being a kind of insurance policy that we take out against making decisions that are far-reaching, potentially dangerous, and irreversible. Each of these factors is important. We make many decisions that are relatively irreversible. In deciding to to learn to play chess, I could predict in view of my general interest in games that some portion of my free time was going to be preempted, and that it would not be easy to give up the game once I acquired a certain competence. But I could also know that my whole life-style was not going to be jeopardized in an extreme manner. Further, it might be argued that even with addictive drugs such as heroin, one's normal life plans would not be seriously interfered with if an inexpensive and adequate supply were readily available. So this type of argument might have a much narrower scope than appears to be the case at first.

A second class of cases concerns decisions made under extreme psychological and sociological pressures. I am not thinking here of the making of the decision as being something one is pressured into—for example, a good reason for making duelling illegal is that, unless this is done, many people might have to manifest their courage and integrity in ways in which they would rather not do so—but rather of decisions such as that to commit suicide that are usually made when the individual is not thinking clearly and calmly about the nature of the decision. In addition, of course, this comes under the previous heading of all-too-irrevocable decisions. There are practical steps that a society could take if it wanted to decrease the possibility of suicide—for example, not paying social security benefits to the survivors, or, as religious institutions do, not allowing such persons to be buried with the same status as those who died natural deaths. I think we may count these interferences with the liberty of persons to attempt suicide; the question is whether they are justifiable.

Using my argument schema, the question is whether rational individuals would consent to such limitations. I see no reason for them to consent to an absolute prohibition, but I do think it is reasonable for them to agree to some kind of enforced waiting period. Since we are all aware of the existence of temporary states, such as great fear or depression, that are inimical to the making of well-informed and rational decisions, it would be prudent for all of us to have some kind of institutional arrangement whereby we were restrained from making a decision that is irreversible. What this would be like in practice is difficult to envisage, and it may be that if no practical arrangements were feasible we would have to conclude that there should be no restriction at all on this kind of action. But we might have a "cooling off" period, in much the same way that we now require couples who file for divorce to go through a waiting period. Or, more farfetched, we might imagine a Suicide Board composed of psychologist and another member picked by the applicant. The Board would be required to meet and talk with the person proposing suicide, although its approval would not be required.

A third class of decisions—these classes are not supposed to be disjoint—involves dangers that are not sufficiently understood or appreciated correctly by the persons involved. Let me illustrate, using the example of cigarette smoking:

1. People may not know the facts—for example, that smoking between one and two packs a day shortens life expectancy 6.2 years, or that the costs and pain of the illness caused by smoking are very great.
2. People may know the facts, wish to stop smoking, but not have the requisite willpower.
3. People may know the facts, but not have them play the correct role in their calculations; for example, they discount the danger psychologically because it is remote in time and/or inflates the attractiveness of other consequences of their decisions that they regard as beneficial.

In case 1, what is called for is education, for example, the posting of warnings. In case 2, there is no theoretical problem. We are not imposing a good on someone who rejects it. We are simply using coercion to enable people to carry out their own goals. (Note: There is obviously a difficulty in that only a subclass of the individuals affected wish to be prevented from doing what they are doing.) In case 3, there is a sense in which we are imposing a good on people since, given their current appraisal of the facts, they don't wish to be restricted. But in another sense, we are not imposing a good since what is being claimed—and what must be shown ar at least argued for—is that an accurate accounting on their part would lead them to reject their current course of action. We all know that such cases exist, that we are prone to disregard dangers that are only possibilities, that immediate pleaures are often magnified and distorted.

If, in addition, the dangers are severe and far-reaching, we could allow the state a certain degree of power to intervene in such situations. The difficulty is in specifying in advance, even vaguely, the class of cases in which intervention will be legitimate.

A related difficulty is that of drawing a line so that it is not the case that all ultra-hazardous activities are ruled out, for example, mountain-climbing, bull-fighting, and sports-car racing. There are some risks—even very great ones—that people are entitled to take with their lives.

A good deal depends on the nature of the deprivation—for example, does it prevent people from engaging in the activity completely or merely limit their participation?—and how important to the nature of the activity is the absence of restriction when this is weighed against the role that the activity plays in people's lives. In the case of automobile seat-belts, for example, the restriction is trivial in nature, interferes not at all with the use or enjoyment of the activity, and does, I am assuming, considerably reduce a high risk of serious injury. On the other hand, making mountain-climbing illegal completely prevents people from engaging in an activity which may play an important role in their lives and in their conception of who they are.

In general, the easiest cases to handle are those that can be argued about in the terms that Mill thought to be so important—a concern not just for the happiness or welfare, in some broad sense, of the individual, but rather a concern for the autonomy and freedom of the person. I suggest that we would be most likely to consent to paternalism in those instances in which it preserves and enhances for individuals their ability to rationally consider and carry out their own decisions.

I have suggested in this essay a number of situations in which it seems plasible that rational people would agree to granting the legislative powers of a society the right to impose restrictions on what Mill calls self-regarding conduct. However, rational people who know something about the resources of ignorance, ill-will, and stupidity available to the lawmakers of a society—a good case in point is the history of drug legislation in the United States—will be concerned to limit such intervention to a minimum. In closing, I suggest two principles designed to achieve this end.

In all cases of paternalistic legislation, there must be a heavy and clear burden of proof placed on the authorities to demonstrate the exact nature of the harmful effects (or beneficial consequences) to be avoided (or achieved) and the probability of their occurrence. The burden of proof here is twofold—what lawyers distinguish as the burden of going forward and the burden of persuasion. That the authorities have the burden of going forward means that it is up to them to raise the question and bring forward evidence of the evils to be avoided. Unlike the case of new drugs, when the manufacturer must produce some evidence that the drug has been tested and found not harmful, no citizen has to show with respect to self-regarding conduct that it is not harmful or promotes his or her best interests. In addition, the nature and cogency of the evidence for the harmfulness of the course of action must be set at a high level. To paraphrase a formulation of the burden of proof for criminal proceedings: better ten people ruin themselves than one person be unjustly deprived of liberty.

Finally, I suggest a principle of the least restrictive alternative. If there is an alternative way of accomplishing the desired end without restricting liberty, even though it may involve great expense, inconvenience, etc., the society must adopt it.

Notes

1. John Stuart Mill, *Utilitarianism* and *On Liberty*, ed. Mary Warnock (London: Fontana Library Edition, 1962), p. 135. All further quotes from Mill are from this edition unless otherwise noted.

2. John Stuart Mill, *Principles of Political Economy* (New York: P. F. Collier and sons, 1900), p. 442.

3. Mill, *Utilitarianism* and *On Liberty*, p. 174.

4. *Ibid.*, p. 299.

5. *Ibid.*, p. 207.

6. *Ibid.*, p. 206.

7. *Ibid.*, p. 207

8. *Ibid.*, p. 214.

9. *Ibid.*, p. 207.

10. *Ibid.*, p. 138.

11. J. F. Stephen, *Liberty, Equality, Fraternity* (New York: Henry Holt & Co., n.d.), p. 24.

12. H. L. A. Hart, *Law, Liberty and Morality* (Stanford: Stanford University Press, 1963), p.32.

13. *Ibid.*, p.33.

14. Mill, *Principles* II, p. 448.

15. *Ibid., p. 458.*

16. *Ibid.*, p. 459.

17. *Ibid.*, p. 451.

18. Stephen, p. 49.

19. Mill, *Utilitarianism* and *On Liberty*, p. 197.

20. *Ibid.*, p. 186.

21. *Ibid.*, pp. 235-6.

Chapter 3

Persuasion and Coercion for Health: Ethical Issues in Government Efforts to Change Life-Styles

Daniel Wikler

What should be the government's role in promoting the kinds of personal behavior that lead to long life and good health? Smoking, overeating, and lack of exercise increase one's chances of suffering illness later in life, as do many other habits. The role played by life-style is so important that, as stated by Fuchs, "The greatest current potential for improving the health of the American people is to be found in what they do and don't do for themselves."[1] But the public has shown little spontaneous interest in reforming. If the government uses the means at its disposal to remedy the situation, it may be faced with problems of an ethical nature. Education, exhortation, and other relatively mild measures may not prove effective in inducing self-destructive people to change their behavior. Attention might turn instead to other means, which, though possibly more effective, might also be intrusive or otherwise distasteful. In this essay, I seek to identify the moral principles underlying a reasoned judgment on whether stronger methods might justifiably be used, and, if so, what limits ought to be observed.

Millbank Memorial Fund Quarterly/*Health and Society*, vol. 56, no. 3 (1978), pp. 303-38. Reprinted with permission.

The author acknowledges support of the Joseph P. Kennedy, Jr., Foundation and of the Institute of Medicine, National Academy of Sciences; helpful suggestions from Lester Breslow, Don Detmer, Edmund Pellegrino, Michael Pollard, Bernard Towers, members of the Institute's Social Ethics Committee, and *Health and Society's* referees; and numerous points and ideas from Norman Fost, Gerald MacCallum, John Robertson, Norma Wikler, and, particularly, David Mechanic.

BACKGROUND TO GOVERNMENT INVOLVEMENT
IN LIFE-STYLE REFORM

This inquiry occurs at a time when the governement is widening its scope of involvement in life-style reform. Major prospective health policy documents of both the United States[2] and Canadian governments[3] have announced a change of orientation in this direction. Behind this shift is a host of factors, one of which is the pattern of disease in which an increasing share of ill health is attributed to chronic illnesses and accidental injuries that are aggravated by living habits. This development has caused increased interest in preventive behavioral change, and has been abetted by the current wave of "therapeutic nihilism," an attitude that questions medical intervention and is more friendly to health efforts that begin and end at home.

That life-style reform should be undertaken by the *government*, rather than by private individuals or associations, is part of the general emergence of the government as health-care provider. Encouragement of healthful living may also have a budgetary motive. Government officials may find that life-style reform is one of the most cost-effective ways of delivering health, especially if more effective change-inducing techniques are developed.[4] Indeed, the present cost-containment crisis may propel life-style reform to a central place in health planning before the necessary scientific and policy thinking has taken place.

Further pressure on the government to take strong steps to change unhealthy life-styles might come from those who live prudently. All taxpayers have a stake in keeping federal health costs down, but moderate persons may particularly view others' self-destructive life-styles as a kind of financial aggression against them. They may be expected to intensify their protest in the event of a national health insurance plan or national health service.

Involvement of the government in legislating healthful patterns of living is not wholly new; there have been public health and labor laws for a long time. Still, with the increased motivation for government action in life-style reform, it is time to reflect on the kinds of interventions the public wants and should have to accept. Various sorts of behavior-change measures need to be examined to see if they might be used to induce healthier living. But that is not enough; goals must also be identified and subjected to ethical examination.[5]

The discussion below will examine a small number of possible goals of government life-style reform, and follow with a survey of the principal kinds of steps now contemplated. The approach will be to devote attention to those behavior-change measures that are likely to be unpleasant and unwelcome. Since most techniques now used or contemplated for future use do not have such properties, there is little need to justify or focus on them. The reader should also note that each possible policy goal will be discussed in isolation from others. Although in actuality most government programs would probably be expected to serve several purposes at once, and some might be justified by the aggregate but not by one end alone, it is best for our purposes to consider one goal at a time so as to determine the contribution of each. Finally, my analysis should be understood as independent of certain political currents with which my views might be associated. There is some danger that attention to health-related personal behavior will distract the government and public from examining other sources of illness, such as unsafe working conditions, environmental health hazards, and even social and commercial determinants of the injurious behavior. Further, undue stress upon the individual's role in the cause of illness could lead to a "blame-the-victim" mentality, which could be used as a pretext for failing to make curative services available. Although these matters are essentially external to the issue of reform of unhealthy living habits, they pose ethical questions of equal or greater moral gravity.

GOALS OF HEALTH-BEHAVIOR REFORM

I propose to discuss three possible goals of health-behavior reform with regard to their appropriateness as goals of government programs and the problems arising in their pursuit. The first goal can be simply stated: health should be valued for its own sake. Americans are likely to be healthier if they can be induced to adopt healthier habits, and this may be reason enough to try to get them to do so. The second goal is the fair distribution of the burdens caused by illness. Those who become ill because of unhealthy life-styles may require the financial support of the more prudent, as well as the sharing of what may be scarce medical facilities. If this is seen as unfair to those who do not make themselves sick, life-style reform measures will also be seen as accomplishing distributive justice. The third goal is the maintenance and improvement of the general welfare, for the nation's health conditions have their effects on the economy, allocation of resources, and even national security.

Health as a Goal in Itself: Beneficence and Paternalism

Much of the present concern for the reform of unhealthy life-styles stems from concern over the health of those who live dangerously. Only a misanthrope would quarrel with this goal. There are several steps that might immediately be justified: the government could make the effects of unhealthy living habits known to those who practice them, and sponsor research to discover more of these facts. The chief concern about such efforts might be that the goverment would begin its urgings before the facts in question had been firmly established, thus endorsing living habits that might be useless or detrimental to good health.

Considerably more debate, however, would arise over a decision to use stronger methods. For example, a case in point might be a government "fat tax," which would require citizens to be weighed and taxed if overweight. The surcharges thus derived would be held in trust, to be refunded with interest if and when the taxpayers brought their weight down.[6] This pressure would, under the circumstances, be a bond imposed by the government upon its citizens, and thus can be fairly considered as coercive.

The two signal properties of this policy would be its aim of improving the welfare of obese taxpayers, and its presumed unwelcome imposition on personal freedom. (Certain individual taxpayers, of course, might welcome such an imposition, but this is not the ordinary response to penalties.) The first property might be called "beneficence," and it is generally a virtue. But the second property becomes paternalism,[7] and its status as a virtue is very much in doubt. "Paternalism" is a loaded word, almost automatically a term of reprobation. But many paternalistic policies, especially when more neutrally described, attract support and even admiration. It may be useful to consider what is bad and what is good about paternalistic practices, so that we might decide whether in this case the good outweighs the bad.[8]

What is good about some paternalistic interventions is that people are helped, or saved from harm. Citizens who have to pay a fat tax, for example, may lose weight, become more attractive, and live longer. In the eyes of many, these possible advantages are more than offset by the chief fault of paternalism, its denying persons the chance to make their own choices concerning matters that affect them. Self-direction, in turn, is valued because people usually believe themselves to be the best judges of what is good for them, and because the choosing is considred a good in itself. These beliefs are codified in our ordinary morality in the form of a moral right to noninterference so long as one does not adversely affect the interests of others. This right is supposed to shield an individual's "self-regarding" actions from intervention by others, even when those acts are not socially approved ones and even when they promise to be unwise.

At the same time, the case for paternalistic intervention on at least some occasions seems compelling. There may be circumstances in which we lose, temporarily or permanently, our capacity for competent self-direction, and thereby inflict harm upon ourselves that serves little purpose. Like Ulysses approaching the Sirens, we may hope that others would then protect us from ourselves. This sort of consideration supports our imposed guardianship of children and of the mentally retarded. Although these persons often resent our paternalistic control, we reason that we are doing what they would want us to do were their autonomy not compromised. Paternalism would be a benefit under the sort of social insurance policy that a reasonable person would opt for if considered in a moment of lucidity and competence.[9]

Does this rationale for paternalism support governmental coercion of competent adults to assure the adoption of healthy habits of living? It might seem to, at first sight. Although these adults may be generally competent, their decision-making abilities can be compromised in specific areas. Individuals may be ignorant of the consequences of their acts; they may be under the sway of social or commercial manipulation and suggestion; they may be afflicted by severe psychological stress or compulsion; or be under external constraint. If any of these conditions hold, the behavior of adults may fail to express their settled will. Those of us who disavow any intention of interfering with free and voluntary risk-taking may see cause to intervene when a person's behavior is not under his or her control.

Paternalism: Theoretical Problems. There are a number of reasons to question the general argument for paternalism in the coercive eradication of unhealthful personal practices. First, the analogy between the cases of children and the retarded, where paternalism is most clearly indicated, and of risk-taking adults is misleading. If the autonomy of adults is compromised in one or more of the ways just mentioned, it might be possible to restore that autonomy by attending to the sources of the involuntariness; the same cannot ordinarily be done with children or the retarded. Thus, adults who are destroying their health because of ignorance may be educated; adults acting under constraint may be freed. If restoration of autonomy is a realistic project, paternalistic interference is unjustified. The two kinds of interventions are aimed at the same target, i.e., harmful behavior not freely and competently chosen. But they accomplish the result differently. Paternalistic intervention blocks the harm; education and similar measures restore the choice. The state or health planners would seem obligated to use this less restrictive alternative if they can. This holds true even though the individuals might still engage in their harmful practices once autonomy is restored. This would not call for paternalistic intervention, since the risk would be voluntarily shouldered.

It remains true, however, that autonomy sometimes cannot be restored. It may be impossible to reach a given population with the information they need; or, once reached, the persons in question may prove ineducable. Psychological compulsions and social pressures may be even harder to eradicate. In these situations, the case for paternalistic interference is relatively strong, yet even here there is reason for caution. Persons who prove incapable of absorbing the facts about smoking, for example, or who abuse drugs because of compulsion or addiction, may retain a kind of second-order autonomy. They can be told that they appear unable to accept scientific truth, or that they are addicted, and they can then decide to reconsider the facts or to seek a cure. In some cases these will be decisions that the individuals are fully competent to carry out; paternalistic intervention would unjustly deny them the right to control their destinies. Coercion would be acceptable only if this second-order decision were itself constrained, compelled, or otherwise compromised—which, in the case of health-related behavior, it may often be.

A second reason for doubting the justifiability of paternalistic interference concerns the subjectivity of the notion of harm. The same experience may be seen as harmful by one person and as beneficial by another; or, even more common, the goodness (or badness) of a given eventuality may be rated very differently by different persons. Although we as individuals are often critical of the importance placed on certain events by others, we nevertheless hesitate to claim special authority in such matters. Most of us subscribe to the pluralistic ethic, for better or for worse, that has as a central tenet the proposition that there are multiple distinct, but equally valid, concepts of good and of the good life. It follows that we must use personal preferences and tastes to determine whether our health-related practices are detrimental.

Unfortunately, it is often difficult to defer to the authority of others in defining harm and benefit. It is common to feel that one's own preferences reflect values that reasonable people adopt; one can hardly regard oneself as unreasonable. To the extent that government planners employ their own concepts of good in attempting to change health practices for the public's benefit, the social insurance rationale for paternalism is clearly inapplicable.

A third reason for criticism of paternalism is the vagueness of the notion of decision-making disability. The conscientious paternalist intervenes only when the self-destructive individual's autonomy is compromised. It is probably impossible, however, to specify a compromising condition. To be sure, there are cases in which the lack of autonomy is evident, such as that of a child swallowing dangerous pills in the belief that they are candy. But the sorts of practices that would be the targets of coercive campaigns to reform health-related behavior are less dramatic and their involuntary quality much less certain. Since the free and voluntary conditons of health-related practices cannot be specified in advance, there is obviously considerable potential for unwarranted interference with fully voluntary choices.

Indeed, the dangers involved in disregarding individuals' personal values and in falsely branding their behavior involuntary are closely linked. In the absence of independent critera for decision-making disability, the paternalist may try to determine disability by seeing whether the individual is rational, i.e., whether he or she competently pursues what is valuable. An absence of rationality may be reason to suspect the presence of involuntariness and hence grounds for paternalism. The problem, however, is that this test for rationality—whether the chosen means are appropriate for the individual's personal ends—is not fully adequate. Factors that deprive an individual of autonomy—such as compulsion or constraint—not only affect a person's ability to calculate means to ends but also induce ends that are in some sense foreign. Advertisements, for example, may instill desires to consume certain substances whose pleasures would ordinarily be considered trifling. Similarly, ignorance may induce people to value a certain experience because they believe it will lead to their attainment of other ends. Alcoholics, for example, may value intoxication because they think it will enhance their social acceptance. The paternalist on the lookout for non-autonomous, self-destructive behavior will be interested not only in irrational means but also in uncharacteristic, unreasonable values.

The difficulty for the paternalist at this point is plain. The desire to interfere only with involuntary risk-taking leads to designating individuals for intervention whose behavior proceeds from externally instilled values. Pluralism commits the paternalist to use people's own values in determining whether a health-related practice is harmful. What is needed is some way of determining individuals' "true" personal values; but if these cannot be read from their behavior, how can they be known?

In certain individual cases, a person's characteristic preferences can be determined from wishes expressed before losing autonomy, as was Ulysses' desire to be tied to the mast. But this sort of data is hardly likely to be available to government health planners. The problem would be at least partially solved if we could identify a set of goods that is basic and appealing, and that nearly all rational persons value. Such universal valuation would justify a presumption of involuntariness should an individual's behavior put these goods in jeopardy. On what grounds would we include an item on this list? Simple popularity would suffice; if almost everyone likes something, such approval probably stems from a common human nature, shared even by those not professing to like that thing. Hence we may suspect that, if unconstrained, they would like it also. Alternatively, there may be experiences or qualities that, while not particularly appealing in themselves, are preconditions to attaining a wide variety of goods that people idiosyncratically value. Relief from pain is an example of the first sort of good; normal-or-better intelligence is an instance of the latter.

The crucial question for health planners is whether *health* is one of these primary goods. Considered alone, it certainly is; it is valued for its own sake, and it is a means to almost all ends. Indeed, it is a necessary good. No matter how eccentric a person's values and tastes are, no matter what kinds of activities are pleasurable, it is impossible to engage in them unless alive. Most activities a person is likely to enjoy, in fact, require not only life but good health. Unless one believes in an afterlife, the rational person must rate death as an incomparable calamity, for it means the loss of everything.

But the significance of health as a primary good should not be overestimated. The health planner may attempt to argue for coercive reform of health-destructive behavior with a line of reasoning that recalls Pascal's wager.[10] Since death, which precludes all good experience, must receive an enormously negative valuation, contemplated action that involves risk of death will also receive a substantial negative value after the good and bad consequences have been considered. And this will hold true even if the risk is small, since even low probability multiplied by a very large quantity yields a large quantity. Hence anyone who risks death by living dangerously must, in this view, be acting irrationally. This would be grounds for suspecting that the life-threatening practices were less than wholly voluntary and thus would create a need for protection. Further, this case would not require the paternalistic intervenor to turn away from pluralistic ideals, for the unhealthy habits would be faulted not on the basis of deviance from paternalistic values, but on the apparent lapse in the agent's ability to understand the logic of the acts.

This argument, or something like it, may lie behind the willingness of some to endorse paternalistic regulation of the life-styles of apparently competent adults. It is, however, invalid. Its premises may sometimes be true, and so too may its conclusion, but the one does not follow from the other. Any number of considerations can show this. For example, time factors are ignored. An act performed at age twenty-five that risks death at age fifty does not threaten every valued activity. It simply threatens the continuation of those activities past the age of fifty. The argument also overlooks an interplay between the possible courses of action: if every action that carries some risk of death or crippling illness is avoided, the enjoyment of life decreases. This makes continued life less likely to be worth the price of giving up favorite unhealthy habits.[11] Indeed, although it may be true that death would deny one of all chances for valued experiences, the experiences that make up some people's lives have little value. The less value a person places on continued life, the more rational it is to engage in activities that may brighten it up, even if they involve the risk of ending it. Craig Claiborne, food editor of *The New York Times*, gives ebullient testimony to this possibility in the conclusion of his "In Defense of Eating Rich Food":

> I love hamburgers and chili con carne and hot dogs. And foie gras and sauternes and those small birds known as ortolans. I love banquettes of quail eggs with hollandaise sauce and clambakes with lobsters dipped into so much butter it dribbles down the chin. I like cheesecake and crepes filled with cream sauces and strawberries with crème fraîche . . .
> And if I am abbreviating my stay on this earth for an hour or so, I say only that I have no desire to be a Methuselah, a hundred or more years old and still alive, grace be to something that plugs into an electric outlet.[12]

The assumption that one who is endangering one's health must be acting irrationally and involuntarily is not infrequently made by those who advocate forceful intervention in suicide attempts; and perhaps some regard unhealthy life-styles as a sort of slow suicide. The more reasonable view, even in cases of imminent suicide, seems rather to be that *some* unhealthy or self-destructive acts are less-than-fully voluntary but that others are not. Claiborne's diet certainly seems to be voluntary, and suggests that the case for paternalistic intervention in life-style cannot be made on grounds of logic alone. It remains true, however, that much of the behavior that leads to chronic illness and accidental injury is not fully under the control of the persons so acting. My thesis is merely that, first, this involuntariness must be shown (along with much else) if paternalistic intervention is to be justified; and, second, this can only be determined by case-by-case empirical study. Those who advocate coercive measures to reform life-styles, whose motives are purely beneficent, and who wish to avoid paternalism except where justified, might find such study worth undertaking.

Any such study is likely to reveal that different practitioners of a given self-destructive habit act from different causes. Perhaps one obese person overeats because of an oral fixation over which he or she has no control, while another overeats in a Pavlovian response to enticing television food advertisements. The diminished voluntariness of these actions lends support to paternalistic intervention. Claiborne has clearly thought matters through and has decided in favor of a shorter though gastronomically happier life; to pressure him into changing so that he may live longer would be a clear imposition of values and would lack the justification provided in the other persons' cases.

The trouble for a government policy of life-style reform is that a given intervention is more likely to be tailored to practices and habits than to people. Although we may someday have a fat tax to combat obesity, it would be surprising indeed to find one that imposed charges only on those whose obesity was due to involuntary factors. It would be difficult to reach agreement on what constituted diminished voluntariness, harder still to measure it, and perhaps administratively impractical to make the necessary exceptions and adjustments. We may feel, after examining the merits of the cases, that intervention is justified in the compulsive eater's life-style but not in the case of Claiborne. If the intervention takes the form of a tax on obesity as such, we face a choice: Do we owe it to those like Claiborne *not* to enforce alien values more than we owe it to compulsive overeaters to protect them from self-destruction? The general right of epicures to answer to their own values, a presumptive right conferred by the pluralistic ethic spoken of earlier, might count for more than the need of compulsive overeaters to have health imposed on them, since the first violates a right and the second merely confers a benefit. But the situation is more complex than this. The compulsive overeater's life is at stake, and this may be of greater concern (everything else being equal) than the epicure's pleasures. Then, too, the epicure is receiving a compensating benefit in the form of longer life, even if this is not a welcome exchange. And there may be many more compulsive overeaters than there are people like Claiborne. On the other hand, the positive causal link between tax and health for either is indirect and tenuous, while the negative relation between tax and gastronomic pleasure is relatively more substantial.[13] Perhaps the firmest conclusion one may draw from all this is that a thoroughly reasoned moral rationale for a given kind of intervention can be very difficult to carry out.

Paternalism: Problems in Practice. Even if we accept the social insurance rationale for paternalism in the abstract, there are theoretical reasons to question its applicability to the problem of life-styles that are injurious to health. It is still possible that in some instances these doubts can be laid to rest. We may have some noncircular way of determining when self-destructive behavior is involuntary; we may have knowledge of what preferences people would have were their behavior not constrained; and there may be no way to restore their autonomy. While at least a prima facie case for paternalistic intervention would exist under such circumstances, I think it is important to note several practical problems that could arise in any attempt to design and carry out a policy of coercive life-style reform.

First, there is the distinct possibility that the government that takes over decision-making power from partially incompetent individuals may prove even less adept at securing their interests than the individuals would have been if left alone. Paucity of scientific data may lead to misidentification of risk factors. The primitive state of the art in health promotion and mass-scale behavior modification may render interventions ineffective or even counterproductive. And the usual run of political and administrative tempests that affects all public policy may result in the misapplication of such knowledge as is available in these fields. These factors call for recognizing a limitation on the social insurance rationale for paternalism. If rational persons doubt that the authorities who would be guiding their affairs during periods of their incompetence would themselves be particularly competent, they are unlikely to license interventions except when there is a high probability of favorable cost-benefit trade-off. This yields the strongest support for those interventions that prevent very serious injuries, and in which the danger posed is imminent.[14]

These reflections count against a rationale for government involvement in vigorous health-promotion efforts, as recently voiced by the Secretary of Health, Education, and Welfare[15] and found elsewhere.[16] Their statements that smoking and similar habits are "slow suicide" and should be treated as such make a false analogy, precisely because suicide often involves certain imminent dangers of the most serious sort in situations in which there cannot be time to determine whether the act is voluntary. This is just the sort of case that the social insurance policy here described would cover; but this would not extend to the self-destruction that takes thirty years to accomplish.

Second, there is a possibility that what would be advertised as concern for the individual's welfare (as that person defines it) would turn out to be simple legal moralism, i.e., an attempt to impose the society's or authorities' moral prescriptions upon those not following them. In Knowles's call for life-style reform the language is suggestive:

> The next major advances in the health of the American people will result
> from the assumption of individual responsibility for one's own health. This
> will require a change in lifestyle for the majority of Americans. The cost of
> sloth, gluttony, alcoholic overuse, reckless driving, sexual intemperance,
> and smoking is now a national, not an individual, responsibility.[17]

All but the last of these practices are explicit *vices*; indeed, the first two—sloth and gluttony—use their traditional names. The intrusion of nonmedical values is evidenced by the fact that of all the life-style habits that affect health adversely, only those that are sins (with smoking excepted) are mentioned as targets for change. Skiing and football produce injuries as surely as sloth produces heart disease; and the decision to postpone childbearing until the thirties increases susceptibility to certain cancers in women.[18] If it is the unhealthiness of "sinful" living habits that motivates the paternalist toward reform, then ought not other acts also be targeted on occasions when persons exhibit lack of self-direction? The fact that other practices are not ordinarily pointed out in this regard provides no *argument* against paternalistic life-style reform. Both those who favor pressuring the slothful to engage in physical exercise might ask themselves if they also favor pressure on habits that, though unhealthy, are not otherwise despised. If enthusiasm for paternalistic intervention slackens in these latter cases, it may be a signal for reexamination of the motives.

A third problem is that the involuntariness of some self-destructive behavior may make paternalistic-reform efforts ineffective. To the extent that the unhealthy behavior is not under the control of the individual, we cannot expect the kind of financial threat involved in a "fat tax" to exert much influence. Paradoxically, the very conditions under which paternalistic intervention seems most justified are those in which many of the methods available are least likely to succeed. The result of intervention under these circumstances may be a failure to change the life-threatening behavior, and a needless (and inexcusable) addition to the individual's woes through the unpleasantness of the intervention itself. A more appropriate target for government intervention might be the commercial and/or social forces that cause or support the life-threatening behavior.

Although the discussion above has focused on the problems attendant to a paternalistic argument for coercive health-promotion programs, I have implicitly outlined a positive case for such interventions as well. A campaign to reform unhealthy life-styles will be justified, in my view, so long as it does not run afoul of the problems I have mentioned. It may indeed be possible to design such a program. In any case, the relative weight of the case against paternalistic intervention can be lessened by making adjustments for the proportion of intervention, benefit, and intrusion. Health-promotion programs that are only very mildly coercive, such as moderate increases in cigarette taxes, require very little justification; noncoercive measures such as health education require none at all. And the case for more intrusive measures would be stronger if greater and more certain benefits could be promised. Moreover, even if the paternalistic rationale for coercive reform of health-related behavior fails completely, there may be other rationales to justify the intrusion. It is to these other sorts of arguments that I now turn.

Fair Distribution of Burdens

The problem of health-related behavior is sometimes seen as a straightforward question of collective social preference:

> The individual must realize that a perpetuation of the present system of high cost, after-the-fact medicine will only result in higher costs and greater frustration . . . This is his primary critical choice: to change his personal bad habits or stop complaining. He can either remain the probem or become the solution to it; Beneficent Government cannot—indeed, should not—do it for him or to him.[19]

A good deal of the controversy is due, however, not to any one person's distaste for having to choose between bad habits and high costs, but rather some people's distaste for having to accept both high costs and someone *else's* bad habits. In the view of these persons, those who indulge in self-destructive practices and present their medical bills to the public are free riders in an economy kept going by the willingness of others to stay fit and sober. Those who hold themselves back from reckless living may care little about beneficence. When they call for curbs on the expensive health practices of others, they want the government to act as their agent primarily out of concern for their interests.

The demand for protection from the costs of calamities other people bring upon themselves involves an appeal to fairness and justice. Both the prudent person and the person with unhealthy habits, it is thought, are capable of safe and healthy living; why should the prudent have to pay for neighbors who decide to take risks? Neighbors are certainly not permitted to set fire to their houses if there is danger of its spreading. With the increasing economic and social connectedness of society, the use of coercion to discourage the unhealthy practices of others may receive the same justification. As the boundary between private and public becomes less distinct, and decisions of the most personal sort come to have markedly adverse effects upon others, the state's protective function may be thought to give it jurisdiction over any health-related aspect of living.

This sort of argument presupposes a certain theory of justice; one who wishes to take issue with the rationale for coercive intervention in health-related behavior might join the debate at the level of theory. Since this debate would be carried out at a quite general level, with only incidental references to health practices, I will accept the argument's premise (if only for argument's sake) and comment only upon its applicability to the problem of self-destructive behavior. A number of considerations lead to the conclusion that the fairness argument as a justification of coercive intervention, despite initial appearances, is anything but straightforward. Underlying this argument is an empirical premise that may well prove untrue of at least some unhealthy habits: that those who take chances with their health *do* place a significant financial burden upon society. It is not enough to point to the costs of medical care for lung cancer and other diseases brought on by individual behavior. As Hellegers[20] points out, one must also determine what the individual would have died of had he not engaged in the harmful practice, and subtract the cost of the care which that condition requires. There is no obvious reason to suppose that the diseases brought on by self-destructive behavior are costlier to treat than those that arise from "natural causes,"

Skepticism over the burden placed on society by smokers and other risk-takers is doubly reinforced by consideration of the nonmedical costs and benefits that may be involved. It may turn out, for all we know prior to investigation, that smoking tends to cause few problems during a person's productive years and then to kill the individual before the need to provide years of social security and pension payments. From this perspective, the truly burdensome individual may be the unreasonably fit senior citizen who lives on for thirty years after retirement, contributing to the bankruptcy of the social security system, and using up savings that would have reverted to the public purse via inheritance taxes, had an immoderate life-style brought an early death. Taken at face value, the fairness argument would require taxes and other disincentives on *non*-smoking and other healthful personal practices which in the end would sap the resources of the healthy person's fellow citizens. Only detailed empirical inquiry can show which of these practices would be slated for discouragement were the argument from fairness accepted; but the fact that we would find penalties on healthful behavior wholly unpalatable may weaken our acceptance of the argument itself.

A second doubt concerning the claim that the burdens of unhealthy behavior are unfairly distributed also involves an unstated premise. The risk-taker, according to the fairness argument, should have to suffer not only the illness that may result from the behavior, but also the loss of freedom attendant to the coercive measures used in the attempt to change the behavior. What, exactly, is the cause cited by those complaining of the financial burdens placed upon society by the self-destructive? It is not simply the burden of caring and paying for care of these persons when they become sick. Many classes of persons impose such costs on the public besides the self-destructive. For example, diabetics, and others with hereditary dispositions to contract diseases, incur unusual and heavy expenses, and these are routinely paid by others. Why are these costs not resisted as well?

One answer is that there *is* resistance to these other costs, which partly explain why we do not yet have a national health insurance system. But even those willing to pay for the costs of caring for diabetics, or the medical expenses of the poor, may still bridle when faced by the needs of those who have compromised their own health. Is there a rationale for resisting the latter kinds of costs while accepting the former? One possible reason to distinguish the costs of the person with a genetic disease from those of the person with a life-style-induced disease is simply that one can be prevented and the other cannot. Health-behavior-change measures provide an efficient way of reducing the overall financial burden of health care that society must shoulder, and this might be put forward as the reason that self-destructive persons may have their presumptive rights compromised while others with special medical expenses need not.

But this is not the argument we seek. The medical costs incurred by diseases caused by unhealthy life-styles may be preventable, if our behavior-modifying methods are effective; but this fact shows only that there is a utilitarian opportunity for reducing costs and saving health-care dollars. It does *not* show that this opportunity makes it right to burden those who lead unhealthy lives with governmental intrusion. If costs must be reduced, perhaps they should be reduced some other way (e.g., by lessening the quality of care provided for all); or perhaps costs should not be lowered and those feeling burdened should be made to tolerate the expense. The fact that money could be saved by intruding into the choice of life-styles of the self-destructive does not *itself* show that it would be particulary fair to do so.

If intrusion is to be justified on the grounds that unhealthy life-styles impose unfair financial burdens on others, something must be added to the argument. That extra element, it seems, is *fault*. Instead of the *avoidability* of the illnesses and their expenses, we point to the *responsibility* for them, which we may believe falls · upon those who contract them. This responsibility, it might be supposed, makes it unfair to force others to pay the bills and makes it fair for others to take steps to prevent the behaviors that might lead to the illness, even at the cost of some of the responsible person's privacy and liberty.

The argument thus depends crucially on the premise that the person who engages in an unhealthy life-style is responsible for the costs of caring for the illness that it produces. "Responsible" has many senses, and this premise needs to be stated unambiguously. Since responsibility was brought into the argument in hopes of contrasting life-style-related diseases from others, it seems to involve the notions of choice and voluntariness. If the chronic diseases resulting from life-style were not the result of voluntary choices, then there could be no assignment of responsibility in the sense in which the term is being used. This would be the case, for example, if a person contracted lung cancer from breathing the smog in the atmosphere rather than from smoking. But what if it should turn out that even a` person's smoking habit were the result of forces beyond the smoker's control? If the habit is involuntary, so is the illness; and the smoker in this instance is no more to be held liable for the costs of treatment than would, say, the diabetic. Since much self-destructive behavior is the result of suggestion, constraint, compulsion, and other factors, the applicability of the fairness argument is limited.

Even if the behavior leading to illness is wholly voluntary, there is not necessarily any justification for intervention *by the state*. The only parties with rights to reform life-styles on these grounds are those who are actually being burdened by the costs involved. Wealthy people who retained their own medical facilities would not justifiably be a target of any of these interventions, and members of a prepaid health plan would be liable to intervention primarily from others in their payments pool. Those members with unhealthy life-styles would then, of course, have the option of resigning and continuing their self-destructive ways; or they might seek out an insurance scheme designed for those who wish to take chances, but who also want to limit their losses. These insured parties would join forces precisely to pool risks and remove reasons for refraining from unhealthy practices; preventive coercion would thus be out of the question. Measures undertaken by the government and applied indiscriminately to all who indulge in a given habit may thus be unfair to some (unless other justification is provided). The administrative inconvenience of restricting these interventions to the appropriate parties might make full justice on this issue too impractical to achieve.

This objection may lose force should there be a national health insurance program in which membership would be mandatory. Indeed, it might be argued that existing federal support of medical education, research, and service answers this objection now. But this only establishes another ground for disputing the responsibility of self-destructive individuals for the costs of their medical care. To state this objection, two classes of acts must be distinguished: the acts constituting the life-style that causes the disease and creates the need for care; and the acts of imposing financial shackles upon an unwilling public. Unless the acts in the first group are voluntary, the argument for imposing behavior change does not get off the ground. Even if they are voluntary, the acts in the second class might not be. Destructive acts affect others only because others are in financial relationships with the individual, relationships that cause the medical costs to be distributed among them. Thus, if the financial arrangement is mandatory, the individual may not have *chosen* that his or her acts should have these effects on others. The situation will have been this: an individual is compelled by law to enter into financial relationships with certain others as a part of an insurance scheme; the arrangement causes the individual's acts to have effects on others that the others object to; and so they claim the right to coerce the individual into desisting from those acts. It seems difficult to assign to this individual responsibility for the distribution of financial brdens. He or she may (or may not) be responsible for getting sick, but not for having the sickness affect others adversely.

This objection has certain inherent limitations in its scope. It applies only to individuals who are brought into a mandatory insurance scheme against their wishes. Those who join the scheme gladly may perhaps be assigned responsibility for the effect they have on others once they are in it; and certainly many who will be covered in such a plan will be glad of it. Further, the burden imposed under such a plan does not occur until persons who have made themselves sick request treatment and present the bill to the public. Only if treatment is mandatory and all financing of care taken over by the public can the imposition of burden be said to wholly involuntary.

In any case, certain adjustments could be made in a national health insurance plan or service that would disarm this objection. Two such changes are obvious: the plan could be made voluntary, rather than mandatory; and/or the public could simply accept the burdens imposed by unhealthy life-styles and refrain from attempts to modify them. The first of these may be impractical for economic reasons (in part because the plan would fill up with those in greatest need, escalating costs), and the second only ignores the problem for which it is supposed to be a solution.

There is, however, a response that would seem to have more chance of success: allowing those with unhealthy habits to pay their own way. Users of cigarettes and alcohol, for example, could be made to pay an excise tax, the proceeds of which would cover the costs of treatment for lung cancer and other resulting illnesses. Unfortunately, these costs would also be paid by users who are not abusers: those who drink only socially would be forced to pay for the excesses of alcoholics. Alternatively, only those contracting the illnesses involved could be charged; but it would be difficult to distinguish illnesses resulting from an immoderate life-style from those due to genetic or environmental causes. The best solution might be to identify persons taking risks (by tests for heavy smoking, alcohol abuse, or dangerous inactivity) and charge higher insurance premiums accordingly. This method could be used only if tests for these behaviors were developed that were non-intrusive and administratively manageable.[21] The point would be to have those choosing self-destructive life-styles assume the true costs of their habits. I defer to economists for devising the best means to this end.[22]

This kind of policy has its good and bad points. Chief among the favorable ones is that it allows a maximum retention of liberty in a situation in which liberty carries a price. Under such a policy, those who wished to continue their self-destructive ways without pressure could continue to do so, provided that they absorbed the true costs of their practices themselves. Should they not wish to shoulder these costs, they could submit to the efforts of the government to induce changes in their behavior. If the rationale for coercive reform is the burden the unhealthy life-styles impose on others, this option seems to meet its goals; and it does so in a way that does not require loss of liberty and immunity from intrusions. Indeed, committed immoderates might have reason to welcome the imposition of these costs. Although their expenses would be greater, they would thereby remove at one stroke the most effective device held by others to justify meddling with their "chosen" life-styles.[23]

The negative side of this proposal stems from the fact that under its terms the only way to retain one's liberty is to pay for it. This, of course, offers very different opportunities to rich and poor. This inequality can be assessed in very different ways. From one perspective, the advantage money brings to rich people under this scheme is the freedom to ruin their own health. Although the freedom may be valued intrinsically (i.e., for itself, not as a means to some other end), the resulting illness cannot; perhaps the poor, who are denied freedom but given a better chance for health, are coming off best in the transaction. From another prospective, however, it seems that such a plan simply adds to the degradation already attending to being poor. Only the poor would be forced to submit to loss of privacy, loss of freedom from pressure, and regulation aimed at behavior change. Such liberties are what make up full citizenship, and one might hold that they ought not to be made contingent on one's ability to purchase them.[24]

The premise that illnesses caused by unhealthy habits impose financial burdens on society does not automatically give cause for adopting strong measures to change the self-destructive behavior. Still, it *may* do so, if the underlying theory of justice is correct and if its application can skirt the problems mentioned here. Besides, justification for such programs may be derived from other considerations.

Indeed, there is one respect in which the combined force of the paternalistic rationale and the fairness argument is greater than the sum of its parts. The central difficulty for the fairness argument, mentioned above, is that much of the self-destructive behavior that burdens the public is not really the fault of the individual; various forces, internal and external, may conspire to produce such behavior independently of the person's will. Conversely, a problem for the paternalist is that much of the harm from which the individual would be "protected" may be the result of free, voluntary choices, and hence beyond the paternalist's purview. The best reason to be skeptical of the first rationale is doubt over the *presence* of voluntariness; the best reason to doubt the second concerns the *absence* of voluntariness. Whatever weighs against the one will count for the other.

The self-destructive individual, then, is caught in a theoretical double-bind: whether the behavior is voluntary or not, there will be at least prime facie grounds for coercive intervention. The same holds true for partial voluntariness and involuntariness. This consideration is of great importance for those wanting to justify coercive reform of health-related behavior. It reduces the significance of the notion of voluntariness in the pro-intervention arguments, and so serves to lessen concern over the intractable problems of defining the notion adequately, and detecting and measuring its occurrence.

Public Welfare

Aside from protecting the public from unfair burdens imposed by those with poor health habits, there may be social benefits to be realized by inducing immoderates to change their behavior. Health-behavior change may be the most efficient way to reduce the costs of health care in this country, and the benefits derived may give reason to create some injustices. Further, life-style reform could yield some important collective benefits. A healthier work force means a stronger economy, for example, and the availability of healthy soldiers enhances national security.

There may also be benefits more directly related to health. If the supply of doctors and curative facilities should prove relatively inelastic, or if the economy would falter if too much of our resources were diverted to health care, it may be impossible to increase access to needed medical services. The social goal of adequate treatment for all would then not be realizable unless the actual need for medical care were reduced. Vigorous government efforts to change life-styles may be seen as the most promising means to this end.

The achievement of these social goals—enhanced security, improved economic functioning, and universal access to medical care—could come at the price of limits to the autonomy of that segment of society that indulges in dangerous living. If we do not claim to find fault with them, it would be unreasonable to insist that the immoderate *owed* the loss of some of their liberties to society as a part of some special debt—while continuing to exempt from special burden those with involuntary special needs due to genes or body chemistry. The reason for society to impose a loss upon the immoderate rather than upon the diabetic would be, simply, that it stood to benefit more by doing so.

Whether it is permissible to pursue social goods by extracting benefits from disadvantageously situated groups within society is a matter of political ideology and justice. Our society routinely compromises certain of its citizens' interests and privileges for the public good; others are considered inviolate. The question to be decided is whether the practices that we now know to be dangerous to health merit the protection given by the status of right. The significance of this status is that considerations of utility must be very strong before curbing the practice can be justified. Unfortunately, I see no decisive argument that shows that smoking, sloth, and other dangerous enjoyable pastimes are or are not protected by rights. It is worth mentioning, however, that many behaviors of interest to health planners are almost certainly of too trivial significance to aspire to such protection; freedom to drive at sixty-five miles per hour rather than fifty-five is an example, as is the privilege of buying medicine in non-childproof containers. Consideration of social utility would seem to justify much that is being currently overlooked in prevention of injury and illness through behavior change.

Even those whose ideology would not ordinarily accept government intervention on these grounds might make an exception for reform of unhealthy habits. Even if the real motivation for the reform efforts were to achieve the social goals mentioned above, some of the intervention might in fact be justifiable on paternalistic grounds; and even the intervention that is not thus justified confers some benefit in the form of promise of better health.

MEANS OF HEALTH BEHAVIOR REFORM

Two questions arise in considering the ethics of government attempts to bring about healthier ways of living. The first question is: Should coercion, intrusion, and deprivation be used as methods for inducing change? The other question is: How do we decide whether a given health-promotion program is coercive, is intrusive, or inflicts deprivations? These questions are independent of each other. Two parties who agreed on the degree of coerciveness that might be justifiably employed in a given situation might still assess a proposed policy differently in this regard, and hence reach different conclusions on whether the policy should be put into effect.

Disagreement over the degree of coerciveness of health-behavior-change programs is to be expected, not least because of the vagueness of the notion of coercion itself. Some of the most difficult problems addressed in the philosophical literature[25] arise in the present context: What is the difference between persuasion and manipulation? Can offers and incentives be coercive, or is coerciveness a property only of threats? And can one party be said to have coerced another even if the latter manages to accomplish that which the first party tried to prevent?

The answers to these and similar queries will affect the evaluation of various kinds of health promotion measures.

Health Education

Health education seems harmless. Education generally provides information and this generally increases our power, since it enhances the likelihood that our decisions will accomplish our ends. For the most part, there is no inherent ethical problem with such programs, and they do not stand in need of moral justification. Still, there are certain problems with some health-education programs, and these should be mentioned.

Health education *could* be intrusive. Few could object to making information available to those who seek it out. But if "providing information" were taken to mean making sure that the public attained a high level of awareness of the message, the program might require an objectionably high level of exposure. This is primarily an esthetic issue, and is unlikely to cause concern.

Can education be coercive? Information can be used as a tool for one party to get another to do its bidding, just as threats can. But the method is different: Instead of changing the prospective consequences of available actions, which is what a threat does, education alerts one to the previously unrecognized consequences of one's acts. Educators who hope to increase healthful behavior will disseminate only information that points in that direction; they cannot be expected to point out that, in addition to causing deterioration of the liver, alcohol helps certain people feel relaxed in social settings. It is difficult to know whether to regard this selective informing as manipulative. Theoretically at least, people are free to seek out the other side on their own. Such measures acquire more definite coercive coloration when they are combined with suppression of the other side; "control over the means of persuasion" is another option open to reformers.[26]

The main threat of coerciveness in health-education programs, in my opinion, lies in the possibility that such programs may turn from providing information to manipulating attitude and motivation. Education, in the sense of providing information, is a means of inducing belief and knowledge. A review of the literature indicates, however, that when health-education programs are evaluated, they are not judged successful or unsuccessful in proportion to their success in *inducing belief*. Rather, evaluators look at *behavior change*, the actions that, they hope, would stem from these beliefs. If education programs are to be evaluated favorably, health educators may be led to take a wider view of their role[27]. This would include attempts to motivate the public to adopt healthy habits, and this might have to be supplied by covert appeals to other interests (''smokers are unpopular,'' and so on). Suggestion and manipulation may replace information as the tools used by the health educators to accomplish their purpose.[28] Indeed, health education may call for actual and deliberte *mis*information: directives may imply or even state that the scientific evidence in favor of a given health practice is unequivocal even when it is not.[29]

A fine line has been crossed in these endeavors. Manipulation and suggestion go well beyond providing information to enhance rational decision-making. These measures bypass rational decision-making faculties and thereby inflict a loss of personal control. Thus, health education, except when restricted to information, requires some justification. The possible deleterious effects are so small that the justification required may be slight, but the requirement is there. Ethical concerns for this kind of practice may become more pressing as the educational techniques used to induce behavior change become more effective.[30]

Incentives, Subsidies, and Taxes

Incentive measures range from pleasantly noncoercive efforts, such as offering to pay citizens if they will live prudently, to coercive measures such as threatening to fine them if they do not. Various noncoercive measures designed to facilitate healthful life-styles might include: providing jogging paths and subsidizing tennis balls. Threats might include making all forms of transporation other than bicycling difficult, and making inconvenient the purchase of food containing saturated fats.

Generally speaking, justification is required only for coercive measures, not for incentives. However, the distinction is not as clear as it first appears. Suppose, for example, that the government wants to induce the obese to lose weight, and that a mandatory national health-insurance plan is about to go into effect. The government's plan threatens the obese with higher premiums unless they lose their excess weight. Before the plan is instituted, however, someone objects that the extra charges planned for eager eaters make the program coercive. No adequate justification is found. Instead of calling off the program, however, some subtle changes are made. The insurance scheme is announced with higher premiums than had been originally planned. No extra charges are imposed on anyone; instead, discounts are offered to all those who avoid overweight. Instead of coercion, the plan now uses positive incentives; this does not require the kind of justification needed for the former plan. Hence the new program is allowed to go into effect.

The effect of the rate structure in the two plans is, of course, identical: The obese would pay the higher rate, the slender the lower one. It seems that the distinction between coercion and incentive is merely semantic. But this is the wrong conclusion. There is a real difference, upon which much ethical evaluation must rest; the problem is in stating what that difference amounts to. A partial answer is that a given measure cannot be judged coercive or noncoercive without referring to a background standard from which the measure's effects diverge favorably or unfavorably. Ultimately, I believe, the judgment required for the obesity measure would require us to decide what a fair rate would have been for the insurance; any charges above that fair rate would be coercive, and any below, incentive.[31] The rate the government plans to charge as the standard premium might not be the fair rate; and this shows that one cannot judge the coerciveness of a fee structure merely by checking it for surcharges.

Even if we are able to sort the coercive from the incentive measures, however, we may have reason to hesitate before allowing the government unlimited use of incentives. A government in a position to make offers may not necessarily coerce those it makes the offers to, but it is relatively more likely to get its way; in this sense its power increases. Increased government power over lifestyles would seem generally to require some justification. In particular, there is inevitably some danger that, given the present scientific uncertainty about the effects of many habits, practices might be encouraged that would contribute nothing to health or that would even be dangerous. A further problem with financial incentives is that if they are to affect the behavior of the rich they must be sizable, and this may redistribute wealth in a direction considered unjust on other grounds.

The imposition of financial penalties as a means of inducing behavior raises questions that have been touched on above. The chief issue, of course, is the deprivation this method inflicts. Even when justifiably applied to induce behavior change, no *more* deprivation ought to be used than is necessary; but there are administrative difficulties in trying to obey this limitation. Different persons respond to different amounts of deprivation—again, the rich person will absorb costs that would deter the poor one. A disincentive set higher than that needed to induce behavior change would be unfair; a rate set too low would be ineffective. The amount of deprivation inflicted ought, then, to be tailored to the individual's wealth and psychology. This may well be administratively impossible, and injustice would result to the degree that these differences were ignored.

Regulative Measures

The coercive measures discussed above concentrate on applying influence on individuals so that their behavior will change. A different way of effecting a reform is to deprive self-destructive individuals of the means needed to engage in their unhealthy habits. Prohibition of the sale of cigarettes would discourage smokng at least as effectively as exhortations not to smoke or insurance surcharges for habitual tobacco use. Yet these regulative measures are surely as coercive, although they do not involve direct interaction with the individuals affected. They are merely one more way of intervening in an individual's decision to engage in habits that may cause illness. As such, they are clearly in need of the same or stronger justification as those involving threats, despite the argument that these measures are taken only to combat an unhealthy *environment*, and thus cannot be counted as coercing the persons who have unhealthy ways of living.[32] What distinguishes these ''environmental'' causes of illness from, say, carcinogens in the water supply, is the active connivance of the victims. ''Shielding'' the ''victims'' from these external forces must involve making them behave in a way they do not choose. This puts regulative measures in the same category as those applied directly to the self-destructive individuals.

CONCLUSIONS

I have been concerned with clarifying what sorts of justification must be given for certain kinds of government involvement in the reform of unhealthy ways of living. It is apparent that more is needed than a simple desire on the part of the government to promote health and/or reduce costs. When the measures taken are intrusive, coercive, manipulative, and/or inflict deprivations—in short, when they are of the sort many might be expected to dislike—the moral justification required may be quite complex. The principles that would be used in making a case for these interventions may have limited scope and require numerous exceptions and qualifications; it is unlikely that they can be expressed in simple slogans such as ''individuals must be responsible for their own health'' or ''society can no longer afford self-destructiveness.''

My goal has been to specify the kind of justification that would have to be provided for any coercive life-style reform measure. I have not attempted to reach a judgment of right or wrong. Either of these judgments would be foolhardy, if only in view of the diversity of health-promotion measures that have been and will be contemplated. Yet it might be appropriate to recall a few negative and positive points on life-style reform.

Inherent in the subject matter is a danger that reform efforts, however rationalized and advertised, may become ''moralistic,'' that is, become an imposition of the particular preferences and values of one (powerful) group upon another. Workers in medicine and related fields may naturally focus on the medical effects of everyday habits and practices, but others may not. From this perspective, trying to induce the public to change its style of living would represent an enormous expansion of the medical domain, a ''medicalization of life.'' The parochial viewpoint of the health advocate can reach absurd limits. A recent presidential address to a prominent professional health organization, for example, came close to calling for abolition of alcohol simply on the grounds that the rate of cirrhosis of the liver had increased by six per 100,000 over the last forty years. In this instance, health is being imposed upon us as a goal from above; perhaps medicine would serve us best if it acted to remove the dangers from the pursuit of other goals.

When the motivation behind life-style reform is concern for taxpayers rather than for self-destructive individuals, problems of a different kind are posed. Insistence that individuals are "responsible" for their own health may stem from a conflation of two different phenomena: an individual's life-style playing a causal role in producing illness, and that individual being at fault and accountable for his or her life-style and illness. The former may be undeniable, but the latter may be very difficult to prove. Unless difficulties in this view are acknowledged, attention may be diverted from the various external causes of dangerous health-related behavior, resulting in a lessening of willingness to aid the person whose own behavior has resulted in illness.

On the positive side, two points made earlier bear repetition. First, although I have emphasized the difficulties in justifying coercive measures to induce life-style change, I have done so in the course of outlining the sort of case that might be made in support of these measures. It is entirely possible that such measures might be fair and desirable; at least, this is consistent with the principles I have claimed are relevant to deciding the issue. Second, few of the steps called for in either the professional or lay literature have been very coercive or intrusive in nature. Little of what I have said goes against any of these. Indeed, one hopes that these measures will be funded and used to the extent they are effective. An increase in the number and scope of such research, education, and incentive programs may be the best result of the current attention to the role of life-style in maintaining health. This would serve two goals over which there cannot be serious dispute: enabling people to be as healthy as they want to be, given the costs involved; and reducing overall medical need so as to make room in the health-care system for all who still require care.

Notes

1. V. R. Fuchs, *Who Shall Live?* (New York: Basic Books, 1974).
2. Department of Health, Education and Welfare, *Forward Plan for Health FY 1977-81* (Washington, DC: U.S. Government Printing Office, June, 1975).
3. M. Lalonde, *A New Perspective on the Health of Canadians* (Ottawa: Government of Canada, April, 1974).
4. Although there is much dispute over the effectiveness of many health-promotion measures, efficient techniques may be developed in step with the progress of behavioral medicine generally. See E. Ubell, "Health Behavior Change: A Political Model," *Preventive Medicine* 1(2):209-221; O. Pomerleau, F. Pass, and V. Crown, "Role of Behavior Modification in Preventive Medicine," *The New England Journal of Medicine* 292(24):1277-82; and R.J. Haggerty, "Changing Lifestyles to Improve Health," *Preventive Medicine* 6(2):276-89.
5. I am not attempting to determine what the actual goals of the government are in intervening in lifestyle; indeed, it may make little sense to speak of specific goals at all. (See G.C. MacCallum, "Legislative Intent," *Yale Law Journal* 75(5):754-87.) The rationale for legislation, as voiced by the legislature, may have the purpose of establishing the legal basis for the legislation rather than that of exhibiting the legislators' goals in passing the measures or of identifying the need to which the measure was a response.

For example, a bill requiring motorcyclists to wear helmets might be accepted by the public on paternalistic grounds, but the personal motivation of the legislators may have been harassment of the cyclists. And the measure might be upheld in court as a legitimate attempt to prevent the public from being saddled with the cost of caring for injured cyclists who could not afford to pay for medical care.

My inquiry into the goals of a proposed health policy has the sole purpose of determining whether the goal of the policy and the means to it are legitimate. Thus, if it is decided that such a helmet law is unwarranted, even on the paternalistic grounds that seem most applicable, it will not concern us that the law could be cleared through the courts by nimble use of the possibility of the cyclists becoming public charges. This is not to denigrate the use of such methods in the practice of legislation and legal challenge; but these pursuits are different from those undertaken here.

6. This measure was concocted for the present essay, but it shares its important features with others that have actually been proposed.

7. "Coercive beneficence" is not a fully correct definition of paternalism, but I will not attempt to give adequate definition here. (See G. Gert and C. Culver, "Paternalistic Behavior," *Philosophy and Public Affairs* 6(1):45-57.) The term itself is unnecessarily sex-linked; "Paternalism" carries the same meaning without this feature. However, "paternalism" is a standard term in philosophical writing, and a change from it invites confusion.

8. For detailed discussions of paternalism in the abstract, see J. Feinberg, *Social Philosophy* (Englewood Cliffs, NJ: Prentice Hall, 1973); G. Dworkin, "Paternalism," in R. Wasserstrom, ed., *Morality and the Law* (Belmont, CA: Wadsworth Publishing, 1971), pp.107-26; M.D. Bayles, "Criminal Paternalism," in J.R. Pennock and J.W. Chapman, eds., *The Limits of Law: Nomos XV* (New York: Lieber, Atherton); and J. Hodson, "The Principle of Paternalism," *American Philosophical Quarterly* 14(1):61-9.

9. Dworkin, "Paternalism," pp. 107-26.

10. Agnostics should adopt the habits that would foster their own belief in God. If they do and God exists, they will receive the infinite rewards of paradise; if they do and God does not exist, they were only wasting the efforts of conversion and prayer. If they do not try to believe in God, and religion is true, they suffer the infinitely bad fate of hell; whereas if God does not exist they have merely saved some inconvenience. Conversion is the rational choice even if agnostics estimate the chances of God's existing as very remote, since even a very small probability yields a large index when multiplied against an infinite quantity.

11, Readers of the previous footnote might note that a similar difficulty attends Pascal's wager. If agnostics took steps to foster belief in every deity for which the chance of existing was greater than zero, the inconvenience suffered would be considerable after all. Yet such would be required by the logic of the wager.

12. Craig Claiborne, "In Defense of Eating Rich Food," *The New York Times*, December 8, 1976, pp. C1, C13.

13. For a fuller discussion of this type of trade-off, see Bayles, "Criminal Paternalism."

14. Feinberg, *Social Philosophy*.

15. Department of Health, Education and Welfare, *Forward Plan*.

16. T. McKeown and C.R. Lowe, *An Introduction to Social Medicine*, 2nd ed. (Oxford: Blackwell's, 1974).

17. J. H. Knowles, "The Struggle to Stay Healthy," *Time*, August 9, 1976, pp. 60-62. Elsewhere, however, Dr. Knowles emphasizes that "he who hates sin, hates humanity" (J.H. Knowles, "The Responsibility of the Individual," in J.H. Knowles, ed., *Doing Better and Feeling Worse* [New York: W.W. Norton, 1977], pp. 57-80). Knowles's argument in the latter essay is primarily nonpaternalistic.

18. T.B. Medawar, "Signs of Cancer," *New York Review of Books* 24(10):10-14.

19. Knowles, "Responsibility of the Individual."

20. A. Hellegers, personal communication, 1978.

21. It may be that the only way to separate those smokers and drinkers taking risks from those not taking risks is to wait until illness develops or fails to develop. Perhaps smokers could save their tax seals and cash them in for refunds if they reach the age of sixty-five without developing lung cancer!

22. The reader may sense a paradox by this point. Taxes on unhealthy habits would avoid inequities involved in life-style reform measures, such as taxes on unhealthy habits. And it is true that some of the steps that might be taken to permit those with unhygienic life-styles to assume the costs incurred might resemble those that could be used to induce them to give up the habits. Despite this, and despite the fact that the two kinds of programs might even have the same effects, I believe that they can and ought to be distinguished. The imposition of a fat tax has a behavior change as its goal. It is this goal that made it a topic for discussion in this paper. The tax would not be imposed to cover the costs of diseases stemming from unhealthy life-styles—indeed, as the reader will recall, the funds obtained through the tax were to be kept in trust and returned later if and when the behavior changed. In contrast, the taxes being mentioned as part of a pay-as-you-go plan would not be imposed as a means to changing behavior. Such a proposal would constitute one way of financing health costs, a topic I am not addressing in the present paper. These taxes would, of course, tend to discourage the behavior in question; but this welcome effect would not be their purpose nor provide their rationale (more precisely, *need* not be their purpose). Any program, of course, can serve multiple needs simultaneously. The pay-as-you-go tax would succeed as a program even if no behavior change occurred, and the behavior-modifying tax would succeed if behavior did change even if no funds were raised. In any case, surcharges and taxes would be but a few methods among many that might be used to induce behavior change, but they could constitute the whole of a policy aimed to impose costs upon those incurring them.

23. D.E. Detmer, "A Health Policy, Anyone? or What This Country Needs Is a Market Health Risk Equity Plan!" *The Public Affairs Journal* 6(3):101-2.

24. It might be possible to devise charges that would be assessed proportionately to income, so that the "bite" experienced by rich and poor would be about the same. This has not been the pattern in the past; all pay the same tax on a pack of cigarettes. In any case, this adjustment is in no way mandated by the fairness argument. The purpose of the charges would be to permit self-destructive individuals to "pay their own way" and hence remain free to indulge in favored habits. Reducing the amounts charged to low-income persons fails to realize that end; the costs of medical treatment for the poor are not any lower than for the rich. Indeed, being poor may increase the likelihood that the costs of treatment would have to be borne by the public. This suggests a scheme in which charges are assessed *inversely* proportional to income.

25. R. Nozick, "Coercion," in S. Morgenbesser, P. Suppes, and M. White, eds., *Philosophy, Science and Method: Essays in Honor of Ernest Nagel* (New York: St. Martin's Press, 1969), pp. 440-72; V. Held, "Coercion and Coercive Offers," in J.R. Pennock and J.W. Chapman, eds., *Coercion* (New York: Aldine Atherton, 1972), pp.49-62; M.D. Bayles, "A Concept of Coercion," in Pennock and Chapman, *Coercion*, pp. 16-29; and J.R. Pennock, "Coercion: An Overview," in Pennock and Chapman, *Coercion*, pp. 1-15.

26. Although this most clearly recalls the banning of liquor and cigarette advertising from the airwaves, I do not believe that the suppression of information was generally involved. The advertisements did not stress the delivery of information. The quoted phrase is from Michael Walzer, "Review of C. Lindblom, *Politics and Market*," *New York Review of Books*, July 20, 1978, pp. 40-42.

27. I.M. Rosenstock, "What Research in Motivation Suggests for Public Health," *American Journal of Public Health* 50(3): 295-302.

28. American Public Health Association, "Statement of Prevention," *The Nation's Health* 5(10):7-13; D.P. Haefner and J.P. Kirscht, "Motivational and Behavioral Effects of Modifying Health Beliefs," *Public Health Reports* 85(5):478-84; N. Milio, "A Framework for Prevention: Changing Health-Damaging to Health-Generating Life Patterns," *American Journal of Public Health* 66(5):435-39.

29. A problem noted by Lalonde, "A New Perspective."

30. See Ubell, "Health Behavior Change." It might be objected that the kind of manipulation I am speaking of is practiced continuously by commercial advertisers, and that no justification is provided by or demanded from them. It certainly is true that these techniques are used, but this does not show that

there is not a need for justification when they are used in the course of a government health-promotion campaign. The fact that the commercials are tolerated may indicate not that the manipulative techniques are themselves unobjectionable, but rather that private interests enjoy first amendment freedom from regulation in their attempts to communicate with the public. The rationale for this freedom—if it exists—may not apply to government communications. The government *per se* is not an entity with interests that must be protected by rights in society; the same holds true (officially, at least) of health-education advocates, when agents of the government.

31. For an account of this complex subject, see Nozick, "Coercion."

32. M. Terris, "A Social Policy for Health," *American Journal of Public Health* 58(1):5-12. For a discussion of this indirect form of paternalism, see Dworkin, "Paternalism."

Chapter 4

Medical Paternalism

Allen E. Buchanan

I

Among the physicians in this country, the medical paternalist model appears to be a prevalent way of conceiving the physician-patient relationship. I contend that the practice of withholding the truth from patients or their families, a particular form of medical paternalism, is not adequately supported by the arguments advanced to justify it. Further, I shall argue that the distinction between "ordinary" and "extraordinary" therapeutic measures both expresses and helps perpetuate the dominance of the medical paternalist model.

Paternalism is usually characterized as interference with a person's liberty of action, when the alleged justification for the interference is that it is for the good of the person whose liberty of action is thus restricted.[1] To focus exclusively on interference with liberty of *action*, however, is to construe paternalism too narrowly. If a government lies to the public or withholds information from it, and if the alleged justification of its policy is that it benefits the public itself, the policy may properly be called paternalistic.

On the one hand, there may be a direct connection between such a policy and actual interference with the citizen's freedom to act. In order to withhold information from the public, agents of the government may physically interfere with the freedom of the press to gather, print, or distribute the news. Or government officials may misinform the public in order to restrict its freedom to perform specific acts. The police, for example, may erect signs bearing the words "Detour: Maintenance Work Ahead" to route unsuspecting motorists around the wreckage of a truck carrying nerve gas. On the other hand, the connection between withholding of information and actual interference with freedom of action may be

Allen Buchanan, "Medical Paternalism," *Philosophy & Public Affairs* 7, no. 4, pp. 371-90.

indirect at best. To interfere with the public's freedom of information the government need not actually interfere with anyone's freedom to act—it may simply not divulge certain information. Withholding information may preclude an *informed* decision, and it may interfere with attempts to reach an informed decision, without thereby interfering with a person's freedom to decide and to act on his decision. Even if I am deprived of information that I need to make an informed decision, I may still be free to decide and to act.

Granted the complexity of the relations between information and action, it seems plausible to expand the usual definition of paternalism as follows: Paternalism is interference with a person's freedom of action or freedom of information, or the deliberate dissemination of misinformation, when the alleged justification for interfering or misinforming is that it is for the good of the person who is interfered with or misinformed. The notion of freedom of information is, of course, unsatisfyingly vague, but the political examples sketched above, along with the medical examples to follow, will make it clearer.

A more serious difficulty with this expanded definition, however, is that it too fails to cover some cases of paternalism. It is sometimes possible to interfere with a person's decision-making by forcing information upon her, rather than by withholding it. For example, a physician might override a patient's request that she not be given certain information about her condition; the patient may wish to make a decision without taking certain information into account or she may wish not to be the one to make certain decisions at all. At least some cases in which a person's decision not to be given certain information is overridden (allegedly for that person's own good) are properly called paternalism.[2] To include these cases as well as those discussed earlier might broaden our definition even further:

> Paternalism is the interference with a person's freedom of action or freedom of information, or the dissemination of misinformation, or the overriding of a person's decision not to be given information, when this is allegedly done for the good of that person.

Somewhat more briefly, we might say that paternalism occurs whenever a person's opportunities for deciding or acting, or her decisions about the conditions under which she shall or shall not decide, are interfered with, allegedly for her own good.

Whether or not this third definition includes all and only cases of paternalism, it does seem to be an improvement on the earlier proposals and it appears to cover most of the paternalistic practices that occur in medicine. However, since the overwhelming majority of instances of paternalism in medicine seem to be cases of withholding information rather than of forcing it upon the patient, I shall concentrate on examining the former in this essay. We can now turn to a brief consideration of evidence for the claim that medical paternalism is a widespread phenomenon in our society.

II

The evidence for medical paternalism is both direct and indirect. The direct evidence consists of survey findings that systematically report physicians' practices concerning truth-telling and decision-making, and of articles and discussions in which physicians and others acknowledge or defend paternalistic medical practices. The indirect evidence is more subtle. One source of indirect evidence for the pervasiveness of medical paternalistic attitudes is the language we use to describe physician-patient interactions. Let us consider some of the direct evidence.

Although there are many ways of classifying cases of medical paternalism, two distinctions are especially important. We can distinguish between the cases in which the patient is legally competent and those in which the patient is legally incompetent, and between those cases in which the intended beneficiary of paternalism is the patient himself and those in which the intended beneficiary is the patient's guardian or one or more members of the patient's family. The first distinction classifies cases according to the *legal status of the patient*, the second according to the *object of paternalism*.

A striking revelation of medical paternalism in dealings with legally competent adults is found in Donald Oken's essay, "What to Tell Cancer Patients: A Study of Medical Attitudes."[3] The chief conclusion of this study of internists, surgeons, and generalists is that "there is a strong and general tendency to withhold" from the patient the information that he has cancer. Almost ninety percent of the total group surveyed reported that their usual policy is not to tell the patient that he has cancer. Oken also notes that "no one reported a policy of informing every patient." Further, Oken reports that some physicians falsified diagnoses:

> Some physicians avoid even the slightest suggestion of neoplasia and quite specifically substitute another diagnosis. Almost everyone reported resorting to such falsification on at least a few occasions, most notably when the patient was in a far-advanced state of illness at the time he was seen.[4]

The physicians' justifications for withholding or falsifying diagnostic information were uniformly paternalistic. They assumed that if they told the patient he had cancer they would be depriving him of all hope and that the loss of hope would result in suicidal depression or at least in a serious worsening of the patient's condition.

A recent malpractice suit illustrates paternalistic withholding of information of a different sort. As in the Oken study, the object of paternalism was the patient and the patient was a legally competent adult. A bilateral thyroidectomy resulted in permanent paralysis of the patient's vocal cords. The patient's formerly healthy voice became frail and weak. The damage suit was based on the contention that by failing to tell the patient of the known risks to her voice, the physician had violated his duty to obtain informed consent for the operation. The physician's testimony is clearly paternalistic:

In court the physician was asked, "You didn't inform her of any dangers or risks involved? Is that right?" Over his attorney's objections, the physician responded, "Not specifically . . . I feel that were I to point out all the complications— or even half the complications—many people would refuse to have anything done, and therefore would be much worse off.[5]

There is also considerable evidence of medical paternalism in the treatment of legally incompetent individuals through the withholding of information from the patients or their guardians or both.[6]

The law maintains that it is the parents who are primarily responsible for decisions concerning the welfare of their minor children.[7] Nonetheless, physicians sometimes assume primary or even total responsibility for the most awesome and morally perplexing decisions affecting the welfare of children.

The inescapable need to make such decisions arises daily in neonate intensive-care units. The most dramatic decisions are whether to initiate or not initiate, or to continue or discontinue, life-sustaining therapy. Three broad types of cases have been frequently discussed in recent literature. First, there are infants who are in an asphyxiated condition at birth and can be resuscitated but may suffer irreversible brain damage if they survive. Second, there are infants with Down's syndrome (mongolism) who have potentially fatal but surgically correctable congenital cardiovascular or gastrointestinal defects. Third, there are infants with spina bifida, a congenital condition in which there is an opening in the spine and which may be complicated by paralysis and hydrocephaly. New surgical techniques make it possible to close the spine and drain the fluid from the brain, but a large percentage of the infants thus treated suffer varying degrees of permanent brain-damage and paralysis.

A. Shaw notes that some physicians undertake the responsibility for making decisions about life and death for defective newborns in order to relieve parents of the trauma and guilt of making a decision. He cites the following comment as an example of this position.

At the end it is usually the doctor who has to decide the issue. It is . . . cruel to ask the parents whether they want their child to live or die . . . . [8]

We have already seen that the information which physicians withhold may be of at least two different sorts. In the cases studied by Oken, physicians withhold the diagnosis of cancer from their patients. In the thyroidectomy malpractice case the physician did not withhold the diagnosis but did withhold information about known risks of an operation. The growing literature on life or death decisions for defective neonates reveals more complex paternalistic practices. Some physicians routinely exclude parents from significant participation in decision-making either by not informing the parents that certain choices can or must be made, or by describing the child's condition and the therapeutic options in such a skeletal way as to preclude genuinely informed consent.

A case cited by Shaw is a clear example of a physician withholding from parents the information that there was a choice to be made.

> Baby A was referred to me at 22 hours of age with a diagnosis of esophageal atresia and tracheoesophageal fistula. The infant, the firstborn of a professional couple in their early thirties, had obvious signs of mongolism, about which they were fully informed by the referring physician. After explaining the nature of the surgery to the distraught father, I offered him the operative consent. His pen hesitated briefly above the form and then as he signed, he muttered, "I have no choice, do I?" He didn't seem to expect an answer and I gave him none. The esophageal anomaly was corrected in routine fashion, and the infant was discharged to a state institution for the retarded without ever being seen again by either parent.[9]

The following description of practices in a neonate intensive-care unit at Yale Medical Center illustrates how parents may be excluded because of inadequate information about the child's condition or the character of various therapeutic options.

> Parents routinely signed permits for operations though rarely had they seen their children's defects or had the nature of various management plans and their respective prognoses clearly explained to them. Some physicians believed that parents were too upset to understand the nature of the problems and the options for care. Since they believed informed consent had no meaning in these circumstances, they either ignored the parents or simply told them that the child needed an operation on the back as the first step in correcting several defects. As a result, parents often felt completely left out while the activities of care proceeded at a brisk pace.[10]

Not every case in which a physician circumvents or overrides parental decision-making is a case of paternalism toward the parents. In ignoring the parents' primary legal responsibility for the child, the physician may not be attempting to shield the parents from the burdens of responsibility—he may simply be attempting to protect what he perceives to be the interests of the child.

These examples are presented, not as conclusive evidence for the claim that paternalistic practices of the sorts discussed above are widespread, but as illustrations of the practical relevance of the justifications for medical paternalism, which I shall now articulate and criticize.

III

In spite of the apparent pervasiveness of paternalistic practices in medicine, no systematic justification of them is available for scrutiny. Nonetheless, there appear to be at least three main arguments that advocates of paternalism could and sometimes do advance in justification of withholding information or misinforming patients or their families. Since withholding information seems to be more commonly practiced and advocated than outright falsification, I shall consider the three arguments only as justifications of the former rather than the latter. Each of these arguments is sufficiently general to apply to each of the types of cases described above. For convenience we can label these three arguments (A) the Prevention of Harm Argument, (B) the Contractual Version of the Prevention of Harm Argument, and (C) the Argument from the Inability to Understand.

The Prevention of Harm Argument is disarmingly simple. It may be outlined as follows:

1. The physician's duty—to which she is bound by the Oath of Hipprocrates—is to prevent or at least to minimize harm to her patient.
2. Giving the patient information X will do great harm to him.
3. (Therefore) it is permissible for the physician to withhold information X from the patient.

Several things should be noted about this argument. First of all, the conclusion is much weaker than one would expect, granted the first premise which is that it is the physician's *duty* to prevent or minimize harm to the patient, not just that it is *permissible* for her to do so. However, since the weaker conclusion—that withholding information is permissible—seems more intuitively plausible than the stronger one, I shall concentrate on it.

Second, the argument as it stands is invalid. From the claims that (1) the physician's duty (or right) is to prevent or minimize harm and that (2) giving information X will do the patient great harm, it does not follow that (3) it is permissible for the physician to withhold information X from the patient. At least one other premise is needed: (2') giving information X will do greater harm to the patient on balance than withholding the information will.

The addition of (2') is no quibble. Once (2') is made explicit we begin to see the tremendous weight that this paternalistic argument places on the physician's power of judgment. She must not only determine that giving the information will do harm or even that it will do great harm. She must also make a complex comparative judgment: Will withholding the information result in less harm on balance than divulging it? Yet neither the physicians interviewed by Oken nor those discussed by Shaw even mention this comparative judgment in their justifications for withholding information. They simply state that telling the truth will result in great harm to patients or their families. No mention was made of the need to compare this expected harm with harm that might result from withholding the information, and no recognition of the difficulties involved in such a comparison was reported.

Consider two of the examples described above: the patient with terminal cancer and the thyroidectomy malpractice suit. In order to justify withholding the diagnosis of terminal cancer from the patient, the physician must not only determine that informing the patient would do great harm but that the harm would be greater on balance than whatever harm may result from withholding information. Since the notion of great harm is vague unless a context for comparison is supplied, we can concentrate on the physician's evidence for the judgment that the harm of informing is greater than the harm of withholding. Oken's study shows that the evidential basis for such comparative judgments was remarkably slender:

> It was the exception when a physician could report known examples of the unfavorable consequences of an approach which differed from his own. It was more common to get reports of instances in which different approaches had turned out satisfactorily. Most of the instances in which unhappy results were reported to follow a differing policy turned out to be vague accounts from which no reliable inference could be drawn.

Oken then goes on to focus on the nature of the anticipated harm:

> It has been repeatedly asserted that disclosure is followed by fear and despondency which may progress into overt depressive illness or culminate in suicide. This was the opinion of the physicians in the present study. Quite representative was the surgeon who stated, "I would be afraid to tell and have the patient in a room with a window." When it comes to actually documenting the prevalence of such untoward reactions, it becomes difficult to find reliable evidence. Instances of depression and profound upsets came quickly to mind when the subject was raised, but no one could report more than a case or two, or a handful at most . . . . The same doctors could remember many instances in which the patient was told and seemed to do well.[11]

It is not simply that these judgments of harm are made on the basis of extremely scanty evidence. The problem goes much deeper than that. To say that physicians base such judgments on weak evidence is to overlook three important facts. First, the judgment that telling the truth would result in suicidal depression is an unqualified psychiatric generalization. So even if there were adequate evidence for this generalization or, more plausibly, for some highly qualified version of it, it is implausible to maintain that ordinary physicians are in a position to recognize and properly assess the evidence in a given case. Second, it is doubtful that psychiatric specialists are in possession of any such reliable generalization, even in qualified form. Third, the paternalistic physician is simply assuming that suicide is not a rational choice for the terminally ill patient.

If we attempt to apply the Prevention of Harm Argument to cases in which the patient's family or guardian is the object of paternalism, other difficulties become apparent. Consider cases of withholding information from the parents of a neonate with Down's syndrome or spina bifida. The most obvious difficulty is that premise (1) states only that the physician has a duty (or a right) to prevent or minimize harm to the patient, not to his family. If this argument is to serve as a justification of paternalism toward the infant patient's family, the advocate of paternalism must advance and support one or the other of two quite controversial premises. She must either add premise 1' or replace premise 1 with premise 1":

1'. If X is a guardian or parent of patient Y and Y is the patient of physician Z, then X is also a patient of physician Z.

1″. It is the duty of the physician to prevent or minimize harm to her patient and to the guardian or family of her patient.

Since both the law and common sense maintain that one does not become a patient simply by being related to a patient, it seems that the best strategy for the medical paternalist is to rely on 1″ rather than on 1′.

Reliance on 1″, however, only weakens the case for medical paternalism toward parents of defective neonates. For now the medical paternalist must show that she has adequate evidence for psychiatric predictions the complexity of which taxes the imagination. She must first determine all the relevant effects of telling the truth, not just on the parents themselves, but on siblings as well, since whatever anguish or guilt the parents will allegedly feel may have significant effects on their other children. Next she must ascertain the ways in which these siblings—both as individuals and as a peer group—will respond to the predicted anguish and guilt of their parents. Then the physician must determine how the siblings will respond to each other. Next she must consider the possible responses of the parents to the responses of the children. And, of course, once she has accomplished all this, the physician must look at the other side of the question. She must consider the possible harmful effects of withholding information from patients or of preventing them from taking an active part in decision-making. The conscientious paternalist must consider not only the burdens that the exercise of responsibility will allegedly place upon the parents, and indirectly upon their children, but also the burdens of guilt, self-doubt, and shame that may result from the parents' recognition that they have abdicated their responsibility.

In predicting whether telling the truth or withholding information will cause the least harm for the family as a whole, the physician must first make intrapersonal comparisons of harm and benefit for each member of the family, if that information is available. Then she must somehow combine these various intrapersonal net-harm judgments into an estimate of the total negative effect that divulging the information will have on the family as a whole. Then she must ask similar intrapersonal and interpersonal net-harm judgments about the results of *not* telling the truth. Finally she must compare these totals and determine which course of action will minimize harm to the family as a whole.

Although the problems of achieving defensible predictions of harm as a basis for paternalism are clearest in the case of defective neonates, they are in no way peculiar to those cases. Consider the case of a person with terminal cancer. To eliminate the complication of interpersonal net-harm comparisons, let us suppose that this person has no relatives and is himself legally competent. Suppose that the physician withholds information of the diagnosis because she believes that knowledge of the truth would be more harmful than withholding the truth. I have already indicated that even if we view this judgment of comparative harm as a purely clinical one—more specifically a clinical psychiatric judgment—it is difficult to see how the physician could be in a position to make it. But it is crucial to note that the concepts of harm and benefit appropriate to these deliberations are not exclusively clinical concepts, whether psychiatric or otherwise. In taking it upon herself to determine what will be most beneficial or least harmful to this patient, the physician is not simply making ill-founded medical judgments that might someday be confirmed by psychiatric research. She is making *moral* evaluations of the most basic and problematic kind.

The physician must determine whether it will be better for the patient to live his remaining days in the knowledge that his days are few or to live in ignorance of his fate. But again, this is a gross simplification: it assumes that the physician's attempt to deceive the patient will be successful. E. Kübler-Ross claims that in many, if not most, cases the terminally ill patient will guess or learn his fate whether the physician withholds the diagnosis from him or not.[12] Possible harm resulting from the patient's loss of confidence in the physician or from a state of uncertainty over his prospects must be taken into account.

Let us set aside this important complication and try to appreciate what factors would have to be taken into account in well-founded judgment that the remainder of a person's life would be better for that person if she did not know that she had a terminal illness than if she did.

Such a judgment would have to be founded on a profound knowledge of the most intimate details of the patient's life history, her characteristic ways of coping with personal crises, her personal and vocational commitments and aspirations, her feelings of obligation toward others, and her attitude toward the completeness or incompleteness of her experience. In a society in which the personal physician is an intimate friend who shares the experience of families under his care, it would be somewhat more plausible to claim that the physician might possess such knowledge. Under the present conditions of highly impersonal specialist medical practice it is quite a different matter.

Yet even if the physician could claim such intimate personal knowledge, this would not suffice. For he must not only predict, but also evaluate. On the basis of an intimate knowledge of the patient as a person, he must determine which outcome would be best for that person. It is crucial to emphasize that the question which the physician must pose and answer is whether ignorance or knowledge will make possible a life that is better *for the patient herself*. The physician must be careful not to confuse this question with the question of whether ignorance or knowledge would make for a better life for the physician if the physician were terminally ill. Nor must he confuse it with the question of whether the patient's life would be a *better life*—a life more valuable to others or to society—if it ended in ignorance rather than in truth. The question, rather, is whether it would be better *for the patient herself* to know or not to know her fate.

To judge that a certain ending of a life would be best for the person whose life it is, is to view that life as a unified process of development and to conclude that that ending is a fitting completion for that process. To consider a human life as a unified process of development, however, is to view it selectively. Certain events or patterns of conduct are singled out as especially significant or valuable. To ascertain the best completion of a person's life for that person, then, is to make the most fundamental judgments about the value of that person's activities, aspirations, and experiences.

It might be replied that we do make such value judgments when we decide to end the physiologic life of a permanently comatose individual. In such cases we do make value judgments, but they are not judgments of this sort. On the contrary, we believe that since this individual's experience has ended, her life-process is already completed.

When the decision to withhold information of impending death is understood for what it is, it is difficult to see how anyone could presume to make it. My conjecture is that physicians are tempted to make these decisions in part because of a failure to reflect upon the disparity between two quite different kinds of judgments about what will harm or benefit the patient. Judgments of the first sort are estimates of how a particular decision will affect the patient's health and fall within physicians' competence as highly trained medical experts. Judgments of the second sort are evaluations of another human being's life as a whole. There is nothing in their training that qualifies physicians to make judgments of the second sort. Further, once the complexity of these judgments is appreciated and once their evaluative character is understood, it is implausible to hold that the physician is in a better position to make them than the patient or her family. The failure to ask what sorts of harm/benefit judgments may properly be made by physicians in their capacities as physicians is a fundamental feature of medical paternalism.

There is a more sophisticated version of the attempt to justify withholding of information in order to minimize harm to the patient or her family. This is the Contract Version of the Prevention of Harm Argument. The idea is that the physician-patient relationship is contractual and that the terms of this contract are such that the patient authorizes the physician to minimize harm to the patient (or her family) by whatever means he, the physician, deems necessary. Thus if the physician believes that the best way to minimize harm to the patient is to withhold information from her, he may do so without thereby wronging the patient. To wrong the patient the physician would either have to do something he was not authorized to do or fail to do something it was his duty to do and which was in his power to do. But in withholding information from the patient he is doing just what he is authorized to do. So he does the patient no wrong.

This version is vulnerable to the same objections raised against the non-contractual Prevention of Harm Argument. The most serious of these is that in the cases of paternalism under discussion it is very doubtful that the physician will or even could possess the psychiatric and moral knowledge required for a well-founded judgment about what will be least harmful to the patient. In addition, the Contract Version is vulnerable to other objections. Consider the claim that the patient-physician realtionship is a contract in which the patient authorizes the physician to prevent or minimize harm by whatever means the physician deems necessary, including the withholding of information. This claim could be interpreted in either of two ways: as a descriptive generalization about the way physicians and patients actually understand their relationship or as a normative claim about the way the physician-patient relationship should be viewed or may be viewed.

As a descriptive generalization it is certainly implausible: there are many people who do not believe they have authorized their physician to withhold the truth from them, and the legal doctrine of informed consent supports their veiw. Let us suppose for a moment that some people do believe their relationship to their physician includes such an authorization and that there is nothing morally wrong with such a contract so long as both parties entered into it voluntarily and in full knowledge of the terms of the agreement. The first thing to notice is that when the patient actually authorizes the withholding of information it appears that we no longer have a case of paternalism, since what is done with permission is no longer an *interference* of the sort that the definition of paternalism describes.[13]

But from the fact that withholding information with explicit authorization may be neither paternalistic nor wrong nothing follows about cases in which explicit authorization is lacking. The fact that some people authorize physicians to withhold information from them would not justify the physician in acting toward other patients as if they had done so. The physician can only justify withholding information from a particular patient if this sort of contract were entered into freely and in full knowledge *by this* patient.

The medical paternalist might reply that patients or their families often give verbal or linguisitic clues that lead the physician to assume that there is authorization, even if it is not explicit. The physician should be careful, however, not to assume that a remark or a bit of behavior which indicates an inclination not to be told is reliable evidence that the person's strongest preference is that he or she should not be told. People often have conflicting inclinations, and when there is no explicit authorization the physician may often not be in a position to assess the relative strength of the patient's conflicting inclinations. But even when this is possible, it is still not enough, because an inclination, even a strong inclination, is not the same as an authorization. An authorization is a purposeful act of communication of a very special sort, an often highly ritualized or at least conventional expression of *resolve,* a determination of *will*, intended to create or waive obligations on the part of others. Granted that this is so, the physician should not confuse behavioral or linguistic evidence of the patient's or the family's inclination not to be told with an authorization not to tell. It appears, then, that the descriptive generalization—the claim that patients or their families authorize physicians to withhold information when they see fit—is implausible.

There is an equally serious difficulty with the normative claim that the physician-patient relationship should or may be viewed as including an authorization for physicians to withhold information whenever they see fit. Even the more extreme advocates of medical paternalism must agree that there are some limits to the contractual relationship between physician and patient. Hence the obligations of each party are conditional upon the other party's observing the limits of the contract. The law, the medical profession, and the general public usually recognize that there are such limits. The patient may seek a second opinion, or she may terminate the relationship altogether. Moreover, it is acknowledged that to decide to do any of these things the patient may—indeed perhaps must—rely on her own judgment. If she is conscientious she will base such decisions on whether the physician is doing a reasonable job of rendering the services for which he was hired.

There are general constraints on how those services may be rendered. If the treatment is unreasonably slow, if the physician's technique is patently sloppy, or if he employs legally questionable methods, the patient may rightly conclude that the physician has not lived up to the implicit terms of the agreement and she may terminate the relationship. There are also more special constraints on the contract stemming from the special nature of the problem that led the patient to seek the physician's services. If you go to a physician for treatment of a skin condition, but he ignores that problem and sets about trying to convince you to have cosmetic nose surgery, you may rightly terminate the relationship. These general and special constraints are limits on the agreement from the patient's point of view.

Once it is admitted that there are any such terms—that the contract does have some limits and that the patient has the right to terminate the relationship if these limits are not observed by the physician—it must also be admitted that the patient should be in a position to discover whether those limits are being observed. But if the patient were to authorize the physician to withhold information, she might deprive herself of information relevant to determining whether the physician has observed the limits of the agreement.

I am not concerned with arguing that authorizing a physician to withhold information is logically incompatible with the contract being conditional. My point, rather, is that to make such an authorization would indicate either that (a) one did not view the contract as being conditional or that (b) one did not take seriously the possibility that the conditions of the contract might be violated or that (c) one simply did not care whether the conditions were violated. Since it is generally unreasonable to expect a patient to make an unconditional contract or to ignore the possibility that conditions of the contract will be violated, and since one typically does care whether these conditions are observed, it is generally unreasonable to authorize the physician to withhold information whenever he sees fit. And if it is generally unreasonable, then it is implausible to contend that simply because she has entered the relationship the patient may or should be viewed as having authorized the physician to withhold information whenever he sees fit. I conclude, then, that on both the descriptive and the normative interpretations, the Contract Version of the Prevention of Harm Argument is not much of an improvement over its simpler predecessor.

There is one paternalist argument in favor of withholding information that remains to be considered. This may be called the Argument from the Inability to Understand. The main premise is that the physician is justified in withholding information when the patient or his family is unable to understand the information. This argument is often used to justify paternalistic policies toward parents of defective infants in neonate intensive-care units. The idea is that either their lack of intelligence or their excited emotional condition prevents parents from giving informed consent because they are incapable of being adequately informed. In such cases, it is said, "the doctrine of informed consent does not apply."[14]

This argument is also vulnerable to several objections. First, it too relies upon dubious and extremely broad psychological generalizations—in this case, psychological generalizations about the cognitive powers of parents of defective neonates.

Second, and more important, it ignores the crucial question of the character of the institutional context in which parents find themselves. To the extent that paternalistic attitudes shape medical institutions, this bleak estimate of parental capacity for comprehension and rational decision-making tends to be a self-fulfilling prophecy. In an institution in which parents routinely sign operation permits without having even seen their newborn infants and without having the nature of the therapeutic options clearly explained to them, parents may indeed be incapable of understanding the little that they are told.

Third, it is a mistake to maintain that the legal duty to seek informed consent applies only when the physician can succeed in adquately informing parents. The doctor does not and cannot have a duty to make sure that all the information she conveys is understood by those to whom she conveys it. Her duty is to make a reasonable effort to be understood.[15]

Fourth, exactly why is it so important not to give parents information that they allegedly will not understand? If the reason is that a parental decision based on inadequate understanding will be a decision that is harmful to the *infant*, then the Argument from the Inability to Understand is not an argument for paternalism toward *parents*. If this argument is to provide a justification for withholding information from parents for *their* benefit, then the claim must be that their failure to understand will somehow be harmful to *them*. But why should this be so? If parents will not only fail to understand but become distressed because they realize that they do not understand, then the Argument from the Inability to Understand turns out not to be a new argument at all. Instead, it is just a restatement of the Prevention of Harm Argument examined above—and is vulnerable to the same objections. I conclude that none of the three justifications examined provide adequate support for the paternalistic practices under consideration. If adequate justification is to be found, advocates of medical paternalism must marshal more powerful arguments.

<h1 style="text-align:center">IV</h1>

So far I have examined several specific medical paternalistic practices and criticized some general arguments offered in their behalf. Medical paternalism, however, goes much deeper than the specific practices themselves. For this reason I have spoken of "the medical paternalist model," emphasizing that what is at issue is a paradigm, a way of conceiving the physician-patient relationship.

Indirect evidence for the pervasiveness of this model is to be found in the very words we use to describe physicians, patients, and their interactions. One widely used distinction that expresses and helps perpetuate the paternalist model is the distinction between "ordinary" and "extraordinary" therapeutic measures.

Many physicians, theologians, ethicists, and judges have relied on this distinction since Pius XII employed it in an address on "The Prolongation of Life" in 1958. In reply to questions concerning conditions under which physicians may discontinue or refrain from initiating the use of artificial respiration devices, Pius first noted that physicians are duty-bound "to take the necessary treatment for the preservation of life and health." He then distinguished between "ordinary" and "extraordinary" means:

> But normally one is held to use only ordinary means—according to circumstances of persons, places, times, and culture—means that do not involve any grave burden for oneself or another.[16]

Although he is not entirely explicit about this, Pius assumes that it is the right of the physician to determine what will count as "ordinary" or "extraordinary" means in any particular case.

In the context of deciding when a highly trained specialist is to employ sophisticated life-support equipment, it is natural to assume that the distinction between "ordinary" and "extraordinary" means is a distinction between higher and lower degrees of technological sophistication. The Pope's unargued assumption that the medical specialist is to determine what counts as "ordinary" or "extraordinary" reinforces a technological interpretation of the distinction. After all, if the distinction is a technological one, then it is natural to assume that it is the physician who should determine its application since it is he who possesses the requisite technical expertise. In my discussions with physicians, nurses, and hospital administrators I have observed that they tend to treat the distinction as a technological one and to argue that since it is a technological distinction the physician is the one who should determine in any particular case whether a procedure would involve "ordinary" or "extraordinary" means.[17]

Notice, however, that even though Pius introduced the distinction in the context of the proper use of sophisticated technical devices and even though he assumed that it was to be applied by those who possess the technical skills to use such equipment, it is quite clear that the distinction he explicitly introduced is not itself a technological distinction. Recall that he defines "ordinary" means as those that "do not involve any grave burden for oneself of another." "Extraordinary" means, then, would be those that do involve a grave burden for oneself or for another.

If what counts as "extraordinary" measures depended only upon what would constitute a "grave burden" to the patient himself, it might be easier to preserve the illusion that the decision is an exercise of medical expertise. But once the evaluation of burdens is extended to the patient's family, it becomes obvious that the judgment that a certain therapy would be "extraordinary" is not a technological or even a clinical, but rather a *moral*, decision. And it is a moral decision regardless of whether the evaluation is made from the perspective of the patient's own values and preferences or from that of the physician.

Even if one is to evaluate only the burdens for the patient himself, however, it is implausible to maintain that the application of the distinction is an exercise of technological or clinical judgment. For as soon as we ask what would result in "grave burdens" for the patient, we are immediately confronted with the task of making moral distinctions and moral evaluations concerning the quality of the patient's life and his interests as a person.

Sometimes "extraordinary" means are defined somewhat more broadly as "those which, in the circumstances, would no longer serve any meaningful purpose." It should be obvious that the phrase "meaningful purpose," like the phrase "grave burdens," is not a medical one, but rather an evaluative term that summarizes an indefinite and unarticulated set of moral judgments. The judgments that lead an individual to conclude that continued treatment would serve no meaningful purpose usually include quite controversial moral judgments concerning the "quality" or "value" of the patient's life. For example, whether or not resuscitative efforts that will prolong a senile patient's life for a week or two "serve any meaningful purpose" cannot be ascertained simply through medical judgment. Nor will it do to say that whether any meaningful purpose would be served depends upon the "quality" of the life thus prolonged, and that judgments about the quality of life are the province of medical expertise.

First of all, it is a moral question, not a medical one, as to *which* notion of "quality of life," if any, is relevant to such decisions. "Quality of life" may be used in either a comparative or a non-comparative sense. In the former sense, quality-of-life judgments are interpersonal ranking judgments: the worth or value of one individual is compared with that of others according to some conception of social utility or in terms of the individual's "contribution to society." In the latter, non-comparative sense, a quality-of-life judgment is one in which we assess the value or quality of an individual's life to or for *that individual,* irrespective of how society or would-be calculators of social utility evaluate it relative to that of other individuals.

Second, even after the moral decision has been made to use one or the other of these radically different conceptions of quality of life, moral judgment is still required to determine what counts as an acceptable level of quality of life if we are to arrive at the conclusion that a certain treatment would or would not "serve any meaningful purpose," and hence count as "ordinary" or "extraordinary." Here, as with Pius's definition, the apparently simple distinction between "ordinary" and "extraordinary" measures masks moral perplexities; the widespread belief that it is a medical distinction and hence properly left to medical experts is clearly false.

When pressed for an explanation of how physicians actually apply the distinction between "ordinary" and "extraordinary" therapeutic measures, the director of a neonate intensive-care unit explained to me that what counts as "ordinary" or "extraordinary" differs in "different contexts." Surgical correction of a congenital gastrointestinal blockage in the case of an otherwise normal infant would be considered an "ordinary" measure. But the same operation on an infant with Down's syndrome would be considered "extraordinary".

I am not concerned here with criticizing the moral decision to refrain from aggressive surgical treatment of infants with Down's syndrome. My purpose in citing this example is simply to point out that this decision *is* a moral decision and that the use of the distinction between "ordinary" and "extraordinary" measures does nothing to help one make the decision. The use of the distinction does accomplish something though: it obscures the fact that the decision *is* a moral decision. Even worse, it is likely to lead one to mistake a very controversial moral decision for a value-free technological or clinical decision. More important, to even suggest that a complex moral judgment is a clinical or technological judgment is to prejudice the issue of *who* has the right to decide whether life-sustaining measures are to be initiated or continued. Once controversial moral decisions are misperceived as clinical or technological decisions, it becomes much easier for the medical paternalist to use the three arguments examined above to justify the withholding of information. Once it is conceded that her medical expertise gives the physician the right to make certain decisions, she can then argue that she may withhold information where this is necessary for the effective exercise of this right. By disguising complex moral judgments as medical judgments, then, the "ordinary/extraordinary" distinction reinforces medical paternalism.

V

It is plausible to contend that the strongest arguments against paternalism must be *rights-based* arguments. Such arguments, if successful, would show that paternalism is unjustified because it violates individuals' rights. The rights in question may be either of two sorts: general or special. General rights are said to accrue to persons independently of their participation in certain voluntary interactions and independently of their standing in certain special relationships to others. Among the general rights that some have sought to defend are the right to life and the right to liberty. Special rights are said to be generated by promises, by the making of contracts, and by voluntary participation in certain cooperative enterprises, or are said to be based on special relationships such as that of child to parent.

In contrast to rights-based attacks, there are strictly consequentialist criticisms of paternalism. My criticisms of the Prevention of Harm Argument and of the Argument from the Inability to Understand are of this type. In the former I attacked the paternalist's assumption that the physician, rather than the patients or their families, will typically, or even frequently, be in a position to judge what would be most harmful or beneficial to the patients or families in the cases in question. In the latter, I attacked the paternalist's generalizations about the cognitive deficiencies of patients and their families when faced with life or death decisions.

The Contractual Version of the Prevention of Harm Argument is not itself strictly consequentialist, but rather is an argument based on the premise that the physician-patient relationship is in fact or should be viewed as a contractual relationship that authorizes the physician to withhold information whenever he sees fit. But in my criticism of this argument, as in my criticisms of the two preceding paternalist arguments, I did not rely upon premises ascribing general or special rights to patients or their families and then argue that the paternalist violates those rights when he withholds information without explicit authorization.

There are good reasons for attempting to criticize paternalism without recourse to the rights arguments. The success of general rights-based critiques of paternalism depends ultimately upon whether a coherent theory of general rights can be articulated and given a rational foundation. If, as seems likely, the relevant general right is a right to liberty, there is the difficulty not only of justifying the claim that there is such a right, but also of specifying just what its content is. While it seems clear enough that a right to liberty, if it exists, is a limited right, the task of articulating its limits is an onerous one. Further, what counts as a violation of the right and what counts as a legitimate limitation of it must be distinguished in such a way that the question is not begged against paternalism.

On the other hand, one might attempt to base the critique of paternalism upon a special right to informed consent (or a special right to information of some kind). However, if we merely assume that patients enjoy a moral (as distinct from a legal) right of informed consent simply by virtue of the special nature of the physician-patient relationship, or if we merely assume that such a right is generated by the making of a contract between physician and patient, the medical paternalist—who has a different conception of the relationship or the contract—may again accuse us of begging the question.

It is for these reasons that I have so far eschewed talk about rights, whether general or special. But this strategy comes at a price. Insofar as my criticisms of the Prevention of Harm Argument and of the Argument from the Inability to Understand are strictly consequentialist, it might be thought that they are vulnerable to a strictly consequentialist rejoinder. Alan Goldman has offered the following paternalist rejoinder:

"You are quite right to point out that judgments about what would be most harmful or beneficial to the patient or her family are often extremely complex and difficult to make with accuracy. But what you say about the fallibility of the judgment that withholding information will be most beneficial to the patient or her family also applies to the judgment that divulging information will be less harmful. So here, as in all cases of medical judgment, the physician must rely upon her own judgment, while recognizing, of course, her fallibility. Similarly, the judgment that the patient or family will be able to undertand the information if it is divulged is just as complex and difficult to make as the judgment that the information would not be understood. But here, too, since the physician's duty is to minimize harm, the best she can do is to estimate the consequences as accurately as she can and then either divulge or withhold information accordingly.[18]

It is here that the temptation to rely upon rights becomes almost irresistible. For claims of right are characteristically thought of as "trumping" considerations of welfare, whether it be the general welfare or the welfare of the right-holder himself. To take rights seriously is to refuse to allow valid rights-claims to be overridden by considerations of the personal or social utility that could be gained by overriding those claims.

According to a less rigorous and more plausible understanding of rights, to take rights seriously is to refuse to allow rights-claims to be overriden by appeals to social utility or the utility of the right-holder himself, except perhaps where the utility to be gained by overriding the right-claim would be *very great*. The difficulty with this weakened version, of course, is that the exception-clause threatens to render rights-claims impotent. For even if there are some cases in which the gain in utility would be so great as to justify overriding a valid right-claim, they will presumably be not only relatively infrequent but also difficult to identify (except perhaps in retrospect), granted human fallibility and the complexity of the judgments of harm and benefit in question. If this is so, it seems plausible to add the following epistemic requirement: to take rights seriously is to refuse to override valid rights-claims for the sake of utility, except when the utility to be gained is very great *and* when the prediction concerning the gain in utility enjoys a very high degree of certainty.

This epistemic condition is especially plausible in the medical context for two reasons. First, as we have already seen, the non-medical harm/benefit judgments in question are so enormously complex that reliable predictions of utility are very hard to come by. Second, because physicians are trained to reason consequentially about purely medical matters, and because they are highly motivated to act for the patient's welfare and tend to define their role in terms of maximizing benefit or avoiding harm, they are especially susceptible to being overconfident in their consequentialist judgments. The evidence of paternalistic practices adduced earlier supports this hypothesis. If the rigorous notion of rights is accepted, rights-based arguments against the paternalist's practices examined above will always be decisive; but even in the less rigorous interpretation, rights-claims will, in virtually all the cases considered, block appeals to the patients' or families' welfare, because the epistemic condition will not be satisfied.

It would be a mistake, however, to conclude that the only fully effective reply to the paternalist must be rights-based. Insofar as the consequentialist rejoinder assumes that the harm/benefit judgments in question are simply medical judgments (judgments that the physician's medical expertise qualifies her to make) it again conflates judgments of medical expertise with complex and controversial moral and psychological judgments. From the fact that the physician must often make difficult medical judgments, even though she knows she is fallible, it does not follow that training as a physician qualifies her to make moral and psychological judgments. Even if a physician is often required to make highly problematic medical judgments and even if she is often in no worse a position to make the moral and psychological judgments in question than the patient or family, this is not sufficient to show that it is the physician who should make them.

But even more important, I think I have shown that in many, if not most, of the cases under consideration, especially under the impersonal conditions of highly specialized medical practice, the physician is *less* likely than the patient or family to be in a position to make even roughly accurate judgments of the sort required. Similarly, in criticizing the Argument from the Inability to Understand, I think I have shown both that physicians' judgments that patients and families are often unable to understand are based on inadequate evidence and that what evidence there is is largely an artifact of the same paternalistic practices which that evidence is supposed to justify. To put it differently, since the physician is advancing the claim that patients and their families typically or at least frequently cannot understand certain information and since, as I have argued, that information, if properly presented, is not technical, the burden of proof is on the physician to present evidence for her generalization about the cognitive deficiencies of patients and families in those situations. I have argued that this burden of proof has not been borne and that there is some reason to think it cannot be borne successfully. I conclude, therefore, that even when limited to strictly consequentialist considerations, my arguments are a serious challenge to most instances of medical paternalism and to the medical paternalist model, which assumes that paternalism toward patients and their families is frequently justified.

One can go beyond strictly consequentialist arguments without going all the way to rights-based arguments. Even without assuming that there is a *right* to informed consent, or a *right* to liberty, one can assume, quite plausibly, that there are valid moral principles of other sorts, including rules that forbid lying and other forms of deception and that require telling the truth at least where others' vital legitimate interests are affected. Although it may prove difficult to provide a sound theoretical underpinning for such principles, they are intuitively plausible and do seem to constitute an important part of our common moral code. If this is so, then it appears that anyone who abridges these principles incurs a burden of proof—he must show either that these rules are to be rejected outright or that the conduct in question constitutes a legitimate exception to the relevant rule. In either case, there is a moral *presumption* to be rebutted. Even though moral presumption against lying, or deception, or withholding information relevant to someone's decisions about his or her legitimate vital interests may not be as strong as the presumption entailed by a moral *right* to informed consent, it must be taken seriously if the moral principles in question are acknowledged as intuitively plausible elements of our shared morality. But if this is so, then the burden of rebutting the presumption lies squarely on the shoulders of the medical paternalist who would disregard those principles. The antipaternalist consequentialist arguments I offered earlier can therefore be reinterpreted as arguments to show that the presumption against the physician's lying or withholding information in the cases discussed has not been rebutted, and that this can be shown to be so without reliance upon rights, whether special or general.

The paternalist who accepts the moral rules in question might insist that although these principles are generally valid, they do not apply to the singular case of the physician-patient relationship. This reply, however, will not do, as my earlier arguments show. Presumably the claim that physician-patient relationship is such that the physician is not subject to the moral principles that generally apply to us all either rests upon the descriptive claim that the relationship *is*, or the normative claim that it *should* be, one in which the patient authorizes the physician to withhold information whenever he sees fit; or it rests upon the assumption that the physician typically or very frequently is in a better position to make certain very complex moral and psychological judgments than the patient or her family. I have argued both against the claim about the factual or normative character of the physician-patient relationship and against the assumption of the physician's qualifications for making the judgments in question.

If, however, it is admitted that patients and their families have a *right* to informed consent (or a right to active participation in decision-making that vitally affects their legitimate interests), my case against paternalism becomes correspondingly stronger, because of the greater strength of the presumption against withholding information which such a right implies. In sum, my arguments can be viewed in three different ways: (1) as strictly consequentialist arguments, (2) as arguments showing that the paternalist's consequentialist justifications for overriding the moral presumption against withholding information do not adequately rebut that presumption, or (3) as arguments showing that even if there are cases in which consequentialist considerations qualify or even outweigh the right to informed consent, such cases are much rarer and much more difficult to identify prospectively with any degree of certainty than the medical paternalist assumes.

VI

In this paper I have attempted to articulate and challenge some basic features of the medical paternalist model of the physician-patient relationship. I have also given an indication of the powerful influence this model exerts on medical practice and on ways of talking and thinking about medical treatment.

There are now signs that medical paternalism is beginning to be challenged from within the medical profession itself.[19] This, I believe, is all to the good. So far, however, challenges have been fragmentary and unsystematic. If they are to be theoretically and practically fruitful, they must be grounded in a systematic understanding of what medical paternalism is and in a critical examination of the justifications for medical paternalistic practices. The present paper is an attempt to begin the task of such a systematic critique.

Notes

1. See, for example, Gerald Dworkin, "Paternalism," in S. Gorovitz et al., *Moral Problems in Medicine* (Englewood Cliffs, NJ: Prentice-Hall, 1976), p. 185. (Reprinted as chapter 2 of this book.)

2. Donald VanDeVeer makes this point in "The Contractual Argument for Withholding Medical Information," *Philosophy & Public Affairs* 9, no. 2, 1980, p. 203.

3. Donald Oken, "What to Tell Cancer Patients: A Study of Medical Attitudes," in Samuel Gorovitz et al., *Moral Problems in Medicine* (Englewood Cliffs, NJ: Prentice-Hall, 1976), p. 112. Oken's study was first published in 1967.

4. *Ibid.* p. 113.

5. *Malpractice Digest* (St. Paul, MN: The St. Paul Property and Liability Insurance Company, July-August 1977), p. 6.

6. It is interesting to note that, according to both the usual and the expanded characterization of paternalism stated earlier, only people who have certain physical and mental capacities can be objects of paternalism, since it is only when these capacities are present that it is correct to speak of interfering with those individuals' freedom of action, misinforming them, or withholding information from them.

7. For a helpful summary, see J.A. Robertson and N. Fost, "Passive Euthanasia of Defective Newborn Infants: Legal Considerations," *The Journal of Pediatrics* 88, no. 5, 1976, pp. 883-89.

8. A. Shaw, "Dilemmas of 'Informed Consent' in Children," *The New England Journal of Medicine* 289, no. 17, 1973, p. 886.

9. *Ibid.*, p. 885.

10. R. Duff and A. Campbell, "Moral and Ethical Dilemmas in the Special-Care Nursery," *The New England Journal of Medicine* 289, no. 17, 1973, p. 893.

11. Oken, pp. 112, 113.

12. Elisabeth Kübler-Ross, excerpts from *Death and Dying*, quoted in *Moral Problems in Medicine*, p. 122.

13. VanDeVeer, pp. 201-2.

14. Duff and Campbell, p. 893.

15. I would like to thank John Dolan for clarifying this point.

16. Pius XII, "The Prolongation of Life," in Stanley Joel Reiser, Arthur J. Dyck, and William Curran, *Ethics in Medicine* (Cambridge, MA: MIT Press, 1977), pp. 501-4.

17. These discussions occurred in the course of my work as a member of a committee that drafted ethical guidelines for Children's Hospital of Minneapolis.

18. Alan Goldman discusses this paternalist rejoinder in *The Moral Foundation of Professional Ethics* (Totowa, NJ: Roman and Littlefield, 1980), pp. 175-6.

19. See, for example, A. Waldman, "Medical Ethics and the Hopelessly Ill Child," *The Journal of Pediatrics* 88, no. 5, 1976, pp. 890-2.

Chapter 5

Paternalism and the Mildly Retarded

Daniel Wikler

In many states, the mildly retarded must submit to the guidance of competent persons or authorities before making important decisions.[1] These include the decision to marry, to have children, to enter into financial contracts, and to live alone. Generally speaking, adults of normal intelligence may make these decisions without obtaining the consent of anyone, and they value this autonomy. When persons of normal intelligence, acting through the state, take custody of the retarded, they do not seek the consent of the retarded, who acquire protection but lose their legal rights. If we claim that relative intellectual superiority justifies restricting the liberties of the retarded, could not exceptionally gifted persons make the same claim concerning person of normal intelligence? I propose to examine the moral importance of relative intellectual superiority, and to consider whether it can serve as adequate grounds for denying full citizenship to the mildly retarded.

I. THE CASE FOR RESTRICTING THE CIVIL LIBERTIES OF THE MENTALLY SUBNORMAL

The standard reason for denying full freedom of decision to the mildly retarded is the alleged danger to themselves and to others. Each of these grounds may be

Daniel Wikler, ''Paternalism and the Mildly Retarded,'' *Philosophy & Public Affairs* 8, no. 4. Copyright © 1979 by Princeton University Press. Reprinted by permission. This paper was originally prepared for a reading at the Hastings Center, Institute of Society, Ethics and the Life Sciences, part of a project supported by National Science Foundation grant number OSS76-14793. Opinions and recommendations expressed herein are those of the author and do not necessarily reflect the views of the Foundation. The author gratefully acknowledges the support of both institutions, and of the Joseph P. Kennedy, Jr., Foundation. The paper was materially improved by criticism and suggestions by Norman Fost, Samuel Gorovitz, Michael Green, and John Robertson.

disputed. The latter is often recognized as dubious, and the former probably exaggerated.[2] One might even argue that the danger posed by mildly retarded persons to themselves is less serious than that posed by a paternalistic bureaucracy endowed with broad powers, questionable wisdom, and inconstant motivation. Still, it seems likely that there exist at least some mildly retarded persons who would in fact damage their own interests if given full civil liberties and who would be protected from this harm by restrictions.

In the liberal tradition, the expectation of doing harm to oneself is certainly part of any strong argument for a paternalistic denial of liberties (doing so merely to impose a benefit would be harder to defend).[3] Still, again within that tradition, an expectation is not itself sufficient to make a case for restrictions. Persons of normal intelligence may also pose a danger or risk to their own interests. They can make impulsive contracts, enter into disastrous marriages, and choose occupations in which they are likely to perform poorly. Despite this, they insist on freedom of choice in such matters; not only freedom to make good choices, but also freedom to fail. Although it is not absolute, a standard liberal principle allows us to do as we please as long as the interests of others are not unfairly threatened. The fact that we are about to act against our own interests is not (generally) enough excuse to restrict us.[4]

Thus, the fact that some retarded persons pose a threat to their own welfare is not *in itself* sufficient reason to deny them the liberty to do so. This denial derives from an exception clause in the liberal principle. While it would be wrong to place restrictions on normal persons posing exactly the same threat to their own interests, restrictions on retarded persons would seem to be justified by their mental disability. Some persons of normal intelligence, however self-destructive, are capable of making their decisions on their own; they have the capacity to understand what is at stake, to weigh the alternatives, and to take responsibility for the result. The mildly retarded, however, by dint of their retardation, cannot. We normal people must decide for them, just as we must for the temporarily insane, the comatose, and others unable to reason.

Or so the argument goes. As it stands, it is vulnerable to criticism at several points. One is the vagueness of the concept of "retardation." "General" intelligence is not easily characterized, let alone tested and measured. And even so, the fact that people have been labeled "retarded" through our social sorting mechanisms is by no means a sure guide to their intellectual abilities. But I do not want to press these objections here.[5] Rather, I want to examine the presupposition that there are but two possible statuses, however uncertain their boundary: one of impaired and one of unimpaired intellect, the one lacking a right to self-direction, the other possessing it. Even if we recognize an intellectual deficit in the mildly retarded person when compared to the person of normal ability, there is no ovbious and compelling reason to attach such moral significance to it. The moderately retarded have this deficit when compared with the mildly retarded; and the normal person might have the same when compared with the gifted.[6] We may recognize, then, an array of such cognitive statuses. Do these differences correspond to a large number of distinct moral statuses? If the average, now deemed "normal," is "impaired" from the point of view of those of higher intellectual status, are persons of average intelligence subject to a paternalistic denial of civil liberties for this reason?

It would seem that if the intellectual superiority of normal persons legitimates their controlling the decisions of the mildly retarded, the same difference in intellect would justify their being regulated by the gifted. Our right to self-direction, however, is a right to be free from constraint by any person, whether of normal, subnormal, or high inteligence. This right is supposed to hold even when our decisions are poor and when others happen to know better. We are in the position, then, of using relative intellectual superiority as our rationale for regulating the retarded, while rejecting the possibility of the same rationale being imposed upon us. Unless the apparent inconsistency is resolved, we shall have to either find new foundations for our paternalistic policy towards the mildly mentally handicapped or abandon it.

II. TWO CONCEPTIONS OF COMPETENCE

The inconsistency of claiming immunity from paternalism on the part of our superiors while claiming the right to impose it on our inferiors rests, I believe, upon a certain conception of mental capacity.[7] On this view, which I will call relativism, mental capacity is an attribute admitting of "more" and "less." The mildly retarded have less capacity than normal persons who, in turn, are less endowed than gifted persons might be. No categorization of a group as "mentally impaired" makes sense, in this view, except when understood as relative to the perspective from some other level. Normal persons, those of average intellectual powers, are impaired relative to the gifted, and the mildly retarded are well-endowed relative to the severely retarded. Intelligence, like wealth, is open-ended. As there is no point at which one is "fully wealthy," only more so and even more so, no one can be "fully intelligent." We may be able to distinguish various levels of mental ability through tests, but any line drawn between mentally "impaired" and mentally "unimpaired" is arbitrary. The line could be drawn anywhere else on the scale with equal justification.

The point of this relativist view can be illustrated by reference to the specific components of what are thought to make up the retarded person's deficit. Mildly retarded persons, according to one authority, are unable to think about and deal with more than one or two aspects of a complex situation.[8] They are unable to defer gratification so as to make choices most likely to be of benefit over the longest run, and to foresee long-term consequences of present acts. Similarly they will be markedly less adept than normal persons in handling abstract concepts, and in making the kinds of judgments conducive to smooth social functioning.

The average or "normal" person does somewhat better at all these tasks. But it is plain that normal performance could be improved. An exceptionally gifted individual may have the ability to consider nearly all the aspects of a very complex situation, to defer gratification as needed, to look far into the future, and to be at home with the loftiest of abstractions. "Normal," in this context, then, will mean no more than "average," and "unimpaired" will simply mean as good as most others.

Any definition of normality in mental capacity which is based upon IQ scores is susceptible to a relativist interpretation. According to the American Association of Mental Deficiency:

> A person's mental capacity usually is determined by reference to whether he has the ability to manage his affairs with ordinary or reasonable prudence, is of sound mind, has demonstrated rational understanding or intellectual comprehension, is capable of making a full deliberation of matters presented to him, has the mental capacity to make choices and to formulate requisite judgments about those choices, has demonstrated an ability to engage in meaningful intellectual process, has sufficient intellectual capacity to grasp concepts, or has substantial capacity to understand and appreciate the nature and the consequences of a specified matter or to give intelligent consent to a specified procedure.[9]

These criteria could not be met even by very bright men and women if we set high standards for "full delibertation" or "consent." Nor does this passage indicate why "ordinary or reasonable prudence" should be enough. On the relativist conception, there is nothing intrinsic to average status that earns its rights vis-à-vis its superiors that other levels will lack vis-à-vis theirs. Average mental capacity, which normal persons conveniently label "full" capacity, is simply what happens to be typical for our species at this moment in its evolutionary history. In this view, there can be nothing to convince the gifted that normal capacity is "unimpaired" or "full." As a consequence, our liberal principle, that persons of unimpaired intellect must be free to place their welfare at risk if they so choose, loses its apparent reasonableness.

The inconsistency could be resolved by abandoning our liberal principle. We could accept the rule that superiors may impose their paternalistic guidance upon inferiors who may be mildly retarded, normal, or even bright persons, depending on the circumstances. It is not *immediately* clear that we do not accept this view now. As Nozick observes, we must reflect on our principles to determine whether they do in fact give such rights to superiors; the difference between such rules and the liberal principle cited above is not evident in our dealings with the retarded. We would be forced to choose between them in practice only if confronted by some race of super-beings.

Ought we endorse this benevolent hierarchy? No definitive judgment on paternalism by the gifted can be made independently of a comprehensive moral theory. Still, some education of our intuitions might be in order. It is important not to confuse the value (to normal persons) of the advice proferred by those with superior minds with the propriety of that advice of being imposed, whether accepted or not. Many normal persons might consent to a regime in which the gifted made important decisions for them. Others, perhaps noting that the lives of the retarded have not been rendered blissful by the intervention of *their* intellectual superiors, might not. Does the relative intellectual inferiority of normal persons to the gifted exempt the former from the protection of the liberal principle? I presume not; there is little difference, in a given instance, between a gifted person better able to deduce future consequences of a present decision and a normal person who knows these consequences through access to the relevant information. Both know better what the future will bring than does a normal person lacking the genius or the data or both. The liberal principle restricts paternalism on the part of governments composed of normal persons who may know better; presumably it does the same for gifted persons who know better.

Any persisting intuition that the gifted would be justified in imposing their opinions on the nongifted might be a product of the following reasoning. Normal persons are capable of understanding that the gifted person is more intelligent than they; hence they would, if rational, accept advice from the gifted person; hence, any person of normal intelligence who did not consent to follow the prescriptions of the gifted would have to be suffering from mental disability. Were this true, even normal persons would be suitable targets for paternalism under the liberal principle's "exception clause." Any nonoptimal decision would be taken as the product of an incompetent mind, and the liberal principle would have much less scope.

In any case, we can reject the benevolent hierarchy, save the liberal principle, and still keep our rationale for paternalistic restriction of the retarded by countering the relativist view of mental capacity itself. This requires that "full" mental capacity be understood as a "range property,"[10] one which is possessed in equal measure by all who process it. Such a conception requires us to determine a nonarbitrary threshold, so that all standing above it are equally endowed and all falling below it are unendowed. The point of the relativist argument is that there can be no such line when the property in question is general intelligence. We need not dispute this claim; rather, we may seek a different (though related) property that, unlike intelligence, has the bipolar structure we require. The idea involved is simple and familiar, and will already have occurred to the reader. Mental capacity ought to be seen not as a matter of intellect, but of *competence*: intellect's power in meeting a challenge. A given challenge may be wholly and fully met by the use of a certain amount of intelligence, if the challenge is not too great. Although some persons may have more intelligence than others, they will be no more competent at performing certain tasks; their added power is simply unused surplus. Those lacking enough intelligence for the task will be incompetent to perform it, while those having sufficient intelligence will be equally competent, however great the difference in their intellectual levels.

We have, then, a nonrelative kind of mental impairment, at least as concerns tasks for which superior intelligence is of, at most, marginal additional advantage. There is a similar kind of threshold for other tasks. It will often be the case that, though added intelligence may increase the benefit to be derived from a given task or opportunity, a lesser talent is all that is needed to understand how to avoid harm. Geniuses may be no more adept than normal persons in determining the safest investments on the stock market, though they may be in better position to get rich. The threshold here distinguishes those unable to comprehend and avoid the "downward" risks from those who can; all in the latter category are equal in this respect. Relativism applies, in such a case, only to capacity for realizing "upward" gain.

This conception of mental impairment and competence seems to support some use of the liberal principle. In the case of challenges for which a given level of intelligence is wholly sufficient, persons of superior intelligence are not of superior competence. Hence, they could not use the principle's exception, which covers the case of impairment, to justify the assumption of decision-making power. The same will hold even for the second sort of challenge mentioned above, in which added intellect assists one only in realizing gain. As we noticed in the first section, the strongest argument for paternalism applies when the aim is to protect from harm rather than to ensure a benefit. If a given level of intelligence is sufficient to avoid danger in a given task, those of greater intellect cannot use this principle to restrict a person's liberty in hopes of increasing his or her gain.[11]

If the foregoing is correct, we have shown the possibility, relative to certain sorts of tasks, of a threshold dividing the mentally impaired from those of full capacity and competence. If this is to help in justifying our restriction of civil liberties of the retarded, we need to show that the threshold happens to fall precisely at the level of intelligence just below what we consider normal. The relativist, we recall, finds no reason to suppose that the level of intelligence currently typical of our population is just the level of intelligence required to master the key tasks a person faces.[12] Without such assurance, it will continue to seem arbitrary to pick average mental capacity as that to which a general right to self-direction attaches.

There is a natural-sounding response to this query which, though mistaken, deserves mention. This is that our capacities are suited to our tasks because of natural selection. It would be pointless for the relativist to ask why it should be that we have just enough lung capacity to serve us in our typical pursuits, or why we have just enough blood cells to avoid fatigue most of the time. The answer in both cases, of course, is that neither is an accident. Both traits are admirable adaptations to our environment and its challenges. There is, with most such characteristics, a certain threshold below which the organism is unable to thrive and above which additional increments do not aid in avoiding destruction. The same process which ensures that average humans will have just enough of the necessary physical capacities might be expected to shape their intellectual endowment.

However successful in explaining why we have the lung capacity we do, natural selection does not resolve the problem of mental competence. The complexity and difficulty of the challenges facing the intellect in modern society are largely reflections of society itself. The magnitude of that part of human intelligence which is inheritable was presumably fixed, however roughly, before the challenges that now typically occupy us in society were set. Evolution might have endowed us with the mental means to design and build shelter, or to distinguish poisonous berries from nutritive ones, but it cannot have been supple enough to set our abilities at precisely the level required to fill out Form 1040 of the Internal Revenue Service.

These reflections, however, do suggest what must be the correct reply to the relativist's query. The threshold of competence in our society falls at or just below average because, first, the level of difficulty involved in key life tasks is in large part socially determined; and, second, because society stands to gain by setting this level so as to render the average person competent.

The social component of a task like that of completing a tax form is obvious. We need not marvel at the invisible hand of evolution for making us bright enough to compute our own tax deductions; those who designed the form are charged with with the responsibility of gearing its difficulty to the level of intelligence that evolution and environment happen to have provided. Importantly for our purposes, this social component is prominent in most of the decisions that are denied to the mildly retarded under laws restricting their civil liberties. For example, those who enter into financial contracts assume an obligation to fulfill their part of the bargain and they forswear certain kinds of excuses for not doing so. If an individual is buying an appliance on the installment plan, he obligates himself to send in payments and cannot default because of inconvenience, second thoughts, or even moderate hardship. At the same time, there are certain excuses which he does not forswear; the safeguards represented by bankruptcy laws may be seen as part of this complex transaction. These socially defined characteristics of contracts set the level of intelligence needed to understand and assume responsibility for risk. Insufficient intellect will prevent people from foreseeing the difficulties involved and thus to risk overextending themselves. At the same time, however, the severity of the penalties is kept within certain limits by the bankruptcy laws and by consumer-interest laws.

Essentially conventional, these arrangements might have been different. Society might have instituted rules allowing persons to annul contracts if they proved inconvenient or if the contractors misjudged their resources at the time of bargaining. Similarly, the burden of a decision to procreate would have been lighter had custom not assigned to parents the responsibility for caring for their offspring. Under these conditions, persons whose mental powers are much weaker than the average would be competent to enter contracts, marry, and make other important decision without regularly risking serious reverses that they could not predict and understand. The threshold of competence and mental impairment would be set that much lower.

If it is, in theory, within society's power to arrange itself so as to render the mildly retarded fully competent, why does it not do so? Mere prejudice, a society made up mostly of persons of normal intelligence concerned only for themselves, need not be the answer. There is considerable social utility, at least for normal persons, in setting the threshold about where it is. Contracts which are void when misunderstood or inconvenient would not facilitate the exchange of goods. An appliance-seller hands over the product in exchange for a piece of paper because he or she believes that payments will follow. If such expectation were lacking, no one, regardless of competence, would have a way of obtaining appliances without cash. The value of contracts and other arrangements, the very ones subject to control in our paternalistic restriction of the retarded, depends on their having features that make them hazardous to those with limited ability. Normal persons make the world safe for normality, but not necessarily safe for retardation.

The same holds true with respect to other abilities and capacities. The strength a person must have to be "unimpaired" is not set by biological limits but by the demands of society. It is, then, no surprise that those who design manual gearshift mechanisms and who set the size of grocery bags manufacture products that presuppose something like the average amount of strength. The majority of normal persons in the society benefit (in a purely economic sense) by having the requirements this high. We could make do with levers and containers that even the very weak could handle, but these would undoubtedly be of less use to us. It is also worth noting that current practice sets the threshold for physical competence, and thus renders equal all those at or above the threshold. Those of average strength are just as competent as the very strong in moving gearshift levers; the advantages of exceptional strength lie in other, more esoteric pursuits. Increments of strength, like increments of intelligence, are important if they put one over the socially-defined threshold of "full" or "unimpaired" performance. Superiority past that point counts much less, both for individuals' welfare and for our moral theorizing about them.

Of course, the average requirements, whether for intelligence or for physical strength, could also be set much higher than they presently are. A society designed by and for persons who are by present standards gifted would be a risk-laden environment for persons of merely normal intelligence. They would find themselves unable to understand the nature of the contracts and other social arrangements to which they would be parties, and they would probably be branded incompetent. This seems, after all, to find for the relativist: the argument that is supposed to show that we may restrict the liberties of the mildly retarded would also show that the gifted have the right to impose restraints upon us, provided, however, that the environments in question also differ in relative difficulty.

Does this argument in fact undermine the standard grounds—need together with incompetence—for denying liberties to the retarded? Only if, as before, we insist that the gifted would not have the right to deny liberties to normal persons in the gifted society. Those who support our present treatment of the retarded on the basis of the liberal principle might wish to abandon this insistence, thereby removing any appearance of inconsistency in their approach to the two groups. But I do not think the liberal can abandon it. The intuition behind the liberal principle remains firm: We have a right to make unconstrained choices, shoulder risks, and even court disaster; and we have this right because of our rational faculty. Being placed in a demanding environment, such as a society designed for the gifted, does not diminish our intellectual endowment. To accept paternalistic treatment of normal persons in the gifted society because of the severity of the challenges would commit us to accept also paternalistic denial of liberty in our present society in those circumstances in which a normal person meets a strenuous challenge. Since this is exactly what liberals reject, they must refuse to endorse paternalistic treatment of the normal person by the gifted person.

The liberal should argue instead the normal persons who find themselves in a society created for the gifted would realize that their powers are inadequate for achieving an understanding and mastery of the tasks besetting them. They would, therefore, seek guidance from a friendly gifted person; or if they did not, they would at least be in a position to assess the risks attendant on making their own decisions. While, by hypothesis, they are incompetent to make many kinds of decisions that society requires them to make, they remain fully competent to recognize their limitations and to decide to seek help. In the liberal view, their intellectual powers will be sufficient to allow them to shoulder responsibility for what might happen, and this is enough to render a paternalistic denial of liberty to those of normal intelligence unjustified.

Again, however, the relativist has a response to the liberal. The relativist can claim that humility, the disposition to recognize one's own limitations, emerges not with a given level of intelligence but with certain traits of character and temperament (indeed, it *is* such a trait). Besides, retarded persons are often capable of understanding the principle, "seek guidance when you need it." Their alleged problem is in knowing when it is needed.[13] The same problem might well afflict persons of average intelligence who find themselves in the troubling environment of the society of the gifted. The notion that a right to self-direction attaches to those of a given level of intelligence, simply because of that mental ability and regardless of environmental circumstances, seems impossible to defend. Attempts to found such a moral right on the metaphysical properties of *persons* offer no help to average human beings (or retarded ones); in these theories, "person" is an ideal, the maximally rational reflective agent. As Daniel Dennett has argued, few if any human beings are "persons" in the sense that Kant and Rawls seem to require.[14] Human beings of average intellect, living in their own society, can insist on autonomy not because they are "persons" in this ideal sense, but because, with respect to the challenges they have fashioned for themselves, they are nearly on a par with persons.

III. DISTRIBUTING THE BURDENS OF INCOMPETENCE

Before applying these conclusions to the moral issue of civil liberties for the retarded, it will be useful to review and summarize the arguments thus far presented. Restrictions on the mildly retarded are usually justified by citing the dangers these persons can inflict on themselves. This, in turn, is thought to legitimate paternalistic intervention because retarded persons, being mentally deficient, do not have the right to self-direction claimed by normal persons. We may grant that many so-called retarded persons are in fact normal, and that many of those who are not are capable of living freely and independently without unacceptable risk to their welfare. The question which remains, then, is whether restrictions are defensible for those who are in fact retarded and who do seem likely to encounter trouble if granted full citizenship. If the right to take risks is to be denied the retarded by normal persons on the basis of the latter's intellectual superiority, one would think it legitimate for exceptionally gifted persons to do the same to normal persons. The right to self-direction claimed by normal persons, however, seems to be a claim of immunity against the paternalistic interventions even of those who are more gifted.

I have sought to relieve this apparent inconsistency, and to show that, for certain important tasks, persons of merely normal intelligence are fully the equal of their intellectual superiors. But the moral issue is not yet settled. My argument, while showing that the threshold between mental incompetence and competence is not arbitrary,[15] also shows it to be set by society. As such, it could also be changed. Arrangements could be made to create the conditions under which the retarded would be in the same position to claim autonomy as those of normal and superior intelligence. We would need to show that fairness does not compel us to make these changes before we could regard the restriction of liberties of the retarded as justified.

There is no simple solution to the problem. We may say at once that society, through consumer laws, for example, ought to make its institutions, customs, and practices as safe as possible insofar as it can do so without compromising their utility. This would serve to make the risks involved understandable to those with limited intelligence and hence in some matters give them the status of competent persons with a right to make their own decisions. To change society so that mild mental retardation would be no handicap in any of the tasks in question might reduce the economic and social value of the relevant practices, thereby shifting hardships from the retarded onto those of normal high intelligence. I have no way of estimating the degree of hardship at stake. If it is substantial enough to seriously impede economic and social functioning, perhaps the majority, which consists of normal persons, would have no obligation to change present practices so radically. *Some* redistribution of burdens, however, is undoubtedly in order.

The fairness of denying civil liberties to the mildly retarded depends, then, on the legitimacy of giving higher priority to general social welfare than to doing what is necessary to achieve equal liberty for all. Given our concern that the mildly retarded not be pushed out into a dangerous world in which they may come to ruin, we have two choices. We may change the world so as to render it safer for all. Or we may refrain from allowing the retarded access to it. The morality of paternalism reduces to a question about distributive justice.

Notes

1. The term "guidance" is not strictly accurate in describing the relation of a legally incompetent person to his or her legal guardian. Technically, retarded persons are (usually) denied the right to make the decisions at all; for example, contracts made by these persons are void, and marriages entered into

by them may be annulled. The differences among these legal arrangements do not affect the present argument. See Michael Kindred, "Guardianship and Limitations upon Capacity," in *The Mentally Retarded Citizen and the Law*, ed. Michael Kindred et al. (New York: The Free Press, 1976), pp. 63-87.

2. This is partly because many persons labeled retarded are in fact not mentally deficient, having been mislabeled by inaccurate testing and sorting processes (see Jane Mercer, *Labelling the Retarded*, Berkely: University of California Press, 1973); and partly because the wide range of support services available to many retarded persons enables them to function adequately on their own.

3. See Joel Feinberg, "Legal Paternalism," *Canadian Journal of Philosophy* I, no. I (1971): 105-24. (Reprinted as Chapter 1 of this book.)

4. It must be reemphasized that this claim is not absolute and that there will be occasions in which it is fair to restrict persons of normal intelligence out of concern for their own interests. But since normal persons claim a prima facie right to do as they please, why should not the mildly retarded also claim this right? Although our behavior towards normal persons is occasionally paternalistic, toward the mildly retarded it is routinely so.

5. The lack of attention to these points in the present paper is not meant to suggest that they are unimportant. Indeed, as recent case law has shown, they are themselves sufficient arguments against public policies that fail to distinguish between degrees of retardation, that rely solely on group IQ tests, and that fail to take into account the particular abilities and social resources a retarded individual may possess. Such policies thus extend the protection of the legal status of "retarded person" to people without regard to their real needs. More important, it also extends the burden of that status, stigmatizing the individual and legitimating the segregation and discrimination that have historically been the lot of those placed in this category. Thus, one powerful argument for granting civil liberties to the mildly retarded is that such equal treatment helps avoid stigmatization and its adverse consequences. This gain may offset the risks involved. The argument appeals to our concern for the retarded person's welfare, rather than to any right of self-direction, and it stands (or falls) independently of the issue addressed in this paper.

6. Robert Nozick poses a related question in his *Anarchy, State and Utopia* (New York: Basic Books, 1974). His concern is with a policy of "Utilitarianism for animals, Kantianism for people," in which beings of higher status may use beings of lower status as means and not as ends. The issue discussed in this essay concerns only behavior toward an individual for his own good, whether it is paternalistic benevolence or respect for autonomy; but perhaps the latter is a particularly Kantian moral attitude. Nozick's own resolution, incidentally, seems open to the objections raised below.

7. This conception of competence and that which follows it below have structural similarities to the "statistical" and the "pathological" models of normality, respectively, of Jane Mercer's *Labelling the Retarded*.

8. Travis Thompson, in an address to the Behavior Control Group, Hastings Center, New York, 1977. Some of Thompson's observations were published in his article, "The Behavioral Perspective," *Hastings Center Report* 8, no. 3 (June, 1978), pp. 29-32. Thompson's claim that the mildly retarded have recognizable intellectual and behavioral deficits is quite controversial. One reason is that the faulty labeling process produces such a heterogeneous population within the social category of "retarded person" that few nontrivial general observations can be made; the present paper concerns those who are "really" retarded. Another reason is that admitting to group differences between the retarded and the rest of the populace is seen as a political act, legitimating and even causing unequal treatment in areas having little relation to such actual deficits as a retarded individual may have (see note 5).

9. *Consent Handbook*, Special Publication No. 3 (American Association on Mental Deficiency, 1977), p. 7.

10. John Rawls, *A Theory of Justice* (Cambridge, MA: Belknap Press of Harvard University Press, 1971), p. 508.

11. No *general* distinction between "benefit" and "harm" need be insisted upon here. The harms in question in this discussion can be enumerated: they are those visited upon people who engage in

unwise exercise of those liberties denied to the mildly retarded. The seriousness of these harms (not "harms" in general) is what makes paternalism a plausible policy in the areas mentioned in the introduction.

12. Different tasks, of course, require different levels of intellectual ability for their successful completion. Any adequate social policy of paternalism vis-à-vis the retarded will employ a notion of "selective competence" in which the retarded person is judged incompetent with respect to specific tasks and (perhaps) competent in other respects. The present, general argument rests on an assumption that many of the important liberties denied the mildly retarded require about the same level of intelligence. The argument does not apply to the liberties that do not.

13. See Thompson "Behavioral Perspective," pp. 31-2.

14. Daniel Dennett, "Conditions of Personhood," in *The Identities of Persons*, ed. Amelie Rorty (Berkeley: University of California Press, 1976), pp.175-96.

15. The boundary is, of course, a vague one. The decision to draw the line at some precise point between average intelligence and severe retardation is arbitrary. What is nonarbitrary, according to my argument, is the drawing of the line at some point *below* the average rather than above it.

Chapter 6

Paternalistic Grounds for Involuntary Civil Commitment: A Utilitarian Perspective

Rolf Sartorius

My purpose in this paper is to offer an interpretation of what I believe to be the central argument underlying the position taken by John Stuart Mill in his classic essay *On Liberty*, and to explore the implications of the argument for *paternalistic* justifications of the involuntary civil commitment of the mentally ill. Although much of what I say will obviously apply to nonpaternalistic justifications of involuntary commitment as well (e.g., posing a threat of harm to others), my central concern is with the morality of the laws and institutional practices reflected in statements of the following sort.

From the American Psychiatric Association's revised position statement on involuntary hospitalization of the mentally ill:

> The American Psychiatric Association is convinced that most persons who need hospitalization for mental illness can be and should be informally and voluntarily admitted to hospitals in the same manner that hospitalization is afforded for any other illness . . . .
>
> Unfortunately, a small percentage of patients who need hospitalization are unable, because of their mental illness, to make a free and informed decision to hospitalize themselves. Their need for and right to treatment in a hospital cannot be ignored. In addition, public policy demands that some

Rolf Sartorius, "Paternalistic Grounds for Involuntary Civil Commitment: A Utilitarian Perspective," in *Mental Illness: Law and Public Policy*, eds. B.A. Brody and H. Tristram Engelhardt, Jr. (Dordrecht, Holland: D. Reidel Publishing Co., 1980), pp. 137-45. Copyright © 1980 D. Reidel Publishing Company.

form of involuntary hospitalization be available for those mentally ill patients who constitute a danger . . . to themselves . . . .[1]

From the Washington, D.C., Hospitalization of the Mentally Ill Act:

[involuntary hospitalization is authorized if a person] is mentally ill, and because of that illness, is likely to injure himself . . . if allowed to remain at liberty.[2]

The operative notions in these statements—"in need of treatment" and "dangerous (or potentially harmful) to oneself"—are hopelessly vague and may be so broadly construed as to be virtually coextensive with the equally vague concept of mental illness itself.[3] They may embrace everything from the risk of suicide at one extreme to being maladjusted and presumably standing to benefit from the benevolent ministrations of a mental-health-care professional at the other. Must we, then, in order to examine paternalistic justifications for civil commitment, consider all the points on the spectrum suggested? Or should we try to draw a line—in terms of the magnitude and likelihood of the harm in question, perhaps—on one side of which would fall those cases in which involuntary commitment was justified and on the other side of which it was not? Neither of these potentially tortuous routes need be taken, of course, unless one believes that there are some cases in which involuntary commitment is justifiable on paternalistic grounds. It is precisely this belief that, following Mill, I intend to oppose. Before turning to Mill's argument, though, some further preliminary remarks are in order.

In 1968 Alan Dershowitz estimated that there were some one million persons locked behind the doors of state mental hospitals.[4] No discussion of involuntary commitment of the mentally ill would be complete without noting that they most likely represent merely a small proportion of those who are committed against their will and who would not be were it not for the existence of statutes authorizing involuntary commitment. Many of those who "voluntarily" commit themselves to mental institutions do so on the basis of the often well-founded belief that if they do not commit themselves voluntarily they will be committed involuntarily, with the added trauma of the procedures necessitated by formal commitment proceedings. The number of persons who fall into this category is almost impossible to estimate, but I am sure that it is substantial. Any assessment of the social consequences of involuntary civil commitment as an institutional practice must surely take such persons, and their undesired loss of liberty, into account.

As the preceding remarks suggest, it is the justifiability of a set of institutional practices defined by law and given life by the customary behaviors of judges, attorneys, health-care professionals, and others that is at issue. Few of us would be at a loss to describe the details of a particular case, real or hypothetical, in which we would have no reservations about the involuntary commitment of a mentally ill person as a means of protecting that person against himself or herself *within the framework of existing law and institutional practice*. But this says absolutely nothing about the justifiability of the practices themselves. When acts of a certain kind are legally permitted, it may be that people on occasion ought to perform them. But it may also be the case that they ought not to be permitted in the first place.

It is worth noting that neither the American Psychiatric Association's Statement nor the D.C. Hospitalization Act provides for the involuntary commitment of those who are simply (a) mentally ill, and (b) dangerous to themselves. The D.C. Act requires that the latter (dangerousness) be "because of" the former, while the APA Statement requires that "because of" mental illness the patient be unable "to make a free and informed decision" to hospitalize himself or herself. Indeed, on one interpretation the APA Statement does not require dangerousness to self (or others) at all, but in fact proposes two independent paternalistic grounds for involuntary commitment: (a) mental illness plus dangerousness to self, (b) mental illness in virtue of which the patient is incapable of making a rational decision about commitment. For the sake of the argument, I would like to consider a proposal that may be more restrictive than either the APA or the D.C. Act. It would authorize involuntary commitment (on paternalistic grounds) only when (a) the patient is mentally ill, (b) the patient is dangerous to self in some quite clear and uncontroversial sense, (c) the patient is incapable of making a rational decision to commit herself or himself, and (d) both (b) and (c) are due to (a).[5]

I have framed the above criteria for involuntary commitment on the grounds of dangerousness to self with a view toward at least partially meeting the frequently heard objection that justifying interferences with individual liberty on such grounds would surely justify too much. For there are many activities that pose considerable danger only to those voluntarily choosing to engage in them, and with which we would yet feel it illegitimate to interfere on the basis of paternalistic concerns. But how are we to distinguish the mentally ill who are dangerous to themselves from sky divers, mountain climbers, heavy drinkers and smokers, and those who refuse available treatment for serious physical disorders? The difference, when there is one, lies in the capacity of individuals to make a rational choice to change their ways. And even when such a capacity may be lacking—as in the case of individuals who are just too stupid to appreciate the dangerousness of their activities—it may not stand in the appropriate causal relationship to the dangerous activity. But when it does, criteria analogous to those framed for mental illness can surely be satisfied, and when they are paternalistic interferences with individual liberty are surely as justifiable as they are in the case of the mentally ill. Drug addiction and alcoholism are clear cases in point. Indeed, given the argument which I shall shortly develop, it will turn out that paternalistic interference with individual liberty may be justified in some such cases but not in the case of those who are dangerous to themselves by virtue of being mentally ill. At any rate, what I am suggesting is that those who are in favor of paternalistic treatment of the mentally ill must admit to the acceptance of a quite general criterion of the following sort: If individuals are in some condition (C) in virtue of which they are both dangerous to themselves and incapable of making rational decisions to adopt patterns of thought and action which will render them less dangerous, the state may legitimately interfere with their liberty as a means of preventing them from harming themselves. Such a principle does not require that the state have and make available means of ameliorating C (treatment in the case of mental illness), but it should be understood to require that the disvalue associated with the loss of liberty in question be outweighed (for a rational agent) by the benefit attached to the avoidance of the potential harm (this to be calculated in terms of both its magnitude and its likelihood of occurrence).

Mill's *On Liberty* is unequivocal in its opposition to any such paternalistic position. It is devoted, writes Mill, to the defense of

> one very simple principle, as entitled to govern absolutely the dealings of society with the individual in the way of compulsion and control . . . . That principle is that the sole end for which mankind are warranted, individually or collectively, in interfering with the liberty of action of any of their number is self-protection. That the only purpose for which power can be rightfully exercised over any member of a civilized community, against his will, is to prevent harm to others. His own good, either physical or moral, is not a sufficient warrant.[6]

Mill, as an act-utilitarian, is committed to the overarching moral principle that the morality of any particular act is to be determined by an evaluation of *its* consequences—in terms of the production of satisfaction and dissatisfaction—for all those who will be affected by it. How, then, could he consistently propose an *absolute* prohibition upon any *kind* of act, let alone paternalistic legislation or particular acts motivated by paternalistic considerations? In attacking Mill's principle in 1882, James Fitzjames Stephen contended that this question simply could not be consistently answered.[7] His argument is that no matter how great the value of human liberty, utilitarians are committed by the very nature of their position to deciding each case (of possibly justified paternalism) on its individual merits.

> If . . . the object aimed at is good, if the compulsion employed is such as to attain it, and if the good obtained overbalances the inconvenience of the compulsion itself, I do not understand how, upon utilitarian principles, the compulsion can be bad.[8]

Stephen's argument has been accepted by many recent commentators on Mill's position. Gerald Dworkin, for instance, writes that "A consistent Utilitarian can only argue against paternalism on the grounds that it (as a matter of fact) does not maximize the good. It is always a contingent question that may be refuted by the evidence."[9] Mill's utilitarian arguments against paternalism, Dworkin contends, must be understood as being accompanied by a second line of (quite non-utilitarian) argument that places an absolute value upon the autonomy of human choice.[10] Joel Feinberg has explicitly endorsed Dworkin's account, claiming that the argument in favor of an absolute prohibition upon paternalism must rest upon the recognition of an "abstract right" to freedom of choice, the violation of which would be "an injustice, a wrong, a violation of the private sanctuary which is every person's self . . . whatever the calculus of harms and benefits might show."[11]

Let us look, then, at the text of *On Liberty* with a view to determining whether or not Mill's arguments are sufficient to support his absolute stance against paternalism without being supplemented with a non-utilitarian appeal to an abstract right of self-determination.

> But the strongest of all the arguments against the interference of the public with purely personal conduct is that, when it does interfere, the odds are that it interferes wrongly and in the wrong place. On questions of social morality, of duty to others, the opinion of the public, that is, of an overruling majority, though often wrong, is likely to be still oftener right, because on such questions they are only required to judge of their own interests, of the manner in which some mode of conduct, if allowed to be practiced, would affect themselves, But the opinion of a similar majority, imposed as a law on the minority, on questions of self-regarding conduct, is quite as likely to be wrong as right, for in these cases public opinion means, at the best, some people's opinion of what is good or bad for other people . . . [12]

> The interferences of society to overrule his judgment and purposes in what only regards himself must be grounded on general presumptions; which may be altogether wrong, and even if right, are as likely as not to be misapplied to individual cases . . . . All errors which the individual is likely to commit against advice and warning are far outweighed by the evil of allowing others to constrain him to what they deem his good.[13]

While Dworkin describes it as "fairly weak"[14] and Feinberg as "at best strong"[15] they are one in agreeing that "arguments of this merely statistical kind . . . [only] create a . . . rebuttable presumption against coercion of a man in his own interest."[16] Both writers, I believe, miss the thrust of Mill's arguments. They are correct in claiming that Mill's arguments establish only a presumption in any particular case, but fail to see that they are sufficient (assuming that they have a sound empirical foundation) to establish an absolute prohibition upon paternalism at the level of law and institutional practice. If the considerations that Mill relies upon are applied not to the question "Do we coerce the Joneses for their own good?" but to the question "Do we permit legal authorities to ever coerce anyone for his or her own good?" it is obvious that it is an absolute prohibition of a certain kind of conduct rather than a rebuttable presumption against the permissibility of particular acts of that kind that is thereby established.

The argument which Mill described as "the strongest of all arguments" in favor of his anti-paternalistic principle is a powerful one, and would appear to be the only kind of argument to which the utilitarian could consistently appeal in an attempt to give Mill's principle the absolute status that he quite rightly required for it. In addition, it would seem to be the only kind of argument that is not damaged by the admission that there are specific instances in which particular acts would be justified on paternalistic grounds if they were not antecedently generally prohibited. The general schema of the argument, I suggest, is the following. Assume (a) that most acts of kind K are, on utilitarian grounds, wrong, although (b) some acts of kind K are, on utilitarian grounds, right, but that (c) most attempts to identify exceptions to the rule of thumb "Acts of kind K are wrong" are mistaken because there is no reliable criterion by means of which exceptions to the rule may be identified. When these conditions are all satisfied, the act-utilitarian has good reason, other things being equal, for acting so as to prevent anyone from ever performing an act of kind K. Whereas (a) and (b) by themselves establish only a rebuttable presumption as to how one ought to act in particular cases, the addition of (c) provides the grounds for an absolute prohibition on the kind of activity in question.

One would surely be inclined to argue this way on the constitutional level with respect to first-amendment freedoms: (a) Most governmental attempts at interferences with, e.g., freedom of the press, have had bad consequences and are thus wrong on utilitarian grounds; (b) But one can, of course, think of specific instances in which legal interference with a particular publication would have good consequences; (c) On the other hand, were government to have the legal power to decide that something was an exception to the hands-off policy indicated by (a), more often than not decisions to interfere would be mistaken, with bad consequences in specific cases, and a chilling effect on the press in general, stemming from well-founded fears that the power would be abused. Therefore, an absolute prohibition on legal interference with the press is the policy choice that will have the best consequences in the long run. Although this may not be very elegant as a piece of constitutional analysis, it should suffice to remind us of what is a familiar and totally reasonable pattern of argument that is wholly consistent with an act-utilitarian position. That the *act* in question is in this case one of the choice of consitutional *rule* makes it no less an act. I therefore contend that Mill's argument is a valid one; the conclusion that he reaches does follow from the premises that he puts forward in support of it, the conclusion being that "mankind are greater gainers (in the long run) by suffering each other to live as seems good to themselves, than by compelling each other to live as seems good to the rest."[17]

Although valid, the soundness of Mill's argument in any particular application will depend upon the truth of the empirical assumptions embodied in the corresponding instantiation of the argument schema outlined above. Surely some forms of paternalism are justified—Mill himself admitted exceptions to which most of us would be willing to add.[18] But although his objections to paternalism may be overdrawn (even though I do not think by very much), Mill's argument does force us to address the central issue when any particular form of paternalism is involved, namely: What are the likely long-run consequences in terms of human well-being of the adoption of the laws, policies, and institutional practices that provide the framework without which it is (typically) impossible to raise the question of the proper disposition of particular cases?

What, then, are the implications of Mill's argument with respect to the involuntary civil commitment of the mentally ill on the grounds that they are dangerous to themselves? Recall that for the sake of argument we are considering a quite stringent criterion, authorizing involuntary commitment only when the individual was found to be not only mentally ill and dangerous, but also incapable of making a rational decision to commit himself, and it was also found to be the case that the dangerousness to self and the requisite incapacity were caused by the mental illness. The acceptability of any such criterion must hinge upon both the reliability with which it can be applied and the consequences of applying it to a population of a certain assumed composition. *When the characteristic to be identified is relatively rare, and the costs of its misidentification at all appreciable, virtually any criterion short of one which is not 100% effective will be clearly unacceptable, even assuming that the benefits associated with the identifications it correctly makes are very considerable.* Modifying only slightly a hypothetical example found in the classic paper by Livermore, Malmquist, and Meehl,[19] let us assume that there is a certain form of mental illness such that virtually all those who have it will commit suicide if left at liberty, and that the other conditions of our proposed criterion are satisfied as well. Again, assume that one person in a thousand suffers from the illness in question, and that our criterion is reliable, distinguishing with 95% effectiveness between those who will commit suicide in virtue of the illness in question from those who will not. In a population of 100,000, ninety-five of the 100 who would commit suicide would be identified and presumably benefited by being involuntarily committed. Five persons would go undetected and—unless they met a natural death first—commit suicide. But out of the 99,900 people who would not commit suicide, 4,995 would also be identified and committed as suicidal!

Is the involuntary civil commitment of the mentally ill on the grounds of dangerousness to self morally justifiable? The question posed by Livermore, Malmquist, and Meehl surely answers itself: "If, in the criminal law, it is better that ten guilty men go free than that one innocent man suffer, how can we say in the civil commitment area that it is better than fifty-four harmless people be incarcerated least one dangerous man be free?"[20]

Notes

1. American Psychiatric Association, "Position Statement on Involuntary Hospitalization of the Mentally Ill (Revised)," *The American Journal of Psychiatry*, vol. 130, no. 3 (1973), p. 392.

2. Quoted in Gerald Dworkin, "Paternalism," *The Monist*, vol. 56, no. 1, p. 66.

3. See Alan M. Dershowitz, "Psychiatry in the Legal Process: A Knife That Cuts Both Ways," *Judicature*, vol. 51, 1968.

4. *Ibid.*

5. As Dershowitz notes, not all of those who are mentally ill are incapable of making an informed decision to commit themselves.

6. John Stuart Mill, *On Liberty*, (Indianapolis, IN: Bobbs-Merrill, Inc., 1956), p. 13.

7. Parts of the following discussion are taken from Rolf Sartorius, "The Enforcement of Morality," *Yale Law Journal*, vol. 81, no. 5, 1972.

8. James Fitzjames Stephen, *Liberty, Equality, Fraternity* (New York: Henry Holt and Co., 1882), p. 50.

9. Dworkin, "Paternalism," p. 193.

10. Ibid., pp. 193-4.

11. Joel Feinberg, "Legal Paternalism," *Canadian Journal of Philosophy*, vol. 1, no. 1 (1971), pp. 108-9.

12. Mill, *On Liberty*, p. 102.

13. *Ibid.*, p. 95.

14. Dworkin, "Paternalism," p. 194.

15. Feinberg, "Legal Paternalism," p. 108.

16. *Ibid.*

17. Mill, *On Liberty*, p. 10.

18. Mill recognized children and "the uncivilized." Dworkin, pp. 186-7, lists a number of other plausible candidates.

19. Joseph Livermore, Paul Malmquist, and Paul Meehl, "On the Justifications for Civil Commitment," *University of Pennsylvania Law Review*, vol. 117, no. 1 (1968), p. 84.

20. *Ibid.*

Part II

Chapter 7

Paternalism: Some Second Thoughts

Gerald Dworkin

> *"I changed my mind."*
> *"Oh, yeah? Does it work any better?"*
>
> > *From a Mae West movie*

I

As seems appropriate for second thoughts (see chapter 2 for my first thoughts), I shall begin at the beginning—the definition of paternalism, Earlier, I defined the concept as

> interference with a person's liberty of action justified by reasons referring exclusively to the welfare, good, happiness, needs, interests, or values of the person being coerced.[1]

A number of critics have objected that confining the concept to interferences with liberty is too restrictive in scope.[2] Given the problem I was interested in, i.e., the proper limits of state coercion, this restriction was reasonable, although even here one ought to be aware that the state has other ways of influencing people's behavior. It may refuse to enforce contracts, give in-kind rather than cash aid, set up licensing boards, require manufacturers to install seat-belts as original equipment, and so forth.

If, however, one wishes to consider the issue of paternalism in other contexts, for example, in the professions, one will need a broader definition. Not all paternalistic acts are acts of the state. Not all paternalistic acts involve interference with liberty. The doctor who lies to her terminally ill patients, the parent who stipulates in her will that a child may not inherit an estate before the age of thirty, the psychiatrist who tells his adolescent patient that he must inform her parents of her drug usage, the professor who refuses to recommend her Ph.D. student to a certain university because he will be "out of his league"—these are all cases of paternalism that do not involve the use of coercion or force and, therefore, on standard views of liberty do not involve restrictions on liberty.

How should one broaden the definition? One way is to include such specific elements as deception. Buchanan, for example, characterizes paternalism as

interference with a person's freedom of action or freedom of information, or the deliberate dissemination of misinformation.[3]

Given a suitably broad notion of freedom of information, this definition will include not only the case of a doctor acting paternalistically toward a patient by misinforming him or by not revealing information, but also the case of a doctor telling the patient more than he wants to know. A patient may make it quite clear that he does not want to know something about his condition and a doctor may insist on telling him the whole truth for his own good.

Still this definition seems too restrictive in scope. There are other ways to paternalize besides coercing or manipulating one's information set. Suppose, for example, we play tennis together and I realize that you are getting upset about the frequency with which you lose to me. So, for your own good and against your wishes, I refuse to play with you. My refusal to engage in a form of social cooperation does not seem to me an infringement of your liberty. But it also seems to me a case of paternalism.

On the other hand, the attempt to broaden the notion by including any violation of a moral rule is too restrictive because it will not cover cases such as the following.[4] A husband who knows his wife is suicidal hides his sleeping pills. He violates no moral rule. They are his pills and he can put them wherever he wishes.

This example, as well as that of the doctor who tells the patient the truth against his wishes, also works against defining paternalism in terms of acts that violate the rights of the person in question. The wife does not have a right to those pills, nor does the patient have a right not to be told the truth.

It begins to look as if the only condition that will work is one that depends upon the fact that the person who is being treated paternalistically does not wish to be treated that way. The wife has no right to the pills, but she does not want her husband to hide them. The patient has no right to not be told the truth, but he doesn't want to hear it. But something more must be present in order to include a case like the following:

Consider a father (a lawyer) who wants his daughter to become a lawyer. The daughter believes that she would make a very good lawyer. Indeed, she believes it likely that she would be more successful professionally than her father, who has managed to survive only on a marginal basis. Because she believes that such success would make her father very unhappy, the daughter decides to become a doctor instead. Here is a decision made against the wishes of another person for that person's own good. Yet, I think that this is not a case of paternalism. The daughter does nothing to interfere with the self-determination of the father. She does not act in accordance with her father's judgment, but neither does she act in such a fashion as to substitute her judgment for that of her father.

There must be a violation of a person's autonomy (which I conceive as a distinct notion from that of liberty) for one to treat another paternalistically. There must be a usurpation of decision-making, either by preventing people from doing what they have decided or by interfering with the way in which they arrive at their decisions.

An implication of this view is that there are no methods of influencing people that are necessarily immune to being used paternalistically. It is not as if rational argument cannot be paternalistic while brute force must be. Some people may want to make their decisions impulsively, without rational deliberation; insisting that they hear arguments (for their own good) is paternalism. On the other hand, brute force used to prevent someone from crossing a washed-out bridge need not be paternalism.

What we must ascertain in each case is whether the act in question constitutes an attempt to substitute one person's judgment for another's, to promote the latter's benefit.

It is because of the violation of the autonomy of others that normative questions about the justification of paternalism arise. The denial of autonomy is inconsistent with having others share the ends of one's actions—for if they would share the end, it would not be necessary to usurp their decision-making powers. At one level, therefore, paternalism seems to treat others as means (with the important difference that it is as a means to their ends, not ours). But, at the same time, because we know that the relation between the good of a person and what that person wants is not a simple one, because what is in a person's interests is not always what satisfies his or her current desires, and because we can conceive of situations in which we would want to have our autonomy denied, the possibility of justifying some paternalistic intervention emerges.

One useful heuristic to guide our judgments about the justifiability of such interventions is to ask under what conditions does A's attempt to substitute his or her judgment for B's constitute treating B as less than a moral equal.

II

It is useful to distinguish between "hard" and "soft" paternalism. By soft paternalism, I mean the view that (1) paternalism is sometimes justified, and (2) it is a necessary condition for such justification that the person for whom we are acting paternalistically is in some way not competent. This is the view defended by Feinberg in his article "Legal Paternalism."[5] More precisely, his view is slightly stronger since the necessary condition is either that the conduct in question be substantially nonvoluntary, or that we need time to determine whether the conduct is voluntary or not. By hard paternalism, I mean the view that paternalism is sometimes justified even if the action is fully voluntary.

In arguing for a "hypothetical consent" scheme for justifying paternalism, I did not make clear whether I regarded the argument as *always* resting upon some deficiency in competence against which we wished to protect ourselves. I spoke of "irrational propensities, deficiencies in cognition and emotional capacities, and avoidable and unavoidable ignorance[6] as being rational reasons for agreeing (hypothetically) to limitations of our conduct, even when others' interest are not affected. I also spoke of insuring ourselves against making decisions which are "far-reaching, potentially dangerous, and irreversible." One set of considerations focuses on the agent; the other on the character of the decision. The former raises questions of rationality and competence; the latter of danger and harm.

The example of forcing people to wear seat-belts illustrates the difficulty I felt both about the correctness of paternalistic intervention and about the proper basis for its justification in such cases. Since I felt that intervention was legitimate, I sought to show that persons who do not fasten their seat-belts (at least most of them) are in some way failing in rationality. They either put an unreasonably high negative weight on what is at most an inconvenience, or discount unreasonably the probability or seriousness of future injury.

I think now that the issue must be faced more squarely. While it is possible to relate such cases to the soft paternalist thesis by claiming ignorance or weakness of the will, the strategy seems too ad hoc to be convincing. In any case, there will be other situations (for example, not allowing individuals to become slaves) in which this approach seems implausible. I propose, therefore, to consider three cases which are difficult for the soft paternalist, and to examine the strategies for dealing with them.

The first set of cases I shall call "safety cases." These include requiring motorcyclists to wear helmets, hunters to wear brightly colored jackets, sailors to carry life-preservers, and drivers to wear seat-belts. These are all instances of making people buy and use various items. They also include cases of preventing people from buying and using various things—bans on Red Dye No. 2, firecrackers, heroin.

The second set of cases is illustrated by the issue of putting fluoride in the community water supply. These cases differ from safety cases since, for example, we do not *require* anybody to drink fluoridated water. We just make it easy for those who wish to receive fluoride to do so and we make it correspondingly more difficult for those who do not wish to do so to avoid it. Since the argument for such measures involves a claim that there are certain actions that should be done collectively, I shall refer to these cases as "collective decisions."

The third set of cases are those forbidding people to sell themselves into slavery or to sell body parts to others. I shall refer to such cases as "slavery cases."

For all three types of cases I shall be making the assumption that there is no convincing reason for regarding the actions of the parties (not to wear helmets, not to be fluoridated, to enter into slavery) as necessarily less than voluntary.

Therefore, if one believes that the restrictive actions are justified, and if one believes that the justification is at least in part paternalistic, we have test cases for soft paternalism.

Of course, one can reject these as counter-examples by claiming that it would be wrong or unjustifiable to prevent people from becoming slaves or to force sailors to carry life-preservers. I confess that I do not see how to progress further with the argument if this is the point of disagreement. These judgments (that it is wrong to prevent people from becoming slaves, etc.) are part of a perfectly consistent positon and one that is not in any way crazy. Of course, those who accept this consequence may do so because they are convinced on independent grounds that hard paternalism is unjustifiable. If so, one may be able to show that their arguments are not sound. But if the disagreement centers on these intuitions, I find it hard to see how it can be resolved.

The first strategy is to argue that the assumption I make about these cases is not valid. Anybody who would agree to become a slave or who would object to carrying a life-preserver must be in some way distracted, misinformed, impetuous, weak-willed, self-destructive, or so forth. In effect, this move denies that these are test-cases for soft paternalism. The contention seems implausible. One cannot argue a priori that persons who do such things are acting nonvoluntarily. Nothing in the concept of becoming a slave prohibits one doing this freely.

While there might be empirical evidence for the nonvoluntary character of many such actions, it is unlikely that all such acts will be nonvoluntary. I do not see how one can rule out the possibility that hard paternalism may be the only position which can justify restrictions on such actions.

The most likely response is that while interference may be justified in such cases, it may be for nonpaternalistic reasons. The justification is based on the interests of third parties who are affected in ways that they have a right to be protected against.

The argument in the "safety" cases is that persons who are injured or killed because of their risky behavior impose costs on the rest of us. When the costs are economic, such as the costs of medical care, the obvious reply is that this might show that we can require such individuals to purchase medical insurance, but it does not show that we can require them to actually wear safety helmets.

Note that in purely economic terms it is quite likely that the effect of requiring motorcycle helmets is to cause badly injured persons to survive (requiring costly medical care) who might otherwise might have died from head injuries!

If the costs result from the efforts involved in rescue operations and so forth, one could again require compensation for such effort as a matter of contract or tort law. But there will be certain individuals who intentionally or otherwise will not insure themselves and who may not be in a position to make financial compensation.

What do we do in the case of such individuals? The libertarian answer is that we announce ahead of time that such individuals will not be aided by us. But surely this imposes a psychic cost on us—that of ignoring or abandoning people in distress. There does seem to be an argument for interference here, because the rest of us do not want to be put in such a position.

In the case of hunters who are shot by other hunters because they do not wear brightly-colored clothing, there is another kind of cost. People have to bear the knowledge that they have caused harm (perhaps death) to another.

Ultimately I am left with the feeling that these arguments either are not relevant to justifying restrictions on behavior (although they may justify compulsory insurance) or, if they are relevant, do not seem strong enough to tip the scale by themselves. In the final analysis, I think we are justified in requiring sailors to take along life-preservers because it minimizes the risk of harm to them at the cost of a trivial interference with their freedom.

The second set of cases, those of "collective decisions," create difficulties for any consent scheme that requires unanimous consent; it is implausible to suppose that one can argue for the rationality of such consent without making various ad hoc assumptions about the extent to which we share common values, religious outlooks, and risk-taking preferences.

We are faced with the following problem. Suppose that most people in a community would consent to a certain practice, but that a minority would not. Although the best solution would be to exempt the minority, considerations of administrative and economic efficiency may make this solution very expensive. It is both more effective and cheaper to put flouride in the community water supply than it is to distribute fluoride pills to those who want them or to supply nonfluoridated water to those who do not want fluoride.

If justice takes precedence over efficiency, the solution is clear. But this is not a question of determining the basic structure of society. It is more a constitutional question of deciding what powers to give the legislature. I am inclined to think that some balancing of interests is appropriate here. Knowing that we will be in the minority on some issues, and in the majority on others, it is reasonable not to demand unanimity for certain issues.

The relevant conditions are: (1) that the majority interest must be important (such as health); (2) that the imposition on the minority must be relatively minor (they have to buy their own water); and (3) that the administrative and economic costs of not imposing on the minority would be very high. However, fairness requires that if there are economic costs to the minority (such as purchasing nonfluoridated water), they should be borne by those who gain.

In this analysis, the restriction on the minority is not motivated by paternalistic considerations, but by the interests of a majority who wish to promote their own welfare. Hence, these are not paternalistic decisions, and do not count against soft paternalism.

Finally, we come to "slavery cases," in which people are not allowed to enter into certain voluntary agreements that would result in great loss of liberty or serious risk of bodily injury. While there may be a presumption in light of what we know about human nature that such choices are usually not fully voluntary, this is a presumption that may be rebutted in particular cases. These are also difficult cases for soft paternalism.

In these cases, however, there is a different line of argument open to the soft paternalist. Since the issue is whether a certain contract will be enforced rather than whether there will be a first-order restriction on the conduct itself, one might argue that different principles apply. Refusal to enforce such agreements may frustrate desires, but it is not a direct interference with liberty.

Again, one may look for third-party considerations. Most of us do not want to live in a society in which, for example, we are legally obligated to return runaway slaves to their owners. Such considerations underlie the general doctrine in contract law which does not require specific performance for the breach of a personal-service contract.

In my original paper, I argued that our objection to allowing voluntary slavery was linked to the promotion of the very value against which paternalism offends— autonomy. If we conceive of autonomy as the capacity of individuals to critically reflect on and take responsibility for the kind of persons they want to be, then we stop people from becoming slaves in order to preserve their future ability to define the kind of lives they want to lead. While I still find this argument plausible, my more recent reflections on autonomy raise the following theoretical problem. There is nothing in the idea of autonomy which precludes a person from saying:

> I want to be the kind of person who acts at the command of others. I define myself as a slave and endorse those attitudes and preferences. My autonomy consists in being a slave.

If this is coherent, and I think it is, one cannot argue against such slavery on grounds of autonomy. The argument will have to appeal to some idea of what is a fitting life for a person and, thus, be a direct attempt to impose a conception of what is "good" on another person.

If, as I suspect, any person who adopted the above attitude would argue for it on grounds of maximizing some other good, the case may reduce to a safety-case as one of mistaken calculation about the best way of securing a person's good as conceived by her or him. The hard theoretical position may never be reached.

Notes

1. Gerald Dworkin, "Paternalism," *The Monist* 56, no. 1, January 1972, p. 65. (Reprinted as chapter 2 of this book.)

2. See, for example, Bernard Gert and Charles Culver, "Paternalistic Behavior," *Philosophy and Public Affairs* 6, no. 1 (Fall, 1976), pp. 45-57.

3. Allen Buchanan, "Medical Paternalism," *Philosophy and Public Affairs* 7, no. 4 (Summer, 1978), p. 372. (Reprinted as chapter 4 of this book.)

4. This condition is Gert and Culver's.

5. Joel Feinberg, "Legal Paternalism," *Canadian Journal of Philosophy* 1, no. 1, pp. 106-24. (Reprinted as chapter 1 of this book.)

6. I would like to thank Daniel Brock, Leslie Francis, and Eric Mack for helpful comments on an earlier draft.

Chapter 8

Paternalism, Freedom, Identity, and Commitment

Donald H. Regan

Some years ago, I wrote an essay entitled "Justifications for Paternalism."[1] That essay is here revised, and expanded by the addition of a new topic. Many readers of the original version did not understand that the two principal sections presented arguments that were quite independent. I would therefore emphasize that in the present version the *three* principal sections (II, III, and IV) are separable one from another. Not surprisingly, in an essay so disconnected, I reach no general conclusions I have much confidence in. I suspect the reason for the failure is that I have been insufficiently daring in rejecting common premises for thinking about the problem. That, however, is a story for another time.

I

It may be useful to rehearse briefly the main points of what I take to be the standard dialectic of paternalism. In the context of a traditional utilitarian approach to the problem of paternalism, there is one necessary and sufficient condition for paternalistic coercion—namely, that the coercion will result in more pleasure or happiness overall for the person coerced. If some individual will be happier overall if she abstains from cigarettes, or from heroin, or if she wears seat-belts in cars or a helmet when riding a motorcycle, we should coerce her to do all those things. That is all there is to it. But this singleminded pleasure-maximizing approach does not satisfy us. Anyone who suggests that we are always justified in compelling people to do that which will make them happiest is ignoring another value that is not the same as happiness, the value of freedom of choice. Among our intuitions we seem to find the idea that individuals have a right to make their own choices, even if they are bad ones. In cases in which paternalistic coercion would be justified on utilitarian grounds, two important values, pleasure or happiness on the one hand and freedom on the other, seem to be irreconcilably opposed.

We might try to resolve the conflict by a rule-utilitarian move. It seems plausible to suppose that in many cases, perhaps most, individuals have a better idea what will make them happy than do remote legislators. If that is so, paternalistic legislation may be misguided more often than not, and a general principle forbidding such legislation, possibly enshrined in a constitution, might make good sense. This is a significant argument. In the end, it may be the strongest argument that can be made for a general prohibition on paternalism.[2] However, it leaves the defense of freedom dependent on a contingency. If there is any intrinsic value in freedom, this argument does not give that value its due. I shall therefore eschew this and other rule-utilitarian arguments in what follows. Except where I specify otherwise, I shall consider the question of when coercion would be justified from the point of view of an idealized paternalist, who not only knows everything about the individual he is coercing and the consequences of various choices by that individual but who also has at his disposal means of coercion that can discriminate perfectly between different individuals and different acts. My hypothetical paternalist does not make mistakes; he need not worry about possible overbreadth in general prohibitions; and he operates in a system in which paternalistic legislation had no bad effects on the administration of the legal system generally. I am ignoring serious practical problems, because it seems to me that before we can decide what sorts of paternalism are justified in practice, we need to have some idea of what sorts would be justified for my ideal paternalist.

We might also try to resolve the conflict between happiness and freedom by saying that some considerable degree of freedom is a necessary condition of being happy. Unfortunately, this claim is not obviously true—witness the cases of nuns, soldiers, and others who manage to be happy inside total institutions— and even if it were true it would still seem to subordinate to happiness something which is an independent value of equal stature.

Another move, still within the standard dialectic, is more promising. It is often suggested that paternalism may be justified when the individual coerced lacks relevant information about the consequences of her acts. Presumably this justification for paternalism gets its force from a feeling that ignorance is a sort of unfreedom. Since the person who lacks information is unfree even if we do not intervene to constrain her choice, we are not really decreasing her freedom by intervening, and the conflict between freedom and happiness never arises. Just why being uninformed is a way of being unfree is an interesting question. Certainly it smacks more of a lack of "positive" freedom than of a lack of "negative" freedom. Still, as an excuse for paternalism, ignorance is in reasonably good repute even with advocates of negative freedom.

If our justification of paternalism is simply people's ignorance, it might seem that we have a warrant not for coercion, but only for education. If the reason we feel justified in forbidding drugs is that we don't think users realize the danger to themselves, should we not concentrate on informing them of the danger, and then let them do as they please? In fact, there are a variety of claims we might put forth to justify coercion in particular cases. Sometimes there simply will not be time to educate the party coerced, as when someone threatens to act in a way that will do her irreparable damage before we can convince her of what the facts are. In other cases, the party to be coerced may lack the expertise to understand or use the information she should have.

Stretching the concept of information a bit, we might suggest that even when expertise is not in question, an individual might have all the facts within her cognitive grasp and still not really appreciate them. For example, someone might know all the medical facts about cigarettes, emphysema, and lung cancer, and still fail to appreciate just how unpleasant the possible consequences of smoking are. In a similar vein, we might suggest that most people are simply incapable of taking very small probabilities properly into account, and this could be regarded as a sort of ignorance about consequences. With these arguments, we can defend a good deal of paternalism with some persuasiveness on the ground that we are interfering only when people lack information.

Another move, similar to the appeal to ignorance, is the claim that paternalism is justified when the subject of coercion is acting under psychological compulsion or under unusual social pressure. In these cases also, we might claim not to interfere with freedom, since the subject of coercion is already unfree, and we might nonetheless open up very considerable opportunities for benevolent intervention.

We have now reached approximately the point Gerald Dworkin reaches at the end of his deservedly influential essay on paternalism.[3] After canvassing much the same justifications for paternalism as those I have mentioned, Dworkin concludes, in effect, that paternalism is acceptable so long as ''we are simply using coercion to enable people to carry out their own goals.''[4] Ignorance, psychological compulsion, or even outright weakness of will may prevent people from achieving their goals, and paternalistic coercion is an appropriate remedy. To be sure, Dworkin does not say we are justified in coercing the ignorant or the weak-willed just to maximize their pleasure or their happiness. He speaks rather of enabling them to accomplish their own goals, whatever those may be. Still, Dworkin's conclusion is troublesome, for two quite different reasons.

On the one hand, it is not clear that even after we limit paternalism as Dworkin would limit it (to cases of ignorance and the like), we have given freedom of choice its due. We are so seldom fully informed of the consequences of our acts, and we are so seldom unaffected by psychological and social pressures of various kinds, that our whole lives might be subject to paternalistic supervision if the approach we have been expounding were taken seriously. Furthermore, this approach fails to take into account a very important fact, which is that making choices, including bad ones, is an essential way in which people acquire information, learn to resist compulsion, and develop strength of will. Freedom, in the sense of the ability to make a genuinely free choice, is not merely something one has or does not have at any point in time with respect to any particular choice. It is a general capacity that one acquires and improves as one exercises it. The achievement of freedom is impossible unless one is allowed to make some decisions that are not fully free. To be sure, Dworkin's statement about enabling people to carry out their own goals (and other similar statements) could be construed as taking this need for "exercise in freedom" into account. But the possible conflict between enabling someone to make the present choice which will further her goals and enabling her to develop a capacity for improved choice in the future goes unnoticed. A related point, less important but worth mentioning, is that we may not value equally Smith's achieving her goals with paternalistic help and Smith's achieving her goals on her own. In other words, we may think there is an important difference between Smith's goals being achieved and *Smith's* achieving them.

My other objection to the approach summarized in the quote from Dworkin is that it assumes each person has, or can be regarded as having, something describable as "her" goals. This is mildly problematic even if we consider only the moment of the choice we propose to interfere with—few people have goals that are fully worked out, and the vaguenesses and gaps might be important. What really troubles me, however, is the implicit assumption that people's goals are stable over time. People change over time, and their goals change with them. Two of the three sections that follow will consider ways in which this fact affects the analysis of paternalism.

II

In the preceding section, we considered one standard approach to minimizing the conflict between our paternalistic impulses and our inclination to value freedom. We saw that if we regard as unfree acts that are performed in ignorance, or under pressure, or as a result of weakness of will, we can indulge in a great deal of paternalism without interfering with freedom at all. This approach, however, threatens to justify more paternalism than we are comfortable with.

In this section, I shall consider a quite different approach to minimizing the conflict between our paternalistic impulses and our concern for freedom. The approach is suggested by John Stuart Mill's discussion of a contract for slavery.

Mill says that although we generally enforce contracts, out of respect for individuals' free choices, we should not enforce contracts for slavery. Mill writes of the would-be slave:

[B]y selling himself for a slave, he abdicates his liberty; he foregoes any future use of it beyond that single act. He therefore defeats, in his own case, the very purpose which is the justification of allowing him to dispose of himself. He is no longer free; but is thenceforth in a position which has no longer the presumption in its favor, that would be afforded by his voluntarily remaining in it. The principle of freedom cannot require that he should be free not to be free. It is not freedom to be allowed to alienate his freedom.[5]

There is a certain looseness here. A person might have what seems to her a very strong reason for wanting to sell herself into slavery. It might, for example, be the only way she could secure the money for an expensive operation necessary to save the life of her child. In such a case, a prohibition on contracts for slavery would be a genuine barrier to achieving the person's goals. It would be a genuine denial of freedom.[6]

Still, Mill has a point. It seems quite natural to argue that even if the act of selling oneself into slavery can be an exercise of freedom, the act in question destroys much more freedom than would be destroyed by prohibiting the act. The person who wants to sell herself into slavery and is not allowed to is less free in regard to her present desire, but she will be freer, in the long run, overall. Therefore, our valuing freedom does not weigh against prohibiting contracts for slavery. It supports it. Whatever the basis of our original impulse to forbid the contract for slavery, that impulse does not conflict in this case with our concern for freedom. The apparent conflict is illusory.

What we have done, in effect, is to substitute for the deontological principle that an agent's freedom must not be interfered with, a teleological principle that the agent's total freedom should be maximized over time. Of course, neither the deontological principle nor the teleological principle could be regarded as the only principle relevant to cases of the sort we are discussing. Freedom is not all that counts. But the point remains that a deontological principle weighs against *every* paternalistic interference with the freedom of the moment, whereas the teleological principle weighs against some such interferences and supports others. The teleological principle will conflict less often with impulses to paternalism from other sources.

It might be objected that in substituting the teleological "freedom-maximization" principle for the deontological "freedom-respecting" principle, we are suggesting an unacceptable "utilitarianism of rights." Whatever the general force of this criticism, it is surely blunted here by the response that we are not invading one person's rights to enhance another person's rights. Rather, we are invading one person's right (if we concede so much to the objection) to enhance that same person's total enjoyment of the same right over time.[7] In this essay, at least, I do not recommend interpersonal freedom-maximization.

I have introduced the freedom-maximization approach in the context of the slavery case because Mill's discussion of that case so clearly suggests it. I do not claim that once we have formulated the freedom-maximization principle, we have said all there is to say about the slavery case. A full discussion of contracts for slavery would take us far beyond the topic of paternalism. Let us therefore turn to a simpler problem.

Consider cigarette-smoking. I am inclined to think that it would violate no one's rights (and that it would probably be a good thing) if the sale and use of cigarettes were prohibited. It may be that a ban on cigarettes can be justified by the arguments considered in the first section of this paper. Many cigarette-smokers remain ignorant about the risks of smoking. Many smokers who are aware of the risks in some sense do not imagine them vividly or do not respond appropriately given the small probabilities involved. Many smokers acquired the habit under social pressure. And so on. But surely there are some smokers who are covered by none of these arguments. Perhaps we ought really not to interfere with those remaining smokers, or my ideal paternalist with his powers of perfect discrimination ought really not to interfere with them. I have a lingering feeling, however, that it may be permissible to prevent cigarette-smoking even by a smoker who has no family, who is as clear-headed and as free of neuroses as a person can be, who is well informed about the chances of getting cancer or emphysema and the general diminution of life expectancy, who has seen close-up the effects of cancer and emphysema, and who just doesn't give a damn.

The freedom-maximization approach allows us to explain why it is permissible to coerce the well-adjusted, well-informed, would-be smoker. To be sure, the smoker does not destroy her freedom completely, as Mill's would-be slave is trying to destroy his. But cigarette-smoking will diminish the smoker's freedom, at least statistically speaking. It will shorten her life-expectancy and increase the likelihood of debilitating disease. (The appeal to statistics is somewhat inconsistent with my intention to consider the problem of paternalism from the viewpoint of an omniscient ideal paternalist. I would concede that if the ideal paternalist can separate those smokers who will suffer bad effects from those who will not, he should coerce only the former. Since we in the real world are unable to make this distinction, it is convenient to talk in terms of statistics and in terms of all smokers suffering a statistical harm, although this raises problems that I am going to ignore.) It seems to me that the expected loss of freedom caused by smoking (taking into account both the magnitude of the various possible losses and their probability) is greater than the loss imposed directly by the prohibition on smoking.

It could be objected that smoking does not cause any loss of freedom. Disease and death are not ordinarily regarded as "unfreedom." Whatever their ill effects, the issue of freedom is not involved. My answer to this is that we are not trying to minimize unfreedom but to maximize freedom, and what I mean by "freedom" in this connection includes abilities, capacities, and in general whatever is a precondition for any human activity. What we desire is that the largest number of people should have the widest possible range of effective choice about what to do with themselves. From this point of view, it is clear that death and injury and disease all diminish freedom.

The objector might persist, with the suggestion that a loss of freedom from disease, say, is less important than an equal loss of freedom attributable to direct paternalistic intervention. I do not necessarily deny this. I shall suggest a reason shortly why it might be true. For the moment, I would say that the expected loss from smoking is so much greater than the loss from paternalistic intervention to prohibit smoking that even if the latter is given some extra weight to reflect the fact that it flows from external intervention and not from the natural consequences of chosen actions, the balance still favors the paternalistic course.

An obvious difficulty with the freedom-maximizing approach is that it assumes freedom is quantifiable, at least to some extent. It assumes that we can compare "bundles" of freedom, and (barring omniscience) lottery tickets with bundles of freedom as payoffs. Now, I cannot give complete directions for comparing bundles of freedom, or lottery tickets, but I can say a few things about how freedom is measured. First of all, it is clear that we do not determine the extent of a person's freedom just by counting up the actions available to her at all relevant times and saying that the greater the number of actions, the greater her freedom. For one thing there is no obviously satisfactory criterion for individuating actions. More important, however, is the fact that freedom to do some things is much more important than freedom to do others. Any criterion based on mere counting would ignore such differences. In deciding how great a person's freedom is, we need to consider not merely how many different things she can do, but what the things she can do are. Freedom to do X will presumably count for more than freedom to do Y whenever X is more pleasurable to the particular individual than Y, or more highly valued by a rational individual than Y, or more essential to the individual's sense of personal identity than Y, and so on. The considerations just listed do not exhaust the possibilities, and each must be taken as including the qualification "other things being equal," if only because the considerations listed might conflict for particular values of X and Y.

It may seem that in the last paragraph I replace a nearly hopeless problem (how to count up actions) with an utterly impossible one (how to evaluate bundles of freedom in terms of the relative importance, according to various criteria, of the available actions). I do not think that is the case. We are no closer to a well-defined procedure for ranking bundles of freedom, but the new problem is more amenable to acceptable intuitive judgments than the old one. If the criterion for ranking bundles of freedom is simply the number of available actions, my intuition says that almost all the bundles that arise in practice are going to contain the same infinite number of actions, and therefore be equally valuable. My intuition also says, however, that the conclusion that almost all bundles of freedom arising in practice are equally valuable is ludicrous. Once the criterion is expanded to include reference to the importance of the actions, I find that I can make some intuitive judgments, like the one I have already revealed regarding where the "balance of freedom" lies if we are considering prohibiting cigarettes.[8]

The notion of freedom-maximization may require judgments that are controversial and incapable of definitive establishment, but in this respect it does not differ from the notion of utility-maximization. Many people have been utilitarians, and many more have agreed that utility-maximization should play some role in moral decision-making, despite uncertainty about just what actions maximize utility, or even just what utility-maximization means. If the notion of freedom-maximization strikes a responsive chord from somewhere among our moral intuitions, perhaps we should struggle along with it just as we do with other notions equally vague.

The freedom-maximization idea seems to me useful in other cases besides the slavery case and the case of cigarettes. Laws against drugs like heroin and laws requiring the use of seat-belts in cars or the wearing of helmets when riding motorcycles present much the same problem as laws against cigarettes. My intuition is that, in each of these cases, paternalistic intervention is likely to maximize freedom overall.

I do not suggest, however, that we would be justified in forbidding all risky activities. Consider mountain-climbing. Although there are substantial risks involved in mountain-climbing, the freedom that would be lost if mountain-climbing were forbidden looms much larger, to my mind, than the freedom that is lost if cigarettes are prohibited or seat-belts required. For one thing, mountain-climbing is likely to be much more important to people who want to climb mountains than cigarettes are to people who want to smoke cigarettes. Climbing is likely to be a source of greater pleasure, especially when we consider not merely the time spent on the mountain, but time spent planning and preparing for trips, talking to other climbers, and so on. Also, climbing is more likely to be closely linked with the would-be participants' sense of identity. A person might describe herself as a mountain-climber in the way that someone else would describe herself as a chess-player, a gardener, or a philosopher. Who would think of describing herself as a cigarette-smoker in the same way?

Beyond all of that, I am inclined to think that mountain-climbing is intrinsically a more valuable activity than cigarette-smoking. It is no accident that people think of themselves as mountain-climbers in a way they do not think of themselves as cigarette-smokers. There is something about the activities themselves that accounts for this difference in attitude. Indeed, while mountain-climbing is plainly an "activity," that word seems out of place as applied to cigarette-smoking.

The claim that some activities are intrinsically more valuable than others is controversial. I lack both the space and the arguments to defend the claim here, although I hope to defend it at some time in the future. Nonetheless, it is part of what accounts for my differing reactions to mountain-climbing and cigarette-smoking; I suspect it contributes to some other people's differing reactions; and I suggest that the reader who reflects on the ways we *talk* about mountain-climbing and cigarette-smoking will be led to see some of the differences that I think make the one intrinsically more valuable than the other.

One other problem that invites attention in a discussion of freedom-maximization is the problem of suicide. In all probability, most of my readers will share the view that suicide should not be unconditionally forbidden. And yet it would seem that there can be no act more destructive of freedom than suicide. If we allow suicide, what has become of freedom-maximization?

People want to commit suicide in various circumstances, and I have no room here for a detailed discussion of the problem. Speaking briefly and generally, there are two points to be made on how freedom-maximization may be reconciled with allowing suicide. First, in any case where the would-be suicide's desire to commit suicide persists (and I am prepared to admit that it is only in such cases, if we can identify them, that suicide should be allowed), the freedom that will be preserved by forbidding suicide will be substantially devalued by the possessor's lack of interest in it and lack of inclination to put it to good use. Second, the person who is prevented from committing suicide (and whose desire persists) is likely to be very unhappy during her remaining life. Considerations of utility-maximization argue in favor of allowing the suicide, and may simply outweigh considerations of maximizing freedom. In other cases, we have often implicitly assumed that our paternalistic impulses were prompted by utility-maximization, so we have been arguing in effect that freedom-maximization and utility-maximization pointed in the same direction. But they need not always do so, nor need either always prevail over the other when they conflict.

One final observation: Although I have been discussing freedom-maximization as a principle which focuses on maximizing the range of choice available to an individual over time (restricting choice now in order to preserve opportunities later on), the same phrase, "freedom-maximization," could encompass an idea I mentioned in the preceding section of the essay, namely, the idea that we want to allow, or perhaps even help, individuals to develop the ability to make choices. We are interested *both* in people's having opportunities for choice *and* in their having capacities for making well-thought-out choices and sticking to them. Unfortunately, a paternalistic intervention that will maximize opportunities for choice in the long run may also interfere with the development of the ability to choose.

I do not conclude that we should abandon range-of-choice-maximization. In cases like the cigarette case, for example, the potential for an individual to learn from her own experience is small, just because the major costs of smoking are likely to appear long after the important initial decisions. Even here, of course, one person may learn from the experience of another, and for any individual who will *not* smoke, it is almost certainly better, on "ability-maximizing" grounds, that she make the decision and stick to it by herself than that she do so with paternalistic assistance. In general, this ability-maximizing aspect of freedom-maximization may account for the feeling noted earlier that a loss of freedom as a natural consequence of some earlier choice is not as objectionable as the loss of an equal amount of freedom, in the range-of-choice sense, as a result of paternalistic intervention. The first loss is more likely than the second to be educational. The point is just that the idea of freedom-maximization is complex. Even so, it is a way of giving content to the value (or values) of freedom that we cannot ignore.

III

At the end of the first section of this essay, I suggested that one weakness of traditional arguments about paternalism is an implicit assumption that people do not change over time. In this section and the next, I shall explore some arguments that take change over time specifically into account.

The central tenet of most arguments against paternalism is Mill's proposition that "the only purpose for which power can be rightfully exercised over any member of a civilized community, against his will, is to prevent harm to others."[9] Paternalism presents a problem because it involves exercising power over an individual, not to prevent harm to others, but to prevent harm to the individual herself. If there were some good reason for regarding the harm done as done to a person other than the agent, the problem would disappear. In many cases in which paternalism seems justified there *is* a good reason for thinking of the harm as done to someone other than the agent. To illustrate that reason, it will be useful to consider a few cases, starting with one that has nothing directly to do with paternalism.

Suppose that, ten years after the occurrence of an act of embezzlement, we finally discover the identity of the embezzler. Suppose also that we hold a retributivist view of punishment. A crime has been committed. We have at last identified the criminal. It would seem that she should be punished. But when we consider the person before us, the "criminal" we are supposed to punish, we discover that she is a different person from the person she was ten years ago. She squandered all her ill-gotten gains in the first six months. Since then she has lived a blameless life. She has punctiliously fulfilled all obligations of trust. She has not (in this hypothetical case) repaid the money she originally embezzled, but that is because her blameless life has been a modest one, and she has had no funds to spare. I think we would be most reluctant to punish in this case. Although the criminal was (and perhaps timelessly is) deserving of punishment, the criminal is no longer accessible to us. Inhabiting the criminal's body and social role, we find a new woman.[10]

Consider next a slightly different case. Imagine a smoker who smokes for twenty years, then quits for ten, and then turns up with lung cancer, of which his smoking is a causal antecedent. Would it not seem to us that nature has been unfair? Perhaps someone who has smoked for twenty years has no ground for complaint if *he* gets cancer, but in this case the person who gets the cancer is an abstainer of ten years' standing. That ought to count for something.

To be sure, accusing nature of unfairness is only a manner of speaking, but it is a manner of speaking that suggests a bridge between the problem of punishment and the problem of paternalism. It seemed unfair to punish the reformed embezzler. It seems "unfair" to "punish" the reformed smoker. The reason is that in each case the person who suffers is not the person who (arguably) deserves to. But if the reformed smoker is not the same person as the unrepentant nicotine-fiend, that may be relevant to the issue of paternalism. If we step in and prevent the would-be smoker from smoking, can we not claim that we are protecting a different person, the smoker's later self? (It may occur to the reader that I am skipping over some problems involving the question of whether, or under what conditions, the smoker will or would reform. I shall discuss these problems presently.)

Actually, I think the suggestion that the smoker becomes a different person is an essential prop for a more standard line of argument in favor of paternalism, at least if the standard line is to amount to anything more than straight utility-maximization. Consider, for the sake of variety, another case in which a cyclist is bound by a statute that makes it an offense to ride a motorcycle without wearing a helmet. Such statutes are frequently attacked on the ground that if the cyclist wants to run the risk of serious injury, that is her own business. A defender of the statute is likely to respond as follows: "Anyone who rides a motorcycle without a helmet risks serious injury. If she is seriously injured, she is likely to become a public charge. She will be cared for in a public hospital or, even if she can afford private care, she will end up unemployed and drawing public compensation. This may not happen in every case, but certainly in statistical terms the helmetless cyclist imposes a burden on public assistance funds. Since public funds must be raised by taxation, the helmetless cyclist hurts someone besides herself."

The argument just stated is not very satisfying. For one thing, when we consider what the statistical burden the cyclist imposes on the public treasury comes to, it may well be that the harm the cyclist does to others by this route is outweighed by the utility to her of riding without a helmet. Further, the tenuousness of the connection between the conduct and the harm gives the argument something of the false ring of rationalization. In any case, the opponent of the helmet statute, in order apparently to avoid the force of the argument, has only to steel himself and say: "You go too fast. You say that the cyclist will be a burden on public assistance funds, but the cyclist never asked for public assistance. The cyclist I have in mind values her freedom, and she realizes that the price of freedom is to suffer the consequences of her choices. If she suffers a serious injury, leave her to manage as best she can. Leave her to private charity, or let her die in the street. So long as you are prepared to do that, her riding without a helmet doesn't hurt anyone but herself."

At this stage, the defender of the statute might reply: "We can't leave her in the street. That would be inhuman. It would cost us more in suffering to leave her in the street than it would cost to care for her properly. So you see, she has harmed us, either way." The obvious retort is: "If you value freedom at all, you must admit that one person's mere emotional distress at another's behavior is no justification for making that behavior a crime. If the cyclist insists on dying in a public thoroughfare, let us remove her, as we would any other offensive exhibitionist. But so long as she is out of the public eye, she is as entitled to die as to read a dirty book."

In rebuttal, the defender of the statute will say: "It's not simply a matter of squeamishness that makes me want to help the injured cyclist. I have a moral obligation to. Being denied assistance when one is injured is a punishment too great to visit on anyone's head just for making a foolish choice, even if the choice was precisely to risk that punishment. The cyclist may have made her original choice with full knowledge, but she must regret it now. My general duty to help people in need would be satisfied here only if the cyclist did not want help at the time she needs it. The fact that she decided to do without help before she needed it is quite irrelevant.'' The defender of the statute adds that being put in a position where one must undertake some burden or expense if one is to satisfy a *moral* obligation (as opposed to reacting on the basis of feelings of pity or horror) is harm, so the cyclist has harmed someone after all.

The defender of the statute is now in a strong position. He may have won the argument. What remains to be observed is that if he has won the argument, he has done so by hitting on a suggestion that makes most of the argument as I have described it superfluous. If we really have an obligation to help the injured cyclist regardless of whether, when she decided to ride without a helmet, she expected help or wanted it, the most plausible explanation is that the cyclist before the accident and the cyclist after the accident are in some sense different people. That is the simplest explanation of why an initial willingness to forego aid is not definitive. But if the cyclist is a different person at the later time, then the cyclist at the time of her original decision has harmed another person. The decision to run the risk was not the original cyclist's "own" business.

It is all very well to suggest that the embezzler, the smoker, or the cyclist may each be different people at different stages of their lives. What exactly makes them different? To say that it is mere passage of time—to say that each of us is a different person on every day of her life—would completely subvert our ordinary notions of personhood. If the mere passage of time does not make the difference, what is it? How do we decide whether the embezzler, for example, has changed in such a way that she no longer deserves to be punished?

I would say, roughly, that the embezzler is a different person when we discover her ten years later if she is no longer the sort of person who would embezzle if placed in the same situation in which she did so originally. What this means, of course, is far from clear. Many moralists, concerned about preserving freedom of the will, might want to hold that the question "Would Jones, if placed in the following situation, embezzle?" often has no well-defined answer. My suggestion about retributive punishment seems to require that the question "Is Jones the sort of person who, if placed in the following situation, would embezzle?" should have an answer. In that case, the second question, about what sort of person Jones is, cannot be the same as the first question, about what Jones would do. Perhaps the second question is about what Jones would probably do, or would be strongly disposed to do, or might do without greatly surprising those who knew Jones well, or something along those lines.

Assuming that further reflection would provide us with a satisfactory sense of "the sort of person who . . . ," we now observe another important point. Our embezzler may, after ten years, be the same person for some purposes and yet be a different person for other purposes. Thus, suppose that at the time she committed embezzlement, the embezzler also committed an unrelated aggravated assault. It is at least conceivable that after ten years the embezzler has grown much more conscious of duties of trust without becoming any more disposed to control a volatile temper that produces occasional physical aggression. In such a case, I think we might hold it inappropriate to punish the embezzler now for her embezzlement, but appropriate to punish her for the assault.[11]

What about the cyclist who rides without a helmet? What makes her a different person after her accident? The answer, I think, is that the cyclist is a different person, in the relevant respect, if she is no longer the sort of person who would ignore her future well-being for the sake of small increments of present utility. Of course, it is not certain that having the accident will produce any such change in the cyclist. But it seems likely to. In many cases, I should think, the cyclist will not merely wish she had behaved differently in the past. She will have a new appreciation of the virtue of prudence and will alter her attitude toward risk in the future. If the cyclist changes in this way, she is a different person, who deserves protection against the foolish behavior of her earlier self.

The reader may have noticed something odd about that last sentence. If the cyclist learns prudence as the result of an accident, she may then be a person who deserves protection, but it is too late to protect her. The harm she deserves to be protected against has already occurred. Looking at the matter from the other end, if we compel the imprudent original cyclist to wear a helmet, the other, prudent, cyclist may never come into existence. Can we really interfere with the first cyclist for the benefit of a later cyclist who may never exist and whose existence our interference is intended to make less probable?

There are a number of questions here. Some of them arise because we do not know whether the cyclist will be injured if she rides without a helmet and whether she will become a new person if she suffers injury. In this essay I am generally ignoring such questions. I am interested in how the situation looks to an ideal paternalist. The ideal paternalist does know whether, if the cyclist rides without a helmet, she will be injured, and he does know whether, if she is injured, she will develop a new attitude to risk as a result.

Now, on the theory I am suggesting, there is no ground to interfere with the cyclist unless she will both be injured and be changed by the experience.[12] Suppose that the ideal paternalist is confronted with a cyclist who will be injured, if she rides without a helmet, and who will be changed. Can the ideal paternalist intervene? The answer is still not obvious. We assume that if the paternalist intervenes, the cyclist will *not* be injured and will not change. But this means that if the paternalist intervenes, he will not be protecting any actual person. He will be protecting a possible later self of the cyclist, whom he prevents by his intervention from becoming actual. If he doesn't intervene, the possible person he could protect will exist and will suffer the effects of a serious accident. But if he does intervene, she will not exist at all.

I think the ideal paternalist can intervene to protect the prudent cyclist, even though she is only a possible person, whose existence the paternalist's intervention will prevent. What is appropriate to do on behalf of possible persons is a complicated issue, and one that I shall not discuss at length even though perhaps I should. There are two points that I think distinguish this case from others in which intervention on behalf of possible persons seems more problematic. First, the possible person the paternalist can protect here is one who *will* exist and suffer *unless* the paternalist interferes with another agent's decision. This is quite different from, say, the case of forbidding birth-control, where the possible person on whose behalf we might act will *not* exist unless we interfere with the potential parents' choice. It seems that we have more reason to act on behalf of possible persons who will exist without our help than to act on behalf of possible persons who need our help to exist in the first place. Second, the possible person we are concerned with in the cyclist case, if she exists, will be connected by physical continuity with an actual person (the original cyclist) who exists regardless of the paternalist's decision. The possible person we are concerned with in this case is unusually well-rooted in actuality, as possible persons go. She deserves protection.

One final point merits brief discussion. Let us refer to the view I have been expounding, on which different temporal stages of one physically connected "person" may be different persons for certain moral purposes, as the "time-slice view." It might be urged against the time-slice view that agents have a greater right to impose risks or harms on their future selves (or time-slices) than to impose risks or harms on unconnected others. It is worth noting that this can be true without destroying the force of the time-slice view as a defense of paternalism. Most people think that there are situations in which it is wrong to impose harms on unconnected others, even though the act imposing the harm would maximize utility. If this is correct, it is a stronger principle against harming others than I think the time-slice approach justifies with regard to one's future selves. I would not suggest that an agent must not harm a future self even if overall utility is thereby maximized. I would suggest only that an agent should not harm a future self and diminish overall utility into the bargain, and that an agent who threatens this may be prevented. Even that is enough to justify more paternalistic intervention than is justified on the view that the agent should be left alone so long as she harms no one but "herself," present or future.

It might be suggested, of course, that the position I have just indicated is untenable. The argument goes as follows. If we believe that one person may not harm another even though she thereby maximizes utility, and if we genuinely regard future selves as other persons, we must be prepared to protect a future self from harm by a present self even though the present self would maximize utility by her choice. If we are not prepared to protect future selves in this way, we do not truly regard them as other persons. That this argument is correct is not self-evident. Might there not be different degrees of otherness, with different moral consequences? If that is held to be impossible—if all others must be treated the same as unconnected others—I think there is as much to be said for the view that unconnected others should *not* be protected against acts that harm them but that maximize utility, as there is to be said for the view that unconnected others deserve a greater protection than this and that future selves deserve either the same greater protection against the agent's present self or no protection at all.

IV

In the preceding section I suggested that we could prevent an imprudent cyclist from riding without a helmet and harming a later, prudent, self. In effect, I suggested that the earlier cyclist's choice should not be held to bind the later cyclist. It is the inability of the earlier cyclist to bind the later that opens the way to "paternalistic" interference.

There is a different sort of case in which it is often suggested that the justifiability of paternalistic interference depends precisely on the fact that a person *can* bind herself. A standard example is the story of Odysseus and the Sirens. I shall argue that attempts at self-binding are no more effective in cases of this sort than they were in the cases of the preceding section. Paternalistic interference that can be justified only by reference to self-binding decisions is not justified at all.

Whereas the general tendency of the two preceding sections was to provide new arguments in favor of paternalism, the general tendency of the present section (not necessarily the only tendency, as we shall see) is to undercut an accepted argument for paternalism.

Consider Odysseus. In order to be able to hear the Sirens' song without being tempted to his death, Odysseus commands his crew to bind him to the mast of his ship and not release him until the Sirens have been passed and left behind. It is often suggested that even if, with the Sirens' song in his ears, Odysseus pleads to be released, the crew are justified in ignoring his pleas because of his original command. In brief, Odysseus' original command is regarded as binding him, and as justifying the crew's protective action, until the command expires by its own terms.[13]

I agree that Odysseus' crew are right to keep him tied to the mast, even if we consider only Odysseus' interests and not the crew's need for a captain. But if we ask why the crew are right, Odysseus' command has very little to do with it. The command has some relevance, for reasons I shall discuss below, but it is neither a necessary nor a sufficient condition for the rightness of the crew's behavior.

To see that the command is not a necessary condition, we have only to suppose that Odysseus has not given the command, believing that he can sail by the Sirens, listen to their song, and preserve himself by sheer strength of will. If Odysseus has attempted this and is mistaken, and if the crew see him poised to jump overboard and swim to his death, surely they are justified in stopping him, tying him to the mast if need be, with no by-your-leave.

128   DONALD H. REGAN

To see that the command is not a sufficient condition, we must alter the facts a bit more. Suppose that the Sirens' song casts no irresistible spell, but is merely extremely beautiful. Suppose that the song is most beautiful when heard from near the Sirens' isle, which is surrounded by dangerous rocks. And suppose that if Odysseus swims to the rocks, he will not be killed but will suffer some physical injury. Surely if we bring all these assumptions together in the right relation, we can imagine a situation in which either swimming to the Sirens or not swimming to them would be a choice a reasonable person might make. Suppose now that Odysseus, approaching the Sirens' isle, decides he wants to sail by. Not trusting himself to stick to this decision, he commands the crew to tie him to the mast, as in the standard version of the tale. When he hears the Sirens' song, however, he changes his mind, not because of any sinister compulsion in the Sirens' song, but just because the song is more beautiful than he imagined, or because he discovers that he cares more about hearing it than he realized. If we remember that the decision to swim to the Sirens can be a reasonable one, then surely Odysseus is entitled to change his mind. (If we like, we can hypothesize further that Odysseus will have no other opportunity to hear the Sirens' song. It is now or never.) The crew ought to release him, despite the earlier command.

If what I have just said is correct, the command is neither necessary nor sufficient to justify the crew's decision to keep Odysseus aboard. What justifies their decision in the standard version of the tale is the fact that swimming to the Sirens is understood to be an irrational choice, with fatal consequences, made under preternatural compulsion.

I shall say more about why Odysseus is entitled to change his mind, but first I should tie up a loose end. I mentioned earlier that the command has some relevance to what the crew should do. One reason is that, in practice, the crew do not know Odysseus perfectly. Even if swimming to the Sirens would be reasonable for some people, the crew must make a decision, when Odysseus asks to be released, whether it is reasonable for him. We could understand their supposing that what Odysseus thought before he was tied to the mast is important evidence concerning what is reasonable for Odysseus now. In addition, if the crew decide wrongly not to let Odysseus swim away when he wants to, they are less to blame if there was an earlier command than if there was not. They can be more easily forgiven for choosing incorrectly between Odysseus' inconsistent commands than for restraining him improperly on their own unprompted initiative.

If we set out to explain more fully why Odysseus is entitled to change his mind, provided that his new decision is a reasonable one, we encounter a difficulty. To speak of Odysseus' changing his mind seems to assume that Odysseus is the same person throughout the episode we are considering. The discussion of the preceding section, however, suggests the possibility that in "changing his mind" Odysseus is really changing his identity. Does it matter how we describe the change in Odysseus? Ultimately I do not think it matters, in this kind of case, how we describe the change in Odysseus. I think the later choice, whether it be of the original Odysseus or of a new one (and provided always that it is a reasonable choice at the time it is made), should control. But the fact that we can describe the change in Odysseus in two different ways complicates the issue. Some people, I predict, will disagree with my conclusion and will believe both that Odysseus does not change identity and that his not changing is an essential part of the explanation why his first choice should control. Others will disagree with my conclusion but will believe that Odysseus *does* change and will believe that his *changing* is an essential part of the reason that his first choice should control. I shall deal with both positions in turn.

First, on the assumption that Odysseus is the same person, is he entitled to change his mind? Many people seem to have the intuition that someone may reasonably want to bind herself for the future by a present decision, and that provided we really are talking about a single person—that is, about a present person binding a future person who is still *herself*—such self-binding decisions ought to be recognized and, where appropriate, enforced.

My intuition runs the other way, and I see two general reasons that support the freedom to change one's mind. One reason is that, other things being equal, the later decision is likely to be a better one. The agent is likely to have more information and to have had more time to reflect on her goals. To be sure, the first decision may have been better. It may have been more carefully considered, or the agent may simply have forgotten something important in the time between the decisions. Nonetheless, in the absence of extrinsic evidence about which decision is more deliberate or better-informed, the mere passage of time suggests considerations which favor the second.

In addition, allowing changes of mind will tend to develop strength of purpose, part of which is precisely the ability to resist vacillation without outside help. I have suggested before that we might sometimes want to let an individual do something foolish, which would harm her in the future, in order to encourage her to develop the ability to make good choices. I now suggest that we may want to inform the agent that we will not, despite her present request, undertake to prevent her doing something foolish, or rather something she currently regards as foolish, in the future. She should master herself. Her fate is in her own hands.

The reasons I have suggested for allowing changes of mind may seem significant but not overwhelming. Is there anything more to say? It is natural to look for examples, discussion of which will move possessors of the conflicting intuitions closer to agreement. Unfortunately, it is not easy to produce examples that shed light on the question. Most examples that present the question seem merely to present it, without illuminating it. Perhaps it is worth mentioning some legal examples, since they are a sort of example about which we have codified views (though not necessarily correct ones). We allow people to revoke or rewrite wills. We allow people to retract offers before they are accepted. Even after an offer has been accepted and a contract formed, we allow the contracting parties to modify the contract or rescind it by mutal agreement. Legislatures, persons of a sort, can repeal legislation. I could go on.

Unfortunately, listing cases in which we allow changes of mind suggests a similar list of cases in which we do not. If there are revocable licenses, there are irrevocable licenses also, often in the form of easements. There are revocable, but also irrevocable, trusts. Gifts, once completed, are irrevocable by the donor. Offers become contracts upon acceptance, binding the offeror unless she is released by the offeree. On a higher level, one might suggest that a constitution embodies decisions by which the whole body politic binds itself.

If we ask what distinguishes decisions that are revocable from decisions that are not, the proponent of the intuition that favors self-binding is apt to suggest that the crucial factor is precisely whether the decision is *intended* to be self-binding. When a decision is intended to be self-binding, it is.

The truth of the matter is complex, and whether one intends to bind oneself is no doubt *relevant* to whether one actually does so. But I think an intent to bind oneself is far from a sufficient condition for self-binding. I cannot discuss all the examples at length. I shall comment briefly on two of them.

Regarding constitutions, the key point is that a constitution is not ordinarily intended to bind (or at least does not ordinarily bind) the same entity that adopts it. A constitution is adopted by the people at large for the purpose of binding the organs of day-to-day government. The people at large, who adopt the constitution, can always change their minds by amending it.[14]

Contracts are different. A contract does bind the agent who enters into it. It is tempting to say that a party to a contract is bound only because someone else's interests are involved. If this were a fully adequate explanation of the bindingness of contracts, the contract case could be dismissed as bearing no analogy at all to the case of Odysseus. Unfortunately, I do not think the proponent of Odysseus' freedom to change his mind can rest here. The bindingness of a contract is *not* fully explained just by saying someone else's interests are involved. Someone else's interests are involved because people rely on contracts. People rely on contracts in part because contracts are known to be binding. In short, bindingness and reliance are a package, and must be explained together. Not until we have the right explanation of the package can we be sure that the reason contracts bind, whatever it is, does not cover Odysseus' decision as well.

The believer in effective self-binding might now suggest that we make contracts binding because the agent who enters a contract benefits from being able to bind herself. Her ability to bind herself is the prerequisite to her getting something she wants. In the contract case, to be sure, being able to bind herself is a prerequisite to getting something she wants *from the other party*. But there might be cases in which ability to bind herself is a prerequisite to her getting something she wants even though no other party is involved. Remember Odysseus: When he asks to be bound to the mast, he wants not to swim to the Sirens. The only way he can be certain of achieving this is by having himself bound and having a crew who will ignore any change of mind. If we make contracts binding so that people can get what they want from other parties, why not make purely self-regarding decisions binding (when they are intended to be binding) so that people can get what they want (at the time of the decisions) from themselves?

One possible answer to the question just posed is that there is a difference in the way self-binding is ''necessary'' in the contract case and in the self-regarding case. Odysseus *could* get what he wants when he tries to bind himself simply by being strong-willed and by not changing his mind. In the contract case, it is not enough that one not change one's mind; the other party needs to *know* that one will not, or cannot effectively, change one's mind.

There is another difference between the two cases, not necessarily deeper, but more interesting. The standard contract case we call to mind to justify our belief that contracts should be binding simply does not involve a change of mind, or even a threatened change of mind, of the kind that occurs in the Odysseus case. I shall explain: Generally speaking, the reciprocal obligations of a contract are performed by the parties at different times. (This is not invariably true, but if contractual performances were always exchanged contemporaneously, we would have much less use for contracts than we have.) The most obvious case in which one party would like not to be bound by her contract is the case in which the other party has performed and she has not. But here it is entirely the time-displacement that accounts for this party's ''change of mind.'' There has been no change in her beliefs or her interests. She just wants to get something for nothing. If we view the transaction as a whole, it is as much in her interest at the later time when she wants out as it was when the contract was made. The question of whether she should be able to ''change her mind'' does not arise in the form in which it arises regarding Odysseus.

To be sure, the desire to breach one's contract *may* result from a genuine change of mind about the transaction as a whole. The party who wishes to breach may be willing to return what she has received under the contract, if that is possible. In this case, if we hold her to the contract, we will prevent an Odysseus-like change of mind. But it is not a desire to prevent Odysseus-like changes of mind, and it is not this case, that leads us to accept the idea of binding contracts in the first place. If people's beliefs and preferences were generally so volatile that Odysseus-like changes of mind were the commonest reason for wanting to break contracts, we would have a very different doctrine of contract from what we have. We would enforce many fewer contracts. Instead of encouraging reliance, and protecting it by making contracts binding, we would save people from relying to their detriment by making it clear in advance that enforcement was not the norm. The doctrine we have, and our standard intuitions about contract, depend on the fact that in ordinary cases parties do not change their minds *in the way Odysseus does*. For that reason, the contract analogy does not suggest that Odysseus should be forbidden to change his mind.

The lesson of the legal examples is ambiguous, but I believe that in the end these examples neither undermine my arguments in favor of freedom to change one's mind nor cast doubt on the intuition that freedom to change one's mind, even after a decision intended to be binding, is the ''normal'' state of affairs.

I have been arguing that Odysseus should be able to change his mind, provided his later choice is a reasonable one, on the assumption that he is at all relevant times the same person. I turn now to the suggestion that Odysseus is *not* the same person if he changes his mind, and to the claim that, precisely because Odysseus is not the same person, his later self should not be able to undo what his earlier self hoped to accomplish. Actually, this suggestion seems quite implausible in the case of Odysseus. I shall therefore consider a somewhat different example, in which the suggestion has more appeal. The example is Derek Parfit's: "Let us take a nineteenth-century Russian who, in several years, should inherit vast estates. Because he has socialist ideals, he intends, now, to give the land to the peasants. But he knows that in time his ideals may fade. To guard against this possibility he does two things. He first signs a legal document, which will automatically give away the land, and which can only be revoked with his wife's consent. He then says to his wife, 'If I ever change my mind, and ask you to revoke this document, promise me that you will not consent.' "[15] I shall call the Russian "Boris." Suppose that as Boris gets older, his ideals do fade. When he inherits the estates, he wishes to keep them. He asks his wife's consent to the revocation of the original document. What should his wife do? Parfit suggests that we can view the older Boris as a different person from the idealistic young Boris who signed the document. If we do, the older Boris's request cannot release the wife from her commitment to the young Boris. The young Boris no longer exists. There is no living person by whom the wife can be released.

Parfit suggests that the commitment is unreleasable. He does not say that because the commitment is unreleasable it must be honored. Parfit is primarily concerned, at this point in his essay, to establish the possibility of viewing the older Boris as a different person from the younger. The general tendency of his essay, as I read it, would support the weakening of *all* obligations based on commitments. Nonetheless, it could be suggested that the unreleasable commitment to the young Boris is a *binding* commitment, which should lead the wife to refuse the older Boris's request. This view I shall call the "rigorist" view.

Note that the rigorist view presupposes Parfit's approach to personal identity (which I share) and applies to cases in which there is an actual change of identity between an earlier and a later occupant of the same body. The rigorist view is quite consistent with the view that so long as there is no change of identity, an agent should be able to change her mind and to release others from commitments to her. Thus, one who holds the rigorist view may believe that in our earlier example, Odysseus can change his mind. This raises a question. Suppose that Odysseus says to his crew: "Bind me, and do not release me. If I ask to be released, ignore me. The request to be released will be proof that I have changed, and that my then-existing self cannot release you from the commitment you now give me." If the crew must accept Odysseus' claim that any change of mind would represent a change of identity, the rigorist view entails that Odysseus can always bind himself firmly, so long as he uses the right formula. I take it, however, that if we accept the rigorist view, the question of whether the original Odysseus has been replaced by a new one is *not* to be settled simply on the basis of what Odysseus at any time says.

What Odysseus says is significant. His assertions about which of his beliefs or preferences or ideals are essential to his identity cannot be ignored. But his assertions, even his *sincere* assertions, are not conclusive.

So much for description of the rigorist view. Is it reasonable? Why, when the older Boris asks his wife to revoke the document, should she care about her commitment to the young Boris at all? The young Boris no longer exists. He can neither enjoy nor even be aware of the satisfaction of his preferences. Why should his preferences, or the commitment to him, count?

In response we might note that people frequently have preferences about what happens after their death or, more generally, about what happens without their knowledge. It is not easy to explain why the satisfaction of such preferences should not be regarded as valuable without falling into a theory which locates all value in mental states. I shall not argue that the preferences of the "deceased" young Boris should not count at all. On the other hand, they might count without counting as heavily as the preferences of the Boris who is still alive. This would tend to undercut the rigorist view. I think there are reasons for devaluing the young Boris's preferences, at least in this case.

Parfit suggests by implication that the wife's promise to the young Boris is like a deathbed promise to a parent to help his or her children.[16] Certainly the promises are alike in that the promisors cannot be released. But they are very different in another respect. The promise to the dying parent is to *help* the children. The promise to the young Boris is to *oppose* Boris the Old. (It might be suggested that the promise to the young Boris is a promise to help the peasants. In a general analysis of whether to keep the promise, that would surely be relevant. But it does not eliminate the difference between the promise to the parent and the promise to Boris that I wish to focus on.) On the face of it, a deceased's preference that the goals of his or her survivors (which we assume are reasonable and morally permissible goals) be opposed seems entitled to less weight than a deceased's preference that the goals of her or his survivors be furthered.

Young Boris is unlike the dying parent because there is a conflict between the goals of the younger Boris and the older. Suppose that we ask directly which Boris ought to prevail. To say that the older ought to prevail just because he is alive might beg the question, although I am not sure it would be a mistake. There may, however, be another way to look at the matter. It would not be implausible to suggest that if the wife honors her promise to the young Boris, she will harm the older Boris. "Harm" is a problematic concept. It might be said that merely not inheriting vast estates cannot be a harm. On the other hand, if we say that the older Boris is deprived of his patrimony, that does sound like harm. At least, the use of the word "harm" is not implausible. It is much less plausible, however, to say that if the wife gives in to the older Boris, she *harms* the younger. Even if postmortem preferences (preferences about what happens after one's death) count, it does not seem that the dissatisfaction of one's postmortem preferences can be a harm. Harms are peculiarly grievous losses. Death may not close the accounts on a life completely (and it does not if postmortem preferences matter), but death arguably puts one beyond the reach of really serious loss. If one way of resolving the conflict between the younger and the older Boris imposes what can plausibly be regarded as a harm, and if the other way does not, should not the latter way (favoring the older Boris) be preferred?

Once we emphasize the fact that the young Boris's specific intention is to oppose the preferences of a later person, we cannot help but see that the proliferation of binding and unreleasable commitments of this sort would be undesirable. One response, short of abandoning the rigorist view, would be to weaken our view of the bindingness of commitments generally. If we wish to retain the idea that commitments are strongly binding and that commitments such as that to the young Boris are as binding as any others, then surely there is a different concession we must make. We must admit that such commitments should not be undertaken lightly, and often should not be undertaken at all.

It is tempting to say that Boris's wife is free to promise what the young Boris asks if she chooses to. After all, it is only Boris's interests that are affected. But this will not do. There may be two Borises. Indeed, the young Boris's request makes sense only because he fears that there will be another Boris, whose interests he wishes to prejudice in advance. In these circumstances, Boris's wife is not free to give her promise just because the young Boris asks for it.

The wife might perhaps give a promise limited to the "life" of the young Boris. Such a promise could not become unreleasable. But then, such a promise could not accomplish what the young Boris wants.

The final point against the young Boris and the rigorist view is this. If the older Boris exists (as a person different from the young Boris), and if the rigorist view is rejected, then the older Boris will have certain interests of the young Boris within his control, to the young Boris's detriment. But the young Boris has it largely within his control whether the older Boris exists at all. Young Boris can murder Old Boris in his cradle if he will merely develop the strength to maintain his own convictions. That opportunity, surely, is all young Boris deserves.

In sum, where no unconnected person's interests are affected, neither the agent who changes his mind (Odysseus) nor the agent who changes his identity (Boris) ought to be bound at a later time by an earlier choice.[17]

V

The arguments of this essay obviously justify no simple conclusion. I do have some final comments.

First, I would emphasize that the freedom-maximization argument of section II and the time-slice argument of section III are independent, even though they may seem most appealing as applied to the same range of cases, involving smokers, motorcyclists, and so on. Some readers may find themselves inclined to meld the two arguments into a third argument to the effect that we can interfere with the smoker, for example, in order to prevent a loss of freedom to the smoker's later, different, self. This argument differs from my time-slice argument if it assumes that the *only* relevant harms to later selves are losses of freedom, and it differs from my freedom-maximization argument in assuming the time-slice view of personal identity. There is in fact some conflict between the general tendencies of the freedom-maximization argument and the time-slice argument. The time-slice argument breaks people down into successive selves and emphasizes discontinuities, whereas the very notion of freedom seems to require some degree of continuity, of integration of personality over time.

If we compare the time-slice argument of section III with the argument against the possibility of binding self-regarding commitments in section IV, there is an apparent similarity. In both cases, it seems, the later self (or else the later decision of a continuing self) prevails. But the parallel is not perfect. Under the time-slice view of section III, as I have described it, the later self does not prevail if the earlier self wishes to make a choice that, although it harms the later self, maximizes utility. The point of the time-slice argument is not that the later self always prevails. The point is that the later self *counts*, and deserves some protection against the earlier. In situations in which we are considering whether to enforce a commitment intended to be self-binding, the later self does prevail. The reason, roughly, is that the earlier self needs help to achieve its goals (unlike the earlier self in a motorcycle case, which needs only to be let alone), and because the earlier self has no persuasive claim to our help once its time has passed.

The argument of section IV can be viewed as one of freedom-maximization, like the argument of section II, but again there are differences. The argument of section II is primarily designed to maximize freedom as range of choice. The argument of section IV seems more likely to maximize freedom as ability to choose, by encouraging people to develop strength of will. In section IV, the range of choice the later Odysseus gains if we refuse to regard commitments as binding seems essentially the same as the range of choice the earlier Odysseus loses. It could be argued, of course, that the later Odysseus gains more than the earlier Odysseus loses. The later Odysseus gains a freedom to jump overboard, while the earlier Odysseus loses only the freedom to *bind himself* not to jump overboard, which may seem less worthy. Similarly, the freedom gained by the later Odysseus may count for more than the freedom lost by the earlier if, as I have suggested, there is some general reason to count the interests of those who are present (at the time when our decision must be made) more heavily than the interests of those who are past. Perhaps it is the timing of the decision about intervention that accounts more than anything else for the different feel of section II cases and section IV cases. But some difference there certainly is.

The arguments of all four of the preceding sections reveal that the sources of our difficulty about paternalism are more various than is usually recognized. The sources are at least three. One source is the conflict between freedom and other values, such as pleasure or happiness. A second source is the complexity of what we value as freedom, which includes both range of choice and ability to choose rationally and effectively. A third source is the discrepancy between the ideal and the actual. We have an ideal of a person who is both rational at each moment and integrated over time. Actual people are neither. The question arises: Ought we to treat actual people as if they embodied the ideal, or ought we to intervene in their lives in hopes of bringing them closer to the ideal in the future?

Notes

1. Donald H. Regan, "Justifications for Paternalism," in *Nomos XV: The Limits of Law*, eds. J. Roland Pennock and John W. Chapman (New York: Lieber-Atherton, 1974), pp. 189-210. There is a useful critical discussion of that essay in C. L. Ten, *Mill On Liberty* (Oxford: Clarendon Press, 1980), pp. 119-23, which came to my attention too late for me to incorporate responses into the present revised version.

2. This argument is well developed in Rolf E. Sartorius, "The Enforcement of Morality," *Yale Law Journal*, 81 (1972), 891-910.

3. Gerald Dworkin, "Paternalism," in *Morality and the Law*, ed. Richard A. Wasserstrom (Belmont, CA: Wadsworth, 1971), pp. 107-26. Reprinted as chapter 2 of the present volume. When I was writing my earlier essay on paternalism, I discovered Dworkin's essay at the last minute. The footnote in which I mentioned his essay did not do it justice. I appreciate it more now, for the sole reason that I have read it more carefully.

4. Dworkin, p. 124.

5. John Stuart Mill, *On Liberty* (London: J.M. Dent, 1910), p. 158.

6. It might be suggested that the nonenforcement of contracts for slavery involves no real denial of freedom because it involves only governmental inaction, and because there can be no objection on antipaternalistic grounds to mere failure to act. This will not do. First, since we generally enforce contracts (at least partly because freedom to contract enhances freedom in general, increasing the agent's control over her life), the refusal to enforce a particular kind of contract cannot be passed off as mere nonintervention. Second, in a case in which the buyer of the slave was able to enforce the contract without judicial assistance by physical coercion, we would not be inclined (if we opposed contracts for slavery in the first place) to recommend government nonintervention. We would hold open the nonwaivable possibility of a civil action for assault or false imprisonment on the part of the slave, and we would regard the buyer as subject to criminal prosecution regardless of the slave's preference in the matter.

7. The argument I will make in the next section suggests a response to the claim at this point in the text. The response is that we are invading one person's right in order to enhance the freedom of that person's later self, who may be a different person for the relevant moral purposes. I am content to note that in order to make this response to the argument of this section, the opponent of paternalism must open himself up to a different attack in the next.

8. I do not suggest that a perfectly discriminating ideal paternalist should ban smoking by every would-be smoker. There may be smokers who, if they could not smoke, would be so persistently wracked by nervous tension they could not otherwise assuage that they would be fit for no other activity. Such smokers should be allowed to continue. I assume such smokers are rare.

9. Mill, *On Liberty*, p. 73.

10. The suggestion that for purposes of apportioning blame and punishment our ordinary criteria of personal identity may be inadequate goes back at least to Locke. See *An Essay Concerning Human Understanding*, Bk. II, ch. xxvii, §§ 16-26. The leading modern proponent of the sort of view about personal identity that I suggest in this essay is Derek Parfit. See, for example, his "Personal Identity," *Philosophical Review* 80 (1971), p. 3, and "Later Selves and Moral Principles," in *Philosophy and Personal Relations*, ed. Alan Montefiore (Montreal: McGill-Queen's University Press, 1973), pp. 137-69.

11. I shall say no more about punishment in the text. There are two points which merit some supplementary discussion.

1. Some readers may think something like the following: "It's all very well to decide not to punish an embezzler after ten years, but what about, say, Adolf Eichmann? Surely nothing could affect the appropriateness of punishing him, wherever and whenever he was found." To the extent that

punishment is justified in terms of deterrence, or in terms of appeasing public desires for vengeance, or in terms of other utilitarian goals, it may well be appropriate to punish Eichmann at any time. But on a retributivist view, whether one that makes desert a justification for punishment or one that makes desert merely a necessary condition for punishment, I think it is a serious question whether Eichmann ought to be punished after twenty years. On the theory I have suggested, the answer ultimately depends, of course, on whether and how Eichmann has changed. I shall not speculate about all the possibilities. For the reader who insists that Eichmann *must* be punishable, I note that it may be possible to accommodate even that claim within my general approach. Eichmann's crime was enormously evil. It may be part of our retributive theory that there is a maximum rate at which eligibility for punishment can be shed over time. If that is so, then it is plausible to believe that an embezzler could shed all eligibility over ten years, while Eichmann could not be cleansed in many lifetimes. A related suggestion would be that a crime such as Eichmann's must have resulted from moral defects much more fundamental and therefore much harder to change than whatever was the cause of an ordinary embezzlement.

2. An untoward consequence of the theory I am suggesting is that it might place a great strain on our adherence to another principle, the prohibition against punishing innocents even when good consequences would result. My theory, if taken seriously, might require nonpunishment of many persons for crimes that earlier inhabitants of the bodies they are attached to unquestionably did commit. The theory might therefore entail that any system of judicial punishment would convict so many innocent persons that it would be insupportable. My own inclination, in the face of this difficulty, is not to abandon the suggested view of personal identity, but to reconcile myself to punishing more innocents (as defined by my theory) so long as there really are good consequences to be acheived.

12. There is actually a further complication, suppressed in the text. It might be the case that the cyclist will be injured in an accident, will *not* alter her attitude toward risk as a result of the accident, but *will* alter her attitude toward risk at some later point in her life. Does this cyclist deserve protection? It is tempting to say that in the circumstances described, the cyclist who suffers the injury is still the same person as the imprudent cyclist (even though she is going to change later) and therefore is not entitled to protection. But what about the still-later, prudent, self? If she suffers any after-effects of the injury, the imprudent cyclist will have hurt her too. For that matter, the post-accident-but-still-imprudent cyclist could be viewed as hurting her later, prudent, self by maintaining an attitude that, if the suggestion just made is correct, deprives all selves after her of protection from the first self. In the end, I think we must protect any later selves who will have learned prudence, from whatever experience or reflection. The imprudent cyclist can be interfered with unless no later self will be prudent.

13. The reader may wonder whether the Odysseus example really raises the problem of paternalism at all. At the point when the crew bind Odysseus to the mast, they are doing so with his consent. At the point when they refuse to release him, they are arguably not doing anything to him at all. The fact that the crew need only ignore Odysseus at the crucial point, instead of actively restraining him, makes it somewhat easier to accept their behavior. But I think it would make no difference to the result if Odysseus' original command were not, "Tie me to the mast, and do not release me," but rather, "If I start to jump overboard, grab me and stop me." This command would require active intervention at the crucial time, but the "paternalistic" course, intervention, would be no less justified. For what it is worth, in the Homeric version of the story, the crew are instructed that if Odysseus asks to be released, they should not ignore him but should add to his bonds. He does, and they do.

14. I have here excised, as too extravagant, a long footnote in the Conference version of the paper on unamendable constitutional provisions.

15. Parfit, "Later Selves," note 10 above, p. 145.

16. Ibid., p. 144.

17. In the text, I argue in effect that paternalism cannot be justified simply by the prospective consent of the person to be coerced. For similar reasons, retrospective consent is neither a necessary nor a sufficient condition for the justifiability of paternalistic intervention. A good and justified effort to educate a child may simply fail, and fail so utterly that the child never sees that the parents' attempts were appropriate. Therefore, retrospective consent is not necessary. On the other side, brainwashing

might produce retrospective consent, so retrospective consent is not sufficient. It might be objected that brainwashing would not produce a "free" retrospective consent, and that a free retrospective consent would be sufficient. This is certainly the most plausible claim that can be made for the necessity or sufficiency of retrospective consent, but it still fails. Consider an Odysseus case, in which either swimming to the Sirens or not might be reasonable. Suppose that when the ship is sailing past the Sirens, Odysseus wants to swim to the Sirens but the crew, on their own initiative, restrain him. Some days later, Odysseus announces that he has reconsidered his views about the relative importance of aesthetic pleasure and physical integrity, and he thanks the crew for having held him back. This announcement by itself does not establish that the crew were right. To be sure, retrospective consent may be relevant, for some of the same reasons as prospective consent. But it is not determinative. Nor does the time-slice view of the previous section suggest that retrospective consent settles the issue in the cases there considered. Whether an act threatens or causes unacceptable harm to a reformed later self of the agent, and whether the agent will come to be glad to have been prevented from performing the act, are related but distinct questions.

Chapter 9

A Paternalistic Theory of Punishment

Herbert Morris

I

Nothing is more necessary to human life, and fortunately nothing more common, than parents' concern for their children. The infant's relatively lengthy period of helplessness requires that others nourish and protect it. And the child's existence as a vital being with an interest in the world, a capacity for eagerness and trust, and a sense of its own worth, all depend upon its receiving loving care, understanding, and attention. With time, the normally developing child relinquishes its almost total dependence; it acquires the capacity to conceive of itself as an agent, to set out on its own, and to live in a world less dominated by its bodily needs and by its parents. Inevitably, this growth in competence and strength brings greater potential for self-harm, for the child's fantasies of its power and knowledge stand in marked contrast to the reality of its relative ignorance and vulnerability. In the ordinary course of events, the more powerful and knowledgeable parent often interferes with the child's choices in order to prevent harm and to bring about good. The reason for this is frequently, if the appropriate degree of parental selflessness is present, the child's own best interests, not primarily the interests of the parents or others.

Concern for the child often, of course, is manifested in allowing and encouraging experimentation, just as it sometimes is in forceful intrusion. The child's developing individuality and sense of personal responsibility require that

Reprinted from *American Philosophical Quarterly*, vol. 18, no. 4 (October, 1981), pp. 263-271. The author is especially grateful for helpful comments made at the Lutsen Conference by Professors Vicki Harper and Tibor Machan, to colleagues at the UCLA Law School, and to Professor John Deigh.

others encourage in it a sense of its own power and competence, support its venturing out, and exercise judgment in forbearing from intrusion, permitting it to err and to learn some painful truths from painful consequences suffered. God commanded Adam and Eve but left them free to disobey, thereby providing evidence of both love and respect. The Devil, preferring for humans a state of permanent infantilism, would, no doubt, have acted differently, as Dostoevsky's "Grand Inquisitor" nicely illustrates.[1]

The rational love of parents for their children guides the parents' conduct so that their children may one day be fortunate enough to say with St. Paul, "when I became a man, I put away childish things." A central drama of many lives is a result of imbalance in the relations between parents and children in this area—of being left too much on one's own or too little, of counting on one's parents too much, or of not being able to count upon them enough, of parental conduct that fosters too much dependence or conduct that imposes upon the child too much personal responsibility, creating in the child not self-confidence but a sense of being alone and insecure in a threatening world.

Paternalism as a social phenomenon is prefigured in this elemental and universal situation of solicitous parental conduct that has its roots in our common humanity. But paternalism is of philosophic interest, not because of the way parents legitimately relate to their children—indeed there is oddity in describing this conduct as "paternalistic"—but rather because something like this practice is introduced into relations among adults. If our responses to adults mirror intrusive and solicitous parental responses to children, we behave paternalistically.

Contemporary discussions of paternalism, understood in this way, proceed by focusing primarily on specific laws, laws that either prohibit or require certain conduct and that, arguably, have as their principal or sole reason for existence the good of those individuals to whom they are addressed. My focus in this paper is entirely different, for I consider paternalism, its meaning and its possible legitimacy, not in the context of specific laws prohibiting or requiring conduct, but rather with regard to the existence of a system of punitive responses for the violation of any law. I shall consider several issues and make a number of proposals. First, I define my particular version of a paternalistic theory of punishment. Second, I argue for, and consider a variety of objections to, this paternalistic theory. Third, I argue that the paternalistic theory I have constructed implies, in a more natural way than other common justifications for punishment, certain restrictions on the imposition of punishment.

II

Let us turn to the first topic. My aim here is to describe the paternalistic theory of punishment I later defend. I set out a variety of moral paternalism, for the good that is sought is a specific moral good.

In order to punish paternalistically, we must be punishing. I assume that the human institution of punishment presupposes, among other things, that certain conduct has been determined to be wrongful, that what are generally recognized as deprivations are imposed in the event of such conduct, that these deprivations are imposed upon the wrongdoer by someone in a position of authority, that wrongdoers are generally made aware that the deprivation is imposed because of the wrongdoing, and that the context makes evident that the deprivation is not a tax on a course of conduct or in some way a compensation to injured individuals, but rather a response to the doing of what one was not entitled to do.

I have placed a logical constraint on the concept of punishment that is not customarily explicitly associated with it. I have claimed that in order for a person to be punished there must be an intention—one normally simply taken for granted—to convey to the wrongdoer and, where it is punishment for breach of a community's requirement, to others as well, that the deprivation is imposed because of wrongdoing. A communicative component is a defining characteristic of punishment, and in part distinguishes it from mere retaliation or acting out of revenge when the goal of bringing about evil for another may achieve all that one desires. The paternalistic theory I present relies essentially on the idea of punishment as a complex communicative act—the components of which I hope will become clear as I proceed.[2]

A central theme in paternalism is to justify one's conduct out of a concern for the good of another. And so a paternalistic theory of punishment will naturally claim that a principal justification for punishment and a principal justification for restrictions upon it are that the system furthers the good of potential and actual wrongdoers. This contrasts with views—although many of the practices supported may be the same—that it is justice that requires that guilty persons be punished or that it is the utility to society that necessitates punishment. The theory I put forward emphasizes what retributivist and utilitarian theories largely, if not entirely, ignore, that a principal justification for punishment is the potential and actual wrongdoer's good. The theory should not, however, be confused with "reform" or "rehabilitative" theories. First, these theories may be based not on consideration of what promotes the good of actual and potential wrongdoers, but on what promotes value for society generally. Second, reform theory may countenance responses ruled out under the paternalistic theory proposed in these pages. And, finally, reform theories usually fail to address the issue of how instituting a practice of punishment, meaning by this both the threat of punishment and its actual infliction, may promote a specific moral good. This is a central feature of the theory I propose.[3]

I also assume that paternalistic measures characteristically involve disregard of, indeed conflict with, a person's desires. Giving people what they want and being motivated to do so for their own good is benevolence, not paternalism. And so, if a longing for punishment were characteristically the way in which people responded to the prospect of its imposition, there would, I think, be no role for a paternalistic theory regarding the practice, for it would simply be a practice that generally supplied people with what they acknowledged wanting. We may speak meaningfully of a paternalistic theory of punishment for two reasons: first, punishment by its nature characteristically involves a deprivation that individuals seek to avoid, with the implication that there is some conflict between what people want and what they get; second, the practice is such that people's desires at the time of the deprivation are not determinative of what they receive. Thus, while there are obviously persons guilty of wrongdoing who desire punishment, this fact will not affect either its being punishment that is meted out to such a person or the punishment being possibly based on paternalistic considerations, for what is customarily viewed as a deprivation is being imposed independently of the individual's desires.

Most important, the theory I am proposing requires that the practice of punishment promote a particular kind of good for potential and actual wrongdoers. The good is a moral one, and it is, arguably, one upon which all morality is grounded.

What is the character of this good? It has a number of component parts, but it is essentially one's identity as a morally autonomous person attached to the good. This statement obviously needs explanation.

First, it is a part of this good that one comes to appreciate the nature of the evil involved for others and for oneself in one's doing wrong; this requires empathy, a putting oneself in another's position. It also requires the imaginative capacity to take in the implications for one's future self of the evil one has done. It further requires an attachment to being a person of a certain kind. The claim is that it is good for the person, and essential to one's status as a moral person, that the evil underlying wrongdoing and the evil radiating from it be comprehended, comprehended not merely, if at all, in the sense of one's being able to articulate what one has done, but rather comprehended in the way remorse implies comprehension of evil caused. A person's blindness about such matters—this view assumes—is that person's loss. The Devil's splendid isolation is his hell.

Of course, this element of the good makes it apparent that for this theory, as for other moral justifications for punishment, the rules defining wrongdoing, the rules whose violation occasions punishment, themselves must meet certain minimal moral conditions. I assume, and do not argue for the view, that attachment to the values underlying these rules partly defines one's identity as a moral being and as a member of a moral community, that it gives one a sense of who one is and provides some meaning to one's life, and that the price paid for unconcern is some rupture in relationships, a separation from others, a feeling ill at ease with oneself, and some inevitable loss of emotional sustenance and sense of identity. I further assume that attachment to these values is a natural byproduct of certain early forms of caring, understanding, and respect, and that the practice of punishment applies to those with such an attachment, and not to those who because of some early disasters in primary relationships might value nothing or possess values we might attribute to the Devil.

Second, it is a part of the good that one feel guilt over the wrongdoing, that is, that one be pained at having done wrong, that one be distressed with oneself, that one be disposed to restore what has been damaged, and that one accept the appropriateness of some deprivation, and the making of amends. Not to experience any of this would be to evidence an indifference to separation from others that could only, given the assumptions I have made, diminish one as a person.

Third, it is also part of the good that one reject the disposition to do what is wrong and commit oneself to forbearance in the future. I assume that this makes possible, indeed that it is inextricably bound up with, one's forgiving oneself, one's relinquishing one's guilt, and one's having the capacity to enter fully into life.

Finally, it is part of the good that one possess and vividly retain a conception of oneself as an individual worthy of respect, a conception of oneself as a responsible person, responsible for having done wrong and responsible, through one's own efforts at understanding and reflection, for more clearly coming to see things as they are with a deepened attachment to what is good. This conception of oneself is further nourished by freely accepting the moral conditions placed upon restoring the relationships with others and with oneself that one has damaged.

It is a moral good, then, that one feel contrite, that one feel the guilt that is appropriate to one's wrongdoing, that one be repentant, that one be self-forgiving, and that one have reinforced one's conception of oneself as a responsible being. Ultimately, then, the moral good aimed at by the paternalism I propose is an autonomous individual freely attached to that which is good, i.e., those relationships with others that sustain and give meaning to a life.

The theory I propose claims that the potential of punishment to further the realization of this moral good is one principal justification for its existence. From the perspective of this form of paternalism, there must be full respect in the design of the practice of punishment for the individual's moral and intellectual capacities. The good places logical and moral constraints on the means that are permissible to realize it. This is the principal reason that I earlier emphasized the communicative aspect of punishment, for on this theory we seek to achieve a good entirely through the mediation of the wrongdoer's efforts to understand the full significance of the wrongful conduct, the significance of acceptance of that punishment. Thus, unacceptable to this theory would be any response that sought the good of a wrongdoer in a manner that bypassed the human capacity for reflection, understanding, and revision of attitude that may result from such efforts. Any punitive response to a fully responsible being—and it might be no more than the giving of an evil-tasting pill or some form of conditioning—that directly in some causal way, with or without the agent's consent, sought to bring about a good (for example, instantaneous truth or aversion to acting violently) would be incompatible with this constraint. There is, then, a good to be achieved but one cannot, logically or morally, be compelled to obtain it. Throughout, there must be complete respect for the moral personality of the wrongdoer; it is a respect, as I later argue, that must be given despite the wrongdoer's consent to be treated otherwise.

It is evident that this paternalistic goal is not to make people feel less burdened or more content. Once the good is achieved, these may be likely results; they are not, however, what is sought. It is important, too, to recognize that this good differs markedly from those particular goods associated with specific paternalistic legislation. It is not one's health, it is not even one's moral health with respect to any particular matter that is sought to be achieved; it is one's general character as a morally autonomous individual attached to the good.

III

What might be said in favor of such a theory and what might be objections to it? Two major issues will be considered. First, can a plausible case be presented that punishment is connected with the good as I have defined it? Second, is there anything morally offensive or otherwise objectionable, as there often is with particular legislation, in having as one's goal in limiting freedom the person's own good?

Let us direct attention again to the relationship between parent and child with which I commenced this essay and in which paternalist-like elements seem clearly and appropriately present. The range of situations here is very wide. Parents coercively interfere, sometimes to protect the child from hurting itself, sometimes to assure its continued healthy growth, sometimes so that the child will learn to move about comfortably in a world of social conventions. But sometimes, of course, coercion enters in with respect to matters that are moral; certain modes of conduct are required if valued relationships among individuals within the family and outside the family are to come into existence and be maintained.

Such values as obedience, respect, loyalty, and a sense of personal responsibility are slowly integrated into the young person's life. This happens to a considerable degree—of course not entirely and in differing degrees in different stages of development—when the child's conduct occasionally meets with unpleasant responses. Written vividly upon children are lessons associated with some loss or some pain visited upon them by those to whom they are attached. It is important for my purposes that a difference in the significance of the painful responses be noted. The pain experienced by the child subjected to a parent's anger or disapproval has the significance of punishment only if the parent deliberately visits upon the child some pain because of the perceived wrongdoing. The parent's spontaneous anger, disapproval, or blame cause the child distress. They may motivate future compliant conduct. They may arouse in the child guilt. They are not, however, by themselves requital for wrongdoing, and by themselves do not relieve guilt. My view is that punishment has some special and logical relationship to wrongdoing and to the possibility of a child's acquiring the concept. Because of this relationship, punishment is connected with the good that I have described in a way that blame or disapproval by themselves are not.

First, because of punishment, children come to acquire an understanding of the meaning of a limit on conduct. Logically connected with the concept of wrongdoing is the concept of a painful response that another is entitled to inflict because of the wrongful conduct.[4] Second, a punitive response conveys to children the depth of parental attachment to the values underlying the limit. Just as children know from experience that they are disposed to strike out when they or what they care for are injured, so they come to appreciate the seriousness of their parents' attachment to the limit and to the values supported by its existence by the parents' visiting some pain upon them. The degree of punishment, then, conveys to the child the importance parents attach to their child's responding to the limit and promotes in children not just an appreciation that something is wrong, but how seriously wrong it is. It conveys, too, the significance of different degrees of fault in the doing of what is wrong. Further, particular punishments that are chosen often communicate to children the peculiar character of the evil caused by their disregard of the limit, the evil to others and the evil to themselves. Thus, even young children will find it particularly fitting to penalize a cheater by not permitting, for a time at least, further play, for such punishment conveys the central importance of honesty in the playing of the game and one's placing oneself outside the community of players by dishonesty. "If you will not abide by what makes this segment of our lives together possible, suffer the consequence of not being here a part of our lives."

Finally, punishment "rights the wrong." It has, in contrast to blame and disapproval, the character of closure, of matters returning to where they were before, of relationships being restored. Just as a limit being placed upon conduct serves to provide a bounded, manageable world for the child, so the punitive response to a breach defines a limit to separation that is occasioned by wrongdoing. The debt is paid; life can go on.

The young hero in Styron's *Sophie's Choice* gives in to a desire for an exciting ride with a friend and forgets his agreement to tend the fire before which his invalid mother sits for heat in the freezing weather. The young man is guilty and remorseful. Why, we may wonder, was he grateful to his father for placing him for a period of time in a shed without heat? The answer seems clear. It diminished the young boy's guilt, diminished it in a way that it would not have been had the father merely said, "You did something dreadful; I know you feel bad. Don't let it happen again!" The young boy's guilt and remorse were painful, but because they were not deprivations imposed because of wrongdoing, they could not serve to reestablish what had been upset in the relations between parents and child.

What I have described is familiar. What needs emphasizing is that this parental practice of punishing is a complex communication to the child. It aids the child in learning what, as a moral person, it must know: that some things are not permitted, that some wrongs are more serious than others, that is is sometimes responsible for doing wrong and sometimes not, and that its degree of blameworthiness is not always the same. Further, the child's response to wrongdoing by feeling guilt, its willingness to accept some deprivation, and its commitment to acting differently in the future all play an indispensable role in its restoring relationships it has damaged, relationships with others and with itself. The claim, then, is that this practice is, in fact, a significant contributing factor in one's development as a moral person.

What more acceptably motivates a parent when it punishes its child than the desire to achieve a goal such as I have described? It would be perverse if the parent were generally to punish primarily from motives of retributive justice or optimal utility for the family. These ends are secondary to, although with retributive ends, to some extent essential to, the child's acquiring the characteristics of a moral person. This much may seem plausible but also quite beside the point. The topic is, after all, punishment in the adult world, and there are significant differences between adults and children that may carry fatal implications for a paternalistic theory. I do not believe this is so, but before moving on I want to note a phenomenon that may cast doubt upon the legitimacy of the parental practice itself.

Parents sometimes say, when imposing some deprivation upon their children, "I'm only doing this for your own good!" There is, I think, something offensive about this. Does it affect the legitimacy of parental concern primarily for the child's moral development in inflicting punishment?

The answer I think is clearly "no." The offensiveness of those words is not limited to situations in which punishment is imposed. Giving some unpleasant medicine or compelling the child to eat some distasteful but allegedly nourishing food, if accompanied by a statement that it is for the child's own good, is equally offensive. The words are customarily uttered in response to some sign of resistance or anger, and what they neglect to address is the child's unhappiness. They rather defend the parents before the child, making the child feel guilty because of its failure to be grateful for the good done it. And so, imposed upon the child is the burden of getting what it does not want, the burden of checking its understandable anger because of this, and finally, the burden of having to be grateful for getting what it does not want and, if it is not grateful, the burden of feeling guilty. It is not the motive of promoting the child's good that is suspect in these cases; it is communicating to the child what one's motive is, with its distressing consequences for the child, and with the still more serious problem, perhaps, that the parent's own guilt is unconsciously sought to be transferred to the child.

IV

One can acknowledge the place of punishment in the moral development of children and acknowledge, too, that it must to some degree be imposed to further this development, and yet wonder what all this has to do with legal punishment of adults. For the law, as a means of social control, presupposes that the individuals to whom it applies are already responsible persons, responsible both in the sense of having the capacity to govern their actions through an understanding of the meaning of the norms addressed to them, and responsible in the sense that they possess a knowledge of and an attachment to the values embodied in the society's laws. There is, nevertheless, a place for punishment in society analogous to its role in the family. I shall briefly sketch what this is.

Through promulgation of laws, through provisions of sanctions for their violation, and through the general imposition of sanctions in the event of violation, each citizen learns what is regarded as impermissible by society, the degree of seriousness to be attached to wrongdoing of different kinds, and the particular significance—especially when the punishment is in its severity and character linked to the offense—of the evil underlying offenses. Punishment is a forceful reminder of the evil that is done to others and to oneself. Were it not present, or were it imposed in circumstances markedly at odds with criteria for its imposition during the process of moral development, only confusion would result. Brandeis, in a quite different context, observed: "Our government is the potent, the omnipresent teacher. For good or for ill, it teaches the whole people by its example." My point is that law plays an indispensable role in our knowing what is good and evil for society. Failure to punish serious wrongdoing, punishment of wrongdoing in circumstances in which fault is absent, would serve only to baffle our moral understanding and threaten what is so often already precarious.

Further, our punitive responses guide the moral passions as they come into play with respect to interests protected by the law. Among other things, punishment permits purgation of guilt and, ideally, restoration of damaged relationships. Punishment, then, communicates what is wrong and, in being imposed, both rights the wrong and serves as a reminder of the evil done to others and to oneself in the doing of what is wrong.

In addition to holding that punishment may reasonably be thought to play its part, even with adults, in promoting the good of one's moral personality, the paternalist has to have some argument for this as a morally permissible way of proceeding. The paternalist is, I believe, on firm ground here. Guilty wrongdoers are not viewed as damned by wrongful conduct to a life forever divorced from others. They are viewed as responsible beings, responsible for having done wrong and possessing the capacity for recognizing the wrongfulness of their conduct. Further, the evil—as Socrates long ago pointed out—that they have done themselves by their wrongdoing is a moral evil greater than that which they have done others. Their souls are in jeopardy as their victims' are not. What could possibly justify an unconcern with this evil if the wrongdoer is one of us and if we sense, rightly I believe, that there but for the grace of God go we? In considering, for example, why we might wish to have a society of laws, of laws associated with sanctions for their violation, of laws that are in fact enforced against others and ourselves, it would be rational (indeed it would, I think, be among the most persuasive of considerations for establishing such a social practice) to hold that it would promote our own good as moral persons. Thinking of ourselves as potential or actual wrongdoers, and appreciating the connection of punishment with one's attachment to the good, to one's status as a moral person, and to the possibility it provides of closure and resumption of relationships, would we not select such a system, if for no other reason than that it would promote our own good?

V

We have now to consider certain objections to the theory. First, does it fail to respect one as an autonomous being? The answer is that it does not. One's choices are throughout respected, and it is one's status as a moral person that is sought to be affirmed. But is there not something offensively demeaning in instituting punishment for such a reason? More demeaning, one might ask, than addressing the wrongdoer's sense of fear to which others appeal in their theories of punishment? More demeaning than an approach that exhibits indifference to the moral status of the person but that is totally committed to retributive justice? I am not convinced that this is so either. On the theory I propose, one is throughout responded to as a moral person.

But does not a paternalistic theory lead to two unacceptable extremes with respect to punishment, the first that we should always warn before punishing, and wait to see the effects of our warning, the other that we should continue punishing until we achieve the desired effects? The answers here can be brief. First, the announcement of the norm and the provision for punishment in the event of its violation is itself the warning, and to allow a person to disobey and be threatened that next time there will be punishment is to issue not one, but two, warnings. Second, the practice of punishment, given the paternalistic goals I have described, cannot permit open-ended punishments, repeated punishments, or punishments that are excessively severe. For the goal is not repentance at all costs, if that has meaning, but repentance freely arrived at, repentance that is not merely a disposition toward conformity with the norms. Also, the punishment provided for wrongdoing must reflect judgments of the seriousness of the wrong done; such punishment cannot focus on some end-state of the person and disregard the potential for moral confusion that would arise from repeated or excessive punishment.

Another criticism might go as follows: "You have ruled out conditioning people, even with their consent, so that they might not be disposed to do evil in the future. But surely, while it is perhaps an unjustifiable practice without consent, it is acceptable with it, for it provides people with what they freely choose and delivers them from an affliction that promotes evil." Two points need to be made here. First, the theory would not preclude freely chosen forms of conditioning (for example, surgery) in those circumstances in which it is acknowledged that the person is not, with respect to the conduct involved, an autonomous agent. There is nothing wrong, for example, in a person choosing surgery to remove a tumor that is causally related to outbursts of violence over which the person has no control. The class of person, then, whose choice would be accorded respect is made up of those we should be disposed to excuse from criminal liability. Second, the theory would regard as morally unacceptable a response, conditioned or otherwise, that had as its goal not just aversion to doing wrong, but obliteration of one's capacity to choose to do so. What must be aimed at is that the afflicted become autonomous, not automatons. There must be freedom to disobey, for the moral price that is paid in purchasing immunity from temptation and guaranteed conformity is too high.

The most troubling objections to the theory are, I think, these: First, it cannot account for the accepted disposition to punish those who are already, as it were, awakened and repentant. And, second, even more seriously, it cannot account for the disposition to punish those who know what the values of society are, but who are indifferent to or opposed to them. Someone, may feel inclined to say, for example: "Most serious crimes—and your theory surely most neatly fits such crimes, not petty offenses—are committed by individuals who are perfectly aware of what they are doing and perfectly aware that society's values are being flouted. These individuals are not going to be instructed about evil or brought to any moral realization about themselves by punishment. You can't be serious about including them when you speak of repentance. They certainly do not care a jot about paying off any debt, because they do not feel any guilt over what they have done. Your theory so fails to match reality as to be just one more tedious example of a philosopher spinning out fantastic yarns without any genuine relevance to reality." What can be said in response to these points?

As to the first, I would claim that the guilty and repentant wrongdoers are naturally disposed to accept the appropriateness of the punishment provided, both because this will evidence to them and to others the genuineness of their feelings and because the punishment rights the wrong, brings about closure, and restores relationships that have been damaged. The experience of guilt and remorse and the avowal of repentance do not by themselves achieve this.[5] A general practice of pardoning persons who claimed that they were repentant would destroy the principal means of reestablishing one's membership in the community.

Now for the second major objection. A response here requires that attention be paid to certain general features of the theory that has been put forward. The theory is, of course, not intended as a description of any actual practice of legal punishment or even as realistically workable in a society such as ours. Things are in such a state that it is not. What is proposed is a moral theory of punishment and, as such, it includes at least two conditions that may be only marginally congruent with our social world. The first is that the norms addressed to persons are generally just, and that the society is to some substantial extent one in which those who are liable to punishment have roughly equal opportunities to conform to those just norms. The second condition is equally important. The theory presupposes that there is a general commitment among persons to whom the norms apply to the values underlying them. If these two conditions are not met, we do not have what I understand as a practice of punishment for which any moral justification can be forthcoming.

At this point it may be thought, "Fair enough, but then what is the point of the whole exercise?" My response is this: First, the theory is not without applicability to significant segments of our society. Second, it has value, for it provides an important perspective upon actual practices; it throws into relief our society's failure to realize the conditions I have stipulated. And, finally, it assists us in sensitive and intelligent forbearance from putting our moral imprimatur upon practices that the paternalistic model would find unacceptable. Excessively lengthy prison terms and the inhumane conditions under which they are served, for example, can be effectively criticized with a clear conception of the good defined by the paternalistic theory. The theory may serve as a guide in our attempts to adjust present practices so that they more closely accord with moral dictates, to work for precisely that society in which the paternalistic conception provides not just the ring of moral truth but descriptive truth as well.

VI

I want now to shift attention to the issue of restrictions on punishment. The proposed paternalistic theory limits punishment, I believe, in a way that accords more closely with our moral intuitions than do a number of alternative theories. First, it follows from the theory that any class of persons incapable of appreciating the significance of the norms addressed to them cannot justifiably be punished. Absence of a free and knowing departure from the norm makes pointless imposition of punishment. Second, it also follows that excuses must be recognized and that mitigating factors be taken into account, including as an excuse, of course, reasonable ignorance or mistake of law.

Perhaps most significantly, a paternalistic orientation implies a position that matches our moral intuitions more closely than other theories on the issue of what kinds of punishment may be inflicted. Punishments that are aimed at degrading or brutalizing a person are not conducive to moral awakening, but only to bitterness and resentment. But there is also, I believe, another paternalistic route to limitations upon certain modes of punishment, limitations that follow from the conception of the moral good.

Wrongdoers have, as we all do, a basic right to be free. How, we may wonder, are we able to justify our imposing our will upon them and limiting their freedom? One answer is that by wrongful conduct they have forfeited their right to freedom. Wrongdoers are in no position to complain if they meet with a response that is similar to what has been visited by them upon another. Such a theory of forfeiture places great weight upon an individual's choice. It holds that rights are forfeitable, waivable, and relinquishable—just so long as the choice involved is informed and free. Individuals might forfeit their right to life by murdering; others might relinquish their right to be free by selling themselves into slavery. The paternalistic position that I have proposed holds otherwise. It implies that there is a nonwaivable, nonforfeitable, nonrelinquishable right—the right to one's status as a moral being, a right that is implied in one's being a possessor of any rights at all.

When punishment is at issue, such a view makes morally impermissible any response to a person, despite what that person has done, that would be inconsistent with this fundamental right, even though ther person were unattached to it, indifferent to its moral value, and eager to forfeit it. A retributivist might respond in kind to any wrong done. A social utilitarian might calculate the effects on people and society in doing so. A paternalist, attached to the good of the wrongdoer, would reject retributive justice and utility as the sole determinative criteria, and would propose a good to be realized that is independent of these values. Punishment will not be permitted that destroys in some substantial way one's character as an autonomous creature. Certain cruel punishments, then, may be ruled out, not merely because they are conducive to hardening the heart but, more important, because they destroy a good that can never rightly be destroyed. As I see it, this precludes, on moral grounds, punishment that may be like-for-like but that nevertheless violates one's humanity by either destroying one's life or destroying one's capacity for rejecting what is evil and again attaching oneself to the good.

Let me be more specific. Suppose that a sadist has cruelly destroyed another human being's capacity for thought while leaving the person alive. Is there a retributivist argument that would bar a like treatment for the sadist? I do not know of it. Certainly, the lex talionis would seem to sanction it. Is our inclination to forbear from treating the sadist in a like-for-like manner derived exclusively, then from social evils that we foresee might flow from such punishment? I do not find this persuasive. Our moral repugnance precedes such calculation, and findings inconsistent with this repugnance would be rejected. Is it simply revulsion at the thought of oneself or one's agents deliberately perpetrating such acts? Is it a concern for our own good that motivates us? This may play a role, but my conviction is that something else is involved. It is the ingredient to which the moral paternalist draws attention. The wrongdoer possesses something destroyed in another. The wrongdoer may desire to destroy it in himself or herself as well but that is not his or her moral prerogative. It is immune from moral transformations brought about by free choice.

VII

I would like, in conclusion, to make somewhat clearer what I am and am not claiming for the theory proposed in these pages and, further, to draw attention to two ironies connected with it.

I have claimed that to have as one's aim in punishing the good of the wrongdoer counts strongly in favor of the moral legitimacy of punishing. I do not claim, of course, that this is the sole justification for punishment, although I do believe that what it seeks to promote is among the most important, if not the most important, of human goods. The practice of punishment is complex and any justification proposed as an exclusive one must, in my judgment, be met with skepticism, if not scorn. There is, too, as I earlier briefly noted, a significant logical overlapping of this theory with retributivism, although at a certain point, when one considers types of punishment, they diverge. A paternalistic theory, given the good as defined, would support principles that are familiar dictates of retributivism—that only the guilty may be punished, that the guilty must be punished, and that the punishment inflicted must reflect the degree of guilt. Failure to comply with the demands of retributivism would preclude realization of the paternalist's goal. I have also, however, suggested that retributivism needs supplementing if it is to meet our intuitions of what is morally permissible punishment. But, or course, this overlapping of justifications for punishment includes as well some form of utilitarianism, for if our goal is as I have defined it, and punishments are threatened and imposed, deterrent values are also furthered. I do not question the rich over-determination of goods promoted by the practice of punishment. I do urge that weight be given—and on the issue of restrictions on punishment, determinative weight—to paternalistic ends.

There are, finally, two ironies to which I wish to draw attention. The first is this. I have selected as the good to be realized by this paternalistic theory of punishment the very good to which philosophers often make appeal in their principled objections to paternalism with regard to specific prohibitions and requirements. Secondly, I have proposed a theory that justifies forceful intrusion into the lives of people. But it is also an atypical paternalistic theory, for it prohibits certain types of intrusion. I reach this conclusion because the good sought does not allow weight to be given to an individual's free choice when the issue is relinquishment of one's status as a moral being. The paternalistic aspect in this derives from the fact that there is a good for the person to which we are attached, although the person might not be, and that we continue to respect in disregard of the usual consequences of a person's free choice. I would guess that something like these thoughts underlies the view that we possess some goods as gifts from God, and that it is not within our moral prerogative to dispose of them. It is easy to suppose, but a mistake nevertheless, that because we may be favored by the gods that we are one of them.

Notes

1. What is gained and what is lost by allowing a choice to disobey is also brought out in C. S. Lewis's engaging replay of the Adam and Eve myth in his novel *Pelandra*.

2. See Walter Moberly's splendid *The Ethics of Punishment* (London: Faber and Faber, 1968), particularly pp. 201 ff.

3. The reform theories discussed by H.L.A. Hart, and found to be unacceptable as explanations of "the general justifying aim of punishment," differ, then, from the theory developed in these pages. Hart's change of mind in the notes to his collection of essays is occasioned by consideration of theories that still differ markedly from the one I propose. See his *Punishment and Responsibility* (New York and Oxford: Oxford University Press, 1968), pp. 24-27, 240-41.

4. Herbert Fingarette, "Punishment and Suffering," *Proceedings of the American Philosophical Association*, vol. 51 (1977).

5. On the connections between guilt and suffering, see Herbert Morris, *On Guilt and Innocence* (Berkeley and Los Angeles: University of California Press, 1976), pp. 89-110.

Chapter 10

The Limits of Proxy Decision-Making

Allen E. Buchanan

I

In 1968, a committee at Harvard University, composed mostly of physicians, formulated a set of criteria for "brain death."[1] Since that time, the Harvard Criteria, as they have come to be known, have been adopted as the legal definition of death in many jurisdictions in this country. The aim of the Harvard Committee was to develop a new definition of death that would facilitate the removal of transplantable organs and provide a basis for terminating treatment in certain cases of severe and irreversible brain damage.[2]

The Harvard Criteria's limited success in achieving the second aim became all too obvious in the Quinlan case. Although Karen Quinlan was in a vegetative state, with no hope of regaining cognitive functions, parts of her brain exhibited some electrical activity. Since total absence of electrical activity is required to meet the Harvard Criteria of brain death, the respirator could not be disconnected on the grounds that she was already dead.[3]

Working on the assumption that Karen Quinlan was a living person with the full panoply of rights accorded to persons by the law, the New Jersey Supreme Court set about the task of determining which of those rights were relevant to the decision whether to continue treatment of a terminally ill incompetent. No attempt was made to develop a new definition of death or to decide the issue of treatment by holding that an individual in an irreversible vegetative state is no longer a living person. Since *Quinlan*, every major court case dealing with treatment decisions for

I am indebted to Margaret Battin, Leslie Francis, Donald Regan, Michael Root, Richard Wasserstrom, and Daniel Wikler for their helpful comments on an earlier version of this paper.

terminally ill incompetents has followed the New Jersey Supreme Court's lead in assuming that the issue is that of determining and implementing the rights of incompetent persons.[4]

This approach is a prime example of judicial conservatism. From *Quinlan* on, the courts have attempted to avoid the fundamental philosophical and constitutional issues raised by the task of developing a more adequate concept of the person and hence of the death of a person. In each case, the court has evaded the question "Who has rights?" in favor of the question "What rights do these individuals have (and how may they be exercised)?"

II

Once the issue was framed in terms of the rights of incompetent persons, a certain line of development was all but inevitable. A common-law doctrine establishing the right of *competent* patients to refuse treatment, understood as an application of a right of self-determination,[5] was reinforced by the *Roe* v. *Wade* ruling on abortion that the constitutional right to privacy includes a right of self-determination with respect to what is done to one's body.[6]

In *Superintendent of Belchertown State School* v. *Saikewicz* (1977) the Massachusetts Supreme Judicial Court held that once a right to refuse treatment, as an application of the right of privacy or self-determination, is acknowledged for *competent* patients, the refusal to extend the same right to *incompetents* would violate the principle of equal respect for persons (and presumably the fourteenth amendment's "Equal Protection" clause).[7] Subsequent rulings involving decision-making for terminally ill incompetents have been viewed as reinforcing this attempt to extend the rights of competent persons to incompetents.[8]

The major problem was to devise a doctrine of proxy decision-making to implement the incompetents' rights of self-determination, granted that the incompetents themselves could not exercise them. The standard for proxy decision-making that *Quinlan* claimed to employ, that *Saikewicz* later developed in greater detail, and that the more recent *Spring* and *Fox* cases have upheld, is the concept of "substituted judgment." According to this standard, the decision for or against treatment

> should be that which would be made by the incompetent person, if that person were competent, but taking into account the present and future incompetence of the person as one of the factors which would necessarily enter into the decision-making process of the competent person.[9]

It is important to understand exactly why the courts have opted for substituted judgment rather than for alternative standards for proxy decision-making. It was argued that this standard, and this standard alone, permits a genuine exercise of the incompetent's right of self-determination.[10] The right of self-determination, both for competents and incompetents, is understood as including the right to refuse treatment even when to do so would not be in one's best interest nor in agreement with what most rational or reasonable persons would elect to do in similar circumstances. Consequently, proxy decision-making that utilizes either a "best interest" or a "reasonable person" standard cannot be viewed as a proxy exercise of the right of self-determination.

The recognition of a right of self-determination that applies to decisions to accept or refuse medical treatment, and the effort to devise a method for making this right effective for incompetents, are major developments in the common-law theory of rights. The extension of the right of self-determination to incompetents and the recognition that substituted judgment is the appropriate standard for proxy exercise of this right, constitute a significant reduction of the scope of the traditional doctrine of *parens patria*, insofar as the latter is understood as proceeding on the assumption that the state is to act in the incompetent's best interest.[11]

The courts have ruled, however, that for both competents and incompetents, the right in question is not absolute, but may be limited by opposing state interests in (1) the preservation of life, (2) the protection of innocent third parties, (3) the prevention of suicide, and (4) maintaining the ethical integrity of the medical profession.[12] Nonetheless, in each of the cases in which they were considered, with one exception, the court concluded that the right of self-determination was preponderant.[13]

III

Both in arguing that in the cases considered the right of self-determination did not conflict with the state's interest in maintaining the ethical integrity of the medical profession and in devising a procedure for applying the standard of substituted judgment, it was essential for the judiciary to delimit the sphere of medical decision-making. Indeed, since *Saikewicz*, at least, the question of *who* is to decide has been the focal point of the debate.

Joseph Saikewicz was a severely retarded sixty-seven-year-old resident of a state institution who had developed an invariably fatal form of leukemia. Physicians had determined that if Saikewicz were given chemotherapy, his life might be prolonged as much as a year, although the treatment itself would be painful and debilitating and its purpose would be utterly beyond Saikewicz's comprehension. In a momentous decision whose exact interpretation is still under dispute, the Supreme Judicial Court of Massachusetts issued a written opinion that went far beyond the particulars of Mr. Saikewicz's case. After approving an earlier probate court order authorizing withholding of chemotherapy from Joseph Saikewicz, the Supreme Judical Court ruled that the proper tribunal for treatment decisions for terminally ill incompetents is a probate court and that the judge's decision is to be based on the standard of substituted judgment.[14]

By apparently judicializing the decision-making process for a broad class of incompetent patients, the *Saikewicz* ruling provoked alarm and indignation in the medical community. Dr. Arnold Relman, editor of *The New England Journal of*

Medicine, sharply criticized *Saikewicz* as an unwarranted judicial encroachment on sound medical practice. According to Relman, existing medical practice proceeds on the assumption that a physician's duty is to act in the patient's best interest, and that the decision whether to initiate or continue treatment that will not cure, but at best prolong, the incompetent's life is to be made by the physician in consultation with the patient's family, when this is possible.[15]

I have argued elsewhere that the justification which Relman and others offer for the position that the physician qua physician should be the primary decision-maker is based on the medical paternalist model of the physician-patient relationship. I have also argued that the major flaw in this model is that it not only overestimates physicians' knowledge and powers of judgment and underestimates their fallibility, but also systematically confuses judgments of medical expertise with moral judgments.[16] As we shall shortly see, one of the most recent judicial decisions concerning terminally ill incompetents provides tacit approval for medical paternalism, adding fuel to the debate over who should decide.

In spite of their remarkably rapid progress—or perhaps because of it—these recent attempts to forge a conceptually coherent and practicable doctrine of proxy decision-making for terminally ill incompetents now face three serious obstacles: (1) Tenacious in their conviction that only the standard of substituted judgment allows a genuine exercise of the right of self-determination, the courts have attempted to use that standard in cases in which it cannot be defensibly applied. The result has been a degradation of the very right which the courts sought to protect. (2) The *Dinnerstein* decision, reinforced by a recent clarification of *Saikewicz* offered by the latter's author, Judge Paul Liacos,[17] endangers the right of self-determination (for both competents and incompetents alike) by undoing earlier judicial efforts to limit the domain of medical decision-making. (3) Recent interpretations of the state's interest in preventing suicide threaten to emasculate the right of self-determination. Each of these problems, I shall argue, signals a failure to establish the proper limits of the theory of proxy decision-making. Let us consider them in turn.

1. There are two types of cases—each frequently encountered in contemporary medical practice—in which the standard of substituted judgment cannot solve the problem of decision-making for incompetents. In the first type of case the substituted-judgment standard is in principle applicable, but its application yields no defensible result because there is insufficient evidence to determine what the individual in question would want done were that individual competent. If no bona fide "living will" or other reliable evidence is available, clearly indicating the individual's preferences when competent, the substituted-judgment standard yields no defensible answer to the question of treatment.

When faced with actual cases in which there was no reliable and clear evidence for determining whether the patient, if competent, would want treatment, the *Quinlan* court and the *Saikewicz* court adopted different, but equally desperate, strategies for avoiding the uncomfortable conclusion that because the standard of substituted judgment could not be successfully applied, no exercise of the right of self-determination was possible.

After admitting that vague anecdotal testimony from Ms. Quinlan's family concerning her former preferences lacked probative weight, the New Jersey Supreme Court nonetheless held that, if competent, she would not wish to be continued on the respirator in an irreversible vegetative state. The court supported this conclusion by observing that most reasonable people would not want to be maintained in her condition.[18]

It appears that the *Quinlan* court abandoned the substituted-judgment standard in the face of insufficient evidence for its responsible application, tacitly replacing it with the "reasonable person" standard. But if this is so, it is hard to see how the court can claim to have achieved the exercise of Karen Quinlan's right of self-determination. For it should be recalled that the right of self-determination was defined as the right to make one's own choice, even when this does not agree with what most reasonable people would want and even when the choice is not in one's best interest.

The Supreme Judicial Court of Massachusetts first attempted to explain away *Quinlan's* apparent abandonment of the substituted-judgment standard and then proceeded to indulge in equally questionable reasoning when faced with a more radical difficulty in applying that standard. According to *Saikewicz*, it was proper for the New Jersey Supreme Court to appeal to the preferences of most reasonable people as indirect evidence of what Karen Quinlan would have wanted, when adequate direct evidence was lacking.[19]

To be a genuine exercise of the right of self-determination, a decision need not *in fact* diverge from what most persons or most reasonable persons would prefer, but it must at least be *possible* that it diverge. However, by simply appealing to what most people or most reasonable people would prefer, the court ruled out this possibility. Consequently, it is difficult to understand how such a procedure could be seen as a genuine exercise of Karen Quinlan's right of self-determination, since the point of affirming that right was to show respect for the individual's choice, even when that choice might diverge from that of the majority or from that of the majority of reasonable persons. Further, neither *Quinlan* nor *Saikewicz* presented any empirical data to support the generalization that most people would prefer to have the respirator disconnected, and neither court even considered the fact that there are some individuals whose religious convictions or fundamental beliefs about the nature and value of life rule out such a preference.

In the case of Joseph Saikewicz, the court faced an even more serious difficulty. There was no conceivable evidence that could have answered the question "What would *this individual*, if competent, prefer?" Prior to her accident, Karen Quinlan was a competent individual, a being with complex preferences and beliefs, and all the rich conceptual capacities that these presuppose. Joseph Saikewicz, in sharp contrast, was never competent. His lifelong mental disability was so severe that, with an I.Q. of ten and an estimated mental age of about a year, he was never capable of forming the preferences in question because he lacked the concepts that they presuppose. In Karen Quinlan's case, the question posed by the standard of substituted judgment could not be reliably answered due to a paucity of evidence; in Joseph Saikewicz's case the question had no conceivable answer.

To say that Joseph Saikewicz's right of self-determination could not be exercised by proxy because he never had the conceptual capacities required for us to infer *his* preferences about whether or not to be given chemotherapy or, more generally, to have his life prolonged at the cost of considerable pain, is to trivialize the problem. The very notions of self-determination, and hence of a right of self-determination, only apply to beings who have, or have the potential for developing, certain rather complex cognitive functions, including the ability to conceive of the future, to discern alternative courses of action, and to make judgments about their own good. Above all, it makes sense to ascribe a right of self-determination only to beings who are capable of conceiving of themselves as *agents*—beings distinct from, and capable of changing, their environment.[20] Instead of clearly acknowledging the inapplicability of substituted judgment in cases like that of Joseph Saikewicz, the Supreme Judicial Court of Massachusetts made a heroic but confused attempt to ascertain the conceptually sophisticated preferences of an individual who never possessed the requisite concepts, in order to protect a right of self-determination that could never be coherently ascribed to him.[21]

The efforts of *Quinlan* and *Saikewicz* to employ the standard of substituted judgment beyond the range of its defensible application have encouraged a dangerous weakening of the standards of evidence. The recent *Spring* case shows how far the lowering of standards has progressed. Earle Spring, an allegedly senile seventy-eight-year-old man suffering total kidney failure, was expected to live about five years if his dialysis treatments, which had begun before he became senile, were continued. His wife and son petitioned a Massachusetts probate court for authorization to terminate his dialysis treatments. The Appeals Court found that Mr. Spring, if competent, would not wish to be kept alive in his present condition.[22]

As Professors George Annas and Leonard Glantz have observed in a thoughtful brief *amicus curiae* for the case, "the evidence provided by family members, in an attempt to indicate what Mr. Spring would choose, is virtually non-existent." The only consideration adduced was that Mr. Spring was now unable to live the active, vigorous life he had enjoyed when he was competent. Annas and Glantz's reasons for rejecting this vague and anecdotal evidence are convincing.

> It is almost always true as people get older that their level of activity declines, and is often severely curtailed. It does not follow from this that such a person would prefer to cease living because of the curtailment of such activities.[23]

Once it is admitted that there are some cases in which the standard of substituted judgment is either inapplicable or yields no defensible result because of lack of reliable evidence, it seems we are left with two alternatives, neither of which can be seen as an application of substituted judgment, nor as a proxy exercise of the right of self-determination. We might apply the best-interest standard or the reasonable-person standard. When the patient's cognitive disabilities are as great as Joseph Saikewicz's, it might be argued that the notion of interest is reducible to pleasure and the absence of pain. If this is so, to determine whether treatment would be in his best interest we would have to try to weigh the pain of the chemotherapy, along with whatever confusion or terror it might evoke in the uncomprehending patient, against whatever gain in pleasure a few more months of life would bring. If the treatment were sufficiently painful and if the opportunities for pleasure during the extra months of life were very limited, we might conclude that treatment would not be in Mr. Saikewicz's best interest.

Application of the reasonable-person standard might produce the same results, although for different reasons. It may be that many or even most reasonable persons, if queried, would reply that they do not wish to be given chemotherapy if they are reduced to Joseph Saikewicz's condition. But we should not assume that this wish would be based solely on the balancing of pleasure against pain mandated by the best-interest test. Some of us would wish not to be treated, not simply because of a desire to avoid pain, but because of fundamental beliefs we hold about the importance of existing as a rational agent, rather than as a mere locus of pleasure and pain.

If, as these reflections suggest, the best-interest standard and the reasonable-person standard are conceptually distinct and may even yield different answers, depending upon what views the majority of reasonable persons hold about the value of certain forms of existence, which standard are we to use when substituted judgment cannot be defensibly applied? Unfortunately, an attempt to answer this question would exceed the limits of this essay.[24]

Although the *Saikewicz* decision was confused about how the standard for decision-making was to be applied, it did state clearly that the courts, not the physician, were to apply it. The New Jersey Supreme Court in *Quinlan* also noted that the protection of basic individual rights was the business of the judiciary, not a matter within the expertise of physicians, but then went on to blur the crucial distinction between medical judgment and moral decision by its confusing use of the term ''ethics committee.'' After concluding that Karen Quinlan, if competent, would wish to have the respirator disconnected, the court made the following ruling.

> Upon the concurrence of the guardians and family of Karen, should the responsible attending physicians conclude that there is no reasonable possibility of Karen's ever emerging from her present comatose condition to a cognitive, sapient state, and that the life-support apparatus now being administered to Karen should be discontinued, they should consult with the hospital ''Ethics Committee'' or like body of the institution in which Karen is then hospitalized. If that consultative body agrees that there is no reasonable possibility of Karen's ever emerging from her present comatose condition to a cognitive, sapient state, the present life-support system may be withdrawn . . . .[25]

Since the sole task assigned to it by the court was to confirm the medical prognosis that Quinlan was in an irreversible vegetative state, the committee in question was in fact a prognosis review committee. To call such a group an "ethics committee" was extremely misleading because this latter term is usually (and reasonably) understood to refer to a body concerned not exclusively or even primarily with medical prognosis, but with moral issues. By suggesting that the only issue was that of medical prognosis, *Quinlan* encouraged the dangerous illusion that the question of whether to discontinue life-support for a patient in an irreversible vegetative state is a matter of medical expertise and that the court should only be involved to the extent of requiring a mechanism of medical peer review to see that prognosis judgments are made according to acceptable professional standards.[26]

2. In the more recent *Dinnerstein* case, the Massachusetts Court of Appeals took an even more radical and confused step toward obliterating the hard-won distinction between questions falling within the technical expertise of the physician and fundamental moral questions concerning individuals' rights. Shirley Dinnerstein was a sixty-seven-year-old woman suffering from Alzheimer's disease, a degenerative disorder of the brain that results in dementia, coma, and eventually death, and for which there is no known treatment. Her condition was described as "essentially vegetative." Partly paralyzed by an earlier stroke and suffering from heart disease, Mrs. Dinnerstein was not expected to live more than a year. Her family sought declaratory relief from the probate court, asking permission to authorize her physicians not to resuscitate her should she suffer cardiac arrest.[27]

The Appeals Court granted the family's request, arguing that the case was *not* within the scope of *Saikewicz* and that therefore the decision not to resuscitate need not be made by a judicial process. The Appeals Court judge explicitly held that the decision not to resuscitate was a matter of medical judgment, falling within the discretion of the attending physician.[28]

According to the judge, there was an important difference between Mrs. Dinnerstein's condition and that of Mr. Saikewicz, and this difference warranted the conclusion that the treatment decision in the former case was a matter of medical judgment that raised no questions about the rights of incompetents, while in the latter the treatment decision called for a proxy exercise of the incompetent's right of self-determination. The alleged difference was that in the case of Joseph Saikewicz "treatment was available, and . . . therefore presented a substantial question of choice," while in the case of Shirley Dinnerstein there was no significant treatment choice to be made because "death must come soon, probably in the form of cardiac or respiratory arrest . . . ."[29]

The court also emphasized that whereas in Saikewicz's case the proposed treatment (chemotherapy) "would be administered for the purpose, and with some reasonable expectation, of effecting a temporary cure of or relief from the illness or condition being treated," the treatment in Dinnerstein's case (resuscitation) would only achieve "a mere suspension of the act of dying . . . ." The Appeals Court judge also added the following puzzling observation.

[Saikewicz] suffered from leukemia, which was not curable, in the sense of a permanent cure, but which was treatable by chemotherapy, which could cause symptomatic remission, thus making possible an extension of normal, cognitive functioning existence for a period of months or years.[30]

There are two obvious difficulties with this line of reasoning. First, although *some* patients who undergo chemotherapy achieve an extension of "normal, cognitive, functioning existence" for a period of months or years, the medical prognosis for Joseph Saikewicz was that chemotherapy would at best extend *his* life by a year without, of course, any improvement in *his* cognitive deficiencies. Second, granted that Shirley Dinnerstein's life expectancy was about a year, it seems implausible to hold that chemotherapy, which may extend life in the one case, offers a significant choice, while resuscitation, which may extend life for about the same period, merely prolongs the act of dying and presents no significant choice.

Further, the fact that resuscitation could not restore Mrs. Dinnerstein's cognitive functioning seems quite irrelevant to the question of whether that treatment would only be a prolongation of the act of dying—so long as we operate with the Harvard brain death criteria. Indeed, nothing in the medical testimony or in the judge's review of it indicates that Mrs. Dinnerstein's death was so near that it would be any more appropriate to describe her as being engaged in the act of dying than it would be to so describe Mr. Saikewicz.

There are no doubt some cases in which resuscitation might be properly described as merely prolonging the act of dying—cases in which repeated resuscitation will at best restore the functioning of an irreversibly damaged heart for a few moments, or perhaps an hour or so. Especially when the patient is sufficiently sentient to suffer the trauma of violent resuscitation techniques, this sort of "treatment" seems futile, if not perverse. But it must be emphasized that the court pointed to no evidence to show that this was Mrs. Dinnerstein's condition, nor did it clearly limit its ruling to just such cases. Let us refer to these as "type A cases."

In contrast to that just described, we may distinguish another type of case in which resuscitation offers more than a brief extension of life, even though, as the court said of Mrs. Dinnerstein, the patient is "in the terminal stages of an unremitting, incurable mortal illness." Let us call these "type B cases." *Dinnerstein* failed to distinguish between these two types of cases and offered no sound justification for its claim that a case of the second type raises no questions concerning the incompetent's right of self-determination, and hence is not covered by the doctrine of substituted judgment. It is not surprising that many physicians and lawyers interpreted the ruling as saying that the physician "does not have to get a court order to resuscitate a hopeless patient . . . ."[31]

It is essential to see that *Dinnerstein* threatens the rights not only of incompetents but of competent patients as well. The court's argument was that in what it vaguely described as cases in which the situation is "hopeless and . . . death must come soon," resuscitation is a matter of medical judgment because there is no significant treatment choice upon which individuals could (if competent) exercise their right of self-determination. But if there is no room for exercising the right of self-determination, there is no room for its exercise either by proxy on behalf of incompetents or by competent individuals themselves.

One explanation of the *Dinnerstein* ruling's dangerous confusions is that it was attempting, unsuccessfully, to mark off not one but two types of resuscitation situations that it believed do not pose significant treatment choices and hence that do not present opportunities for a proxy exercise of the right of self-determination. The first are type-A cases described above, in which repeated resuscitation will at best restore cardiopulmonary functioning for a very brief period, perhaps at considerable cost to the patient. Even here the decision clearly requires moral judgment. Pretending that it is merely an exercise of the physician's professional expertise is sheer obfuscation. Further, although I will not argue the point here, I believe that a strong case can be made for following patients' wishes, if they are competent, or those of the family, if the patients are not competent. Nonetheless, it may not be plausible to require the legal machinery of proxy decision-making for most cases of this sort.

The second type of case is a subset of the type-B cases described above, "type B'." Here, unlike cases of type A, resuscitation may extend "life" for some considerable period—months or even years—but the "life" thus lengthened will be noncognitive, although the patient will not be dead according to the Harvard Criteria. Both Karen Quinlan and Shirley Dinnerstein would be included in this group. In these cases also it would be plausible to argue that resuscitation is not a significant treatment alternative of the sort that requires proxy decision-making for implementing a right of self-determination, but for quite different reasons than in cases of type A. One could argue that in type-B' cases the doctrine of substituted judgment no longer applies because we are no longer dealing with a living person, a being with a right of self-determination.

The *Dinnerstein* court, like other courts that have dealt with decision-making for incompetents, denied themselves this line of reasoning because they were not willing to question the adequacy of the Harvard Criteria and to grapple with the fundamental philosophical and constitutional issue of which beings have a right of self-determination.[32]

The difficulties raised by the *Dinnerstein* ruling cannot be eliminated by simply refecting the court's position on medical judgment and extending the doctrine of proxy decision-making to what I have called type-B' cases. For, as was noted earlier, there will be many cases in which the standard of substituted judgment will yield no defensible result simply because there is no reliable and clear evidence of what the patient would want if competent. But if, as several defenders of *Saikewicz* have claimed, we must fall back on the best-interest standard in such cases, the result may be quite unsettling.[33] For if the patient is in an irreversible vegetative state, it will not be possible to argue that nontreatment is in that patient's best interest on the grounds that the pain of the treatment outweighs any good it may produce. Instead, granted that the patient is in a vegetative state and therefore will experience no pain from treatment, the best-interest standard would seem to require resuscitation, unless we are willing to make the implausible assertion that it is in the patient's best interest to die, even when life can be preserved without suffering. It may be that the Appeals Court's unsuccessful attempt to exclude Shirley Dinnerstein from the domain of proxy decision-making was a desperate effort to avoid this disturbing conclusion.

The difficulty arises because of the unexamined assumption that the relevant notion of *interests* applies to individuals in an irreversible vegetative state. If these individuals can be said to have interests such that it makes sense to ask whether treatment is in their best interest, this is only because the word ''interest'' is being used in an extremely attenuated sense. We do perhaps operate with such an attenuated sense of the word when we speak of what is good or bad for lower forms of animal life or plants. But if this is the notion of interest we are to apply to an individual in an irreversible vegetative state, it is hard to see how withholding life-support could be in that individual's best interest any more than refraining from watering a plant could be said to be good for it.

It might be suggested that when the substituted-judgment standard yields no defensible result due to lack of evidence about the individual's preferences when competent, and when the best-interest standard yields counter-intuitive results because the applicable notion of interest is so attenuated, we may rely upon the reasonable-person standard. It may be that many reasonable persons would not wish to be maintained in an irreversible vegetative state. But if this is so, I suspect that it is because many reasonable people have a conception of what it is to be a person or a human being which includes the presence of some cognitive activity, or because there are limits on the burdens they are willing to impose on those who would care for them. On the other hand, there are others, including some active in the Pro-Life movement, who have a wider conception of what counts as a person or a human being. Consequently, to say that the reasonable-person test dictates that an individual in an irreversible vegetative state ought not to be resuscitated is to rely implicitly on a certain conception of personhood or upon certain substantive moral views, or both. It is to assume a definite answer to the basic philosophical and constitutional question while pursuing a strategy of trying to evade that question. Even if philosophical argument can show that the appropriate concept of a person includes the capacity for cognitive functioning, the courts could not settle the issue by simply asserting that most reasonable persons adhere to this concept, unless they were willing to employ a more substantive notion of ''reasonableness'' than current legal usage allows.

If the problem cannot be solved by simply defining as unreasonable those who deny that only cognitive existence should be sustained (or sustained at considerable cost to others), appeal to the reasonable-person standard here, as elsewhere, cannot be viewed as an implementation of the incompetent's right of self-determination. If the right of self-determination is a right to choose even when that choice diverges from the preferences of the majority of reasonable people, a procedure that uses a concept of the death of a person that some reasonable people reject is not an exercise of that right.

In sum, it appears that a coherent theory of decision-making for patients in an irreversible vegetative state requires a concept of the death of a person more refined than that of the Harvard Criteria.[34] Once the difficulties noted above of applying the concept of a right of self-determination are recognized, and once *Dinnerstein's* attempts to exclude decision about life-support for irreversibly vegetative patients are seen to be inadequate, an alternative approach becomes attractive. A cognitivist or higher-brain-function concept of death would allow us to replace the question "How can this person's right of self-determination be exercised?" with the question "What rights and interests do the family and the state have in determining what may be done with the mortal remains of what was formerly a person, and how are these rights and interests affected by the rights and interests of a living person in determining what is to be done with his remains when he died?" It is important to emphasize, of course, that even if the being in question is no longer a living person, there may still be significant moral constraints on our conduct toward it, though these constraints will be of a different sort. The advantage of this approach is that it meets the issues head-on where they should be met, thus avoiding the confusions that have plagued the decisions examined above.

3. A third and final problem that threatens to undermine the notion of a right of self-determination—not by stretching it beyond its coherent range of application, but by circumscribing it so severely as to rob it of all substance—is the interpretation of the state's interest in preventing suicide. The Supreme Judicial Court of Massachusetts offered a less than convincing explanation of why the interest in the prevention of suicide did not weigh against the need for proxy exercise of Joseph Saikewicz's right of self-determination.

> The interest in protecting against suicide seems to require little if any discussion. In the case of the imcompetent adult's refusing medical treatment such an act does not necessarily constitute suicide since (1) in refusing treatment the patient may not have the specific intent to die, and (2) even if he did, to the extent that the cause of death was from natural causes the patient did not set the death producing agent in motion with the intent of causing his own death. (3) Furthermore, the underlying state interest in this area lies in the prevention of irrational self-destruction. What we consider here is a competent, rational decision to refuse treatment when death is inevitable and the treatment offers no hope of cure or the preservation of life. There is no connection between the conduct here in issue and any state concern to prevent suicide.[35]

While the *Dinnerstein* ruling apparently did not even deem the question worth considering, the Massachusetts Appeals Court, in the recent *Spring* case, agreed with *Saikewicz*, concluding that "the policy against suicide [is] of no relevance."[36]

The first contention in the passage from *Saikewicz* cited above is dubious. In many cases, competent patients refusing resuscitation or some other life-support therapy will do so with the specific intent of ending their life. The second claim is also questionable because it assumes without argument that there is an obvious answer to the complex question of whether refraining from acting in certain cases counts as causing death. The law of homicide by omission recognizes that one person can bring about another's death by refraining from acting as well as by positive actions. But if one person can be said to cause another's death by refraining from acting, it is hard to see why one cannot cause one's own death in the same manner. It seems, therefore, that what is needed is a coherent account either of why one cannot bring about one's own death by refusing treatment or of why bringing about one's own death by refusing treatment, with the intent to do so, is not a case of suicide.

The third consideration advanced in the *Saikewicz* ruling is in some respects more promising, but it too raises difficulties that none of the subsequent rulings have addressed. The main problem lies in the interpretation of the notion of *rationality* presupposed by the claim that the state's interest is in preventing irrational self-destruction. If "rationality" is to be gauged here by the opinion of most reasonable people, the state's interest threatens to obliterate the right of self-determination understood as a right to make choices—even fatal choices—that the majority may not find reasonable. In the passage cited above, it seems that the Supreme Judicial Court of Massachusetts was able to conclude that the right of self-determination did not conflict with the state's interest in the prevention of suicide only by reducing the right of self-determination to a right to make a "rational decision to refuse treatment." Yet in supporting its original argument that competent patients have a right of self-determination that includes the right to refuse treatment, the Supreme Judicial Court of Massachusetts cited previous rulings that upheld the right of the individual to refuse life-saving treatment on the basis or religious beliefs that most reasonable people may reject.[37]

If, as was suggested earlier, the Harvard Criteria were replaced with a higher-brain-function concept of death, the state's interest in preventing suicide, regardless of how strongly or weakly that interest is interpreted, would be irrelevant in some of the cases discussed. If irreversibly vegetative patients are declared dead, there is no question of exercising their right either of self-determination or of suicide. Granted the momentous nature of such a declaration, a policy of applying a cognitivist conception of the death of a person in such cases would be morally defensible, of course, only within the framework of a set of institutional procedural safeguards. But for other cases, such as that of Joseph Saikewicz, the need to determine the mutual boundaries of the right of self-determination and the state's interest in preventing suicide is inescapable. Until this demarcation is achieved, recent judicial efforts to establish a substantive right of self-determination for competents and incompetents will remain incomplete and precarious.

IV

At the outset of this essay, I noted that recent attempts to develop a common-law doctrine of decision-making for terminally ill incompetents were a prime example of judicial conservatism. Each of the rulings considered above scrupulously avoided raising the fundamental philosophical and constitutional question "Which beings have rights?" in favor of the question "What rights do these individuals have and how may they be exercised (assuming that they have equal constitutional rights)?" Starting from this limited framework, attempts were then made to extend to incompetents a broad and substantive right of self-determination already recognized for competents.

If my criticisms are sound, these efforts are doomed to failure because proxy exercise of the right of self-determination is not possible for all of several types of cases that the courts have included in the class of "terminally ill incompetents." That class must be divided into two subclasses: Those individuals who possess at least the potential for the minimum cognitive functioning required for coherent ascription of the right of self-determination, and those who do not. The Harvard Brain Death Criteria, which the courts have not questioned, are not sufficient for determining the class of individuals to whom the right of self-determination may be ascribed, because those criteria classify as living persons some individuals who will never regain cognitive functioning.

Further, when the standard of substituted-judgment is not applicable, either because of insufficient evidence of the individual's preferences when competent, or because the individual never was capable of having the conceptually sophisticated preferences in question, proxy exercise of the right of self-determination is simply not possible. Efforts to employ the substituted-judgment standard in these cases only weaken the doctrine of self-determination by encouraging a lowering of the standards of evidence concerning what the individual would prefer if competent.

In some of the cases in which the substituted-judgment standard yields no defensible result, a retreat to the traditional doctrine of *parens patria* as acting in the incompetent's best interest will be appropriate. But not all cases in which the doctrine of substituted judgment is inapplicable are cases in which the patient has *interests* in the sense required for applying the best-interest standard. In some cases—those in which the patient is in an irreversible vegetative state—abandonment of the notion of proxy decision-making and recourse to a higher-brain-function concept of death seem inescapable.

In *Roe* v. *Wade*, the United States Supreme Court, by refusing to take a clear stand on the fundamental philosophical and constitutional question "who has rights?" and by concentrating instead on the scope of a woman's right of self-determination (as an application of the constitutional right of privacy) produced a decision that many found incoherent and that fully satisfied no one.[38] If my diagnosis of the inadequacies of the evolving doctrine of decision-making for terminally ill incompetents is accurate, judicial history is repeating itself with no less disturbing results.

Notes

1. The Ad Hoc Committee of the Harvard Medical School listed four criteria: (1) unreceptivity and unresponsivity, (2) no movements or breathing, (3) no reflexes, and (4) two flat electroencephalo-

grams, measured twenty-four hours apart (indicating no functioning in either the higher or lower brain). From "A Definition of Irreversible Coma," *Journal of the American Medical Association*, vol. 205, no. 6 (August, 1968), pp. 337-40).

2. For two interesting discussions of the relationship between these two aims, see H. Jonas, "Against the Stream: Comments on the Definition and Redefinition of Death" in *Philosophical Essays: From Ancient Creed to Technological Man*, (Englewood Cliffs, NJ: Prentice-Hall, 1974), pp. 132-40; and R. Veatch, "The Whole-Brain-Oriented Concept of Death: An Outmoded Philosophical Formulation, *Journal of Thanatology*, vol. 3, no. 11 (1975), pp. 13-17.

3. For arguments in favor of replacing the Harvard Criteria with a cognitivist or higher brain function conception of death, see Veatch.

4. These cases, in chronological order, are as follows: *Superintendent of Belchertown State School* v. *Saikewicz*, Mass., 370 N.E. 2d 417 (1977); *In the Matter of Earle N. Spring*, Mass. App., 399 N.E. 2d 493 (1979); and *In the Matter of Father Philip K. Eichner, S.M., on behalf of Brother Joseph Charles Fox*, Supreme Court, Appellate Division, Mass., Second Judicial Department (1980). A prominent exception, which is discussed below, is *In the Matter of Dinnerstein*, Mass. App., 380 N.E. 2d 134 (1978).

5. After citing case law establishing the doctrine of informed consent for medical treatment, the Supreme Judicial Court of Massachusetts in *Saikewicz* articulated the basis of the right to privacy, understood as a right of self-determination:

> Of even broader import, but arising from the same regard for human dignity and self-determination [as the doctrine of informed consent], is the unwritten constitutional right of privacy found in the penumbra of the Bill of Rights. *Griswold* v. *Connecticut*, 381 U.S. 479, 484, 85, S. Ct. 328, 13 L. Ed. 2d 339 (1965). As this constitutional guaranty reaches out to protect the freedom of a woman to terminate pregnancy under certain conditions, *Roe* v. *Wade*, 410 U.S. 113, 153, 93 S. Ct. 705, 35 L. Ed. 2d 147 (1973), so it encompasses the right of a patient to preserve his or her right to privacy against unwanted infringements of bodily integrity in appropriate circumstances. *In Re Quinlan*, supra 70 N.J. at 38-39, 355 A. 2d 647 (*Saikewicz*, p. 424).
>
> The constitutional right to privacy, as we see it, is an expression of the sanctity of individual free choice and self-determination as fundamental constituents of life. The value of life as so perceived is lessened not by a decision to refuse treatment, but by the failure to allow a competent human being the right of choice. (*Saikewicz*, p. 426).

In the court decision discussed in this essay, the terms "right to privacy" and "right of self-determination" are sometimes used interchangeably. In what follows, I use the latter term, both for the sake of uniformity and because it better expresses the content of the right in question.

6. *Roe* v. *Wade*, 410 U.S. 113 (1973).

7. *Saikewicz*, p. 427.

8. See, for example, *In the Matter of Earle N. Spring* and *In the Matter of Philip Eichner [Fox]*.

9. *Saikewicz*, p. 417.

10. "If a putative decision by Karen [Quinlan] to permit this non-cognitive, vegetative existence to terminate by natural forces is regarded as a valuable incident of her right to privacy, as we believe it to be, then it should not be discarded solely on the basis that her condition prevents her conscious exercise of the choice. The only practical way to prevent destruction of the right is to permit the guardian and family of Karen to render their best judgment, subject to the qualifications hereinafter stated [concerning consultation on prognosis], as to whether she would exercise it in these circumstances." (*Quinlan*, p. 429.) "[T]he goal is to determine with as much accuracy as possible the wants and needs of the individual involved. This may or may not conform to what is thought wise or prudent by most people." (*Saikewicz*, p. 430.) Thus *Saikewicz* explicitly distinguished the application of substituted judgment from "a reasonable-person inquiry" and from a decision according to the best-interest standard. Similarly, *Quinlan* held that the treatment decision was to be made by determining what Karen Quinlan, if competent, would choose, when there is no assumption that her choice must agree with that of most reasonable persons or would be in her best interests.

11. Judge Paul Liacos, author of the *Saikewicz* ruling, emphasized this development in an address to a conference sponsored by the American Society of Law and Medicine:

> . . . one of the fundamental aspects of the *Saikewicz* opinion has been largely overlooked, and that lies in the understanding of the fact that the interest of the state, sometimes defined under the concept of the so-called *parens patria* power, has been redefined so as to give recognition to the rights of individuals to control their own fate to a much larger extent. Those rights have been guaranteed by *Saikewicz*, not only to the competent, but to incompetent individuals as well. From *Medicolegal News*, vol. 7, no. 3 (Fall, 1979), p. 5.

12. *Saikewicz*, p. 425.

13. I examine the relation between the state's interest in preventing suicide and the right of self-determination in section III.

14. *Saikewicz*, pp. 433-4.

15. A. Relman, "The *Saikewicz* Decision: A Medical Viewpoint," *American Journal of Law and Medicine*, vol. 4 (1978), p. 236.

16. A. Buchanan, "Medical Paternalism" *Philosophy & Public Affairs*, vol. 7, no. 4 (Summer, 1978), pp. 370-90 (reprinted as chapter 4 of this book); "Medical Paternalism and Legal Imperialism: Not the Only Alternatives for Handling Saikewicz-type Cases," *American Journal of Law and Medicine*, vol. 5, no. 2 (1979), pp. 100-5.

17. Liacos, p. 6.

18. *Quinlan*, p. 647.

19. *Saikewicz*, pp. 429-30.

20. Although the *Saikewicz* ruling emphasized that the right of self-determination (or privacy) was a recognition of the sanctity of individual *choice*, neither it, nor any of the rulings discussed in this paper, ever considered whether the concept of choice is applicable to all the individuals the courts include under the term "incompetents."

21. *Saikewicz* suggested the following thought-experiment as a way of determining what Joseph Saikewicz would choose if he were competent:

> . . . one would have to ask whether a majority of people would choose chemotherapy if they were told merely that something outside of their previous experience was giong to be done to them, that this something would cause them pain and discomfort, that they would be removed to strange surroundings and possibly restrained for extended periods of time, and that the advantages of this course of action were measured by concepts of time and mortality beyond their ability to comprehend. (p. 430).

The inappropriateness of this "analogy" is obvious: the individuals described lack certain information, but they are nonetheless described as having the conceptual capacities required for choice, or self-determination. In particular, they are assumed to be able to understand language and to recognize that alternatives are being presented from which they are to choose. None of this applied to Joseph Saikewicz.

22. *Spring*, p. 500.

23. G. Annas and L. Glantz, brief *amicus curiae* (*Spring*) on behalf of The American Society of Law and Medicine, Inc. (1980), p. 15.

24. A brief argument can be sketched, however, in favor of the best-interest standard, where substituted judgment is inapplicable, at least in cases such as that of Joseph Saikewicz or Karen Quinlan. It can be argued that in such cases the best-interest standard has the advantage of determining the outcome solely on the basis of the patient's preferences (rudimentary though they may be), rather than on the basis of reasonable persons' preferences, which by hypothesis the patient cannot have. In that sense, the best-interest test does not impose others' values on the patient.

In a recent conversation, Professor John Robertson suggested to me that the *Saikewicz* ruling's version of the substituted-judgment standard can only be understood as a best-interest standard. Robertson also suggested that this latter standard is appropriate in such cases, but that the best interest of the individual should be weighed against certain social interests, granted the scarcity of medical resources. While I agree that an acceptable theory of proxy decision-making must ultimately be integrated with a larger theory of justice, including distributive justice, I cannot explore these systematic issues here. (For an overview of the general implications for health care of various theories of justice, see my essay, "Justice: A Philosophical Review," in *Justice and Healthcare*, ed E.E. Shelp (Dordrecht, Holland: Reidel Publishing, forthcoming).

25. *Quinlan*, p. 647.

26. G. Annas has defended this aspect of the *Quinlan* decision, contending that the court "defined a legally acceptable *medical* standard for decision making . . . " ("Reconciling Quinlan and Saikewicz," *American Journal of Law and Medicine*, vol. 4, no. 4 (1979), p. 371). I have argued that Annas has failed to distinguish between medical judgment (concerning prognosis) and moral decision ("Medical Paternalism and Legal Imperialism," pp. 114-6).

27. *Dinnerstein*, pp. 134-6.

28. *Ibid.*, p. 129.

29. *Ibid.*, p. 138.

30. *Ibid.*, p. 138.

31. *Ibid.*, p. 138.

32. For a briefer critique of *Dinnerstein*, and one with which I am in substantial agreement, see John Robertson, "Legal Criteria for Orders Not to Resuscitate: A Response to Justice Liacos," *Medicolegal News*, vol. 7, no. 3 (February, 1980), pp. 4-6.

33. In "Medical Paternalism and Legal Imperialism" I suggested that, in spite of its professed use of the substituted-judgment standard, the Supreme Judicial Court of Massachusetts in *Saikewicz* fell back on the best-interests test. I also implied that this procedure was appropriate, without noting that there are some cases in which the best-interests standard produces counter-intuitive results.

34. For what appears to be the most perceptive philosophical examination of the concept of brain death, see M. Green and D. Wikler, "Brain Death and Personal Identity," *Philosophy & Public Affairs*, vol. 9, no. 2 (1980), pp. 105-33. Green and Wikler argue in favor of the replacement of the traditional cardiopulmonary criterion for death by the brain-death criterion on the grounds that personal identity does not "survive the kinds of changes which brain death involves." Their view is (1) that for a given patient to be *Jones*, i.e., this particular person, is for him to have certain psychological traits (certain memories, etc.); (2) that "when brain death strips the body of its psychological traits" (p. 118) the patient ceases to be Jones; and (3) that the patient's ceasing to be Jones is Jones's death. Although I believe that the authors' analysis is compatible with all the arguments of the present essay, there are two problems with their approach that can be stated only briefly here. First, if Green's and Wikler's arguments succeed, they show not that brain death *is* the death of the person, but rather that brain death is a sufficient, though not a necessary, condition for that person's death. For brain death is the death of the *whole* brain and it is possible for the lower brain to survive the death of those higher brain centers that, as Green and Wikler acknowledge, are the seat of the psychological traits that constitute personal identity. It follows, then, that if the authors' view of personal identity is correct, it provides the basis not only for replacing the cardiopulmonary criterion by the brain-death criterion, but also for replacing the brain-death criterion by what I have called a higher-brain or cognitive criterion. Second, it is not at all clear that Green and Wikler have succeeded in defending the brain-death criterion as a basis for determining how we ought to treat those who are brain dead without relying implicitly on an "account of the essence or personhood," as they claim to have done (p. 120). At one point, the authors conclude that "If, as has been established above, removal of the conscious, functioning brain leaves us with a body not identical to the person formerly associated with it, surely removal of the dead brain leaves just the same thing; and no more remains when the brain died in place" (p. 127). Yet if we are to draw conclusions that this termination of support is permissible, we must assume that the death of the brain, since it involves the cessation of all psychological traits, implies not only the patient ceasing to be this particular person, but also the patient ceasing to be a person. For it could be argued that it is conceivable that the brain in question could change so radically that *Jones* would cease to exist, although there would still be a person living. And as Green and Wikler admit, we are concerned to preserve the lives of

persons, not just the life of a particular person, Jones. The authors may be assuming that the changes that involve the loss of Jones's personal identity are also incompatible with the existence of any person. But if so, they are tacitly relying upon an account of what it is to be a person, not just upon an account of personal identity.

35. *Saikewicz*, p. 426.

36. *Spring*, p. 502.

37. *Saikewicz*, pp. 424-5. Included here are well-known cases in which the courts have upheld an individual's refusal to be given blood transfusions on religious grounds that the majority may find unreasonable (*In re Brooks Estate*, 32 III. 2d 361, 205 N.E. 2d 435, 1965).

38. As many critics have pointed out, the major difficulty with the decision is that the appeal to the woman's right of self-determination (or privacy) is insufficient justification for abortion unless some reason is given for excluding fetuses from the class of persons. For unless they are so excluded, the antiabortionist can argue that the state's interest in protecting innocent third parties opposes and outweighs the right of self-determination.

Chapter 11

Cooperative Paternalism versus Conflictful Paternalism

Jack D. Douglas

> Receiving bread from us, they will see clearly that we take the bread made by their hands from them, to give it to them, without any miracle, but in truth they will be more thankful for taking it from our hands than for the bread itself! For they will remember only too well that in old days, without our help, even the bread they made turned to stones in their hands, while since they have come back to us, the very stones have turned to bread in their hands. Too, too well they know the value of complete submission! And until men know that, they will be unhappy.

> . . . In his old age he reached the clear conviction that nothing but the advice of the great dread spirit could build up any tolerable sort of life for the feeble, unruly "incomplete, empirical creatures created in jest." And so, convinced of this, he sees that he must follow the council of the wise spirit, the dread spirit of death and destruction, and accept lying and deception, and lead men consciously to death and destruction. He sees that he must deceive them all that way so that they may not notice where they are being led, that the poor blind creatures may at least on the way think themselves happy.

> Fyodor Dostoyevsky,
> "The Grand Inquisitor,"
> from *The Brothers Karamazov*

Since we human beings are "rational" creatures who act to maximize, or, at the least, to optimize what we believe to be "goods" or pleasure for ourselves, those who wish to influence our actions normally do so by trying to show implicitly or

I greatly appreciate the helpful criticisms Margaret Battin and other participants in the conference on paternalism made of an earlier draft of this paper.

171

explicitly that acting in the way they want us to will be "good" for us. Mothers and fathers, friends and enemies, lovers and haters, Popes and generals, Christs and Satans—all must submit to the same devices of self-presentation in terms of our own best interest, if they are to influence us.

Since we human beings know from experience that others who are well intentioned toward us, and especially those who like, care for, and love us, will generally, but not always, *try* to influence us in ways they sincerely believe will lead to our "good," we are normally most influenced by those we believe to have good intentions toward us, especially by those we believe love us or, at least, like us. Priests and advertisers, lovers and seducers, sales agents and swindlers, politicians and kings, autocrats and democrats—all try to convince those they wish to influence, control, or exploit, that they are benevolent, kindly, altruistic, friendly, caring, and loving.

Since we human beings also know from experience that parents are normally very loving toward their children and, because of this, normally try to influence their children in ways that will be to their own best good, regardless of what the children think (which is the definition of paternalistic behavior), maternalism and paternalism have always been among the most successful devices of self-presentation by those who wish to influence others. Popes and kings, village heads and bureaucrats, police officers and psychiatrists, mentors and employers—all have often made use of the ideas of paternalism (or, more rarely, of maternalism) in trying to get others, especially those they consider to be inferiors, to do what they want them to do.

The everyday facts about paternalism are so obvious to common sense that philosophers and legal analysts normally do not take them into consideration explicitly in their complex arguments for and against various ideas and principles of paternalism. It is especially striking that they rarely give explicit consideration to genetic paternalism and maternalism, that is, the paternalism and maternalism actually practiced by genetic (natural) parents. (It is not uncommon for them to state in passing that their arguments do not violate common sense understanding of actual parental behavior. (Dworkin, Gert and Culver, for example, make this statement twice.[1]) But that hardly constitutes a discussion of the everyday relations between parents and children.) There seems to be an implicit assumption that genetic paternalism is unproblematic morally, whereas extensions of paternalism are inherently problematic because they are inherently very different from genetic paternalism. An examination of the everyday realities of paternalism justifies neither of these assumptions and lays the foundations for a different and, it is to be hoped, more realistic and fruitful analysis of the pluses and minuses of paternalism.

THE GENETIC REALITIES OF PATERNALISM

Genetic mother-child and father-child relations are, of course, the bedrock of human society. These relations vary in strength from one culture to another, depending on how extended the family is, the presence or absence of surrogates (such as normatively prescribed relations between mother's brother and sister's son), the degree of everyday interaction, the degree of actual and expected economic dependence on each other, individual variations, and many other factors. But almost everywhere parent-child relations are the closest and most important relations in the early years of a child's life. They are normally built on the powerful emotion of caring love. There are obviously situational and individual variations in the degree to which parents feel caring love, with some parents feeling so little that they can abandon their children (although almost always with the certainty that the other parent or a surrogate will continue to care for them). Because of this variability, and especially because of the willingness of some parents to turn the care of their children over to surrogates for support, societies normally have stern moral rules commanding parental caring for the child. But genetically determined caring love is the core, the immediate source, of the parent-child relationship. Parents who do not feel caring love and who abandon their children are seen by most people as "monsters" who lack the natural instincts.

Caring love inspires in the parents a deep and sincere commitment to "care for" the child, to act in ways they sincerely believe will be for the best interests, the good of the child. The child's best interest is obviously conceived of in the very long-run terms of a lifetime.

Parents willingly sacrifice many of children's short-run pleasures to their lifetime interests, and socially shared moral rules normally prescribe this. In doing so, parents obviously engage in the full gamut of behavior commonly referred to as paternalism, ranging from the "weak paternalism" of attempts to influence behavior indirectly, through direct attempts to control behavior noncoercively and attempts to interfere with liberty of action, to the very "strong paternalism" of severely coercive actions.

It is, of course, biologically necessary that some competent adult do all these things to and for children, first to keep them alive and then to teach them to be competent adults so they can live, propagate, and in turn socialize the new generation to be competent adults. (It is obvious that more extreme forms of coercion, normally called "abuse," are not necessary genetically and can even be highly destructive. But even parents who beat their children severely seem commonly to believe that this is "for their own best interest," especially as a means of teaching the children to live morally. If parents believe in eternal damnation for transgressors, it is easy enough to see how they might be willing to inflict severe pain on their children to prevent their being damned to eternal hellfire. Such parents become Grand Inquisitors in miniature.) The child is necessarily dependent on the parent or parent surrogate. The caring love of the parents is the genetically determined motivational guarantee that maternal and paternal care will, on average, be provided.

It is crucial to note that both the caring love and the *interests* of parents lead them to *sincerely* act in ways they believe are in the best long-run interest of their child, that one of their primary goals in doing this is to teach the child to be a competent adult, and that a large, but culturally variable, degree of independence from paternalistic (and maternalistic) control is a vital part of the competence-training parents provide. Genetic paternalism is, on average, sincerely aimed at helping the child over the long run to become largely independent of paternalism. (If one acts paternalistically for the dependent's best interest, but *not* to make the dependent independent over the long run, I shall call this *minimally cooperative paternalism.*) The biological reason for this is that independence is in fact to children's best survival interests, to the best interests of those who sincerely feel caring love for them (because their interests, while not identical with the children's, largely overlap theirs), to the best economic interests of parents who are supporting them, and to the best biological interest of anyone who shares their genes. (Parents not only train children to become independent, but in most cultures they also teach them to eventually become paternalistic toward the increasingly dependent, aging parents.) Parental love, genetic interest (in the child's producing grandchildren), and economic interest are powerful motives for parents to teach children to become independent.

Genetic paternalism is by far the most important form of *sincerely cooperative paternalism.* Sincerely cooperative paternalism is any form of paternalism (doing good for others in the name of "what is good for them") in which those acting paternally are sincerely acting to help the other person become more independently competent over the long run, and the other person sincerely believes this is the case. Cooperative paternalism is grounded in a *perceived mutuality of interests.* The parents and the children each perceive the other to be sincerely acting in a cooperative dominant (parent) and submissive (child) manner *because they perceive that the other loves them.* Even when children believe that their parents are completely wrong about what is to their best interest, they rarely rebel and will often go along with the parents' desires (especially publicly) as long as they perceive that the parents love them. If they do not perceive love, they will often be distrusting and rebellious, regardless of whether they believe the parents are right about their interests. (It is, of course, possible for one partner to be sincerely cooperative and the other not, or for the child to believe it is not cooperative when it is, in which case we have asymmetric cooperative paternalism. But symmetric relations seem far more common.)

Conflictful paternalism is any form of paternalism that is not aimed at the long-run independent competence and equality of the submissive member of the relation. In conflictful paternalism, individuals may or may not exploit submissive persons materially, but they necessarily exploit them in terms of power and pride. Human beings, like all higher animals,[2] have strong dominance drives. Those who succeed in dominance-striving are rewarded with the powerful feeling of pride; those who fail suffer the tortures of shame. The more the submissive person identifies with the dominant one, the less the feeling of "failing in dominance-striving," because the individual is not striving *against* the other. Since love involves a high degree of self-identification, and thus a relatively high degree of perceived identification of interests, the more love there is between individuals, the less dominance-striving there is, so the less one who is in fact submissive feels shame. Children who love and are loved can be proud of being "dutiful children," rather than feel shameful at being submissive. Cooperative paternalism thus does not generate shame on the part of the submissive partner. But conflictful paternalism does generate pride in the dominant and shame in the submissive in direct proportion to the degree of perceived submission. As the degree of perceived conflict of interests increases, the degree of frustration, envy, and resentment also increases. When the degree of perceived conflict and perceived submission are both high, the dominance-submission relations become almost unbearably painful, and the tendency to rebellion becomes intense.

But open rebellion may still not occur. Individuals accept submission in direct proportion to their feeling a need to do so. *The common pattern is for individuals to accept submission only to the degree that they feel threatened by not doing so.* The more children feel threatened by the world, or threatened by the parents themselves for independence-striving, the more their tendency to remain submissive and dependent; and, conversely, the less they feel threatened by the world and by the parents for independence-striving, the more they reject their submission and strive for independence. As children come to feel more competent at making their own living and managing all the problems of living, they begin to reject submission and to become independent, and then begin to strive for dominance themselves over those with whom they do not feel loving identification. If the parents support this, children rapidly become independent and strive for dominance outside the home. If the parents try to keep them in submission, they will fight back—rebel—in innumerable ways, unless they feel incompetent, and thus too threatened to break loose.

Philosophical and legal discussions of paternalism have normally focused their attention on the *claims* made by those supposedly acting paternalistically that they are acting "in the best interest" of the individuals being treated as dependents, that they are "caring for" the dependents. While we have only unusual instances for doubting this with genetic parents, we shall see that the distinctions between claims, sincere commitments, and real outcomes are of vital importance in evaluating the intents and effects of nongenetic paternalism. But the first and greatest weakness of the philosophical and legal discussions has been their failure to note *the crucial fact of genetic paternalism: that on average it is sincerely aimed at training the child to become independent of the parents, even to replacing them, and that it in fact achieves this in the vast majority of cases with at least minimal success.*

GENETIC AND SOCIAL EXTENSIONS OF PATERNALISM

Parent-child relations are on average inspired far more by what behavioral biologists call *reciprocal altruism* than any other human relations.[3] Reciprocal altruism exists when individuals help each other even when, in the short run, the help rendered is not to the best material interests of the individual giving the help.

In parent-child relations, relations among siblings, and to a rapidly decreasing degree, in other family relations, the short-run losses in survival value to the helper are clearly offset by the long-run genetic interests of increasing the reproductive potential of the one helped. It even "pays" parents genetically to risk their lives up to a point[4] to save the child, and the same is true, although possibly less so, for the child.

In most higher animals, although probably not in all, the extreme reciprocal altruism of such lower animals as ants and bees is replaced by a considerably more "selfish" set of emotions, motives, and patterns of behavior. This is true even within family groups and is very obviously true within human community groups. Genetically, just as Adam Smith and the other liberal economists assumed from their own observations of human beings in action in everyday life, human beings are predominantly governed by self-interest, at least beyond the narrow genetic bonds of the family group. Yet it is also clear that human beings do behave in reciprocally altruistic ways beyond family groups. The crucial question is: Under what conditions does sincere altruistic behavior aimed at the eventual independence of the person helped exist?

The obvious first possibility is that behavior similar to parental behavior, that is, maternalistic and paternalistic behavior, will arise in relations that involve caring-love feelings and long-run reciprocal interests in training the helped individuals to become independent. When we look at the wide gamut of human relations, we find that there are many obvious examples of such paternalistic relations. Friendship relations are normally between roughly equal partners, rather than between independent and dependent partners. But an inherent aspect of friendly relations is that each is dependent on the other emotionally because of the caring love involved. Moreover, friends expect each other to help them when they are in a weaker position, and each expects to help the other in those situations. The normal friendship involves rapid oscillations between being dependent and providing help; and the help provided is aimed at making the other strong enough to be independent, to stand on his or her own feet once again. Friendships thus come to be reciprocally paternalistic relations at times.

The powerful bonds of friendship and their reciprocal paternalism are found in all human societies and the great majority of individuals, especially boys and men, develop these bonds. Some anthropologists, especially Lionel Tiger,[5] have argued that there is a specific genetic bonding of men in hunting groups that leads them to patterns of reciprocal altruism almost as strong as those found within the nuclear family. It is quite true that friendly bonds are most powerful on average in men who face the dangers of warfare, hunting, politics, imprisonment, and similar activities. These sometimes become "sacred bonds" that go beyond caring love and take on overtones of romantic love. But friendships can become that close in any walk of life, with each friend identifying his or her interests extremely closely with those of the other. Montaigne's famous essay on friendship described one of his own friendships in just those terms, while explicitly denying that there was any element of "Greek" feeling (homosexual romantic love) involved. It seems more likely that friendship and its pervasive pattern of reciprocally cooperative paternalism has always been part of human (genetic) nature, and hunting, warfare, and similar dangerous situations are merely situations that commonly elicit the loving feelings and altruistic behavior more than nondangerous situations. (The reciprocal altruism of a team of mountain-climbers fighting against shared dangers and agony has reportedly "welded the team tightly together for life."[6]) In general, it appears that *friendship has developed as a distinctly human bonding to provide help in general to each partner*, thus increasing the adaptation of both partners, and thence spreading the genes that make it possible.

Friendship is only one, although by far the most common, of the many forms of caring, loving, reciprocally altruistic human relations. There are many others that involve far more inequality in decision-making than friendship, thus making them more paternalistic. Because of the fundamental importance in human life of cultural transmission, all human societies have developed role relationships in which older, culturally superior, more knowledgeable members teach younger members valued (and generally adaptive) aspects of the culture. The genetic parents obviously do this cultural training more than anyone else. But even the simplest societies seem to have some nonparental cultural transmission roles. In these role relations, the teachers generally become parent substitutes and behave paternalistically toward the student. These roles commonly involve varying degrees of caring love and reciprocal altruism in which the parent figure controls the learning, and often the other behavior, of the child-figure for the child's own good. Very importantly, this paternalistic relation, just like the genetic one, is aimed at making the child-figure eventually independent of the teacher and equal to the teacher. Indeed, such roles are often used not only to transmit already created culture, but also to create culture, so that teachers are commonly trying to teach students to eventually be superior to themselves.

It is of crucial importance to note that the paternalistic teacher's relation with the student must closely parallel the genetic paternalistic role in order to succeed. That is, the teacher must be closely involved with the student, must know and treat the student as an individual, must show by actions that the teaching is aimed at the best interest of the student, especially at making the student an independent, equal (or even superior) master someday. In short, the teacher must be seen by the student to have the same caring feeling and altruistic behavior as the parents. The student can then feel secure enough in the relationship and identified enough with the master to submit to the master, that is, to become dependent and submissive (thus vulnerable), to develop the dependent-caring love of the child that enables the child to literally identify with the master and to learn to be like the master by being, doing, and feeling with the master. This dependency allows the master to develop and even recreate the life of the student for the student's own good. The master can thus have a profound effect on the emotions, beliefs, behavior, and entire future of the student.

We might note a certain emotional difference in relations between the master and student from those between the parent and child. A child may feel "awe" for the parent, especially in the traditional pattern of the highly patriarchal family. But normally this feeling of "awe" is dominated by a feeling of love, so the child feels an awed-loving. In master-student relations there are, certainly under the most successful conditions, some feelings of love, but these are normally dominated by feelings of "awe," at least in the beginning when the differences in competence and the dominance-submission relations are the greatest. The student feels a loving-awe under the most successful conditions. This dominance of awe, as long as it is combined with caring-love feelings, seems to facilitate submission and identification, so the master may have a greater effect in shaping a student's life than a parent for whom the student feels awed-love. Of course, if submissive individuals feel an awed-fear or fearful-awe, they may remain submissive, but they do not identify with their masters and secretly try to avoid becoming like them.

When the conditions of sincerely cooperative paternalism are not met, these learning roles do not work and are commonly rejected, just as genetic paternalism roles are rejected when they are not *sincerely* cooperatively paternalistic. If students feel that their masters are manipulating them for the masters' interests, they will feel betrayed and will act the way betrayed human beings do. The close personal contact that seems so universal in successful learning relations seems essential in maintaining the caring love and reciprocal altruism of both partners. This close contact also seems essential in maintaining the perception of caring and altruism that enables each partner to feel secure in his or her role with the other. (At the same time, aloofness and awayness inspire more feeling of awe. Loving-awe is inspired by a delicate combination of slightly aloof superiority with caring closeness.) A fatherly Zen master or Vedantic teacher can demand and receive almost complete submission in recreating the life of the student, but an impersonal, bureaucratic university that tries to operate *in loco parentis* will commonly generate only resentment or even open rebellion, unless the student feels too threatened to rebel.

There are also the many arguments over the centuries that the human being is by nature altruistic, either reciprocally or asymmetrically, toward other human beings beyond the limits of family and close personal relations that build on the family relations. One of the clearest and most empirical arguments comes from ancient China during the Period of Troubles in which all the basic arguments over human nature were debated just as hotly as in our modern world. Mencius, taking the Confucian position that human beings are by nature altruistic, and thus normally practice sincerely cooperative paternalism, supported his argument by example. If a person sees an unknown child about to be run over by a cart, the person will grab and save the child. I think we all know innumerable instances in which adults do in fact behave altruistically and paternalistically toward children, even those who are strangers. (Mencius's example is sincerely altruistic because the person clearly acted on behalf of the child's interest, probably with some small risk to self, and it is paternalistic because the person did so for the child's best interest, without consulting the child's will.) Although cultural variables, such as

"Christian charity" (as taught by the Good Samaritan parable), can increase or decrease this paternalistic behavior toward children unrelated to the benefactors, it does appear to be universal. In fact, it closely parallels the same paternalistically protective behavior of other primates toward unrelated children of the same species. Closely connected with this phenomenon of random paternalism toward children is the random feeling of pity and caring love that adults have toward unrelated children and that even small children have toward unrelated babies. Everybody feels caring-love for "cute" babies (and almost all babies are cute).

It is crucial to note that Mencius, like modern charities in their advertisements to get money, used children as his example, especially very small children, defenseless children, noncompetitors. And he mentioned only a situation in which the risk to the benefactor was very small and very brief. Almost anyone will take a small, one-time risk to save a child, but few will take a single large risk or many small risks that add up to a larger one for a nonrelated child, and almost no one will take larger risks for adults when they recognize the risks involved. (Police officers and fire-fighters may take a number of small risks during their careers, but they continually remind us forcefully that they expect to be paid very well in advance, and upon retirement for a lifetime, in return for the small risks.)

Arguments that human beings are by nature more generally altruistic than this, and that they will thus act sincerely in their paternalistic actions to help the other person to become independent, almost always fail to note the simple difference between public presentations and private (secret) motivations. Saints have long been presented as "obvious" examples in Western societies of sincerely altruistic and paternalistic individuals. Yet saints are a very poor example, possibly the worst. Saints are generally individuals striving strenuously to achieve fame and power—dominance—within the hierarchy of Western religion. Edward Wilson has rightly seen behind the public humility of saints to detect the fierce pride of dominance involved in Christian altruism:

> Can culture alter human behavior to approach altruistic perfection? Might it be possible to touch some magical talisman or design a Skinnerian technology that creates a race of saints? The answer is no. In sobering reflection, let us recall the words of Mark's Jesus: "Go forth to every part of the world, and proclaim the Good News to the whole creation. Those who believe it and receive baptism will find salvation; those who do not believe will be condemned." There lies the fountainhead of religious altruism. Virtually identical formulations, equally pure in tone and perfect with respect to ingroup altruism, have been urged by the seers of every major religion, not omitting Marxism-Leninism. All have contended for supremacy over others. Mother Teresa is an extraordinary person but it should not be forgotten that she is secure in the service of Christ and the knowledge of her Church's immortality. Lenin, who preached a no less utopian, if rival, covenant, called Christianity unutterably vile and a contagion of the most abominable kind; that compliment has been returned many times by Christian theologians.

"If only it were all so simple!" Aleksandr Solzhenitsyn wrote in *The Gulag Archipelago*. "If only there were evil people somewhere insidiously committing evil deeds, and it were necessary only to separate them from the rest of us and destroy them. But the line dividing good and evil cuts through the heart of every human being. And who is willing to destroy a piece of his own heart?"

Sainthood is not so much the hypertrophy of human altruism as its ossification. It is cheerfully subordinate to the biological imperatives above which it is supposed to rise.[7]

We would also note that Saint Bernard, like so many other hundreds of thousands of other would-be saints, was at that time on a mission for the forces of the Inquisition. His "fatherly" actions were aimed at suppressing possible heretics for all time, certainly in the name of the public interest and possibly "for their own good," and it is most unlikely he ever had any intention of making anyone independent of church absolutism.

In the last century, Kropotkin rightly pointed out that social Darwinists normally overlooked the many cooperative elements in society, both human and nonhuman. Reciprocal altruism is vital to human life. But he and his successors have normally failed to note that voluntary, cooperative relations are normally built on very clear expectations of reciprocation and on the belief of both parties that they will be better off by the transaction. Although there are isolated acts of sincere paternalism beyond the limits of family and close (caring) relations, especially toward children, these are by far the exception. They appear to be primarily a result of cultural conditioning and individual variations, both of which are unreliable in comparison to the far more reliable genetic drives toward dominance. Given what we know about primate and human nature, protestations of sincere paternalism are far more apt to be public fronts intended to hide attempts to dominate the lives of others than they are to be sincerely altruistic acts aimed at helping and making the individual independent in the long run.

THE GROWTH AND DECAY OF PATERNALISTIC RELATIONS

One of the most common forms of paternalism, one that all civilizations seem to develop to a high degree under certain conditions, is found in the lord-peasant relations known as feudalism. The basic relation of dominance and submission known roughly as *feudalism first develops and prospers in periods of severe perceived military threat*. Although there are always situational differences, European feudalism seems to have been reasonably representative. (The situational variations within Europe were as great as those outside.) As Marc Bloch noted, "Feudalism was born in the midst of an infinitely troubled epoch, and in some measure it was the child of those troubles themselves."[8] The civil wars among the descendants of Charlemagne and the terrifying invasions of Moslems, Hungarians, and Scandinavians made life perilous for the peasants of most of Europe. Unable to defend themselves without leadership and heavier armament than they could provide individually, and without central leadership to protect themselves, they became the dependents (vassals) of the lords in exchange for their independent leadership and, above all, protection by their skill in war. The relations between leader and followers were undoubtedly very close in the beginning. It was precisely because the lord was immediately at hand, whereas any titular king was far away, that he could give more protection. His closeness would also allow the peasants to judge how trustworthy he was, how caring and effective he really was at protecting them. Although we do not know from the records, the relations in the beginning must have been very much like friendship relations except that one partner was clearly meant to provide the independent decision-making of leadership and protection and the other was to be the dependent follower. The difference between leading and following, independency and dependency, must also have been small. In a rough way, the peasants reverted to partially childlike dependency in exchange for the fatherly protection of the lord. The standard translation of the vassals' pledge of their "commendation" to the lord uses the word "guardianship" for the lord's expected relationship to the vassal:

> To that magnificent lord, so and so, I, so and so. Since it is known familiarly to all how little I have whence to feed and clothe myself, I have therefore petitioned your piety, and your good will has decreed to me that I should hand myself over or commend myself to your guardianship, which I have thereupon done; that is to say in this way, that you should aid and succor me as well with food as with clothing, according as I shall be able to serve you and deserve it. And as long as I shall live I ought to provide service and honor to you, suitably to my free condition; and I shall not during the time of my life have the ability to withdraw from your power or guardianship; but must remain during the days of my life under your power or defense.[9]

The peasants probably expected to become independent some day when the invasions were over, but when the invasions ended the lords were stronger than ever and had come to provide the basic services of government. Regardless of what peasants might have preferred, once the threat was past, the lords remained and proceeded to extend their "paternal" relations with the peasants. There is actually considerable evidence[10] that when the immediate threat was past, the relations between vassals and lords were less paternalistic, more voluntary, and included equal exchanges of "aid and counsel." The vassals seemed to have considerable independence through their assemblies of vassals, which counseled the lord on all matters concerning their relationship with him, and even in shifting allegiances to new lords when the old ones were too constraining. Still, in most areas of Europe, where feudalism began in the post-Carolingian time of troubles, it remained. The kernel of paternalistic dependency remained to be expanded later into full-blown dependency as the lords grew in military strength by centralizing and solidifying their pyramid of paternalistic power. Today we are apt to look at those relations as highly exploitive, at least as they were once the original crisis was past. And certainly by the fourteenth century there were enough peasant rebellions, such as that by Nat Tyler and his many followers, to make it obvious that many peasants did too. But we must not forget that, at least in the earlier centuries, most lords remained reasonably close to the land. They thus knew the peasants well and developed caring feelngs for them. Most of them fulfilled their many obligations of providing paternal help to the dependent peasants. If given a completely free choice, it seems very likely the peasants would have chosen to become independent—free. But, of course, they did not have a completely free choice, although from the twelfth century on more and more of them were able to choose to move to the growing free cities. When the initial threat of invasion passed, the peasants were no longer free to choose independence; they were locked into a paternalistic dependence that eventually became increasingly uncooperative, not aimed at their independence but at their perpetual dependence and submission. The lords continued at all times to present the front of sincerely cooperative paternalism, and developed the abstract ethos of "noblesse oblige" to replace more informal, caring relations. But the realities became increasingly clear to the dependents and, thus, increasingly unacceptable to most of them *whenever there appeared to be a way out of the dependency.*

It would appear in general that the paternalistic relations of feudalism were more sincerely cooperative, although probably never intended by the lords to lead to vassal independence, the closer the lords were to their vassals. As the lords centralized their power, they necessarily moved away from the vassals because they had less time. As they moved away, their relations became more formalized, more abstract, more impersonal, more determined by values and laws than by basic feelings and concrete situations. The lords moved from a minimal form of cooperative paternalism to one of conflictful paternalism in which they used their growing power to prevent the increasingly resentful and angry vassals from becoming independent. Still, even with the growing reliance on force to prevent the vassals' escape, in most of Europe and especially in the Mediterranean societies, the front of paternalism was maintained and was probably often vital in preventing successful revolutions.

The paternalism of feudalism evolved into the paternalism of *patronage* or a *patriot system.* Patronage systems are even more widespread in human societies than feudalism, and are probably created wherever there are wide disparities in social knowledge and material goods so that some part of the population can only subsist marginally by depending on the better-off to protect them from the great risks of subsistence-living *when family relations cannot meet this need.* The paternalism of a feudal system, at least one that still functions anywhere near the ideal of European feudalism, is limited by the granting of a fief by the lord to the vassal under conditions that make it difficult for the lord to take away the fief and by the roughly egalitarian requirements that the lord be "counseled" by the vassals concerning their welfare. When fiefs became hereditary in Europe, almost certainly because the vassals had considerable bargaining power once the time of troubles was past, paternalism was distinctly limited until the growing centralization of the lords' power encouraged its increase once again.

Similar limitations appear to exist in the paternalistic system known as the *jajmani system* of India. The jajman-kamin system (also known by many other terms throughout India[11]) has given rise to the same kinds of evaluations in terms of paternalistic "exploitation" that feudalism has in Europe, almost certainly because it has so many of the same features. Wiser's[12] original work on the subject emphasized the dependency of the kamin on the jajman, but also saw their relationship as basically an egalitarian one in which the kamin received services (both social and ritual) and land use in exchange for his own services and produce of the land to the jajman. Beidelman[13] subsequently tried to show that the relationship is literally a feudal one that is overwhelmingly economic and basically exploitative:

> The *jajmani* system is a feudalistic system of prescribed, hereditary obligations of payment and of occupational and ceremonial duties between two or more specific families of different castes in the same locality . . . . The most important power determinant in the *jajmani* system is land. It is almost impossible to over-emphasize land tenure in this respect, and it is this that places the *jajman* in a position far superior to a kamin. This importance of land is due to two factors: (1) land is usually very unequally divided in Indian villages and most tends to be held by only one or a few castes; (2) India is an enormously populous agricultural nation, 75% rural, so that the land is the chief means for security and wealth.
>
> Thus a *jajman* may often be equated with a landlord and a *kamin* with a tenant laborer. The *jajman's* aim is a ready and cheap labor supply, the *kamin's*, some means of gaining access to land or produce and thus security. *Kamins* therefore depend directly or indirectly for most of their food upon the relationship between themselves and their *jajmans*. This principle is at the core of the traditional *jajmani* payments which stress gifts of grain, a form of payment which has increased in importance with the rising population pressure upon the land.
>
> I conclude that although the *jajmani* system is extremely complex its prime determinants rest upon the basis of land, and it is this relationship to the land which assigns roles and power wthin this system. Both land and number favor the *jajman* and such power has been often used by *jajmans* to utilize ceremony and ritual as secondary enforcements of such a position. *Jajmans* occupy the apex in an agrarian socio-economic system (*jajmani* system) which may be considered feudalistic. This power position of the *jajman* enables him to derive preferential payments, prestige, and other benefits and enables him to coerce local integration of caste roles which stabilizes his position despite the tensions within such relationships.[14]

Beidelman stresses the general poverty, lack of land, and the subsistence level living of the kamins as the basic motives for their dependency. He also sees this dependency as all the greater when the kamins' tenancy is uncertain because it is not hereditary:

> In comparison to the *jajmans*, the strength of the *kamins* is much less, and one clearly sees that the locus of power in this system lies with the *jajman*. Such power as the *kamin* does have depends upon his ability to offer a monopolized and necessary service to his *jajman*. If a *kamin* can be replaced or if the *jajman* may dispense with the *kamin's* services, then the *kamin's* strength is utterly lost. The data show cases of *jajmans* shaving themselves, beating drums at their own ceremonies, doing their own carpentry work, etc., when their *kamins* have gone on strike. In such a way *kamins* are very vulnerable indeed. Weakened caste values on forbidden tasks or on the ritual necessity of certain services such as those of a barber or Brahman may thus undermine ritual needs.[15]

This supposedly leads the jajman to be more exploiting.

Although Beidelman's careful survey of the literature is probably the best available, he seems to misunderstand the basic meanings of the paternalistic relations to the participants. He is aware of the vast complexity of these relations in India, but does not seem to realize how important the informal workings of caste relations are, as Srinivas[16] has shown. Social scientists who first studied India mistook the beautifully simple, classical terminology for castes and their interrelations for the reality, and believed that caste operated as a "varna system," a highly structured, highly systematic set of reciprocal rights and obligations. But social reality never works that way, simply because any such highly structured social world would soon grind to a halt or, rather, explode into revolution because it would be so totally incapable of dealing with all the situational contingencies that life is heir to that the members would have to either die or revolt. Caste is actually often ambiguously defined, slowly changing, highly variable from one region to another, and involves considerable competition:

> [T]he caste system of even a small region is extraordinarily complex and it does not fit into the *varna*-frame except at one or two points. For instance, the local caste-group claiming to be Kshatriya may be a tribal or near-tribal group or a low caste which acquired political power as recently as a hundred years ago. The local trading caste again might be similar in its culture to one in the 'shudra' category, and far removed from the Sanskritized Vaishya of the *varna* system. Finally, castes included in the Shurda category might not only not be servants, but landowners wielding a lot of power over everyone including local Brahmins.
>
> Again the *varna*-frame is too rigid to fit the facts of intercaste relations today, and it may be assumed that it was always so rigid. According to *varna*, caste appears as an immutable system where the place of each caste is clearly fixed for all time. But if the system as it actually operates is taken into

consideration, the position of several castes is far from clear. Mutual rank is ambiguous and therefore arguable. This is due to the fact that the caste system always permitted of a certain amount of mobility. This is why mutual position tends to be vague in the middle regions of the hierarchy and not at either extremity. At one extremity no mobility is possible while at the other it is extremely difficult. *Varna* also conceals the considerable diversity which exists between the caste system of one region and another. Studies of caste at the regional level ought to be accorded high priority, and only after a comparison of different regions can statements be made about caste at the all-India level.[17]

All these complexities of caste are the result of and operate on the basis of the vastly complex personal relations that ultimately determine, rather than being determined by, the symbolic values and labels that social scientists call social structure. The paternalistic relations of the jajman-kamin quasi-system are examples of those personal relations. It seems very likely that the paternalistic relations of the jajman-kamin quasi-system vary at any one time in India from one region to another from interdependent, sincerely minimally cooperative paternalism (without the goal of eventual independence on the part of the jajman), to conflictful, exploitative paternalism. But on average it very likely involves a considerable amount of interdependent, sincerely minimally cooperative paternalism. Any system of human relations that exists for centuries must not only be flexible, but must also satisfy the basic drives of the average human beings involved, unless there is a great deal of force applied from outside to prevent change. The jajman needs and gets a labor supply to work the fields and he wants certain services performed that give him dominance and, thus, pride. The dependent, submissive, childlike status of the kamin involves some loss of pride, although every effort is apparently made with ritual and the ideology of interdependence to hide this. (What kamin would not immediately choose to become a jajman, if given the chance? No doubt there are some who would refuse, just as there are people in our society who prefer to be at the lower end of the work scale to avoid the anxieties of responsibility, but there are generally only a relatively few people that insecure.) Very importantly, the shame of submission involved in accepting paternalistic dependency is considerably offset in sincerely cooperative paternalism by the *indirect dominance* the submissive partner gains from the dominance of the patron. (We shall see this ever more clearly in the Spanish patron system.) But in exchange for sacrificing some independence and dominance, the kamin gets some increase in security. The kamin's marginal subsistence level of existence in a world of agricultural uncertainties makes life very insecure without some form of social security system such as the jajman-kamin system provides. Just as the "furnish system" of sharecropping in the American South provided security against crop loss, so does the jajman-kamin system. It is precisely this value of these paternalistic relations that has led the Indian factory workers, with the aid of the Indian government, to insist on introducing such jajman-kamin relations into factory work. Morris's detailed study[18] of the emergence of factory labor in Bombay in the nineteenth and early twentieth centuries makes no significant reference to paternalistic relations. British labor relations seem to have predominated, except that in the early period more laxness in work was allowed. When the owners faced great competition in the 1920s and tried to cut back the work force to increase productivity, the workers reacted violently in general strikes. In post-colonial India, Lambert has found that the factory workers have demanded the application of the ideal jajman-kamin (or purjan) paternalism:

> The carry-over of this general notion of reciprocal obligation between *jajman* and *purjan* into the factory employer-employee is relatively easy. The attention to the workers' property rights in the factory job is evident in the elaborate regulations concerning dismissal and the difficulty factories have in firing a permanent worker merely on the grounds of inefficiency. Both the day-to-day pressure of the Union and the threat of a suit in the labor court act as a margin of safety for the property rights of the worker. The workers' right to compensation in case of layoffs further symbolizes the perquisites of status. At the same time, much of the "indiscipline" and low productivity which Myers refers to as partial commitment, and what the management often takes as an inevitable condition, derive from this same set of interpersonal norms. At the same time, the expectation on the part of the worker is that his status as a worker, so long as he displays proper deference behavior to the owner, entitles him to various perquisites and special favors from the owner or his representative.
>
> The general point is not, then, that the workers are still oriented to a specific village, but to a village-based set of interpersonal relational norms which are infused throughout the traditional society and are carried over into the factory. This outlook explains in part the general lack of anxiety about the job market which our data showed.[19]

In the Western world, feudalism evolved into various forms of patronage systems that are far less formalized, ritualized, legalized, and hereditary than such paternalistic relations as the jajman-kamin system. The patron systems of Spain and various parts of Latin America are among the most highly developed. Kenny has provided a class analysis of traditional patron-client relations in Spain:

> I define *patron* as " . . . someone who is regarded (and who regards himself) at once as a protector, a guide, a model to copy, and an intermediary to deal with someone else or something else more powerful than oneself, whether or not such power is imaginary or real in a single context or in all, and whether or not the advantages to be gained from his patronage are material or intangible." Likewise, a client is " . . . someone who avails himself of a patron's services and who maintains a reciprocally beneficial relationship with him."[20]

Patron-client relations are based very openly on the model of paternalistic family relations, as almost all such systems of dependency are. Since the sixteenth century, Spain has been basically a poor society with a rigid, hierarchialized social system ruled by monarchs, lords, dictators, and, above all, by an absolutist bureaucracy. The people revolted many times in the early centuries, but failed to throw off the impoverishing absolutist dependency forced on them. But, of course, the people have found a way to corrupt the system to make it work more humanely and flexibly and in a more egalitarian way. They have personalized the system by building vastly complex patron-client relations stretching from the poorest peasants to the richest and most successful politicians.

In the towns and cities, the "arranging" of affairs with officialdom becomes the concern of the patronage system. Certificates are required for mere vicinage, social benefits, all kinds of trading activity, voting, and even migration—for a man may be returned to his pueblo unless he can prove that he will live with relatives or has a house to go to. Entry to certain schools may depend on presentation of a certificate of Baptism and perhaps First Communion as well. Most applications for certificates are usually made in triplicate and must be countersigned elsewhere. It is not surprising that many agencies now offer to deal with the whole procedure of official applications for a small fee. Otherwise, the man claiming sickness benefits or seeking a housing permit or the like must lose many mornings' work waiting at government offices. Where his personal presence is not necessary his wife may go in his stead taking her sewing and a sandwich especially if she has to wait for hours at the window-counter marked "URGENT." Once made, the application takes months to clear and its success is always in doubt.

At a higher level in the urban setting where power is more closely associated with wealth, lobbying for the highly prized and exclusive concessions such as import and export licenses reveals a specially intimate type of patronage "pyramid." It is not a question here of considering that one may be entitled to these things by right, for between what is one's right and what is possible lie a thousand indifferent shrugs of the shoulder.

The process of circumventing these obstacles thrown up by authority can only be eased by having an *amigo*—a friend—in the right places. To have *enchufe* (literally meaning "plug") is to be able to make contact with the right people at a judicious moment. It is the new equivalent of the old friend at Court. It is a short cut through the maze of authority which balances the tension between State and community. It is the rule of *amigocracy*.[21]

Kenny emphasizes the reciprocity involved and the way the reciprocity makes the society function in more egalitarian ways than one would imagine from looking at the structure from the outside:

Clients may of course have a number of patrons, for it is always wise to cover oneself. Yet, in stressing the reciprocity rule—equally valid for the patron/patron relationship—one sees that at the back of the material advantages involved there lie a striving to level out great inequalities, a fight against growing anonymity (especially in the urban setting), and a seeking out of the primary personal relationship. For the client, of course, there is as well the material benefit gained: for the patron there is his "investment" in supporters—his clients; between patrons themselves there is a comfortable cementing of relationships. The success or failure of these motivating factors is clearly revealed only in a crisis when protestations of loyalty and support significantly show the alignment of forces and the delineation of patronage "pyramids." Spanish political life has been marked by the maneuvering of such groups until a "strong man" emerges around whom spheres of patronage newly orbit. To a lesser degree, they are evident also in the rival cults of the Virgin and saints who, as patrons of villages or parishes or organizations, are at times used as symbols of hostility between groups.[22]

But, once again, the basis for the system, the ultimate reason for accepting and promoting the system from the ground up, is that this sincerely cooperative paternalism works as an insurance system in a very poor society beset by high risks, a society in which experience (of failure in revolution, to give one important example) has taught a fatalistic acceptance of dependent submission:

> With this singular regard for authority must be associated the emotional satisfaction derived from giving and receiving protection and support as well as that of special treatment in the arranging of difficult matters. This paternalistic satisfaction has peculiar force when the patron and client are closely allied by reciprocal economic ties, for example the landlord-tenant relationship in India. But its potency is more understandable among a people whose stoic consideration of this transient life comes perilously close to fatalism, whose traditional class and whose dependence on more and material support in this largely barren land of the mystics is an almost instinctive "just-in-case" type of insurance.
>
> Hence, the element of change becomes a social force in Spain, startlingly apparent in all walks of life and expressed in one form at least by a wholesale recourse to decision by lot. Ranging from the division of the pine tree common patrimony in a Castilian village and the national selection of young men for the military draft to the fervid playing of the national lottery and the choice of subjects for examining oneself in the central school for diplomats—the results depend on the casting of lots. Luck is fickle; God's ways are mysterious. Patronage, therefore, provides one at least down-to-earth insurance policy.[23]

A similar system of patron-client relations exists in much of Latin America, especially in societies like Brazil's, where large plantations and many slaves prevailed, probably because effective systems of slavery always rely on a considerable degree of paternalism to justify them, and in societies like Peru's in which the Spanish system of open exploitation of Indians has evolved into a more sincerely minimally cooperative paternalism of a "furnish system," a sharecropping system buttressed by much of the family and friendship symbolization of the Spanish patron system. Ford's study of Peruvian large landholders emphasizes the sincerity of the landowners in their belief that they are doing what is in the best interest of the Indians. He also emphasizes that the landowners sincerely believe what any agricultural economist knows, that is, that they could have a far more efficient, profitable agriculture by evicting the Indians and adopting large-scale agricultural engineering; but he also found they were anxious to maintain the less efficient paternalistic system:

> More frequently to be observed in the relations of whites and Indians is an attitude of paternalism on the part of the former—the disappearing type of paternalism one may still occasionally see in the treatment of Negro workers by white bosses in the southern United States. The *patron* of a Peruvian hacienda is likely to exhibit a great deal of personal kindness, to allow indulgences, so long as the work of his Indian laborers and tenants is carried out to his satisfaction. At the same time he will loudly voice his vexation at their slowness, laziness, stupidity, and general inefficiency. His display of injured righteousness in response to the exploitation charges of would-be reformers is not feigned, but quite genuine. He will maintain, often with considerable truth, that far from exploiting his *colonos* (or *yanaconas* or *partidarios*), he allows them to live on the land at a financial loss to himself, since the land could be more profitably farmed under some other system. Like the plantation owner of the Old South, he is puzzled, hurt, and angered at the condemnation of his paternalism, which he regards as Christian charity in the fullest sense.[24]

Contrary to what political critics have charged, such sincerely minimally cooperative paternalistic relations are found over and over throughout the world. Almost always, if they last long, they involve a great deal of reciprocal altruism, of interdependent giving and taking. Dewey, for example, has described a highly interdependent system in Java that involves very few, if any, external constraints:

> Wage labor takes on a special significance in view of the high unemployment and the desire for cash. A man who wishes to have some work done and has the cash to pay wages for it is in a position to allocate it on a patronage basis. Today, especially with the decline in the number and size of plantations, the major source for wage labor is the wealthier farmers. They are almost invariably the influential men in the village and have tied to them, through links of kinship and neighborhood, various of the poorer villagers. The latter have obligations to support their patron politically, give him assistance and small gifts when he gives a feast, do odd jobs and run errands; and they must be available when he needs a large labor force. At harvest time crops must be gathered quickly to keep them from spoiling and get them to market when the price is highest. Since success in farming depends largely on the ability to assemble a sufficient labor force, the patron

must keep the loyalty of his followers. He must help them by lending or giving money and food or other supplies when they are in need, advise them in their dealings with the outside world, and allow them priority when allotting wage labor, thus providing them with opportunities to earn cash. If he fails to do these things he loses their support, which in turn damages his prestige and endangers his economic position.[25]

As they are in India, paternalistic relations are commonly used even in very modern, profit-oriented factory work. This kind of factory paternalism has been used most extensively and effectively in the famous oyabun-kobun relations in Japanese factories. It is first important to realize that the factory oyabun-kobun system has been an adaptation to the situation of industrialization of an already existing system of oyabun-kobun relations in the villages of what is known as Frontier Zone Japan. The Frontier Zone is very poor in comparison to Core Japan. It is close to subsistence-level existence, so that a year of bad crops can spell disaster for the poorer farmers. Just as we would expect from our other sources, the oyabun-kobun system of minimally cooperative paternalism has developed and has been maintained in the Frontier Zone while the better-off families of Core Japan have developed their own forms of family, paternalistic self-help, and other forms of nonpaternalistic self-help. Beardsley, Hall, and Ward[26] have described it in precisely these terms in *Village Japan*. They and Japanese scholars in general have carefully compared villages of Core Japan (such as Niiike referred to below) and those of the Frontier Zone (such as Ishigami). They find that only in the Frontier Zone do oyabun-kobun relationships get built up. Just as in India and elsewhere, these relations can tie together whole groups of fictive kin and be inherited. (These groups of fictive kin relations are known as "dozoku." Groupings of neighbors for self-help with no kin-reference are known as "koju.")

The critical question for conditions favorable to hierarchy is how poor are the poor. If the poorer members of a group are very close to the lower margin of existence, hierarchy becomes a form of life insurance. If any small setback such as a below-average harvest poses a calamity threatening starvation, patronage may be welcomed on almost any terms. Tenants or small landowners who are hard pressed to keep alive under the best of circumstances are in no position to refuse subservience to the house that can help them through hard times. Over the years the habit of dependency hardens and becomes accepted as life's natural course. Any malcontent who attempts to renounce his traditional obligations may find his community mobilized against him, his neighbors being motivated not by love for their mutual patron but by the necessity for quelling any disturbance impeding the smooth functioning of their community. So long as a substantial number of households in a community have little more than subsistence, while a few households have the power given them by surplus, so long can the *dozoku* perpetuate itself.

But in Niiike and most of Core Japan the margin above mere subsistence is considerably wider than in Ishigami and the Frontier Zone generally. In Niiike, by canny double-cropping and skilled techniques, a farmer with only a small bit of land can provide a fair bulwark against minor crises. Furthermore, in times of poor crops he can step up household processing of goods or work at a salaried job to bolster family income. Under such circumstances the security of kin-based hierarchy is less attractive than the freedom and flexibility of equal-level organization. Economic independence fosters attitudes of equality and mutuality. The organization of the *koju* and similar associations among farmers of the Core Zone reflects the relative independence of the participants. In the past, apparently, there was more vertical organization in Niiike and the Core Zone than there is today. But the favorable conditions for agriculture probably have long been a deterrent to the development of such extreme hierarchy as that of Ishigami mura and the Frontier Zone. Urban-industrial influences in the area today give farmers in the Core Zone more economic latitude than ever before, further reducing the poverty that is the best environment for rigid hierarchy.

Of course, the Niiike household must still meet emergencies, often too severe to handle alone. But no one in Niiike need prepare for these crises by serving a patron. The villagers meet emergencies by household groups. Sometimes they fall back on old kinship groupings, as in the case of the attempted murder. But increasingly they rely on the collective resources of neighborhood groupings not only for daily intercourse but for emergencies as well, as in the case of funerals, accident, illness, or crop failure. The *koju* and the various smaller *kumi* or teamwork groups of Niiike offer a collective cushioning against disaster.[27]

Levine[28] has shown that two forms of management-worker relations developed in pre-occupation Japanese firms. In the small firms, the cooperative paternalism of oyabun-kobun developed to provide security of employment, personal feelings of worth (status) by identifying with the higher-ups, on-job training, and many other forms of welfare desired by the new workers. These relations were extremely close, as all sincerely cooperative paternalistic relations must be. As the firms grew in size, the managers could no longer fulfill all the demands of oyabun-kobun paternalism, but they developed a system of linked paternalistic relations that approximated the oyabun-kobun relations as much as possible, so that the workers were related paternalistically to the foremen, who remained identified with the workers rather than with management, and they in turn were linked to the lowest level of management, who in turn linked on up the ladder to the highest manager. This modified oyabun-kobun system was strongly supported, even demanded, by the workers.

Closest possible contact between manager and managed was necessary to carry out the patriarchal approach effectively. In small shops, face-to-face, day-to-day interaction readily occurred. If the enterprise grew larger, management then began to utilize dependable assistants as channels of communication and donors of welfare benefits, and often subdivided the work force into small units, each with its own *oyabun*, thus creating a pyramid of father-child (*oyabun-kobun*) relationships within the larger enterprise organization. In some instances, management suggested that the workers form their own mutual benefit societies in order to facilitate communications and co-ordinate the welfare activities. These organizations might have become means for worker protest, but what little protest they summoned, rather than expressing dissatisfaction with the patriarchal system per se, usually was directed at the employer's failure to carry out his responsibilities in serving the welfare needs of the workers. Although a group of this sort sometimes brought individual grievances to the attention of management, such an organization resembled a trade-union only slightly. As a rule, it made no attempt to challenge management's decision-making authority or to bargain for terms of employment with management.

Subordinates felt a deep sense of obligation and duty to the patriarchal employer, and their common loyalty, fortified by family, religious, and other traditional values, heightened their conformity. Workers readily placed the needs of the enterprise well ahead of their own. At times, they were willing to become self-sacrificing, in some cases even to an extreme degree. So, in all likelihood, was the employer.[29]

The other form of management in pre-occupation Japan was what Levine calls "despotic." Actually, however, Levine himself shows the Japanese continued to use forms of paternalism, even the word oyabun, but now the spirit was different. As firms grew in size, relations necessarily became less direct, less frequent, less personal, less caring—more bureaucratic:

From the outside, despotic systems closely resembled the patriarchal, but the inner spirit fundamentally differed. As firms grew in size, and especially as welfare programs expanded and became more complex, the cost of administering a patriarchal approach overburdened management's time, energy, and resources. Although paternalism was not abandoned, a heavy strain was placed on the sense of mutual obligation between superior and subordinate. Management and workers were likely to be suspicious of one another, simply because it was difficult to reproduce the family structure faithfully in a large plant as levels of authority were added. Welfare programs became the means of controlling or minimizing unrest among the workers. Although managements typically strove to be benevolent in exerting their despotic control, essentially this was a negative approach, in contrast to the positiveness of patriarchalism. No longer did as strong a feeling of self-contained enterprise community exist.

As a result, authoritarianism grew—an experience hardly foreign to most Japanese, who recognized it as part of the traditional family system. The despotic employer also required a considerable staff of assistants, now to serve as a police corps rather than as a means of increasing his sensitivity to subordinates' needs. No risk was taken which might upset the tranquility of the regime. Special pains were taken to recruit docile workers; any worker displaying aggressive tendencies was quickly and surely rooted out even if he did manage to pass through the recruiting sieve. *Oyabun*, or "labor bosses," were relied upon to provide the enterprise with small groups of well-disciplined employees, who usually continued to work together as a unit. In addition, decisions were made at the top, or, if at lower levels, within the meaning of well-defined orders from above.[30]

Relations had actually become conflictfully paternalistic in these larger, more bureaucratic firms. The forms of paternalism were now used as fronts with which to manipulate workers into identifying their interests with that of management and thus to submit to management's decisions.

As Abegglen (1973) has shown in his classic study of[31] the postwar Japanese factory, the oyabun-kobun system does not exist in the strict sense in the big firms (pp. 133-134). But, instead, the system of modified minimally cooperative paternalistic relations has been developed even further and now spans a whole group of "clans" of industries (those linked into the famous "zaiabtsu"). (pp. 163-64)

Abegglen has argued specifically [32] that this paternalistic system of factory relations is a transitional phenomenon, bridging traditional Japanese society and what is evolving. (Although I do not know, I would strongly expect that most factory workers, or a disproportionate number, are immigrants from the Frontier Zone. These would be the rural poor most likely to immigrate to urban factories, the ones most in need of emotional and material support during the transition, and the ones most used to cooperative paternalism.) Many observers of Japan have argued that cooperative paternalism is beginning to break down in the Japanese factory and is being replaced by more individualistic and voluntary self-help patterns of feeling and behavior. Abegglen thinks that, while such changes have been occurring slowly at the "margin of compensation," any major changes of this sort must lie in the future.

Any reasonable view of the past two decades however must conclude that continuity is the predominant fact, and that substantial change, while often heralded, is yet to occur.

Nor is this surprising. The system of employment in Japan is a highly efficient one, and one that is congruent with the main values and behavior patterns of Japanese society. It is in many ways a more human, less brutal system of employment than the West has developed. It certainly is characterized by less conflict. Both its economic effectiveness and its social value work to maintain the system.

Will the system change? Of course. As the society changes, and it is changing, under the impact of affluence, increased leisure, a much altered pattern of family life and a greatly increased interaction with other nations, so patterns of relations in the workplace will change. Changes in the employment system will arise from these more basic social changes, and will reflect in the future as to date the characteristics of the broader society.[33]

While the cultural factor is an important one, and in this case has certainly slowed down the transition, I would expect from all the available evidence that the growing affluence, which makes self-help and voluntary mutual help more possible, will combine with the bureaucratization process to lead workers to want increasing independence. If managers choose to try to retard this development by using paternalism as a front, workers will become increasingly suspicious and resentful, and eventually revolt. There is, in fact, excellent precedent for this in Japan itself. Higher education is precisely the one area in Japanese life in which one would expect the oyabun-kobun type of paternalism to be strongest, because of the universal pattern of mentor-student cooperative paternalism (including that of Zen Master and Student) and because of the high regard the Japanese feel for scholars. No doubt these relations do exist in individual cases, but the remarkable thing is that, rather than acting like good kobun, Japanese students have acted in exactly the opposite way—by revolting. The reason is described by Reischauer as being primarily the large number of students relative to faculty and, thus, the distance and impersonalism of their relations, both of which prevent the development of sincerely caring, cooperative paternalistic relations.

Students who have won admittance to the prestige universities as well as those who have had to settle for lesser institutions often find university life disappointing, and many react to it with apathy or unrest. This is in part a psychological letdown after the years of preparation for the entrance examinations, but it is also a natural response to insufficient intellectual stimulation. One reason for this, particularly in national universities, is the rigidity of the Japanese university system and its strong resistance to changing needs. Another reason is the serious underfinancing of universities, particularly private ones, which results in very large classes, a poor student-faculty ratio, and little personal contact with professors.

While Japan devotes about the same percentage of its national income to elementary and secondary education as do the other advanced countries, it provides notably less for higher education, despite the fact that a considerably higher proportion of young people attend university than in the countries of Western Europe. This underinvestment in higher education is seen particularly in the heavy burden the Japanese place on private universities and the near bankruptcy of these institutions. In other advanced countries, all or most students are in government or government-financed institutions —even in the United States the figure has risen to 75 percent—but in Japan, since the government simply has not met the expanding demand for higher education, some 80 percent of the students are in private universities. None of these have any appreciable endowment or can count on substantial outside giving.

. . . The problem of the government universities is not so much finances as rigidity of organization. This may be in part the product of the German pattern copies in the late nineteenth century and in part the result of a fierce fight for academic freedom waged against the oppressive prewar government, which has left a jealously guarded tradition of autonomy in universities and in their various subdivisions. Universities even at the undergraduate level break up into sharply divided faculties, which have only minimal contact with one another. These faculties in turn are usually divided into chairs (*koza*), each made up of a professor, an assistant professor, and one or a few lecturers and assistants. Both the faculties and the chairs have almost complete autonomy and tenaciously protect their respective academic domains and budgets. Courses of study for students are rigidly prescribed, new fields of study are hard to start, and the mixing of fields of study is almost impossible.

. . . It is not surprising that students in both private and government schools evince considerable disenchantment, which mounts at times to open rebellion. Some students show little interest in their studies, devoting themselves instead to outside activities, such as sports, hobbies, and radical politics. This is particularly true during the first two years, before students settle down in their final years to completing their studies in preparation for the next round of examinations for business or the bureaucracy.

Student government organizations, supported automatically by fees assigned from tuition payments, have for the most part been dominated ever since the war by leftist extremists and have spawned a wide variety of explosively revolutionary splinter groups. These student organizations are usually known by the name of their national federation, the Zengakuren. Student unrest often focuses on intramural issues, such as raises in tuition or the costs of student facilities, rather than genuine academic problems . . . .[34]

There is one final study that shows clearly the conditions under which sincerely cooperative paternalism develops and those under which it decays. Norbeck has shown in *Pineapple Town: Hawaii* that newly arrived Filipino and Japanese workers, generally from poor rural areas, felt a very strong need for material help, emotional support, and protection from the American managers.[35] American managers strongly preferred an impersonal, "rationalized" relation with workers, but they felt forced to take part in cooperative paternalistic relations. They built a company town, developed close personal relations, encouraged oyabun-type labor bosses as the link with the workers, and even participated in the Spanish-type godparent system (compadradzgo) used by the Filipinos. But, as the workers became assimilated and more affluent, paternalism quickly waned and only echoes are now found. Norbeck has tried to explain this primarily in terms of the cultural reluctance of the Americans to take part (*their* desire that workers be independent), the effects of task-specialization in producing competition, and the overall effects of industrialization and the money economy in promoting impersonalism and individualism. No doubt these have the effect of decreasing paternalism, but the decline in the conditions that promote cooperative paternalism seems to be the most important. We should note also that the workers came to look to unions for protection when they no longer found this reliably in management. Union paternalism has been a general alternative to management paternalism at the middle levels of affluence in many nations, especially in nations like Britain where job insecurity has been felt by workers to be an important threat. As workers come to feel more secure on their own, they also give up the dependency fostered by union paternalism, and unions either wane or become more open economic and political weapons.

Paternalistic relations can persist even in otherwise highly individualistic and free cultures if, and only if, the dominant partners maintain close personal contact with, and demonstrate in action their caring for, the submissive partners. Islands of extremely paternalistic relations still exist among Southern whites, in spite of the massive efforts by national unions to destroy them, and in spite of the growing affluence of workers that makes the insurance system provided by paternalism less valuable to them. For example, Cannon Mills, an American maker of textiles, still practices highly paternalistic employee relations at its huge plant in the company town of Kannapolis, North Carolina. Its recently appointed president from the Northeast found that "much of what might have appeared to an outsider as egregious paternalism was in fact a form of leadership that nourished the company's spirit and style" (Burck, 1981). An outsider would presumably have thought the paternalism was exploitative or conflictful, but it appears from the inside to be sincerely minimally cooperative precisely because the managers have maintained close and caring relations with the employees: "Cannon managers have always lived close to the factory floor—in mind and in body, since only a few paces separate the vast Plant No. 1 in Kannapolis from the back door of the chairman's office . . . Cannon's entire industrial relations policy rests on such direct contacts."[36]

THE MYTH OF STATE PATERNALISM

Most of the discussion of paternalism by philosophers and lawyers (e.g., Dworkin; Gert and Culver; and Hodson [37]) has been concerned with state paternalism and has implicitly been concerned with specifying the conditions under which we can be sure that sincerely cooperative paternalism will not become paternalistic despotism, or conflictful paternalism. The states discussed are almost always modern states, so they are discussing the impersonal, rational-legal, bureaucratized paternalism of our so-called "welfare" states. It should be obvious from our discussion of the situations that give rise to and maintain sincerely cooperative paternalism that our modern welfare bureaucracies and legal bureaucracies create exactly the opposite situation. Sincerely cooperative paternalism is sought when individuals feel the need to be cared for, when they believe they face situations that greatly threaten them and that they cannot cope with independently. Sincerely cooperative (caring) paternalism is given by nonfamily members overwhelmingly only when the relations between the dependent and independent (the weak and the strong, the poor and the rich, the ignorant and the knowledgeable) are kept very close and very caring. The distant and impersonal relations of bureaucracies foster the opposite of sincerely cooperative paternalism, that is, conflictful paternalism —exploitative relations in the guise of paternalism. Rostovtzeff [38] long ago noted that the traditional paternalism of the Egyptian Pharaohs, which was obviously a somewhat more cooperative form involving little bureaucracy and considerable contact between the Pharaoh's representatives and the people, was gradually replaced by the Greek Ptolemaic rulers with a massive, rationalized bureaucracy that by its very "impersonalism," its very lack of personal considerations, progressively alienated the people. "They had always blindly obeyed the king and his officials . . . But centuries of evolution had accustomed them to a rather mild paternal form of pressure . . . With the Ptolemies came a marked change. The system remained the same in the main . . . But now the old system was managed in a different way. It was carried on by a huge, complicated, and rather dull and impersonal bureaucratic machine . . . What still remained of the old-fashioned, personal, paternal management of Egypt was more and more replaced by pure bureaucracy, impersonal and exasperating by its very impersonality."[39] This and the related "sinister phenomena" of the Ptolemaic bureaucratic welfare state led in time to growing conflicts, decreasing production efficiency, erosion of the tax base, and eventually to flight from the royal bureaucracies. The rationalism of the Ptolemies was very much like that of our modern state bureaucracies. It is an important cultural factor exacerbating the impersonalism of bureaucracy, but any bureaucracy has a built-in tendency to become more distant, more impersonal, and, thus, to move further away from the conditions that are necessary for maintaining a minimally cooperative form of paternalism.

Exploitative power-seekers have almost always tried to appear cooperatively paternalistic, in the same way they have tried to appear wise, magically powerful (in control of the power of God, etc.), and everything else that is appealing. We have seen that genetic paternalism is on average inherently (genetically) sincerely cooperative in the strongest possible sense. We have seen that there are weaker (on average) extensions of this in friendly, caring-loving relations, especially in friendship and mentor-student relations. We have seen that there are many weaker forms of minimally cooperative paternalism that provide vital help that is deeply desired by human beings in situations in which they feel threatened in ways they cannot cope with by acting independently or by voluntary and equal cooperation. All these have given almost all human beings a high appreciation of the values of sincerely cooperative paternalism. (It is not by accident, or by some genetically perverse desire to be submissive, that human beings so commonly worship a God the Father or a Mother God. In the face of the ultimate threat, death, which we cannot cope with independently, we fervently want an ultimate father or mother to save us, to protect us from the threat.) Those who would exploit human beings by dominating them, by keeping them in dependent submission, have always recognized that they will be the heir of this high esteem, and thus more apt to be dominant, if the potentially submissive people see them as parent-like. So they present themselves in that way. I need hardly go into historical details of the Confucians with their political theory of the links between the emperor as the father of all the Chinese people, or the Fathers of the Church, or even of Horace Mann, the father of compulsory state education in the United States— instituted for the "public welfare," of course.

But I do not mean that only "evil" persons, those consciously setting out to do evil to others, will make use of the rationales of paternalism to continue dominating and exploiting the recipients of paternalism. State bureaucracies necessarily, though certainly to varying degrees, foster distance and impersonalism—the exact opposite of the caring-loving feelings necessary for sincerely cooperative paternalism. They do this necessarily for a very simple reason. All rulers, whether they be monarchs or assembled bodies of the citizens, come to recognize very quickly from experience that government officials will use official powers and goods for their own purposes, those of their families, their friends, and their paternalistic clients (in that order). In short, they come to recognize that officials will become corrupt, both by usurping the power of the ruler and by seizing the goods of the people, so they must institute minute controls to try to contain the corruption. The Confucians, in spite of the fact that their entire system rested on the rationale of close family relations between citizens and mandarins, had to create distance and impersonalism between those very officials and citizens by rotating the officials, regulating them with minute rules and the Powers of the Censorate, thus breaking the ties that did develop. Eisenstadt[40] and his fellow researchers studying imperial state bureaucracies have shown that, in spite of all these measures, officials eventually do expropriate a major portion of the official power and goods for themselves. But the crucial point is that all states, regardless of how paternalistic their values are and regardless of how freventy paternalistic they might start out in practice, must soon institute precisely the distant and impersonal relations that make cooperative paternalism impossible and that make conflictful paternalism a tremendous incentive. What may begin with sincere feelings of caring for the people soon becomes indifference and irritation because the people do not sufficiently appreciate the benevolence and hard work of the bureaucrat; in the end, bureaucratic resentment commonly turns into self-righteous manipulation of the people in the name of their own good, for the secret good only of the bureaucrat. In the American welfare state today, this process of bureaucratic disillusionment and retreat from clients is so standard it is given a stereotypic label—"burnout." The Temptation of the Grand Inquisitor is an extreme outcome of the way in which state bureaucracies necessarily operate. But note that it arose within a massive bureaucracy that started out as a small band of idealists dedicated to parent-like love and charity.

It is, therefore, inherently dangerous to accept any form of state paternalism as truthful or legitimate. And it is especially dangerous to lend the prestige of scholarly analysis to the protestations of state paternalism. Moreover, it is completely unnecessary to accept any state paternalism as necessary to achieve the results desired. The overwhelming goal of the philosophical and legal discussion of paternalism is to legitimize the provision of minimal help for individuals who are temporarily unable to help themselves, and above all to help them avoid irrevocable injury, such as death, when they are temporarily "encumbered"—that is, insane, inebriated, etc. In almost all cases they make a fine, if overly elaborate, justification for someone to act in a sincerely cooperative paternalistic way to provide such help when the individuals are threatened. What they fail to see is that their proposed (or accepted) solution of state intervention is the exact opposite of what is needed to ensure the crucial conditions that alone guarantee the sincerely cooperative nature of the paternalistic help—that is, a close relation and the caring love that can spring from that. They also fail to note that state intervention is not necessary, even if it could achieve those results on average. When individuals are threatened in overwhelming ways, they have recourse to genetic family members, friends, fictive kin, neighborly voluntary groups, and Mencius-figures (Good Samaritans) who will take small risks for short periods of time to help out total strangers. These individuals are precisely the ones who, because of personal relations and concrete situations (such as observing the direness of the situation), are aroused to sincere caring and, thus, are the ones most apt to act sincerely in the interest of the threatened individual. They are also the ones close at hand who know the person and situation well enough to know how to do what is needed most effectively. And they almost always do it, even today in our society in which the rhetoric of state paternalism encourages everyone to "let the government do it." Government bureaucrats are precisely the people who, especially over the long run, are least apt to have the caring feelings and are least apt to know the concrete individuals and situations well enough to act effectively on their behalf. They are the ones most apt to exploit individuals by using the front of paternalism. I see every reason in the world to support sincerely cooperative paternalism and to reject *all* forms of state paternalism.

Notes

1. Gerald Dworkin, "Paternalism," *The Monist,* vol. 56 no. 1 (1972); and Bernard Gert and Charles M. Culver, "Paternalist Behavior," *Philosophy and Public Affairs* 6 (Fall, 1976).

2. Edward O. Wilson, *On Human Nature* (Cambridge: Harvard University Press, 1978) and *Sociobiology: The New Synthesis* (Cambridge: Belknap Press, 1975).

3. R. I. Trivers, "The Evolution of Reciprocal Altruism," *Quarterly Review of Biology*, vol. 46, no. 4 (1971), pp. 35-57; and Wilson, *Human Nature*.

4. Richard Dawkins, *The Selfish Gene* (New York: Oxford University Press, 1976).

5. Lionel Tiger, *Men In Groups*, (New York: Random House, 1969).

6. David Roberts, "Five Who Made It to the Top," *Harvard Magazine*, January/February, 1981, p. 40.

7. Wilson, *Human Nature*, pp. 165-66.

8. Marc Bloch, *Feudal Society* (Chicago: University of Chicago Press, 1961), p. 3. See also Sidney Painter, *A History of the Middle Ages, 284-1500*, London: Macmillan and Co. Ltd., 1964, 1953c; and Joseph R. Strayer and Dana C. Munro, *The Middle Ages (395-1500)* (New York: Appleton-Century-Crofts, Inc., 1942), pp. 96-132.

9. Strayer and Munro, *Middle Ages*, p. 112.

10. *Ibid.*, p. 117.

11. Thomas O. Beidelman, *A Comparative Analysis of the Jajmani System* (Locust Valley, NY: J. J. Augustin Incorporated, Publisher, 1959), pp. 6-7.

12. W. H. Wiser, *The Hindu Jajmani System* (Lucknow: Lucknow Publishing House, 1936).

13. Beidelman, *Jajmani System.*

14. *Ibid.*, pp. 6, 74-8.

15. *Ibid.*, pp. 75-6.

16. M. N. Srinivas, *Caste In Modern India* (New York: Asia Publishing House, 1962).

17. *Ibid.*, pp. 7-8.

18. David Morris, *The Emergence of an Industrial Labor Force in India* (Berkeley: University of California Press, 1965).

19. Richard D. Lambert, *Workers, Factories, and Social Change in India* (Princeton: Princeton University Press, 1963), pp. 92-3.

20. Michael Kenny, "Patterns of Patronage in Spain," *Anthropological Quarterly*, vol. 33, no. 1 (1977), p. 15.

21. *Ibid.*, p. 19.

22. *Ibid.*, p. 22.

23. *Ibid.*, p. 16.

24. Thomas R. Ford, *Man and Land in Peru* (Gainesville, FL: University of Florida Press, 1962), p. 111.

25. Alice G. Dewey, *Peasant Marketing in Java* (New York: The Free Press of Glencoe, 1962), p. 26.

26. Richard K. Beardsley, John W. Hall, and Robert E. Ward, *Village Japan* (Chicago: University of Chicago Press, 1959).

27. *Ibid.*, pp. 274-5.

28. Solomon B. Levine, *Industrial Relations in Postwar Japan* (Urbana, IL: University of Illinois Press, 1958).

29. *Ibid.*, p. 38.

30. *Ibid.*, pp. 38-9.

31. James C. Abegglen, *Management and Worker: The Japanese Solution* (Tokyo: Sophia University/Kodansha International, Ltd., 1973).

32. *Ibid.*, p. 165.

33. *Ibid.*, pp. 48-9.

34. Edwin O. Reischauer, *The Japanese* (Cambridge: The Belknap Press of Harvard University Press, 1977), pp. 174-7.

35. Edward Norbeck, *Pineapple Town: Hawaii* (Berkeley: University of California Press, 1959).

36. C. S. Burck, "Reveille at Cannon Mills," *Fortune*, January 16, 1981, pp. 68-76.

37. Dworkin, "*Paternalism*;" Gert and Culver, "*Paternalist Behavior*;" and John D. Hodson, "The Principle of Paternalism," *American Philosophical Quarterly*, vol. 14, no. 1 (1977), pp. 14-23.

38. M. Rostovtzeff, *The Social and Economic History of the Hellenistic World*, vol. 1 (Oxford: The Clarendon Press, 1953).

39. *Ibid.*, pp. 412-3, 415.

40. S. N. Eisenstadt, *The Political Systems of Empires* (New York: The Free Press, 1963).

Chapter 12

Noncoercive Exploitation

Joel Feinberg

What are the limits to what can be done by a person (to be called A throughout this paper) to another (to be called B) even with the latter's fully voluntary consent? A legal paternalist would not allow A to harm certain of B's interests, even with B's approval or at B's request. I have argued elsewhere[1] that this view shows insufficient respect for B's autonomy, his right to govern himself at his own risk within his own moral domain. What are we to say, however, about the quite different cases in which A can be said to exploit B or "take advantage" of him without necessarily infringing his autonomy or even harming his interests? Can there be such a thing as noncoercive exploitation, willingly consented to? If there is such a thing, may it rightly be prevented by the coercive arm of the state? If so, are the justifying grounds paternalistic, moralistic, or other?

I. EXPLOITATION AND COERCION

Many of the leading examples of exploitation, of course, are also examples of coercion. Still, the concepts, despite their large overlap in application, are quite distinct. Coercion is always a relation between two persons or groups of persons. The word "exploitation," on the other hand, has such wide application that it needn't even involve more than one person, as when one is told to exploit one's own talents or to make the most of one's own opportunities. To exploit something, in this most general sense, is simply to put it to one's use, not to waste it, and there

I wish to thank Bruce Landesman and Martin Golding for their exceptionally perceptive and helpful critical comments on this paper at the Liberty Fund Conference in Lutsen, Minnesota, in September, 1980. I have gratefully adopted various of their suggestions in this revision of the orginal paper, but since some substantive disagreements remain, I hope that each of them will one day publish his own views on exploitation.

is no limit in principle to the sorts of things that can be exploited. Even in this general nonpejorative sense, the exploiter is always a person; diseases, landslides, and tropical storms have never exploited anything. The kind of exploitation with which we shall be concerned here, however, is interpersonal exploitation, in which both exploiter and exploitee are persons. When "exploitation" refers to an interpersonal relationship, it tends almost uniformly to be pejorative. Thus, interpersonal exploitation must be a way of using another person that is somehow wrongful or unfair. We rarely speak of exploitation as justifiable, and in this respect it may differ, at least in degree, from coercion, which is often morally called for.

Despite these differences in sense, exploitation and coercion often go together. Some proposals by A are coercive in their effect on B in that they close or narrow B's options, and are also instances of A's exploitation of B's vulnerability for A's own advantage. To determine whether A has coerced B, we look to the effects of his conduct on B's options. The expected effect on A's own interests (his profit or gain) is relevant only to the further and partially independent question of exploitation. If we define exploitation in terms of A's profit through his relations to B, not all exploitation involves coercive machanisms. In fact there are four possibilities:

1. A's act can be exploitative and coercive, as when his proposal effectively forces B to act in a way that benefits himself (A).
2. A's act can be exploitative and noncoercive, as when he takes advantage of B's traits or circumstances to make a profit for himself, either with B's consent or without the mediation of B's choice at all.
3. A's act can be nonexploitative but coercive, as when A, a police officer, calls out to the murderer-in-hiding to come out with hands up or face lethal fire.
4. A's act can be both nonexploitative and noncoercive, as in an ordinary commercial exchange from which both vendor and purchaser expect to gain (but not at one another's expense).

I shall be concerned primarily with noncoercive exploitation in this paper, and with the other combinations only when useful for purposes of comparison and contrast. Among the contrasting cases, coercive exploitation (1. above) in particular deserves clear characterization, since in some contexts its character as exploitative (even though coercive) will be of interest. When A applies coercive pressure, as opposed to direct compulsion, to B, the "pressure" is applied not directly to B's body (as with pushes, pulls, injections, physical barriers, etc.), but only figuratively (to his will). The alternatives to a given choice are made so unattractive to him that in effect he "has no choice" but the coerced one. More attractive options have been closed by the intervention of the coercer. When the coercion is also exploitative, the coerced choice is one from which A stands to benefit and B stands to lose. It is the desire to gain a benefit for himself that leads A to exert the pressure; it is the desire to avoid even greater loss that leads B to accede to it. When the exploitation in a coercive proposal (threat and/or offer) is excessive, both in terms of A's gain and B's loss, the proposal is often characterized as extortion. B is totally dependent on A for something B vitally needs or intensely wants, and A, aware of his enormous bargaining advantage, "tightens the screws" for all he can get. What makes extortion in this sense possible is the unequal bargaining position of the parties. A exploits B's need and total dependence for excessive personal gain at B's expense.

II. THE ELEMENTS OF EXPLOITATION: WAYS OF USING THE OTHER PERSON

Put very vaguely, all interpersonal exploitation involves one party (A) profiting from his relation to another party (B), by somehow "taking advantage" of some characteristic of B's, or some feature of B's circumstances. When the exploitation is coercive, the characteristic of B that is taken advantage of is his lack of power relative to A, as when A, for example, is in a superior bargaining position. The word "exploitation" is a technical term in Marxist economic theory[2] where it refers to the coercive process by which capitalists hire workers for bare minimal wages because the workers have no alternative except starvation. Then all the wealth created by the workers' labors ("surplus value") goes to the employer. This, of course, is a case of superior power exerting its force extortionately to produce unconscionably harsh employment contracts to which the employees' agreement is considerably less than fully voluntary. There are other examples of exploitation, however, that as John Kleinig has noticed, do not violate the exploited party's autonomy:

A sponger may exploit another's generosity; children may exploit the love of their parents; a man may exploit the insecurity of a woman; advertising firms may exploit the gullibility of the public; politicians may exploit the fears of the citizenry. It would be difficult to argue that these cases of exploitation involve coercion. Rather they involve one party's playing on some character trait of the other for the purpose of securing some advantage.[3]

The key phrase "play on" is very apt. The skilled exploiter plays on the other's character in the way a pianist "plays on" a piano. A may say afterwards to B: "You are what you are (generous, loving, insecure, gullible, or fearful, as the case may be). I don't change that, or infringe it, or exert pressure on it. Rather I *use* it to my profit. *You* have no complaint coming. At most you might be envious of my gain. But I didn't force anything on you; I simply used you as you are."

Common to all exploitation of one person (B) by another (A), whether that exploitation be coercive or not, is that A makes a profit or gain by turning some characteristic of B to his own advantage. That characteristic could be simply a vulnerability to force or deception; it could be some other kind of weakness; or it could be a strength. It could be a trait, or it could be a circumstance. It could be an occurrent state or an underlying disposition, a virtue of character or a flaw, a skill or an ineptitude. In any case, what is necessary is that A use it for his own gain.

Characteristically, B loses, but not always. The essential point is that because of something about B, which A uses in a certain way, A profits. Thus there are three constitutive elements in all exploitation about which we can raise further questions: (1) How A uses B; (2) What it is about B that A uses; (3) How the process redistributes gains and losses (benefits and harms). In addition, exploitation (in the pejorative sense of the term with which we are here concerned) is assumed to be *unfair* ("taking unfair advantage") or otherwise subject to adverse moral criticism.

To begin with the first element, what Kleinig called "playing on" another is also called "using" the other or, in come cases, "manipulating" the other. It would hardly mark an advance in our philosophical understanding, however, if we were to define this element of exploitation as "manipulation," since many dictionaries define "manipulation," in turn, in words that could serve as well to define noncoercive exploitation, and thus we would have a small circle of interdefinable notions. (To manipulate is "to control or play upon by artful, unfair, or insidious means, especially to one's own advantage."[4]) Moreover, manipulation may suggest too active a form of intervention for some sorts of noncoercive exploitation. The exploiter (A) uses more passive techniques when he simply agrees to do what B wants and thereby exploits B's greed, recklessness, or foolishness without any "manipulation" at all. Indeed, he may simply respond to initiative that is entirely B's from the outset. Nonmanipulative exploitation can be illustrated by examples from both competitive and noncompetitive contexts. Thus, in response to B's proposal, A says: "Do you really want to bet $1,000 that you can beat me at billiards (gin rummy, one-on-one basketball, etc.)? All right, I'll be happy to take your money, that is 'exploit your foolishness.'" Imagine that A's remark is more than the usual bravado of conventional badinage. His self-confidence is entirely well founded. We can imagine also that A has not tricked or misled B into underestimating A's talent and B has no illusions or misconceptions under that head. B has never lost a match of this kind before, although he has never played anyone of A's calibre. He is young, brash, and cocky—precisely the traits that A will exploit—but he is free of all coercion, and he knows exactly the risks he is taking.

For a morally parallel example in a noncompetitive context, considered the folowing: B is a professional beggar who is led to believe on good evidence that he can improve his business if he has only a stump instead of an arm. So he offers A $1,000 to amputate his quite healthy arm. A replies: "I think that your values are cockeyed. How could you prefer an increased income to a healthy left arm? Still, it is *your* arm, and if you want me to exploit your foolishness, I will be happy to do so." And he does.[5]

One could argue, of course, that in each example, B consents out of ignorance, so that his action is not fully voluntary after all. In the first example, B believes that he can win, a belief that is proved false by the event, showing that he labored under a voluntariness-diminishing misconception after all. And in the second example, one might argue that B falsely believed that his increased profits would adequately compensate him for the loss of his arm when, in fact, let us suppose, he comes keenly to regret his action in later years. The reply to this argument from ignorance (or mistake) in the first example is that it gives so strong an interpretation of the ignorance condition for nonvoluntariness that no wagers or contests of skill could ever qualify as fully voluntary on both sides. To be sure, B's prediction or anticipation of the outcome turned out to be false, but his belief that he *could* win (given nearly equal skill, fierce competitiveness, and a little bit of luck)—that is, the belief that he had a *chance* to win—might well have been correct even though he lost. And while his taking the risk of losing might have seemed unreasonable to more cautious friends and observers (it was not a risk any of them would have taken), it was not patently irrational, as would be required to vitiate its voluntariness. Much the same may have been true of the second example. B's belief that he would not come to regret his choice may have been false, and even unreasonable in the eyes of others. But again, it was a matter of choosing to risk a future development that no one could foresee with certainty, and if the risk were not manifestly irrational (as we may suppose) there is no reason to deny that it was fully voluntary.

The fact of B's voluntary consent to the risk in these examples, however, does not automatically relieve A of all responsibility for subsequent harms to B. It is at least a somewhat disingenuous reply to criticism for A to say, "B brought it all upon himself. I was a mere passive instrument of his will," for, as Kleinig points out, A actively chose or agreed to be the instrument of B's purposes and cannot escape responsibility for his own free choice. Kleinig's view, which we shall examine in section V below, is that exploitation of another's rashness or foolishness is *wrong*, even when, because of prior voluntary consent, it does not violate the other's right, it does not wrong him, and it does not treat him unjustly. It is wrong because the actor (A) believes on good evidence that it will probably cause harm to B, and deliberately harming another to one's own gain is something we ought not to do, even though the other can have no grievance against us.

More active forms of noncoercive "using" or "playing upon" another person involve a great miscellany of manipulative techniques that fall short of outright coercion or misrepresentation. A can offer inducements, employ flattery, beg or beseech; he can try alluring portrayals, or seductive suggestions; he can appeal in turn to duty, sympathy, friendship, or greed, probing constantly for the character trait whose cultivation will yield the desired response. If he finds it and thereby persuades the other to consent, the other cannot complain of being forced or tricked into it. After all, it was his own true, flawed, but autonomous self whose utilization produced the consent, not some overpowering external force.

III. THE ELEMENTS OF EXPLOITATION: EXPLOITABLE TRAITS AND CIRCUMSTANCES

The next factor to be considered turns our attention away from A to B and to the traits and circumstances in virtue of which he is exploited by A. Virtually any traits or circumstances are in principle exploitable, provided only that they are causally relevant to the exploiter's purposes. Exploitable traits include virtues (excellences) and flaws, both self-regarding and other-regarding, and also occurrent mental states of relatively brief duration, whether or not they instantiate underlying dispositions of character, such as particular states of joy or grief, anger or love. A can exploit such character flaws in B as recklessness, cockiness, or vaingloriousness, as well as other-regarding flaws like greed, vindictiveness, or enviousness. Even B's moral virtues, his unwillingness to cheat, free-load, or break his word, his generosity, and tendency to trust others, make him vulnerable. Indeed, any trait or circumstance of B's that A can subsume under a reliable generalization makes B reasonably predictable, and it is precisely in his predictability to one who has studied him closely that his vulnerability to exploitation often consists. By capitalizing on his knowledge of B's character and his present circumstances, A gets B to respond in the desired manner without using any force or deception whatever. He knows, for example, that B, a conscientious type, can be trusted to do his share of the work, so that A can get away with doing less of his own. Or he predicts that B, a cocky sort, will wager in an unequal contest, so he arranges such a contest and pockets his profit.

Moral Flaws

Exploitation of another party's defect of character is likely to seem the least blamable form of noncoercive, nonfraudulent exploitation. Even fraudulent exploitation of another's moral defects, while blamable on balance, seems to have a mitigating character. Consider, for example, so-called "confidence games." These swindles exploit a weakness in their victims, and trick them by deliberate deception and misrepresentation. Sometimes the victim is badly harmed and the fraudulent exploiter is rightly seen as a heartless villain who deserves severe punishment. But often there is a pleasing element even in the fraud when the victim's exploited trait was itself a moral flaw, particularly when it was an other-regarding moral flaw, like cruelty or greed, so that the victim was hoist with his own petard, and is seen to have got what he had coming, even though it was wrong for the con-artist to have given it to him. One of the reasons that practical jokes at their harmless best are so amusing is that they exploit some appropriate flaw in their victims, as in the story of the prissy London office worker who was excessively protective of his precious derby hat. Every day he found that his head had grown because (unknown to him) his waggish colleagues had substituted identical hats of gradually diminishing size, each with his name and the correct size on the hatband. To be sure, the methods used were deceptive and the victim's role in the joke far from fully voluntary, but the actual harm done (as opposed to perplexed anxiety induced) was minimal, and the trait exploited was an unattractive character flaw. If we add to these elements some profit to the jokesters and subtract the element of fraud, we have a case of noncoercive exploitation that can also please the observer and lead him, at the very least, to modify his adverse judgment of the exploiter.

A noncoercive, nondeceptive, and nonmanipulative case of a similar sort is suggested by a recent newspaper report. The exploiter in that story may seem entirely blameless because the traits of his "victim" that he turned to his own advantage are themselves other-regarding flaws. According to the published report, an Italian engineering company seems to be "exploiting" the Libyan dictator, Colonel Muammar Qaddafi, by turning to its own advantage a somewhat malevolent Libyan scheme, and making its profit at Qaddafi's expense.

> One of . . . Qaddafi's latest plots calls for the building of a wall 187 miles long to seal off his country from Egypt. He plans to hire thousands of Kenyans to build this "El Fateh Line" in North Africa to prevent border attacks by the Egyptians. Engineers say privately that Qaddafi is nuts, that building a wall on shifting sands in territory physically altered by periodic sand storms is silly—"but they're willing to take his money."[6]

If the engineering firm has made its appraisal known to Qaddafi (and not merely "privately"), and Qaddafi's acceptance of the unreasonable risks are entirely due to his own headstrongness and not due to any withholding of information or expert opinion from him, his "consent" to the operation is largely voluntary, and the Italian firm cannot be charged with defrauding him. The firm might yet be morally censured for wrongfully exploiting him but for the fact that his wall scheme is part and parcel of a general foreign policy that involves among other unsavory elements large-scale assassination plots around the world. The exploitation of another's evil propensities pleases in much the manner of the morally apt practical joke, and even more for being profitable.[7]

Moral Virtues, Conscientiousness, and Trust

It is very much otherwise when the exploited trait is a virtue, when, for example, a freeloader takes advantage of the dutiful laborer or the law-abiding farepayer, when the freeloader profits, not necessarily at their expense, but *only* because they were honorable enough to forego themselves the easy gains of the cheater. When A cheats on his phone bill, he may not cause much harm to anyone, since the phone company will pass on its losses in dilute form to all its customers. The evasion of payment exploits the company's trust and also the cooperative forebearance of the other customers who do pay their proper fees. As we shall see in section V, this kind of cheating is generally thought to be the clearest example of *unfair* advantage-taking.

When A and B are close friends, A may sometimes be tempted to exploit B's friendship for his own advantage. When he passes off a burdensome chore to B in full confidence that B will do the task if only out of friendship, he may well be subject to the charge that he takes unfair advantage of his friend. Perhaps he has asked for a favor that he himself would resent having to grant were their roles reversed. In that case, he exploits a complex of B's virtues— friendly good will, loyalty, and trust among them—for his own convenience, and this strikes us as morally akin to cheating or free-loading. On the other hand, A "exploits B's friendship" in a blameless (and hence a not genuinely "exploitative") way when he simply uses his influence with B in a way that costs B no unreasonably burdensome inconvenience. B (or his influence) has become a compliant instrument of A's but B does not feel wrongly used. Loaning his influence costs him little, and he is likely to reassure A that "that's what friends are for."

Misfortunes and Unhappy Circumstances; Coercive Offers

When A, a publisher, exploits a widow's grief (through the pitiless glare of publicity), or when A, as a circus owner, exploits a grotesquely diseased person's revolting appearance (by exhibiting the person for a salary in a sideshow), the results are repugnant. In these cases, it is unfortunate circumstances rather than character traits that are utilized, and even when there is voluntary consent the result is morally ugly, for one person's profit is made possible only because of another person's suffering. The moral repugnance is likely to be greater still when the exploitation is coercive, where, for example, the circus owner has arranged things so that the grotesque person can find no other work, and then offers a low-paying job as the only alternative to permanent unemployment. Exploiters are typically opportunists; they extract advantage from situations that are not of their own making. Coercers, on the other hand, are typically makers, rather than mere discoverers and users, of opportunities. (The model coercer is the person with a gun who *creates* an exploitable situation by using the weapon to back up a threat.) One technique for profiting from the misfortunes of others combines the opportunism of the typical exploiter with the manipulative intervention of the typical coercer, by means of the "coercive offer."

Suppose opportunistic A holds out to unfortunate B the prospect of rescue or cure—but for a price. B is in an otherwise hopeless condition from which A can rescue her if she gives him what he wants. He will pay for the expensive surgery that alone can save her child's life, provided that she becomes for a period his mistress. A thus uses his superior advantages to manipulate B's options so that she has no more choice than she would have if a gunman pointed his pistol at her healthy child's head, and threatened to shoot unless she agreed to become *his* mistress. The difference between the two cases of course is that the lecherous millionare makes no unlawful *threat*. If B declines his proposal her child will die, but that will no more be A's doing than it would be the doing of any other person who was rich enough to pay for the surgery but in fact did not; whereas if B declines the gunman's proposal in the other example, the gunman will commit murder. That is the difference between the two cases that has led many writers to refer, plausibly enough, to proposals like that of the lecherous millionaire as "coercive offers."[8] They are coercive because they manipulate a person's options in such a way that the person "has no choice" but to comply or else suffer an unacceptable alternative.[9] They are "offers" because the proposer does not threaten any harm beyond what would happen in any case without his or her gratuitous intervention. Quite clearly, the coercive proposer *exploits* his superior power and his victim's desperate need, in order to have his way with her, but of course the example does not present a case of *noncoercive exploitation*, which is our main interest here.

More Unfortunate Circumstances: Credulity Born of Desperate Need

Another way of exploiting a person's unhappy situation may be closer to the mark. About 700,000 Americans a year learn that they have cancer, and a sizable proportion of these do not survive the disease. Many are told by their physicians at a certain point that, while symptoms can be treated and the progress of the disease slowed down, cure is impossible and premature death inevitable. It is no wonder that thousands of terminal cancer patients are willing to take a chance on any advertised cure, no matter how low the probability of its success. After all, they have nothing more to lose and everything to gain. And it is no surprise that there are promoters of unproven "wonder drugs" who are willing to exploit cancer patients' desperation for profit to themselves. The most famous of the scientifically disreputable but popular cancer cures is laetrile (also called vitamin B-17), an extract of apricot pits. The Federal Drug Administration and many private laboratories have tested laetrile on animals and found no sign of its alleged effectiveness. Most cancer specialists consider its promotion to be outright quackery. Because its therapeutic value is unproven, the F.D.A. refused to license its use. That decision caused a roar of protest from what had already become a powerful laetrile lobby, and within five years legislatures in twenty-three states had passed legislation legalizing the use of laetrile.

A liberal case for such legislation can be made even on the assumption (now well confirmed) that laetrile is worthless as a cancer cure. In moderate doses, laetrile is harmless. If its legal use required a medical prescription, it would not be likely to cause any harm (or indeed to have any significant effect on health one way or the other). Legislatures could require that a warning label (e.g., "The Surgeon-General has determined that there is no evidence that laetrile is an effective medication for cancer.") appear on every bottle, to obviate fraudulent misrepresentation, and to assure that patient consent is "voluntary." Prescriptions of laetrile could be legally restricted to patients who have been certified as terminal. Thus, if dying persons choose to cling to what they believes is their last desperate chance of survival, no paternalistic intervener will deprive them of their hope. Only the disease itself will do that. "Under the Government's nodding supervision, the purity of the product might then be assured, the flourishing black market in laetrile— which has netted some of its pushers millions of dollars—would finally be broken, and the nostrum could be given despairing patients beyond all hope of conventional medicine."[10] In 1977, the editor of the *New England Journal of Medicine*, arguing on liberal gounds for the legalization of this worthlesss drug, told the press: "If a patient suffering from incurable cancer comes to me and says he wants to go on a pilgrimage to a shrine [one offering the hope of a miraculous cure] I wouldn't deny him that right.[11]

The primary consideration against legalization is the argument from exploitation. Pharmaceutical companies, druggists, and even some physicians will make large and legitimate commercial profit from the sale of the product. These profits will not exactly be at the expense of the customers, since the drug is harmless, and they freely pay their money to keep alive their hope—an exchange that seems reasonable to them, if not to us. Yet some parties will be turning to their own advantage the misery and desperation of others, achieving a gain for themselves only because of their fellows' misfortunes. That is a form of parasitism that tends to offend the objective observer, whether ultimately justifiable or not. It is not pleasant to behold the strong and healthy making their livings off the desperate hopes of the powerless.

"Human Weaknesses"

Another class of conditions whose exploitation is morally suspect are moral weaknesses, largely self-regarding character flaws that incline people to act against their own interests, their own judgment, or their own consciences whenever there is temptation to do so. A exploits the moral weakness of B when he deliberately provides that temptation and takes his own profit from the consequences. Lord Devlin has claimed that "All sexual immorality involves the exploitation of human weaknesses,"[12] and finds considerable support for this opinion in the *Wolfenden Report* that he is criticizing. The latter, in its chapter on the English crime of "Living off the earnings of prostitution," states:

> It is in our view an oversimplification to think that those who live on the earnings of prostitution are exploiting the prostitute as such. What they are really exploiting is the whole complex of the relationship between prostitute and customer; they are, in effect, exploiting the human weaknesses which cause the customer to seek the prostitute and the prostitute to meet the demand. The more direct methods . . . are not the only means by which the trade is exploited; that it continues to thrive is due in no small measure to efforts deliberately made to excite the demand on which its prosperity depends . . . . At the present time, entertainments of a suggestive character, dubious advertisements, the sale of pornographic literature, contraceptives, and "aphrodisiac" drugs (sometimes all in one shop), and the sale of alcoholic liquor in premises frequented by prostitutes, all sustain the trade, and in turn themselves profit from it . . . .[13]

I assume that both Lord Devlin and the authors of the *Wolfenden Report* considered sexual congress with prostitutes to express a "human weakness" because they thought of it as something typically opposed to the customer's interests, his prudential judgment, and his conscience, something succumbed to typically only because of the enticements, allures, and stimulants of the commercial exploiters. In other passages, however, Lord Devlin seems to make a stronger claim, that the impulse to illicit sexual conduct is a human weakness even when it is not in any way dangerous to the actor (apart from rendering him or her liable to criminal prosecution) nor contrary to his or her conscience. This stronger and more puzzling claim won the sympathy of American authors of the *Model Penal Code* and, for a time, at least, of a majority of the United States Supreme Court (which had clearly been influenced by the *Model Penal Code*). Professor Louis B. Schwartz, co-author of the *Code*, wrote that its anti-obscenity provisions were not aimed at any "sin of obscenity" as such, but obliquely at a "disapproved form of economic activity— commercial exploitation of the widespread weakness for titillation by pornography."[14] As Schwartz proceeds to point out, the criminal prohibition of obscenity, so regarded, takes on the "aspect of regulation of unfair business or competitive practices:"

> Just as merchants may be prohibited from selling their wares by appeal to the public weakness for gambling, so they may be restrained from purveying books, movies, or other commercial exhibition by exploiting the well-nigh universal weakness for a look behind the curtain of modesty.[15]

Justice Brennan quoted that passage with approval in his opinion in *United States v. Ginzburg*[16] upholding Ginzburg's conviction (and five-year sentence) for violating a federal obscenity statute. What aroused Justice Brennan's ire, and that of some of his colleagues, was not that obscene materials were produced, disseminated, used, and enjoyed (the justices do not appear in this case to be excessively prudish), but rather that persons should derive a profit from "the sordid business of pandering . . . to the erotic interest of their customers."[17] In the absence of any argument that erotic interest as such is a human weakness, this use of the word "pander" begs the question. We *cater* to people's wishes, and we *minister* to their needs; but we can *pander* only to their weaknesses. In fact, pandering can be well defined as noncoercively exploiting the moral weakness of others by providing them the services they voluntarily seek, even though contrary to their interests or consciences. The legal writers quoted above speak of "human weakness" because that term is less censorious than "moral weakness," and their concern is not to censure the weak parties so much as to condemn the exploiter who profits by serving them.

While there may be genuine doubt that erotic interest is a human weakness, there can be no doubt at all that any *addiction* is a moral weakness of some human beings that renders them especially vulnerable to exploitation by others. But the sort of exploitation I have in mind cannot plausibly be said to be voluntarily consented to; the addict's exploitation is by means of still another kind of "coercive offer."[18] "I'll pour you a drink if you give me a dollar," said to a genuine alcoholic with a final dollar in hand may in effect leave the alcoholic no choice but to hand over the dollar, the compulsion stemming from his own addiction rather than from an external threat. A better example of an undoubted human weakness that is frequently exploited *noncoercively* by others is the desire knowingly to bet against the odds in certain forms of structured gambling for the sake of the thrills involved and the (not too much) less-than-even chance of winning large sums of money. Surely the slot-machines that one sees everywhere in Nevada exploit a human weakness in this way. Hardly anyone is addicted to them even in an appropriately figurative sense, and some even profit occasionally from playing them. But it is a statistical truth that most plays are losing ones and that the machines will win in the long run. Profit is assured for those who "play upon" the very human propensities of the passersby who indulge in them in many cases against their better judgment, "in a weak moment."

Three-Party Cases; Notoriety

Still another sort of human condition that lends itself to exploitation by others is sheer notoriety, or the state of being interesting to others. Exploitation of this condition is often a relation among three parties, or groups of parties. In these cases, the primary party whose traits or circumstances are exploited is not the same as the party (or parties) from whom the profit is derived, although the latter party is also "used" for the exploiter's gain. Norman Mailer's book, *The Executioner's Song*,[19] a "true-life novel" based on the career of Gary Gilmore, the Utah murderer who insisted upon his own execution, illustrates the genre well. The first half of the Mailer book is mainly a narrative of Gilmore's life, his loves, and his crimes, derived in large part from his own words in tapes and letters. Book Two of the "novel" introduces the cast of "literary ambulance-chasers" bent on using the Gilmore story to make as much money as they can. Diane Johnson's review describes how Mailer's book succeeds in both describing and exemplifying this brand of exploitation:

> . . . now enter hordes of people sensing a buck to be made out of Gilmore's refusal to appeal his death sentence, and big money if he gets executed. Into the lives of the sad, consternated people of Provo come reporters, TV people, film people, media lawyers, contracts, names they've heard of (David Suskind, Louis Nizer), names they haven't [Mailer's partner] (Lawrence Schiller) . . . . once you are in the mind of Schiller who becomes the protagonist of Book Two, it becomes obvious why Mailer has kept himself out of the narrative. This account of the exploitation of the poor convict and his relatives is so appalling that the author of the end product—the book you are reading—must seem to be innocent of it, must seem not to be writing it at all, let alone making a reported half a million for starters out of it. It is the "carrion bird" Schiller who must seem the bad guy . . . .[20]

Why should the efforts of journalists to make a profit by selling to their customers the inside story of interesting events and a truthful account of notorious persons strike us as "appalling?" After all, the writers did not stage the events; they simply report, in an organized and interesting fashion, what has already happened and offer their accounts to third parties who voluntarily, indeed eagerly, pay the price. Nobody was tricked, no one was coerced and there was not even much active noncoercive manipulation of motives. But in the end, the writers are enriched and those whose careers they used to their advantage are dead, demoralized, or devastated; only because personal tragedies have occurred has a profit been made at all. The writers have exploited, that is, turned to their own advantage, the misery of others, just as the carrion bird converts to its own substance the victims of misfortunes in which it had no role.[21]

The carrion bird, of course, performs useful services. Why then is it such an appalling symbol for human beings? Prehaps it is because none of us can be comfortable in the presence of others who have a stake in our misfortunes, especially in those *unnecessary* misfortunes that, unlike inevitable death and taxes, come only to those whose deeds or luck are terrible. Physicians also make their livings off the sufferings of others, but their function is to cure, repair, and prevent, and not *simply* to make a profit for themselves. Mailer and Schiller did little *for* Gilmore and his family,[22] and for that matter they did nothing *to* them either; rather, they took them and left them as they found them, having used them exactly as they were to make a killing for themselves.

Exploitation Films

The Mailer example does not clearly illustrate the exploitation of a human weakness. The book is a serious work of high literary merit, appealing only to the natural and quite respectable curiosity of its readers, and avoiding the lurid or sensational. No one can accuse Mailer of "pandering" to his audience. It may seem otherwise with those books and (especially) films for which critics reserve their most contemptuous label, "exploitation work." Movies that are produced by cynical hacks out to make as many bucks as possible by playing on the transitory prejudices, enthusiasms, fads, or foibles of a particular audience, with no effort whatever to employ with, or style, or measure, are called "exploitation films," or, more commonly, "youth exploitation films." All films, of course, attempt to play on some tastes or dispositions of their projected audiences and are usually made with an eye to profit, but exploitation films are made with no other motive than profit, and turn to advantage the mindless or disreputable traits of their audiences.

Bruce Landesman has presented good reasons, however, for denying that producers of exploitation films exploit the individuals who pay to see and enjoy them. What he argues, in effect, is that the producer's service to the consumer in these cases in not truly *pandering* after all. Landesman points out that there is a distinction between A exploiting a person, B, so that we can say that B suffered exploitation and blame A for it, on the one hand, and A exploiting F, some characteristic or circumstance of B. As Landesman rightly maintains, the exploitation of F may be exploitation in the wholly nonpejorative sense of mere using for a purpose, as when a film director "exploits" the peculair intensity of an actor to bring out the proper passion of the character portrayed, without, of course, exploiting the actor himself. One exploits people by exploiting their traits or circumstances, but one can "exploit" their traits or circumstances without exploiting them. Thus Landesman contends that exploitation films "exploit the vulgar tastes and prejudices of the audience, but . . . it may sound too strong to say that audience members are exploited." I think Landesman is right about this because the fully voluntary participation by the audience is not typically contrary of their interests, their judgements, or their consciences, the way acceptance of genuine pandering is. Nevertheless, we may be inclined to condemn it as pejoratively exploitative of vulgarity—although not exploitative of persons— since it strikes us as a peculiarly offensive kind of wrongful gain analogous to profiting in other cases from the suffering or misfortunes of others.

Other Multi-Party Cases

Playboy *centerfolds*. There remain certain common uses of the term "exploitation" that are more difficult to analyze. Other examples of alleged three-party exploitation are especially puzzling. Consider, for example, the commonly voiced complaint of feminists that centerfold photographs of nude female models in such magazines as *Playboy* "exploit women" (as opposed to merely exploiting their traits). The exploiter in this case must be the publisher who presumably makes a gain by means of the photographs well beyond what it costs to pay the model. Those from whom the profit is made are the readers (or voyeurs), mostly men who willingly pay the purchase price at least partly in order to look at the photographs. If we can agree with Lord Devlin, Professor Schwartz, and Justice Brennan that the taste for that sort of thing in the male audience is a "human weakness," it will follow that the publisher makes a profit by pandering to a human weakness. The publisher exploits male readers by turning their lust to advantage.

But how does that process exploit women? The only woman directly involved is the model and, like any other contractor or employee, her relatively weak bargaining position could be exploited if the publisher offered her an inadequate fee for her labors. That would be to "take advantage of her" in the manner of Marxist (coercive) exploitation. But, in fact, that cannot be what feminists mean, for the models often receive pay in four figures for only a few hours' work, even though they can usually be replaced by any of dozens of understudies eager for their chances to be "exploited" in turn. The only obvious sense that I can discern in which the nude models are exploited is the relatively innocuous one in which all persons whose characteristics or skills are used by others for profit are "exploited." The attractiveness of the model is turned to the advantage of the publisher, but if her role in the process is voluntary and she is paid a fair wage, the exploitation is not at her expense, and *ceteris paribus* is not unfair to *her*.

It is clear, then, that if any women are exploited by the nude photographs, they must be persons other than those who do the posing. Some women not directly involved in the transaction feel that *they* have been exploited (perhaps vicariously) insofar as they share the characteristics of the model that are being turned to another's gain, as their own sexual attractiveness is cheapened, and as this is demeaning to them. That state of affairs may well be objectionable, particularly if we accept the premise that the interest of the ogling man betrays a "human weakness," but it rather stretches the meaning of the word "exploitation" even beyond the limits of its extensive elasticity to use it in this way. At the worst, *Playboy* centerfolds may be degrading to women, but they are not, on that gound, exploitative of them.

A better explanation of the prevailing usage is that proposed by Allen Buchanan.[23] The element of exploitation in the nude photographs, on his view, is not so much vicarious as causally indirect. The centerfolds contribute to an environment in which more direct and familiar types of exploitation of women by men are encouraged, and they do this by spreading the image of women as sexual playthings. The pictures then have a direct causal influence on the way the woman's role is conceptualized in society and that, in turn, makes certain kinds of exploitation possible. The exploitation involves four sets of parties: the publisher, the model, other women (the victims), and other men (the direct exploiters). Both the publisher and the model, on this account, are *indirect* exploiters.

IV. THE ELEMENTS OF EXPLOITATION: DISTRIBUTION OF PROFIT AND LOSS

The third element in the exploitation relation is some redistribution of benefits and harms among the related parties. The one essential feature under this head is that the exploiters themselves be gainers. Exploitation in the usual pejorative sense is the wrongful turning to some advantage by one party (A) of some trait or circumstance of another party (B). There are a variety of ways in which B's interests might be affected by the process, but without gain for A, there is no exploitation.

We would not normally speak of exploitation either (at least in any blamable sense) when B himself stands to gain from the use to which A puts him. In the most general nonpejorative sense, physicians "exploit" sick persons by turning to their own profit the unhappy circumstances of their patients. But they achieve this gain by helping the other party and, unless the fee charged is extortionate, patients cannot complain that they were exploited since they too profited from the process. Of course, typically physicians do not rub their hands in gleeful anticipation of their fees when they encounter a person with a serious ailment; their minds are entirely on the cure and their motives may be commendably humanitarian and sympathetic. But even in the rare case of the ambulance-chasing physician motivated entirely by greed, the patient cannot complain of exploitation if the fees were standard and the treatment beneficial. At the most, we can say that the physician's motives or intentions in that case were "exploitative"—all he or she cared for was "what's in it for me." But even then it cannot be true that the physician's conduct exploited the patient in any blamable sense that provides the patient with a moral basis for complaint.[24]

When, on the other hand, B is harmed by the profitable use to which A puts him, that use may be exploitative. In that case, we can say that the exploitation not only benefits A but is also *at the expense of B*. Now we can even speak of B as a victim of A's exploitation. But if the exploitation was noncoercive yet harmful—if A received B's voluntary consent to the conduct that proved harmful to B—the subsequent harm is not unfair to B. It is not an injustice *to him*; it gives him no grievance; it does him no wrong. Yet it may demean or degrade him; it may present him to the world in an unfavorable (although not inaccurate) light; it may cost him dear. The exploiter may not be answerable to *him* in that case but, as Kleinig reminds us, he may nevertheless be answerable to third parties or to his own conscience, or subject to adverse criticism generally.

Perhaps the most philosophically interesting pattern by which exploitation may distribute losses and benefits is that of actions in which A uses some trait or circumstance of B to make a gain for himself, but B is *neither harmed nor benefited* in the process. A's conduct neither helps B nor is at his expense, and yet it is clearly exploitation of B, even in the strongly pejorative sense. The two most familiar species of this puzzling genus are *parasitic profit* and what the law calls "unjust enrichment."

Noncoercive exploiters are often parasites; they make their livings by attaching themselves to others and, without necessarily injuring their hosts, take their own gains as byproducts of the host's activity. The dictionary recognizes a sense of "parasite" in which the parasite may even be an invited guest ("one frequenting the tables of the rich and earning welcome by flattery").[25] In this case, the host's consent is voluntary; he or she doesn't mind at all being used. Indeed, the host has a use in turn for the flatterer, and the exploitation in this case is not only consensual, it is also mutual. If the relationship is also mutually productive, if it is genuinely advantageous for both parties, it resembles not so much parasitism as the biological process of symbiosis, the living together of two dissimilar organisms in a mutually beneficial relationship. We are not inclined to use the word "exploitation" at all for such cases unless it is to indicate that the trait taken advantage of by at least one of the parties is some sort of defect, or weakness, or symptom, as when one party is paid to provide whippings to the other, a sexual masochist. The need for flattery is itself both a character flaw and a human weakness, hence we can speak even of the well-paid parasitic sycophant as an exploiter. Paid flatterers, moreover, are not productive parasites. They live off their host's vanity, and contribute nothing of genuine substance in return, like the drug provider who lives off the host's addiction and provides only more addiction-strengthening drugs in return.

Parasitic profiteers who are most clearly noncoercive exploiters, however, are the people who operate either with the consent of their "hosts" or, more likely, not against the will of their hosts, the latter being either ignorant of, or helplessly indifferent to their own exploitation, which in turn is neither harmful to them nor in any way productive of benefit to them. The Mailer-Schiller exploitation of the Gilmore family fits this model closely. So do all cases, generally speaking, in which A attaches his profit-sucking tubes to some vulnerable place in the social nexus and extracts some advantage from events that occur in B's life, without depriving B of any gain or inflicting any harm upon him. If this way of taking profit is to be condemned as exploitation, as opposed to ordinary commercial initiative, it must be because of the particular traits or circumstances of B's that are utilized by A. If they are moral virtues like cooperativeness or trustworthiness, or innocent personal weaknesses, or tragic personal losses, the utilizer is said to have "exploited" them for personal gain, but if they are other-regarding moral flaws, or routine or happy events, the word "exploitation" is considered too harsh and judgmental.

In cases of purely parastic exploitation, the exploited party doesn't normally "consent" to the actions of the exploiter. In fact, the question of consent doesn't arise at all simply because the exploiter's actions are not harmful. The questions these cases raise for our principles and policies are: Under what conditions are A's benefits taken unfairly "at B's expense?"; and can such benefiting ever rightly be prohibited by the criminal law? At present, a variety of noncriminal remedies are made available by law of restitution under the rubric "unjust enrichment." A has been "enriched" if he has received a benefit (in almost every case from B, the plaintiff) and the enrichment is "unjust" provided that retention of the benefit would be unfair. When B has "officiously" conferred the benefit upon A, he is not later entitled to restitution. Thus companies are not entitled deliberately to send unordered goods to persons and then sue for payment of the bill or return of the product. Nor are benevolent gift-givers entitled to sue for the return of their gifts at a later time when their feelings toward the recipient have changed. These legal rules accurately reflect moral intuitions and are grounded in socially useful policies. If a zealous and crafty book dealer deliberately sends me a twenty-dollar book that I did not order, along with a bill requesting full payment, there is no unfairness if I retain the book and ignore the bill. I could hardly be accused of "exploiting" the book dealer to my own advantage when the traits from which I took my advantage were the dealer's cupidity, officiousness, or deceit. If I keep the book, the "joke" is on the book dealer. The very scheme which was meant to exploit me—to take advantage of my carelessness, gullibility, or some other "human weakness"—was turned back upon the dealer. Moreover, the rule barring restitution for officious benefits prevents me from being inundated with unordered products and charged with the immense inconvenience of returning them all to their senders. Of course, there is no further point in prohibiting officious conferrals by the criminal law. Simply barring restitutional remedies is sufficient to deter unsavory commercial practices and to "protect persons who have had benefits thrust upon them."[26]

When conferrals of benefits are deemed "non-officious," on the other hand, the courts will order restitution of the benefit to the unwitting benefactor on the theory that were A to insist on retaining the benefit, that would be for him to *exploit* some weakness, innocent mistake, or unavoidable misfortune of B. Conferrals of benefits are non-officious when:

1. The benefit is conferred as the result of an innocent *mistake* (except for undetachable improvements of A's land that he does not want or cannot pay for); or
2. The benefit is conferred as the result of fraud or coercion, either from A or from some third party; or
3. The benefit is conferred at A's request; or
4. The benefit is conferred in an emergency in order to save A or some third party from serious harm.[27]

If restitution is not required in these cases, A has unjustly enriched himself at B's expense, that is to say, has taken (or kept) advantage of B. Especially in those cases in which A has had a hand in arranging the beneficial transfer, he can be said to have "exploited" B.

In most cases, perhaps, A's gain from unjust enrichment is exactly the same as B's loss, so that in contrast to the cases of pure exploitative parasitism discussed earlier, B is harmed as well as exploited. An example of A's gain coinciding exactly with B's loss would be the overpayment of a debt to A because of a "mistake of fact" by the debtor B, when "the payee would be unjustly enriched by the amount of the overpayment if he were permitted to keep it and the payor would be unjustly deprived of that amount if he were not permitted to recover it."[28] But there is no necessary relation in unjust enrichment between A's gain and B's loss, and there are numerous interesting cases in which A is enriched unjustly, that is, in a manner that is unfair to B, even though B suffers a smaller loss or even no loss at all. In these cases, B sues to "recover" A's gain rather than to be compensated for any loss of his own.

Dan Dobbs explains very clearly the difference between restitution of unfairly retained benefits and compensation for damages:

> The damages recovery is to compensate the plaintiff, and it pays him, theoretically, for his losses. The restitution claim, on the other hand, is not aimed at compensating the plaintiff, but at *forcing the defendant to disgorge benefits* [italics mine] that it would be unjust for him to keep.[29]

Dobbs then considers the defendant who, as "a conscious wrongdoer," comes upon plaintiff's missing boat, worth $5,000 at the time, "and sells it to someone else at a very good price above the market, say for $10,000."[30] In this case,

> the plaintiff has lost a boat worth $5,000. He could have sold it on the market for such a price and he could replace it on the market for such a price. If he has no special damages, his recovery of damages would be $5,000, because such a sum represents his loss and would fully compensate him. But the bad faith defendant has sold the boat for twice its market price, whether by luck or clever bargaining or the location of a special customer. The defendant thus has gains resulting from his tort [the tort of wrongful conversion]. If it is unjust for the defendant to profit from his tort, he should be made to disgorge these gains. That is exactly what the law of restitution will force him to do.

The plaintiff in such a case obtains a windfall, but this is thought to be
acceptable because it is the major means of avoiding any unjust enrichment
on the defendant's part [italics mine].[31]

The defendant in the Dobbs example has walked into his own trap and the order that he disgorge his ill-gotten gains for the advantage of the plaintiff has a pleasing moral symmetry to it. In a way, the plaintiff has "exploited" *him* to make a "windfall profit," but the traits and circumstances thus turned to the plaintiff's advantage involved the defendant's wrongdoing, turned back on the wrongdoer himself. The very same scheme that was meant to profit the defendant at the plaintiff's expense has boomeranged, and profited the plaintiff at the defendant's expense.

Whether we are talking about "unjust enrichment" in the strict legal sense or in an analogous moral sense, we must notice that unjust enrichment is often a matter of passive recipience rather than active doing or taking. The enrichment is more often like a windfall than it is like reaping the fruits of one's larceny, burglary, or fraud. Consider the author who dumps a messy manuscript on a grossly underpaid and inexperienced typist and demands that it be typed with great care and finished as soon as possible. The typist takes the manuscript and agrees to the proffered terms. Two days later the amazed author learns that the typist has finished the job one full week in advance of the deadline; in addition, the typist has done a perfect job, worthy of the highest paid professionals. The author now feels that unless he pays the typist a bonus, he has exploited (taken unfair advantage of) the typist's supererogatory zeal. If the author does not pay her more, the typist has no complaint coming, for the author will have discharged his side of the bargain anyway. If the typist's labors were disproportionate to the reward, that was her doing, after all, not the author's. And yet, this seems to be one of those strange cases in which a "gratuity" is morally mandatory. But for the typist's consent to the promised fee, the author's failure to pay an additional amount would be unfair-on-balance to her, and even though she freely consented to the terms, the author's gain is "unjust." How could the law possibly rectify this injustice? Unlike overpayment of a debt, the gain in this case cannot be returned, so restitution is impossible. And legal pressure to make the author pay more than originally agreed would interfere with contractual commitments as well as encourage "gratuitous conferrals" in illicit commercial strategies. Consensual exploitation, it seems, is often not subject to legal correction.

V. FAIRNESS AND UNFAIRNESS

What is the difference between one person merely "utilizing" another for gain, and one person exploiting the other? The correct short answer to this question, of course, is that there is an element of *wrongfulness* in exploitation that distinguishes it from nonexploitative utilization. It is more difficult to characterize the nature of the wrongfulness involved in exploitation, however, and that problem in its full complexity cannot be settled here. In some cases, the wrongfulness appears to be identical with *unfair* treatment of the exploited party, or treatment that would be unfair but for the exploited party's consent. In other cases, unfairness may be incidentally involved as one of the consequences of the exploitation, although the wrongdoing that renders the treatment exploitative is, as Landesman shrewdly suggests,[32] a distinctive and irreducibly independent kind of wrongdoing, quite separate from the unfairness of the subsequent gains or losses. In still other cases of exploitation, there may be no unfairness to the exploited party at all, either inherently or consequentially, either actually or hypothetically ("unfair but for his or her consent"). Landesman gives two convincing examples from the latter category. Exploitation films exploit the tastelessness or vulgarity of their audiences in a shameful way, yet they give their audiences exactly what they want for a reasonable, agreed-upon price, so these films are hardly unfair to their audiences. Neither will it do to say that, but for the audience's voluntary consent, the films would have been unfair, as if there were an element of prima facie unfairness in their showing that consent overrides, as there is, for example, in the case of the rash challenge or the foolish request for an amputation. Similarly, when a parasitic exploiter extracts profit from the misery of another without coercion or deception, there may be something morally repugnant about the gain, but it seems implausible to interpret the wrongfulness as unfairness to the party whose misfortune was "utilized." Perhaps there is a wider genus of "injustice" of which unfairness to a mistreated party is only one species. In that case, we might say it is *unjust* that one party cash in on another party's misfortune, or appeal to another party's vulgarity or prejudice, even though the wrongful gain is neither unfair to the exploited parties nor such that it would be unfair but for their consent. On the other hand, gains earned by taking advantage of other parties' desperate credulity, their self-regarding foolishness, rashness, or stubbornness, or their moral weakness, are not only unjust in this generic sense but also specifically unfair as well (or would be so but for consent). Having made this disclaimer, I shall now proceed to discuss the relation of exploitation to injustice with special attention to the cases in which the form of injustice *is* specific unfairness to the exploited party.

How then do we distinguish between merely turning another person's situation to our own advantage and unfairly "taking advantage" of the person? In treating this question, we must remember that even the fair use of others, in a given instance, might not be morally justified-on-balance, all things considered. In judging the use to be fair, we imply only that the used parties themselves have no personal grievance. It may have been wrong for other reasons for the second party to use the first party in that way, but it was not wrong because his or her *rights* were violated. Moreover, A's use of B might be unfair to B yet justified-on-balance, all things considered, as the least of the evils A had to choose from in the situation. There is always a presumption in favor of fairness and against unfairness, but there is no necessary correspondence between on-balance-justification and fairness. They are quite distinct notions and, in this imperfect world, only imperfectly linked.

Fairness and unfairness, while not as comprehensive concepts as justifiability-on-balance and unjustifiability-on-balance, are nevertheless internally complicated themselves. One and the same act may be fair in some respects and unfair in others, or fair to some affected parties and unfair to others. What we must mean by unfair exploitation is: Profitable utilization of other persons that is either unfair on balance to them, or which in virtue of its other unfairness-producing characteristics *would be unfair on balance to them but for their voluntary consent to it.*

To determine whether a given suspect case is an instance of unfair exploitation and to evaluate it morally from the various relevant standpoints, we must determine:

1. Whether A used the situation of B for his own gain, and
2. In case B did not consent, whether A's use of B was unfair to B, and
3. In case B did consent, whether but for that consent A's use of B would have been unfair to B.

If the answers to 1 and either 2 or 3 are affirmative, the case can properly be described as an instance of exploitation. But then we can raise still another question about it:

4. Given that A has exploited B, was he justified-on-balance, in the circumstances, in doing so?

In case the answer to 3 is affirmative, and our case therefore is one of consented-to exploitation, we can ask still another question:

5. Is A subject to adverse moral criticism for his exploitation of B even though B had voluntarily consented to his actions? That is, was A's use of B morally wrong (or "unjust" in itself) even though it was not unfair-on-balance to B?

A fuller account of the characteristics that distinguish exploitation from mere profitable utilization would follow the outline of the main structural elements in exploitation listed above, and their main combinations and variations. Which ways of using or "playing upon" others' traits or circumstances tend to be unfair to them? Which traits and circumstances of B are such that their utilization by A tends to be unfair (exploitative) to B? Which ways of changing the balance of gains and losses between the parties tend to be exploitative and which do not? Precise and detailed answers to these questions may be impossible in the absence of a complete normative moral theory, but we can hope to say of certain elements that insofar as they present in a relationship between A and B, that relationship tends to be unfairly exploitative, and insofar as they are absent, that relationship tends not to be unfairly exploitative. That would not give us a litmus test in the manner of a set of necessary and sufficient conditions, but it would provide a useful start toward a full analysis of the concept of exploitation.

Consider the first element, the nature of A's use of B's situation. It would surely seem that coercive uses have the greatest tendency to be unfair. When they are disadvantageous to the "victim" (as they normally are), and vitiative of consent (as they always are), they are outright inflictions of harm by A on B for the sake of A's own gain. Forcing another to contribute to one's own gain by threatening him with still greater harm as his only alternative, and by intervening oneself forcibly, or indirectly by capitalizing on his vulnerabilities, to close all his other options is surely to "take advantage of him" as well as to coerce him. (But one can coerce him for the sake of some end other than one's own gain, in which case the exploitative element may be lacking.) Coercive offers all tend to be exploitative, including those that take advantage of the offerer's stronger bargaining position, as in wage-gouging, price-fixing, and profiteering. Coercion, whether through threats or offers, of course, is never voluntarily consented to; hence, when it harms its victim it wrongs him as well.

Subtler forms of manipulation by A, however, may be consistent with B's voluntary consent, and thus not unfair-on-balance. But insofar as A's profitable utilization of B is the consequence of manipulative techniques, it also tends to be unfair to B. I have in mind consent won by seductive luring, beguiling, tempting, bribing, coaxing, imploring, whimpering, flattering, and the like, short of deceptive innuendo, threats, or coercive offers (which diminish or vitiate voluntariness). These techniques do not overpower, nor necessarily deceive by misrepresentation. But they appeal to a weakness in their victim. They bring out the victim's worse rather than better self, but a real self nevertheless. And they engage that lesser self in the process of persuasion, so that in a sense the victim acts—not against his will—but against his "better judgment," and his initial disposition. If the manipulative process is excessively long, intense, or emotional, the victim can complain after the fact that his consent was not fully voluntary because of fatigue, clouded judgment, or otherwise diminished rational capacity. But these defenses will be in vain if the process simply brings out the lesser self by a kind of direct appeal or lure that does not impair the victim's capacities so much as engage his vanities or greeds.

Less likely to be unfair are fishing expeditions in which A merely hangs his lure within range of vulnerable B, attracting his voluntary agreement to a scheme that is in fact likely to promote A's gain at B's expense. A may initiate the process by making a proposal to B that B, after due contemplation, but no manipulative persuasion, readily accepts. Least likely of all to be unfair to B are those agreements that B himself initially proposes and to which A reluctantly responds, as in our earlier example of challenges to contests of skill; yet, as we have seen, these voluntary agreements may nevertheless exploit B in a manner that we would characterize as unfair were it not for the fact of B's voluntary consent. Still, because of that consent, the agreement is not unfair-on-balance, and whether or not the exploiter is subject to censure for his role on other grounds depends on a myriad of background factors and expected consequences—the full range of considerations that are implicated in all questions of on-balance moral justification.

The second element to be examined in any effort to determine whether A's profitable utilization of B is also unfair exploitation is the nature of the traits or circumstances of B that A turns to his own advantage. Insofar as the utilized traits

or circumstances are social virtues (especially rule-abidingness, honesty, industry, cooperativeness, friendly goodwill, or conscientious dutifulness), misfortunes, or human weaknesses, the advantage taken tends to be unfair. Whereas,
insofar as the utilized traits are certain defects of moral character (e.g., cruelty or
greed), or unusually good fortune (especially when unearned or underserved), the
utilization has less of a tendency, or perhaps no tendency at all, to be unfairly
exploitative.

The clearest of all examples of unfairness are those cases in which A takes
advantage of B's trust by cheating or free-loading and thus achieves a dishonest
gain for himself. The result in some cases will be a loss for B, but characteristically
the loss will be minimal. (How much do one hundred million telephone owners
lose per capita when one freeloader cheats on his bill?) In other cases, B will not be
harmed at all, as when A, an impatient driver in a traffic jam, moves his car to the
forbidden emergency lane and then accelerates by a long line of stalled law-
abiding motorists, including B. The indignant B, let us suppose, will get to his
destination no later because of A's cheating, so he cannot claim that his interests
were *harmed*, even though he was unfairly taken advantage of, in the sense that
A's gain was made possible only because B and the other motorists in his lane were
too honorable to do the same thing themselves. To be law-abiding is to be
vulnerable in this way, to make possible a cheater's gain that otherwise would have
been impossible. The most flagrant form of moral parasitism is that which takes
advantage of the honorable forbearance of others and thus unfairly exploits their
honesty and trustworthiness.

The wrongful exploitation of misfortunes and unhappy circumstances may
or may not involve specific unfairness, but in either case it produces a form of
unjust gain that offends the moral sense of the observer in a way similar to that of
genuinely unfair freeloading. Part of what seems outrageous in the cheating and
freeloading cases is that A, who is morally defective, should gain relative to B and
the others precisely because B and the others are morally superior to him. This puts
the moral universe out of joint: untrustworthiness is rewarded and honesty is
penalized (or at least unrewarded). A similar asymmetry is involved when A
profits because of, and only because of, B's misfortune. A does not necessarily
harm the grotesque-appearing victim of an exotic disease (B) by contracting to
exhibit him in his circus sideshow,[33] but he does make a good thing for himself out
of the other's misfortune. Similarly, the television news producer who photographs at length and close-up the hysterical grief of a woman whose children have
been killed, down to the last moan, shriek, or howl, for the effects on the television
audience, turns another's disaster to profit. This is a different kind of moral
parasitism from cheating, and surely less egregious, but when it is not clearly
productive of social gain, it too offends the moral sensibility.

The same asymmetry is present, but in considerably weaker form, when the
exploited trait is a "human weakness." Pandering gives the customers what they
want, or what they come to want after succumbing to temptation, so the customers
themselves can have very little grievance. Surely their complaints, if they have any

at all, are substantially less than that of the law-abiding person whose honesty was put unfairly to another's advantage, or even the unlucky person whose personal catastrophe is milked for another's gain. Still, the moral sensibility is offended by A's profits, even when they are not substantially unfair, if it appears that they are possible only as the other side of the coin of B's lust, gluttony, morbid curiosity, sentimentality, envy, or prejudice. Insofar as the weaknesses in question are "dirty," the money made by exploiting them seems dirty too and, insofar as the existence of these flaws is regrettable, making money out of them seems doubly regrettable. Appealing cynically to others' tastelessness is a way of getting down on all fours with them, and thus demeaning oneself in the process; cynically degraded persons present an appearance even more offensive to moral judgment than the moral weaklings they live off.

In all the types of exploitation we have considered, the distinctively offensive element is not that B has suffered a loss but that A has made a profit. We are not indignant that B must pay an additional penny of his telephone bill or that he is frustrated in the traffic jam (where he would be in any case), but that A has made a good thing for himself out of it. We are not angered because bereaved B has suffered his loss (which occurred quite independently of anything A did) so much as that A has made a kind of windfall profit out of it. We are not offended at the flaws of character and taste pandered to by cynical merchants nearly so much as that they make their own living parasitically off them. In each case, there is a preceived asymmetry between something regrettable and a personal gain that is extracted, quite nonproductively, from it.

It is otherwise when the utilized trait is another's moral flaw or when the utilized circumstance is another's undeserved good fortune. There is actually a rather pleasing sort of moral symmetry when a would-be exploiter is hoist with his own petard, when A's untrustworthiness, cruelty, or greed is exploited by B to A's disadvantage, so that A only gets what he has coming. There is nothing flagrantly offensive, in this case, when the exploiter (B) turns the would-be exploiter's (A's) wrong-doing to his own advantage. And in the other case, when B receives a windfall blessing, we are not offended when A, without harming B, cleverly turns B's good luck to his own advantage.

The final set of considerations bearing on the fairness or unfairness of one person's use of another is the effect on the balance of gains and losses of the parties. Insofar as A's use of B is beneficial to B it tends, of course, not to be unfair to B, and insofar as it is harmful—"at B's expense" in a strict sense—it tends to be unfair. The interesting cases are the intermediate ones in which A's utilization of B's situation is neither harmful nor beneficial to B but, nevertheless, in somewhat weaker sense, "at his expense" too. These tend to be less flagrantly unfair than the harmful cases. Still, when A's "parasitic profits" are unshared or shared unfairly with B, or when A has been unjustly enriched, other things being equal, there is unfair exploitation even without harm.

VI. STATE INTERFERENCE

What, if anything, should the law do about exploitation? A large part of this question is easy enough. When A's exploitative conduct is of a sort that could be expected to be *harmful* to B, and is done without B's voluntary consent, it can be prohibited and punished by law in virtue of the harm principle. If it is the harm principle that legitimizes the prohibition, the act is forbidden not because it is exploitative but because it is harmful. The harm principle alone could handle most cases of coercive and fraudulent exploitation since these are objectionable because they harm victims, or subject them to the risk of harm, without their voluntary consent.

The harm principle can also be stretched without strain to handle the cases of cheating and free-loading discussed above. When cheaters take unfair advantage of the law-abiding forbearance of others to achieve a gain for themselves, they may not directly cause harm to anyone, but if their conduct were to become general, it would cause immensely harmful consequences to social practices and institutions in which all have a stake. The ultimate rationale of rules proscribing such conduct is to protect us from social harms by preventing the frequent occurrence of cheating.

That leaves two troublesome categories: (1) when A's conduct both exploits and harms B, but is done with B's fully voluntary consent, and (2) when A's conduct exploits B without harming him (whether or not it was done with B's fully voluntary consent). The former category is not covered by the harm principle as it is usually interpreted, for that principle is generally thought to be mediated in its application by the maxim *Volenti non fit injuria*, so that consented-to harm is not to count as genuine harm for the purposes of the principle. It is useful in this connection to distinguish two senses of "harm." A harms B in the first sense when his behavior invades and sets back one of B's interests; it leaves B worse off than he would otherwise have been. A harms B in the second sense when he *wrongs* B, that is, treats him unjustly, and violates his rights or deserts. In all but a handful of exceptional cases, instances of harm in the second sense (wrongs) will be instances of harm in the first sense (set-back interests), but not vice-versa. A may set back one of B's interests excusably or justifiably, or the invaded interest may be one that B has no right to have protected. The harm may have occurred in a fair competition, or it may have been at B's request, or B may have consented freely to the risk of its occurring. Thus, A's action when consented to by B may harm B in the exclusively interest-related sense but, insofar as B's consent was genuine, the loss cannot count as a harm in the sense of a wrong. And insofar as the harm principle employs only the latter sense of harm, it cannot by itself legitimize prohibitions of conduct to which a prospective "victim" has consented.

If such conduct is to be prohibited at all, it would have to be on either hard paternalistic grounds—to protect B from the consequences of his own fully voluntary choices—or else on the grounds that *exploitation* per se is an evil of sufficient magnitude to warrant prohibition even when, because of consent, it does not wrong its victim. As we have seen, such consented-to exploitation might have tended to be unfair in the sense that, but for the victim's consent, it would otherwise have been actually unfair to him. But even though it was not unfair-on-balance to B (because of B's consent), it might yet be called *unjust* from the point of view of A.[34] Thus, one might argue that prohibition is justified to prevent *unjust gain* even when it is not necessary to prevent *unfair loss* (or "harm" in the sense of the harm principle). In that case, the coercion-legitimizing principle would be neither the harm-to-others principle nor legal paternalism, but rather a version of legal moralism that justifies the prevention of immoral gains even when there is no wronged victim.

The second troublesome category would even more clearly require a moralistic principle to justify its prohibition, for it includes cases in which there is wrongful gain by A without harm *in any sense* to B. Not only has the exploited party suffered no wrong, but he has not suffered any *de facto loss*, and his interests are in no worse condition than they would be in had A not exploited him at all. If nevertheless the law were to prohibit (or otherwise render impossible) A's conduct, it must be purely on the ground that exploitation per se is a prohibitable evil, that the prevention of ill-gotten gain is as legitimate an aim of the law as the prevention of unconsented-to harm.

I cannot argue with any thoroughness in this limited space either for or against the moralistic principle that legitimizes prohibition of exploitation per se. It is sufficiently important, I think, as a preliminary step, to distinguish that principle clearly from other, less reputable, versions of legal moralism, and to point out that frequently *it* is the legitimizing principle that is tacitly invoked in support of what appears at first sight to be "paternalistic" legislation.

John Kleinig points out that in a number of jurisdictions a sharp distinction is made between self-regarding one-party crimes and two-party consensual crimes. Often the law seems to take a stand against paternalism in the one-party case, once satisfied that the individual has acted voluntarily, and yet refuses to accept his voluntary consent as a defense for his partner in the two-party case. "Thus in some places suicide and attempted suicide have been decriminalized, but aiding and abetting suicide have not. Similarly, possession and use of small quantities of marijuana have been legalized, but not its sale."[35] Sometimes, Kleinig points out, the official explanation of this asymmetry invokes "pragmatic considerations" about the difficulty of acquiring evidence, for example, or "the difficulty of being sure [in the two-party case] that the consent was full, free, and informed."[36] Pragmatic considerations may, of course, be involved in the full explanation, but it is hard to understand how they could include reference to any problem about the difficulty of verifying consent. Why should the voluntariness of an act of consenting be any harder to determine than the voluntariness of any other kind of act, for example, the act of shooting oneself or the act of smoking a cigarette? Kleinig is right in suspecting that the true explanation goes deeper, and is not so much concerned with preventing harm to the voluntary actor or consenter, as with preventing exploitation or other wrongdoing by the provider or abettor. But when the abettors or providers do not themselves profit from their role, when, for example, the service is provided gratis out of sympathy or benevolence (as in mercy-killing), the object of crimimal prohibition cannot be simply prevention of exploitation.

In my view, there is at least a certain plausibility in making exploitation an independent target of criminal proscriptions, although, as I shall argue sketchily below, that plausibility is minimal, and will rarely, if ever, weigh enough to outbalance the standing case for liberty. But when both wrongful harm *and* wrongful gain (exploitation) are missing, I can see no case at all for criminalization. If A plausibly believes he is doing B a favor by *giving* him some marijuana, then certainly he is not exploiting B for his own good. And if the transaction followed B's uncoerced and undeceived request, or A's own freely made offer to which B happily consents, then, in virtue of the *Volenti* maxim, B can have no personal grievance against A. If the marijuana turns out to be physically harmful to him, that was a risk he freely assumed. A's kindness to him may then have proved harmful to his health-interests, but it certainly did not *wrong* him. Since no third-party interests are directly involved in this example, it would be an invasion of B's autonomy to prevent the voluntary transaction, and even worse treatment of A if he were punished despite B's consent. To punish A more than B seems downright perverse.

I am not sure that Kleinig would agree with this judgment. He denies that B's consent to (request for) A's action makes A a mere instrument of B's will. Since A did not have to do as B requested, B's consent does not relieve him of all responsibility for the consequences. From this, however, Kleinig concludes that "B's consent to A's act does not change the quality of A's act in any significant way."[37] This seems to me to be an overstatement. To be sure, there is a sense in which all individuals are responsible for all their voluntary behavior. All individuals must answer, at the very least, to their own consciences, for what they have done. For agreeing to do what he did for B, A is subject to moral judgment, at least on some ideal record, and it will be forever to his credit or blame, as a matter of record, that he acted wrongly or rightly, badly or well. What does *not* follow, however, is that A is answerable to B for the harmful consequences of his agreement to do, without thought of personal advantage, what B, with his eyes wide open, and his judgment unimpaired, freely requested of him. That, it seems to me, *is* a significant change in the quality of A's act produced by B's consent. If the law punishes A in this example, it can only be on paternalistic grounds: to "protect" B from the consequences of his own voluntary choice. The harm principle as mediated by *Volenti* would not justify criminalization, and the harm principle unmediated by *Volenti* collapses into paternalism. Whatever plausibility moralism has as a ground for preventing exploitation is absent in cases like this in which personal gain is not involved. If A were to be punished in this example, it would be for permitting another autonomous person to determine the acceptability of his own risks, and doing so in a manner that is not flagrantly irrational.

The moralistic element in the rationale for criminalization becomes more plausible, however, as A's own role becomes more exploitative. Kleinig's main concern is with cases in which A's own judgment of the probability of harm to B (or the reasonableness on balance of the risk of harm to B) differs from B's. B is willing to take his chance of losing from the transaction he proposes to A, and A thinks that B's willingness to assume that risk is foolish or rash. And yet there is likely profit for A in proposed agreement, so he is willing (as the saying goes) to "take B's money." His expectation is then confirmed by the event; he acts as required by the agreement and exploits B's rashness for his own gain. B's interests are harmed, but B cannot complain that A wronged him since B consented in advance to A's conduct, without coercion or deception. Kleinig, however, won't let A walk away free with his ill-gotten gain. A has blame and censure coming; he had no right to harm B's interests even with B's consent, if he could have avoided doing so. So, even though B is in no position to complain of A's conduct, we disinterested third parties can condemn A for exploiting B's foolishness, and the moral record will contain the true judgment that he acted wrongly in doing so. As Kleinig puts it: "The other's foolishness is something he will have to bear, but to exploit it is not to leave responsibility for the consequences on the other's shoulders alone."[38]

We can agree with Kleinig's moral judgment against A, however, without agreeing that the law has any business interfering with A and B in cases like this. Our moral disapproval of A is quite consistent with the judgment that it would have been wrong, and desrespectful to B's autonomy, for any third parties to prevent A from doing B's bidding in the first place.

The transactions we have been considering between A and B have three relevant variables that yield eight possible combinations, only four of which are interesting and controversial. The variables are (1) whether or not harm results to B's interests, and (2) whether or not B consents voluntarily to A's action, and (3) whether or not A's conduct promotes his own gain. The eight possibilities, then, are as follows:

1. B's interests harmed; B consented; A profits.
2. B's interests harmed; B consented; A does not profit.
3. B's interests harmed; B did not consent; A profits.
4. B's interests harmed; B did not consent; A does not profit.
5. B's interests not harmed; B consented; A profits.
6. B's interests not harmed; B consented; A does not profit.
7. B's interests not harmed; B did not consent; A profits.
8. B's interests not harmed; B did not consent; A does not profit.

Combinations (3) and (4) can be dismissed from the present discussion since both are instances of A wrongfully harming B, and it is uncontroversial that the harm principle can validate prohibitions of wrongful harm-doing, whether or not the actor profits personally. Likewise, we can rule out numbers (6) and (8). In both these cases, A acts in a manner helpful or indifferent to B's interests, and without gain to his own. He may make a gift to B out of disinterested benevolence, having first asked B's permission ("Will you accept this?"), or he might place money anonymously in B's bank account without B's consent. In either case, these are examples of innocent behavior that should raise no problems for the law. Surely no one would argue that officious conferrals should be criminalized.

We have already discussed examples in the four remaining categories in which controversy is possible. In section V we considered these combinations in a discussion of the unfairness that is a frequent element in exploitation. Here we must briefly consider whether there is a point in prohibiting actions in any of these four categories by means of the criminal law. Our discussion can hardly be conclusive as it must draw on a very limited number of examples in each category, but it will be a start.

We have already looked at an example in the first category (1), that of the rash challenge (or acceptance of a challenge) to a contest or wager. A exploits B's rashness and cockiness for his own profit and B's loss. Depending on how we fill in the details, we can make A seem blameworthy for the way he uses B, or not. Surely Kleinig's tendency to censure exploiters of this kind is *sometimes* justified. Censure is especially appropriate if we think of A as exploiting an understandable and not altogether unsympathetic human weakness of B. But the phrase "human weakness" is subject to various interpretations. In the Devlin-Schwartz usage it refers to a universal tendency to indulge one's lower tastes in defiance of one's own governing standards. But B's cockiness in the present example is neither universal nor inevitable; it is peculiar to B, part of his distinctive personality profile. In fact, it is a character flaw, albeit of a largely self-regarding kind—in short, a failure of prudence. If we forbid others to exploit it at B's expense, we remove one of the most reliable methods of correcting it to B's own long-range benefit. A does not merely "take B's money;" he teaches B a useful lesson. As a consequence, B's cockiness may be just a bit more discriminating in the future.

The second category (2) includes cases in which B eventually suffers harm from what A did with his (B's) consent, even though B's initial consent did not seem to A to be a patently unreasonable acceptance of risk at the time. A acts either at B's request (e.g., abetting suicide) or his own initiative (offering marijuana), but with no thought to his own gain, and no subsequent profit. No wrongful harm is inflicted upon a "victim" in this example, so the harm principle cannot warrant criminalization, and no moralistic principle aimed at exploitation has plausible application either, since no element of exploitation is involved, neither wrongful loss nor wrongful gain.

In the fifth (5) and seventh (7) categories are the motley cases in which A's gain seems excessive, even though it does not cause a loss to B. The gain may come from a transaction to which B consented (category 5), such as pandering and passive unjust enrichment, or it may derive from activity for which B's consent was not requested, or even from actions in defiance of B's refusal to give his consent (both in category 7). Let us consider pandering again. The habits of using prostitutes and reading or watching pornography are thought to be shameful by the bulk of the population, including no doubt many of the users themselves. Yet these habits, when discharged through voluntary transactions, harm no one's interests and lead to considerable profits for the panderers. The sellers in these transactions are said to pander to a human weakness, but we must note that the exploited trait in question is nothing like the prudential character flaw of the cocky billiards player. Perhaps it is not so much a weakness or a character defect as it is simply a form of crudity or vulgarity, a kind of bad taste. Exploiting it for profit does no harm at all in a strict sense. At most, "Such conduct offends against an ideal of human excellence held by many people; that is why they condemn it."[39] And it offends people of high sensibility to see others getting rich by catering to it. I can sympathize with that feeling of repugance, but I cannot think of any principled way of translating the feeling into an argument for repression. Any such argument would be likely to warrant massive interference in human life. It is, after all, offensive to see people make a killing from exploitation films that not only pander to poor taste, but reenforce and further degrade it, or to see people reap profits from the mass production of expensive comestics, gossip magazines, or astrological horoscopes, thus exploiting such human weaknesses as vanity, morbid curiosity, and superstition. Other panderers service our sentimentality, misplaced anger, or wishful thinking. In fact, the service of "human weaknesses" is perhaps our foremost growth industry. An affirmative program to elevate tastes and promote rational ideals of excellence would be a much more economical way of eliminating these evils than wholesale criminalization.

Passive unjust enrichments, like the author's gain from the supererogatory diligence of the underpaid typist in our earlier example, fits category 5 perfectly. The typist's interests are not harmed by the author's failure to pay a gratuitous bonus, and a fortiori the typist is not wronged by the author's keeping exactly to their bargain; and yet his gain from her zealousness is unjust and permits us to say that he took advantage of her. For all of that, the law cannot require the author to return the unjustly received benefit, or its equivalent, without encouraging an avalanche of officious conferrals and devious tactics for extracting profits from unwilling "beneficiaries." And if the law of restitution has no proper role in these cases, then a fortiori the criminal law is out of place. No one could bring serious criminal charges against individuals on the grounds that they stubbornly keep to the original terms of their bargains. That would make a mockery of the rules of contract.

Examples of cases in category 7 are harder to come by. Here we must think of A leaving B exactly as he found him, neither better nor worse off, after A has made his own gain by turning some aspect of B's situation to his own advantage quite without any consensual agreement. The cases that come most readily to mind are not pure instances of unproductive parasitism, because of the involvement of third parties—book readers or moviegoers—who are benefited. I have already characterized the Mailer-Schiller use of the Gilmore tragedy in category 7 terms, but it has other distractive elements that may make it less than pure—the fact that among the traits exploited were grievous moral failings, for example, and that the exploited circumstances included extreme misfortunes and suffering. A hypothetical example, therefore, may do better.

Suppose that an author with Mailer's talents writes a book about some lonely hero's inspiring life spent against fearsome barriers for the sake of some worthy goal. The author makes a huge killing in the bookstores but she never thinks of sharing a penny of it with the lonely hero. No wrong has been done the man, no promises broken, no harm inflicted. He has been left exactly as he was, no better, no worse, while the author used the hero's life for her own enrichment. Any sensitive observer can sense the injustice in this, but the problem of designing a purely legal remedy defies solution. We could allow suits for restitution, but if they are to put the moral universe back in equilibrium instead of making it further out of balance than ever, they will have to be governed by a novel complex of rules. Saints and heros would have the right to restitution, apportioned to the degree of their moral excellence, whereas newsworthy villains would get not a penny of further profit from their moral crimes. Persons who are newsworthy for reasons other than their moral excellence or moral failings would be rewarded with some intermediate fraction of the author's royalties. Those who are newsworthy because of some great good fortune that came their way would not be allowed to profit (much) more at the expense of the writer who brings their interesting experience to the public. Those whose sufferings are used to whet the public's curiosity would be given a more generous share. In the end, the public interest will be no better served by such rules and their inevitiable misapplications than it would be by a system of distributive justice that allotted each citizen's share of the economic pie directly, according to the principle that "the good guys get the most, the bad guys the least."

One final point. Our survey strongly suggests that efforts to protect persons from noncoercive and even, in some cases, harmless exploitation characteristically invoke in their defense not legal paternalism but rather legal moralism, a family of proposed justifying reasons that, in turn, is more of a miscellany than may writers have noticed. Legal moralism is a class of legitimizing considerations that includes the need to "enforce morality," the need to protect traditional ways of life, to prevent inherently immoral states of affairs, and to prevent other inherent evils that happen not to be harms or violations of individual rights. One form of moralism that is frequently applied tacitly to the problem of consensual exploitation justifies state interference on what might be called "perfectionist" grounds. Its appeal is to the need to promote and protect certain ideals of human excellence, even when those ideals are dissociated from human interests and unlikely to produce gain or prevent loss to any assignable persons. R.M. Hare describes this mode of argument in his discussion of "whether it is wrong for a pretty girl to earn good money by undressing herself at a 'strip club' for the pleasure of an audience of middle-aged businessmen."[40] Questions of gain and loss, benefit and harm, advantage and disadvantage, he reminds us, are likely to seem quite irrelevant to such moral questions:

. . . those who call such exhibitions immoral do not do so because of their effect on other people's interests; for since everybody gets what he or she wants, nobody's interests are harmed. They are likely, rather, to use such words as "degrading." This gives us a clue to the sort of moral question with which we are dealing. It is a question not of interests but of *ideals.* Such conduct offends against an ideal of human excellence held by many people; that is why they condemn it.[41]

It is a form of legal moralism, then, to argue that the protection of some ideal of human excellence can justify the legal prohibition of normally harmless (because freely consented-to) conduct. One might be employing this form of legal moralism if one argued that it should be illegal for A to give B marijuana gratuitously and benevolently, or for A to assist B's suicide entirely out of pity, or for A to pander even without personal profit to B's "weakness" for pornography. The principle that lies behind such judgments is that it is a legitimate function of the state, through its legal apparatus, to promote human excellence, cultivate virtues of character, and elevate tastes. This principle seemed self-evident to the ancients, but it is repugnant to modern liberals.

A second kind of moralism builds on the first but applies strictly to instances of consensual exploitation only, that is, cases in which A turns some aspects of B's situation unfairly to his own advantage, but does this without wronging B, since either he doesn't set back B's interest (as in parasitism) or he has B's consent (as in passive unjust enrichment), or even B's full cooperation (as in pandering). The non-harmful evil that the law is entitled to prevent, according to this brand of moralism, is unjust gain, even when it is not, strictly speaking, gain at another party's expense, that is, gain correlated with the other party's wrongful loss. It is bad enough that a person voluntarily undergoes degradation, according to this view, but it is much worse still that someone else should profit from it. It is the element of deriving gain from an objective evil, even when that evil is not a harm in any relevant sense, that is said to justify, in extreme cases, criminalization. If the evil opposed by the first form of moralism is degradation of an ideal, the evil opposed by the second form is a type of distributive injustice, namely, that which consists in a person becoming better off as a direct consequence of some evil.

I think we can agree that some voluntary transactions are degrading, and that degradation is an evil even when "harmless," and that exploitation of an evil for personal gain is a greater evil still. But none of these evils are necessarily harms, wrongs, invasions of rights, or personal grievances that people can voice on their own behalf. Exploiters can be made, in egregious cases, to disgorge their ill-gotten gains, thus cancelling the distributive injustice, but when restitution is not feasible, the evils that remain "float free," so to speak, without being wrongs to anyone in particular. They are, in a sense, "unjust" without being unfair on balance *to* anyone. Their freefloating character makes it doubtful indeed that they could ever be sufficiently evil to warrant legal coercion by means of the criminal law. That blunt and undiscriminating instrument, unless aimed at serious harms and wrongs, in quite sure to cause more evil than it can possibly prevent.[42]

Notes

1. Joel Feinberg, "Legal Paternalism," *Canadian Journal of Philosophy*, vol. 1, no. 1 (1971), pp. 106-24. (Reprinted in this book as chapter 2.)

2. For a fuller and more accurate account, see Allen Buchanan, "Exploitation, Alienation, and Injustice," *Canadian Journal of Philosophy*, vol. 9, no. 1 (1979), pp. 121-139.

3. John Kleinig, "The Ethics of Consent," in Kai Nielsen and Steve C. Patten, eds., *New Essays in Ethics and Public Policy, Canadian Journal of Philosophy*, supplementary volume VIII (Canadian Association for Publishing in Philosophy, 1982).

4. *Webster's New Collegiate Dictionary*, 3rd ed. (Springfield, MA: G. & C. Merriam Co., 1977), p. 699.

5. The facts in this hypothetical case are very close to those in the actual case of *R.* v. *Wright*, 1 Coke on Littleton 194 (127a, 127b); 1 Hale PC 412. See John Kleinig, "Consent as a Defense in Criminal Law," *Archives for Philosophy of Law and Social Philosophy* (Wiesbaden: Franz Steiner Verlag GMBH, 1979), vol. 65, no. 3, pp. 335 ff. See also the more recent case of *State* v. *Bass*, 255 N.C. 42 (1961); 120 S.E. 2d 580; 86 A.L.R. 2d 259. "A man asked a physician to cut his fingers off so that he could collect insurance money. The physician was convicted of being an accessory to mayhem. The court held that consent of the person was no defense to the charge . . . ." See Jesse Dukeminier "Supplying Organs for Transplantation," *Mich. Law Review* 811(1968). Similar problems are involved in cases about, and legislation governing, the *transfer* of bodily organs. Dukeminier gives some examples: "In some foreign countries live persons are not permitted either to give or to sell their spare organs when delivery is to take place during life. In Italy, such a statutory provision exists as a result of an incident which occurred in the 1930's when a rich man bought a testis from a young Neopolitan and had it transplanted by a surgeon. The public outrage resulted in the passage of a law prohibiting the sale or gift by a live person of an organ if removal of the organ could produce a permanent deficiency. The Italian law was modified in 1967 to permit the removal of kidneys from live persons for transplantation . . . [In America] criminal law sets limits on the ability of a patient to give his informed consent to a surgical operation that is not for his benefit, but . . . exactly what those limits are is unclear. It is clear that one cannot consent to the infliction of death, and consequently an unpaired vital organ such as the liver cannot be consensually removed. Under some circumstances, a person cannot consent to serious bodily injury; the removal of an organ, *even with the donor's consent* [italics mine], may constitute the crime of assault and battery or the crime of mayhem . . . ."

6. *Parade Magazine*, June 29, 1980.

7. The point is well illustrated in the 1973 movie *The Sting*, which tells the story of a large profit made by some swindlers by turning the greed of a ruthless gangster to their own advantage. The comeuppence of the ganster was so "just right"—so much what "he had coming"—that even though his fleecing was thoroughly fraudulent, we would not naturally use the pejorative "exploitation" to describe it.

8. Whether or not it is possible to speak of nonthreatening proposals as coercive has been the source of much recent controversy, partly because of differing analyses of coercion, partly because of different understandings of what threats are. Among the leading contributions to the subject are: Robert Nozick, "Coercion" in *Philosophy, Science, and Method*, eds. Sidney Morgenbesser, Patrick Suppes, and Morton White (New York: St. Martin's, 1969); Harry Frankfurt, "Coercion and Moral Responsibility," in *Essays on Freedom of Action*, ed. T. Honderich (London: Routledge and Kegan Paul, 1973); Virginia Held, "Coercion and Coercive Offers" in *Coercion: Nomos XIV*, eds. J. Roland Pennock and John W. Chapman (Chicago: Aldine-Atherton, 1972); Michael D. Bayles, "Coercive Offers and Public Benefits," *The Personalist*, vol. 55 (1974); Daniel Lyons, "Welcome Threats and Coercive Offers," *Philosophy*, vol. 50 (1975); Vinit Haksar, "Coercive Offers (Rawls and Gandhi)," *Political Theory*, vol. 4 (1976); Donald VanDeVeer, "Coercion, Seduction, and Rights," *The Personalist*, vol. 58 (1977); and Theodore Benditt, "Threats and Offers," *The Personalist*, vol. 58 (1977).

9. Eric Mack protested at the Liberty Fund Conference that it is profoundly misleading to label as "coercion" a proposal whose effect is to create a net *increase* in a person's open options, and surely the woman in our example has one new alternative, after receiving the proposal, that she did not have

234   JOEL FEINBERG

before, so in a sense her *freedom on balance* has been increased. This point must be granted to Mack. Still it remains true, and consistent with Mack's point, that the millionaire has "forced" (or "coerced") her into becoming his mistress.

10. *Time Magazine*, June 20, 1977, p. 54.

11. *Ibid.*

12. Patrick Devlin, *The Enforcement of Morals* (London: Oxford University Press, 1965), p. 12.

13. *The Wolfenden Report: Report of the Committee on Homosexual Offenses and Prostitution* (New York: Stein and Day, 1963), p. 163.

14. Louis B. Schwartz, "Morals Offenses and the Model Penal Code," *Columbia Law Review*, vol. 63 (1963) as reprinted in *Morality and the Law*, ed. Richard A. Wasserstrom (Belmont, CA: Wadsworth, 1971), p. 96.

15. *Ibid.*, p. 97.

16. 383 U.S. 463 (1966).

17. *Ibid.*, p. 467, quoting *Roth* v. *United States*, 354 U.S. 476, 495-96 (1957) (Warren, C.J., concurring).

18. This interpretation of coercive offers is expanded with considerable ingenuity by Harry Frankfurt, "Coercion and Moral Responsibility."

19. Norman Mailer, *The Executioner's Song* (Boston: Little, Brown, 1979).

20. Diane Johnson, "Death for Sale," *New York Review of Books*, vol. 26, December 6, 1979, p. 4. Johnson's reaction strikes me as excessive. Mailer depicts Schiller as someone troubled by his reputation as a "carrion bird," very sensitive to the interests of those he is "exploiting," worried in his conscience, and very determined to be as "professional" as possible. Still, Mailer's attitudes toward Schiller seem ambivalent, and the facts are never altogether clear to the reader, so we can treat the episode as interpreted by Ms. Johnson at least as a "hypothetical example" of great philosophic interest, even if not altogether accurate historically. Whether Schiller was an exploiter or not, there is no doubt that those who sold tickets to the execution, the wax museums who bid for Gilmore's clothes, the sellers of Gilmore T-shirts, and many others were.

21. Consider the uproar when Hollywood's MGM film studio announced plans to base a movie on "the Yorkshire Ripper," who had slain thirteen women in five years of terror. The film company was denounced by the Labour MP for Leeds for "cashing in on other people's tragedies . . ." while the *London New Standard* editorialized: "Leeches suck the blood of others and get fat by it. MGM executives are proposing to exploit the vile deeds of a man who has brought fear and misery to countless women in the North in order to make a 'contemporary mystery thriller' to titillate audiences inured to horror on the screen and ready for new deprivities" (Associated Press Dispatch, London, December 24, 1980).

22. The $50,000 paid to Gilmore for "exclusive rights" and $25,000 to his disturbed girl friend dribble through their hands almost entirely before the book's story is even finished.

23. In his remarks at the Liberty Fund Conference in Lutsen, Minnesota.

24. The public in the United States has traditionally attached a kind of stigma to life-insurance agents and undertakers, but not to physicians. Viviana A. Rotman Zelizer explains why: "The occupational stigma of selling insurance cannot . . . be explained away by an unqualified statement of its relation to death in general. It is the specific nature of that involvement which built its ill-repute. To life insurance salesmen, as to undertakers, death is a moneymaking business. As 'businessmen' of death they are differentiated from the 'professionals' of death, physicians and clergymen, whose connection to death is made legitimate by their service orientation . . . Regardless of the individual motivations of the practitioners—their greed or beneficence—professions institutionalize altruism while business institutionalizes self-interest. To save and to heal is holier than to sell." (*Morals and Markets: The Development of Life Insurance in the United States*, p. 135.)

25. *Webster's New Collegiate Dictionary*, 3rd ed. (Springfield, MA: G.&C. Merriam Co., 1977), p. 832.

26. American Law Institute, *Restatement of the Law of Restitution* (1937), Chap. 1, §2.

27. *Ibid.*

28. *Ibid.*, Chap. 1, §1, comment d.

29. Dan Dobbs, *Law of Remedies* (1973), p. 224.

30. *Ibid.*, p. 223.

31. *Ibid.*, p. 224.

32. In his written commentary on the first draft of this essay, which was distributed at the Liberty Fund Conference in Lutsen.

33. But he would be harmed if the avoidable loss of dignity is a "harm" even when the diseased person does not care about his dignity. Harmful or not, the loss of dignity is an *evil*, and drawing profit from an evil is the nub of what offends in this kind of exploitation.

34. For the distinction between justice as a virtue of actors and justice as the effects of actions on the rights of "the other party," see Josef Pieper, *Justice* (London: Faber and Faber, 1957), pp. 13 ff.

35. Kleinig, "Consent as a Defense in Criminal Law," p. 340.

36. *Ibid.*

37. *Ibid.*, p. 344.

38. *Ibid.*

39. R.M. Hare, *Freedom and Reason* (Oxford: Clarendon Press, 1963), p. 147.

40. *Ibid.*

41. *Ibid.*

42. In fact, however, the anti-exploitation principle may constitute a part or the whole of the actual rationale of various crimes now on the books. If a fortune teller, necromancer, or astrologer (A) takes advantage of B's superstitious credulity to make a profit at his expense, that is a fraudulent swindle and a kind of exploitation. If B acts on the phony advice or prophesy, the profit of A is doubly at his expense. (Imagine that B applies the prophesy by betting on a losing horse or buying a failing stock.) But if precisely the same phony advice is given *gratis*, with precisely the same result, there is no exploitation since A does not gain. The transaction in that case might well be a severe case of malicious mischief, but since there was no "unjust gain," it is probably not a crime in most places. Thus the rationale of some crimes seems aimed more at unjust gain than at unjust harm. The entire rationale of such disparate crimes as ticket scalping and blackmail may be provided (for better or worse) by the anti-exploitation principle. The blackmailer (A), by taking money for not doing what he has a perfect right to do otherwise (reveal the truth about B), seems to be punished for making an unjust gain off B rather than for harming or wronging B. See Jeffrie G. Murphy, "Blackmail: A Premininary Inquiry," *The Monist*, vol. 65 (1981), pp. 22-27.

Chapter 13

Paternalism and Promoting the Good

Dan Brock

> Paternalist: "Recent studies indicate only fifteen percent of Americans use their seat-belts. We ought to do as some European countries have done and make it illegal to drive a car without the seat-belt fastened. It's just downright stupid not to use seat-belts."
>
> Anti-Paternalist: "I agree with you that it's stupid not to use seat-belts, but people have a right to decide for themselves whether to use them, so long as only they are harmed by not using them. No one else has a right to make them use seat-belts for their own good."

Any actual case always turns out to be more complicated than this, but it often seems that, in disputes about whether some particular paternalistic interference is morally justified, once various disagreements about matters of fact have been stripped away, we encounter old familiar antagonists: on the one side, those who appeal to a cost/benefit, or general consequentialist calculus in support of the interference, and, on the other, those who resist the interference with an appeal to a general right to liberty, self-determination, or autonomy. And this in turn suggests that the dispute can be finally settled only by settling the adequacy of a general consequentialist moral theory in comparison with theories that hold that persons have basic moral rights that consequentialist considerations do not, at least sometimes, justify infringing. But this, of course, is about as perennial and deep-seated a dispute as exists in moral philosophy, and it certainly does not appear reasonable to expect an early resolution of it. Pessimism reasonably arises about what we can expect in the way of progress on a theory of paternalism. I, myself, have construed the underlying issue in this way on previous occasions, and I believe many recent philosophical treatments of paternalism, and disputes about paternalism, may be understood in these terms. In particular, many recent accounts of when paternalism is morally permissible seem to presuppose some form of moral rights theory, reflecting, no doubt, the increasing prevalence of such theories in moral philosophy generally. Sometimes this is explicit, as, for example, when Jeffrie Murphy discusses the implications of a finding of incompetence:

> Basic human rights (including the right to do stupid and dangerous things if one so desires) may be set aside, and the incompetent person may be treated as the object of someone's (usually the states') benevolent concern and management.[1]

John Rawls similarly makes weaknesses or infirmities of one's reason or will a necessary condition for infringing on paternalistic grounds the particular liberties whose priority is expressed in the form of rights.[2] In others, the rights-based structure is less explicit, but, I believe, still presupposed. For example, it is widely held that medical treatment of competent, conscious adults is morally, and not just legally, impermissible without their consent. This is commonly explained to be necessary to avoid violating various rights, such as the abstract rights to liberty, autonomy, or self-determination mentioned above, or the somewhat more specific right to control what is done to one's body. In the law, the appeal is often to a legal right to bodily integrity, or to the more general right to privacy; in the absence of free and informed consent, medical treatment generally constitutes a battery.

Some recent general theories of paternalism have been formulated in terms of consent. Rosemary Carter has developed an account of paternalism according to which it is justified only by prior, or certain specifically qualified forms of subsequent, consent.[3] And John Hodson has offered the following principle of paternalism:

> Paternalistic interventions are justified if and only if (i) there is good evidence that the decisions with respect to which the person is to be coerced are encumbered, and (ii) there is good evidence that this person's decisions would be supportive of the paternalistic intervention if they were not encumbered.[4]

As Hodson spells this out (I shall take up the notion of encumbrances in more detail later), this too comes, in effect, to the view that for paternalistic intervention to be justified, it must be that, except for particular sorts of present distortions in individuals' ordinary decision processes, they would consent to the intervention. We strip away the encumbrance, e.g., mental illness, to find what the actual person's will would have been in its absence, and whether he or she would, when unencumbered, consent to the paternalism.

Paternalism is action by one person for another's good, but contrary to their present wishes or desires, and not justified by the other's past or present consent.[5] Given an ordinarily resisting subject, therefore, consent appears an unlikely candidate for justification of paternalism. That many prominent treatments of paternalism can be understood as embodying some form of "in the absence of specified conditions, the subject would consent to the intervention" condition suggests how deeply the rights view pervades this subject. Free and informed consent to another's action can be best understood as a means of waiving the right that that action would otherwise violate. And the requirements in basic moral principles regulating paternalism of free and informed consent, or of potential consent in the absence of specified conditions, seem justified only if moral rights, whose violation is to be avoided, are assumed present. If the goal is merely to maximize the good, on most any common or plausible account of what the good is, the presence or absence of consent would at most create a strong presumption that the action did or did not promote the subject's good. Bur since persons can and sometimes do consent to what does not best promote their good, as well as refuse consent to what would promote their good, consent could not be a requirement, a necessary condition, for justified action undertaken for another's good.

The feature of rights bearing on paternalism that a consequentialist will object to, or at least find problematic and in need of further argument, has already been noted in the quote from Murphy above—"the right to do stupid and dangerous things if one so desires." This is not quite correct, since few would defend a specific right whose content was doing stupid and dangerous things. Rather, the point is that various rights—including ones practically important to paternalism, such as a right to control what is done to one's body, to privacy, or to specific liberties—give the rightholders an entitlement to act as they see fit within the areas of behavior protected by the right, even when the actions in the exercise of the right are stupid or dangerous to the persons themselves. For some actions that are stupid or dangerous to their agent, or more generally that fail to best promote their agent's good, a consequentialist will believe paternalistic intervention justified, while a rights theorist will resist such intervention by appeal to rights.

Nevertheless, no defender of such rights holds that there are no conditions in which people's current choices in the exercise of their rights may be overridden on paternalistic grounds. Three prominent, plausible, and closely related accounts of a necessary condition for permissible paternalistic interference are that the subjects be incompetent, or their choices be encumbered or involuntary. The general idea is that so long as people are competent, or their decisions and conduct are unencumbered or voluntary, they have a right to make even bad choices about how they will act, without paternalistic interference by others. I shall argue in section I of this paper that, in each of these three requirements designed to limit paternalistic interference, there is an ambiguity that raises serious doubts about whether they can successfully fulfill that role. These same doubts make the appeal to moral rights to protect a person's bad or foolish choices problematic as well. I shall suggest in section II that a consequentialist account of paternalism, to the effect that paternalism is justified just in case it maximally promotes the good of the subject, avoids these difficulties without, as often thought, permitting too much paternalism.

Since I consider consequentialist moral theories unsatisfactory in other respects, most especially on distributive questions, and the appeal to moral rights plausible for a considerable range of moral issues, I have strong misgivings about proposing a consequentialist treatment of paternalism. I want to stress, therefore, that it is the special role moral rights commonly play in treatments of paternalism that I will be questioning in this paper, and not their place in acceptable moral theories generally. Later I shall take up briefly whether a consequentialist treatment of paternalism can indeed be successfully kept independent of commitment to a general consequentialist moral theory.

I

The difficulty for the incompetence and encumbrance limitations on the use of paternalism is essentially the same. I shall discuss them together, although noting differences in the conditions when they are relevant to my purposes here. As already noted, many philosophers make some condition of incompetence a necessary condition for justified paternalism. Murphy can again serve as one example. He explicitly argues that incompetence is a necessary condition for justified paternalism, develops three forms of incompetence with regard to decisions of a given sort—being ignorant, compulsive, or devoid of reason with respect to them—and stresses that competence is compatible with foolish or dangerous decisions. Hodson, similarly, makes an encumbered decision a necessary condition of justified paternalism, and defines an encumbered decision as "made in circumstances which are known to affect decision-making in such a way that the person making the decisions sometimes comes to believe the decisions were mistaken or unfortunate.[6] Rawls notes that "in the original position the parties assume that in society they are rational and able to manage their own affairs."[7] He seems to have some form of incompetence or encumbrance condition in mind when he goes on to argue that they will agree to specific forms of paternalism only in circumstances in which this assumption turns out to be false, only "to protect themselves against the weaknesses and infirmities of their reason and will in society."[8] The first part of the quote from Rawls brings out an underlying assumption of each of these views and, I believe, of rights views in general: Ordinary, normal adults, generally have capacities sufficient to order their lives without unwanted interference by others. The complement of this is that paternalism is only permissible when its subjects are incompetent/encumbered with regard to the decision in question, that is, when they lack those capacities necessary for satisfactorily ordering their lives without interference from others. Normal adults will lack the capacity only when they are subject to a specific incompetence/encumbrance to which normal adults are not in general subject, or when they are subject to a specific defect of will or reason adversely affecting their normal deliberating and decision-making capacities. The choices of normal, competent/unencumbered adults then are binding in the sense that they ought not to be interfered with on paternalistic grounds.

While closely related, the concepts of competence and encumbrance are at least different in that an encumbrance is a property of a particular decision, while competence is often considered a capacity for decisions or tasks of specified sorts that endures over time. I want first to examine more closely the concept of competence and, in turn, the conception of incompetence and its rationale as a necessary condition for paternalism. I shall return subsequently to the concept of an encumbrance. Daniel Wikler, in discussing paternalism and the mentally retarded, introduced a distinction between two senses of competence that will be helpful in illustrating the problem with the incompetence requirement for paternalism.[9] What Wikler calls the relativist conception (hereafter competence$_r$) views competence as a matter of mental capacity, an attribute admitting of "more" and "less" and that people have in differing degrees. In this view, where one draws the line between impaired and unimpaired, competent$_r$ and incompetent$_r$, is arbitrary. We draw it somewhere between the levels of capacity of normal adults and of the mildly retarded; relative to the gifted, however, normal adults are impaired or incompetent$_r$. The alternative conception views competence as a range or threshold property (hereafter competence$_t$) possessed in equal measure by all who possess it. General intelligence or intellect is not a threshold property, but competence understood as "intellect's power in meeting a challenge" may be. Wikler states, "A given challenge may be wholly and fully met by the use of a certain amount of intelligence if the challenge is not too great. Though a person may have more intelligence than another, he will be no more competent at performing certain tasks; his added power is simply an unused surplus. Those lacking enough intelligence for the task will be incompetent to perform it; while those having sufficient intelligence will be equally competent however great the difference in their intellectual levels."[10] Although he grants that "added intelligence may increase the benefit to be derived from a given task or opportunity," Wikler understands the competence condition in terms of sufficient capacity "to understand how to avoid harm . . . to comprehend and avoid the "downward risks.'"[11] It is true that most of the usual rights to liberty(ies), autonomy, or self-determination are commonly not extended to young children, the retarded, and many mentally ill persons, yet are fully extended to all normal adults, however much they differ in intelligence. This alone strongly suggests that it is competence$_t$ that is assumed by the rights theorist to be necessary for a person to possess rights. Competence seems generally understood as a minimal requirement, and as implying capability for a minimally satisfactory performance. A competent decision-maker, then, in the sense necessary for possession of a right to liberty with regard to such decisions, need not be a first-rate decision-maker; and a choice, in order to be competent and protected from paternalistic interference, need not be the best choice.

But why *should* the threshold and not the relativist conception of competence be employed in a theory of rights and paternalism? Wikler was seeking an account of competence that would explain how it is consistent for normal persons to act paternalistically toward the mildly retarded while rejecting the right of the gifted or very intelligent to act paternalistically toward them. His point was that the level of difficulty in certain key tasks is in large part socially determined, and that society sets this level so as to render the average person, though not the mildly retarded, competent$_t$. In a theory of moral rights and paternalism, the threshold conception of competence has the effect of requiring a minimal capacity to understand and avoid major harms in an activity in order to possess the relevant rights. Those rights in turn protect the conduct of competent persons, so understood, from paternalistic interference.

The difficulty with allowing this, but only this, restriction on basic moral rights can be brought out in the following way. Why have even a competence$_t$ requirement for the possession and exercise of moral rights? The most natural and plausible answer is that, when such a requirement is not satisfied, for persons to have moral rights that prohibit paternalistic interference with their actions would be contrary to their good by allowing them to cause significant perventable harm to themselves. The prevention of harm is the motivation for the moral-rights theorist allowing any paternalistic interference at all with persons acting as they wish. But this same general motivation supports the relativist, and not merely the more limited threshold, conception of competence. Why, at the level of basic moral principles, should only the avoidance of major downside risks and harms limit possession and exercise of moral rights? Persons undertake activities in the first place in order to obtain the benefits the activities promise, and not merely to avoid the potential danger they carry. They seek to promote their good quite as much by obtaining such benefits as by avoiding such harms, and the former is equally relevant to their capacity or competence to promote their good effectively in an activity. They may fail to act to promote their good as much by failing to secure the benefits they seek as by failing to avoid harms. But if the conception of competence is expanded to include the capacity to secure the benefits of an activity as well as to avoid its risks and harms, the conception of competence will usually be, as Wikler himself agrees, a relativist conception, admitting of considerable differences in degree, and not a threshold conception. And why shouldn't the necessary condition for paternalistic interference be incompetence in this expanded conception, since incompetence$_t$ is only one form, although a particularly gross form, of defect of reason or will, one way in which people's choices and resultant conduct may fail best to promote their good? The other principal form of defect or failure is just what is captured by the expanded conception.

Consider Jones, a fellow of, at best, average intelligence and rather limited imagination, who inherits a moderate sum of money from his parents. He is competent$_t$ to handle his own affairs, and is able to invest his funds so as to avoid disastrous losses, although he thereby barely stays even and never has the additional funds for travel and other opportunities that he had hoped for from his inheritance. Jones is competent$_t$ to handle his own financial affairs, although compared to his friend Smith, a brilliant, imaginative investment counselor, he is incompetent$_r$ or impaired. But incompetence$_r$, that is, incompetence in the expanded sense suggested above, makes Jones's decisions defective and prevents him from best promoting his good just as incompetence$_t$ would. The point of the example is not that Jones's choices should be overridden. The considerations taken up in section II below, as well as Jones's competence, bear on that conclusion. Rather, the point is that Jones's decision-making competence is not captured by the threshold conception restricted to harm avoidance, but requires the broader relativist conception concerned with both potential benefits and harms. Full competence in this broader sense seems nothing less than the capacity to make the best possible choices for promoting one's good.

Hodson's conception of an unencumbered decision is subject to a similar ambiguity regarding whether it must be the decision which best promotes the agent's good. Recall that, for Hodson, paternalism requires "good evidence that the decisions with respect to which the person is to be coerced are encumbered," and encumbered decisions are characterized as decisions "made in circumstances which are known to affect decision-making in such a way that the person making the decisions sometimes comes to believe the decisions were mistaken or unfortunate."[12] Examples Hudson offers of encumbrances are ignorance, emotional stress, compulsion and undue influence, mental illness, and nonrationality. Hodson is explicit that his account asks what the specific person's actual choice would have been in the absence of the encumbrance, and contrasts this with theories that would substitute for an actual person's unencumbered choice what a fully rational being would choose. An unencumbered choice need not be a fully rational choice, and need not be, in that sense, the best choice. The idea of an encumbrance, then, is a specific condition that adversely distorts the actual person's decision from what it would otherwise have been. And this would suggest that the minimally competent investor Jones is not encumbered in his investment decisions. Although I am not certain, I believe this is what Hodson's view of Jones would be. But, however that may be, the important point is that Jones's decisions *are* made in circumstances "known to affect decision-making in such a way that the person making the decisions sometimes comes to believe the decisions were mistaken or unfortunate." They *do* satisfy the condition for encumbered decisions. What makes Jones's decisions ones that he later comes to view as unfortunate or mistaken are not temporary onslaughts, such as emotional stress, that impair his ordinary decision-making capacities, but normal and enduring limitations in those capacities—his modest intelligence and limited imagination. If these are encumbrances, we must say that Jones's decisions are permanently encumbered by these limitations. But then it would seem that *any* conditions, temporary or permanent, that lead Jones to make decisions that he comes to view as unfortunate or mistaken, as failing best to promote his good, are encumbrances or impairments. And, likewise, any decisions that in avoidable ways do not maximally promote his good are encumbered or impaired.

The point can also be put in terms of rights. If the right to self-determination may be overridden on paternalistic grounds when one's decisions are impaired by a temporary encumbrance like unusual emotional stress, why should they not be overridden as well when they are impaired by a permanent encumbrance like limited intelligence? Both create defective decisions that prevent people from best promoting their good. I do not mean to claim that this is Hodson's view, or the view of rights theorists in general. It is not. But the point is that Hodson's concept of an encumbrance, like the concept of incompetence, seems to include *all* decisions and decision-making made in circumstances that do not result in the maximally best decision. If this is so, the necessary condition for paternalistic interference of incompetence or an encumbrance will not do the job intended of protecting some bad decisions and conduct from such interference.

At the risk of belaboring my general argument, I want to consider one other influential treatment of paternalism that I believe is subject to the same sort of difficulty as the incompetence and encumbrance limitations. Joel Feinberg, following Mill, endorses what he calls weak paternalism, which permits paternalistic interference only with an agent's involuntary choices.[13] Voluntary choices are made

> While fully informed of all relevant facts and contingencies, with one's eyes wide open, so to speak, and in the absence of all coercive pressures or compulsions. There must be calmness and deliberateness, no distracting or unsettling emotions, no neurotic compulsion, no misunderstanding. To whatever extent there is compulsion, misinformation, excitement or impetuousness, clouded judgment (as, e.g., from alcohol), or immature or defective faculties of reasoning, to that extent the choice falls short of perfect voluntariness.[14]

Voluntary acts, Feinberg adds, "represent (their agent) faithfully in some important way: they express his settled values and perferences."[15] But then Feinberg goes on to suggest that running unreasonable risks may be done voluntarily, that weak, foolish, or reckless persons may freely (presumably voluntarily) choose to harm or risk harm to themselves, and that it is even possible (however unlikely) that a choice to inflict injury for its own sake on oneself could be voluntary. Is this a coherent account of voluntariness?[16] Perfect voluntariness, as Feinberg characterizes it, would seem to entail that agents make the best choices possible under the circumstances; all possible defects of reasoning or willing, all conditions that might deflect them from a fully rational choice in the promotion of their good, seem to be ruled out by the various elements of voluntariness. This is not to say that the choice must thereby turn out to be for the best, or best to promote the agent's good. There may be, for example, certain information about consequences that no one possesses, and this may result in a choice different from what would have been best had the information been available. One can, therefore, fully voluntarily shoulder a risk that works out badly. But if relevant information is available (could be acquired?), for example, is known by others, such that if one had it one would not have assumed the risk, then its assumption would not be fully voluntary.

Voluntariness, in Feinberg's sense, assures the absence of avoidable factual mistake, of affective distortion in the choice, and of coercion or compulsion, including internal compulsion. Perfectly voluntary choices must maximally or fully "express [a person's] settled values and preferences." But then how could perfectly voluntary choices involve assumptions of unreasonable risks, or be weak, foolish, or reckless? The obvious answer would seem to be that they are the free choices of a weak, foolish, or reckless person. But can we, in fact, coherently describe fully voluntary conduct that is foolish or reckless? Consider several possibilities.

Person A is not normally foolish or reckless, and does not view herself as such or want to be such, but on a particular occasion she makes a choice that she regards as foolish or reckless. Since she does not want to be and is not normally foolish or reckless, could this choice represent her settled values and preferences, or wouldn't it rather have to be explained by some factor like emotional stress or an unconscious neurotic association that made her decide in this instance in a manner that is "out of character" and contrary to her settled values? But such factors are just what would make it nonvoluntary on Feinberg's account.

Person B often engages in foolish and reckless conduct. These are his settled character traits, and so a particular piece of such conduct is fully "in character." B himself views this conduct of his as foolish and reckless. However, he does not want to be a foolish and reckless person, and has tried repeatedly but unsuccessfully to change. I think we ought to say that B's conduct is involuntary as well. B's conduct does express his settled preferences, at least what economists call his "revealed preferences"—this is the way he standardly behaves. But his conduct does not reflect his settled values, or conception of his good, which include *not* being foolish or reckless. B is not able to act as he wants to act. He is foolish and reckless in spite of himself, and so is subject to the particular form of involuntariness philosophers commonly characterize as weakness of will.

Person C may seem to be what we are after, for she is foolish and reckless like B, but content and even pleased with being such as well. She has no desire to change. A particular piece of foolish and reckless conduct is in character, both as being the way she often acts, as with B, but also and unlike B, in conformance with her conception of her good. The conduct unambiguously represents her faithfully; there seems no reason to assume that it is involuntary. But now the problem is whether, as fully voluntary, we can still describe it as foolish and reckless in the necessary way. Suppose C has the habit of dashing across busy streets, narrowly missing being hit by oncoming traffic. Most of us would view such conduct as foolish and reckless, so there is no problem correctly describing it from our different perspective as foolish and reckless; such conduct forms no part of *our* conception of the good, or *our* rational plans of life. But C, let us suppose, just needs and enjoys more risk and danger in her life than most of us do, and this happens to be one way that she gets it; without it, her life begins to feel flat and boring. Can we still describe C's behavior as foolish and reckless from her point of view? I think we cannot, although we can still describe it as dangerous, both from her and our point of view. She might call it daring or exciting, and unlike the overly cautious and deliberate way in which most people cross streets, but not foolish or reckless; this indicates that it embodies the sort of risk-taking and danger that she values and prefers. Reckless behavior is, roughly, behavior that seriously risks or endangers something its agent values without the promise of any compensating benefit gained or loss avoided of comparable value to the agent. But C, as we have had to describe her, *is* getting a benefit to which she attaches comparable value from her street-crossing, and so her behavior, while dangerous, is not reckless. We can vary the case a bit so that even C might grant that, in one sense, her conduct is foolish or reckless; for example, she explains that she engages in this reckless behavior periodically because it makes her husband admire her fearlessness, or makes her cautious neighbor envy the abandon with which she is able to act. Here, the reckless behavior is still a means to another end she values sufficiently (her husband's admiration, her neighbor's envy) to motivate her to freely undertake the behavior. Once again, while it is necessary that C's husband or neighbor view her behavior as reckless, from C's conception of her good the conduct is not foolish or reckless since it serves another end to which she ascribes sufficient value. And so we still have not found foolish or reckless conduct that is fully voluntary.

Perhaps the closest we can come is with person D. D knows and freely grants that he sometimes acts foolishly and recklessly, with no compensating gain, as with C. But, unlike B, he does not want to be different and so fail to identify with the conduct. Perhaps he once did, but he has long since given up trying to change and now just accepts that that's the kind of person he is. He accepts this limitation as, say, a scientist might come to accept that he or she is not sufficiently brilliant to do genuinely important, original work in her or his field. D might say, with an air of resignation, "I freely chose to dash across that busy intersection, and I grant you it was a foolish and reckless thing to do, but that's just the way I am, the way I sometimes choose to behave." I believe this description of D is an unstable one. It is difficult to maintain the right sort of difference between D and our earlier B. If D really does view this as conduct he would be better off without, however much he has accepted that that is just the way he is and there is nothing he can do to change, he must still nevertheless regret that he is unable to rid himself of it. It is still weakness of will, however much he has resigned himself to his weakness, and so behavior which is in turn not fully voluntary.

The general problem here with the involuntariness condition, as a necessary condition for permissible paternalistic interference, is the same as that to which the incompetence and encumbrance conditions are subject. It too fails to protect the "bad" or "non-best" choices that rights are supposed to protect. On the contrary, it provides a plausible criterion, involuntariness, according to which only the maximally best choices are to be protected from interference as fully voluntary and so fully ours. The rights theorist generally attempts to account for two intuitions: first, that there is a wide array of choices and conduct that are only the agents' business, theirs alone to make and determine, even when others may be able to choose more wisely or interfere for their benefit—the intuition that might be expressed by the response, "you might be right, but it's my life and so it's up to me to decide;" second, that there are some instances in which these choices are permissibly interfered with for the agents' own good, with a necessary condition for such interference being involuntariness, or incompetence, or encumbrance. The difficulty is that the involuntariness standard, just as the incompetence and encumbrance standards, would be satisfied just in case the decision is not the best in the circumstances, and so does not serve to protect some "bad" choices, and some conduct not for the best, which was supposed to be the crucial role of rights in limiting paternalism. Quite to the contrary, these standards instead lend support to what I shall call a consequentialist approach to paternalism: When will the interference in fact maximize the subject's good?

Anti-paternalists might, at this point, accept my argument that the incompetence, encumbrance, and involuntariness requirements fail to provide the limits to paternalism they want, and so simply abandon these requirements. Moral rights to liberty or self-determination, they may again insist, permit us to act as we see fit in the area protected by the right, even when our choices may be foolish or dangerous, and contrary to our own interests or good. Rights are rights to make bad choices as well as good ones, to fail as well as to succeed, and they properly limit paternalistic interference. If incompetence, encumbrance, or involuntariness requirements for paternalism undermine this function of rights, these requirements should be abandoned. But the core question I am pressing here is why we should want rights to have this feature. Why should our basic moral principles prevent others from interfering with our doing what we want when their interfering would be for our own good, while our doing what we want would be contrary to our own good? This seems a perverse failure to attend to our own good that no reasonable moral theory should endorse. There is a commonplace view of persons that will help focus this perversity.

Persons are purposive beings. When they act, they act for a reason and for some end; they engage in goal-directed activity. It is tempting, then, to suggest that action in the strict sense, that is, action that is intentional, must be aimed at some apparent good, some end the agent at least takes as desirable or good. But this would, of course, be too simple. As Harry Frankfurt and others have recently stressed, persons are capable of reflecting on the desires and ends they in fact have, of identifying or failing to identify with particular desires, of deciding they do or do not want to have these desires move them to action, or to be their will.[17] They can form what Frankfurt calls second-order desires, desires that have other first-order desires as their object, and it is this second-order reflection and deliberation that enables us to distinguish between the motivational structure persons in fact have at a given time, and their conception of their good. Where they have a second-order desire to have a desire that they in fact do not have, or not to have a desire that they in fact do have (as was true of person B in the example above), then their actual motivational structure is not coincident with their conception of their good. This provides one sort of exception to a general claim that deliberate, purposive action is always aimed at the agent's perceived good; weakness of will is to be construed along these lines. Paternalistic interference with people doing what they want in these cases will not, in itself, entail either action in conflict with those individuals' own conception of their good, or action interfering with their pursuit of their perceived good. Paternalistic interference in these cases will generally be justified by the consent of the subject of the interference, and then is probably not even correctly understood as paternalism. Consider the other cases in which a person's desires and purposes are as he or she wants them to be. Here, we can say that this complex of ends and purposes reflects, or perhaps constitutes, the individuals' conception of his or her good. For convenience, call all actions when our motivating desires are as we want them to be cases of autonomous action; in autonomous action, agents seek their good as they perceive it. [18]

Since a person's desires and purposes often are in conflict, in order to be pursuing one's perceived good when acting on a desire one wants to have, one's desires have to be rationally ordered within a consistent preference system. The only conception of rationality needed here is the relatively minimal instrumental, or more vs. less conception, according to which, crudely put, it is rational to select the action from among available alternatives that maximally promotes one's system of ends. Rationality in this sense does not determine our ends, but rather determines the most effective means for their promotion. In autonomous, rational action, then, we seek maximally to pursue and achieve our good as we perceive it—this is the ideal toward which purposive action is aimed. [19] But, of course, we do not always attain this ideal; we do not always succeed in acting so as maximally to promote our good. This can arise in any number of ways, some of which have already been mentioned; perhaps the most obvious is when we simply miscalculate the consequences of our action. Now, as has already been stressed, rights protect our acting as we see fit without interference from others, even in at least some cases in which what we are doing *will* fail best to promote our good, and even when the interference would, in fact, succeed in *better* promoting our good. But this feature of rights now appears paradoxical, if not a practical inconsistency. In purposive, autonomous, and rational action, persons seek to promote their good. Why, then, when they are in fact failing to do so, and the interference of others would, in fact, better promote their good, is it rational for a purposive, autonomous agent to resist rather than to accept, indeed welcome, the interference? To resist the interference would seem inconsistent with assumptions of rational agency. And the same can obviously be said about the appeal to moral rights to block others from interfering in our action in ways that would better promote our good than would their not interfering; it seems perversely inconsistent with this conception of purposive, autonomous, and free action. Whether put in terms of rights or not, we have on the one hand a conception of human action as seeking its agent's good, and on the other a deliberate refusal to permit the promotion of one's own good when that will be achieved by the paternalistic interference of another. Without giving up this conception of purposive, autonomous action, the resistance to paternalism and defense of this feature of moral rights appear irrational, or at least in need of further explanation.

Perhaps the foregoing sketch of a person and of purposive, autonomous, and rational action can best be taken as raising a challenge to the defenders of moral rights that are to protect nonbeneficial action from paternalistic interference. I think it unlikely that defenders of such rights will want to reject the features of a person and of purposive, autonomous, and rational action that I have noted. More likely, they will urge that there is more to the conception of a person and purposive action that does make appeal to a right to act on one's own nonbeneficial choices plausible and rational. The challenge, then, is to develop that conception of a person and of purposive action, and to show how it supports such a right.[20]

I would stress again that this argument in no way relies on a general rejection of moral rights or on a general acceptance of consequentialism. Nothing in the above implies that the standard defense of moral rights as restricting other consequentialist appeals, and in particular as prohibiting action sacrificing the interests of some individuals in ways that violate their rights, in order to promote the greater good of others, is unsound. My argument does not entail the general abandonment of moral rights in favor of consequentialism. Moral rights may still be necessary in order to prevent the unfair sacrifice of some persons for the greater good of others. The argument is designed to call into question only the appeal to moral rights by the rightholders deliberately to prevent the maximal promotion of their own good; that is, to insist on the sacrifice of their own good without any seeming compensating advantage to themselves *or* others.

II

I have used the examination in section I of incompetence, encumbrance, and involuntariness requirements for paternalism to develop the problematic nature of the appeal to basic moral rights to liberty or self-determination in order to block paternalistic interference in individuals' nonoptimal choices regarding how their good is to be promoted. Moreover, I have suggested that there is a plausible interpretation of each of these three requirements that is consistent with a consequentialist position that paternalism is justified just in case it maximally promotes its subjects' good. If this position is sound, we cannot settle whether paternalism would be justified in hard cases by appeal to moral rights to liberty or self-determination. Let me give two examples that I consider to be hard cases:

Case 1. Evidence of a nearly conclusive sort has accumulated to the effect that regular cigarette-smoking significantly shortens human life and increases substantially the incidence of various illnesses causing serious suffering and disablement. Despite widespread educational programs concerning these harmful effects, large numbers of Americans continue to smoke. Should the government prohibit for paternalistic reasons the production, sale, and use of cigarettes?

Case 2. Anna is planning to marry Adam. Adam is a deeply neurotic misogynist. Anna's best friend is Bertha, an experienced psychoanalyst who knows both Anna and Adam extremely well. Bertha is confident that the marriage will fail and will cause Anna long and severe suffering before it finally ends. She has discussed her misgivings with Anna, but Anna remains determined to go ahead with the marriage. Bertha knows that the one way she can stop the marriage is to tell Anna, falsely, that Adam has been secretly seeing another woman. Should she do so?

In both these cases, the interference does appear to be for the good of the subject. The opponent of such interference may *express* opposition to it by an appeal to rights to liberty or self-determination, but I hope to have cast some doubt on whether such an appeal serves to *justify* the opposition. I believe that it is only considerations of a consequentialist sort that adequately explain why these are hard cases for a theory of paternalism. I want now to explore whether such considerations can satisfactorily illuminate disagreement about cases like these without appeal to moral rights. The remainder of this paper will be devoted to developing briefly some of the more important features of such a consequentialist treatment.

In the consequentialist view, disagreement about whether paternalism is justified should ultimately reduce to disagreement about whether interference with what people currently want to do will maximally promote their good. What is needed then is a theory of the good for persons.[21] Rather than fully develop and defend such a theory here, which is far too extensive a task for this essay, I shall content myself with noting certain features of principal candidates for such a theory that have important implications for the treatment of paternalism and, in turn, with indicating some of the principal considerations that generate restrictions on the use of paternalism.

For present purposes, probably the most important distinction between theories of the good for persons is between what I will call desire theories and ideal theories. On the desire theory, individuals' good consists in the satisfaction of their desires to the maximum extent possible. This, of course, is extremely crude, and ignores many serious issues and difficulties in the nature of such a view. But the point I wish to stress is that there is a strong subjective quality to individuals' good in this view. This subjective quality has both an ontological component—whether something is for a person's good depends on whether that person wants it—and an epistemological component—we can only know something is for people's good by knowing that they want it. The importance of this subjective element is reinforced by two additional points: the desires of different persons will differ in many cases, and persons are generally considered to be in some sort of epistemically privileged position with regard to what they want. On ideal theories, at least some states of affairs obtaining are important components of a person's good independently of whether that person desires those states of affairs to obtain—e.g., the development of certain uniquely human capacities, gaining of knowledge, or participation in nonexploitive personal relations. The good for persons on such ideal theories is often expressed as a particular ideal of human excellence that one ought to strive to realize. In contrast with desire theories, there is a strong objective quality to a person's good in ideal views. This objective quality likewise has an ontological component—whether something is good for people does not depend on whether they in fact want it—and an epistemological component—we can know that something is good for people without knowing whether they want it. There need be no difference between desire and ideal theories about what kind of life is a good life, about the content of a good life, and, for example, about whether it includes nonexploitive personal relations, or whatever; the difference is about what makes the component good, in particular, whether it is in fact desired by the person in question, or whether it is supported by whatever other sort of argument the ideal theorist employs in support of this theory of the good.

It is also misleading to suggest that there is a sharp distinction between desire and ideal theories that yields in turn a sharp distinction between fully subjective and fully objective theories in the sense noted above. It is more accurate to say that different theories of the good for persons lie at different points on a subjective-objective spectrum. Ideal theories rarely deny that anything is *ever* a part of individuals' good simply because desired by them but claim only that *some* things are good independent of whether they are desired. Ideal theories, therefore, generally include subjective as well as objective components in the full conception of a person's good. Different ideal theories can then be located at different points on a subjective-objective spectrum, according to the proportion and importance of the objective components within the full theory. Likewise, there are various ways that any plausible desire theory of a person's good will permit judgments of the form that "x, though now desired by A, is not good for A," and this will be to incorporate an objective component. I shall here mention only two such ways that have considerable practical importance for paternalism. First, any plausible desire theory will be a rational-desire theory, employing some constraints of rationality on the desires whose satisfaction is for a person's good. Different conceptions, and so constraints, of rationality are possible. A relatively minimal, instrumental account of rationality can be characterized in terms of what Rawls called counting principles, which tell us such things as that, when choosing between a course of conduct that satisfies our ends or desires m, n, and o, and one that satisfies these plus some additional end or desire of ours, it is rational and for our good to select the latter.[22] More powerful conceptions of rationality concern, for example, the process by which a person comes to have a desire.[23] Second, an objective component can be generated in a desire theory as follows.[24] If a person has a desire to suffer serious and permanent injury, e.g., the loss of eyesight, for its own sake and for no further reason, that desire is irrational and the satisfaction of it contrary to the person's good. This judgment does not require any knowledge of the person's other desires. But how can this be on a desire theory? The explanation is roughly as follows. As purposive beings, persons have various ends they pursue and whose satisfaction on the desire theory is good. Whatever a person's particular set of ends, or plan of life may be, being sighted will better enable the person to carry out a great many of those ends; eyesight is what Rawls would call a natural primary good. Even if it should somehow turn out that a person never in fact needs to see, the person could not know this will be so, and so has reason to desire not to suffer this injury for its own sake. This is not to say, of course, that a person might not in some instance have good reason, all things considered, to want to forego eyesight, as, for example, if doing so were medically necesary to save the person's life; but that is not to want to suffer serious injury for its own sake. This means that even in the desire theory, given some minimal and noncontroversial empirical facts about all persons, we can know that a particular person has a reason to want some specific things, like avoidance of serious injury, and that avoidance of serious injury is prima facie for his or her good, without knowing any particular facts about the person. I take it that the practical importance for paternalism of these two objective elements in a desire theory of a person's good is obvious. Ideal theories of a person's good can, then, incorporate subjective components, and desire theories will have objective components. A particular version of either theory is not to be located simply on one side or the other of a fixed objective-subjective line, but rather at some particular point on an objective-subjective spectrum.

Whether a theory that a good life is a happy life is to be classified among desire or ideal theories, it will have many of the features of desire theories. What will make people happy is an empirical question, as is what they desire, and there are well-founded empirical generalizations to the effect that, for example, periodic food or nourishment is important for the happiness (or, at least, for the avoidance of unhappiness) of virtually all. Likewise, there are particular kinds of foods or activities whose contribution to happiness, as well as whether they are desired, varies greatly between persons, depending on those persons' particular tastes, talents, and so forth. Moral controversy over paternalism is likely to center in the areas in which desires, contributions to happiness, or ideals, vary greatly between persons.

In both desire theories and ideal theories, some things are only good for people if they, as a matter of fact, want them, and so a significant portion of a person's good on both sorts of theories lies at the subjective end of the spectrum. This provides one significant practical limitation on justified paternalistic interference with people acting as they want: for such subjective components, a person wanting something is the principal, or the only, evidence that it is for that person's good. Significant limitations on paternalism are warranted on both desire and ideal theories to protect our conduct from interference in the areas of the subjective component. The more persons' desires vary in these areas, the greater the practical importance of insuring such protection. But if everyone held a desire theory of the good for persons, and so individuals differed merely in what they desired, only a mistaken confusion about the relevance of whether I would want what you want would lead me to believe that I could promote your good by preventing you from getting what you want. This confusion is of considerable importance in practice, but could be avoided at least in principle by scrupulous attention to whose desires are relevant to assessments of whose good.

There is a feature of most ideal theories which generates deeper difficulties that we have not yet noted. We need a distinction between what I shall call personal and universal ideal theories of the good for persons. Personal, ideal theorists believe that certain states of affairs obtaining with regard to them, e.g., *their* being in nonexploitive personal relations, developing *their* particular talents, are good for them or part of their good, independently of whether they desire them, but they do not believe that such non-desire-dependent ideals need be part of the good of other persons.[25] In short, they hold the ideals for themselves, but not for others. Universal, ideal theorists believe that certain states of affairs obtaining with regard to persons generally, e.g., not being in exploitive personal relations, developing one's particular talents, are good for anyone, part of anyone's good, independently of whether others desire them.[26]

I believe that most who hold ideal theories of a person's good hold them in their universal form. From the standpoint of those who hold universal, ideal theories of the good for persons, others, whose desires run contrary to these ideals, and whose theories of the good run contrary in turn, are simply mistaken about their own good. And this will be a philosophical disagreement, resting on a disagreement about the correct theory of a person's good, unlike disagreement among proponents of a desire theory about whether a particular course of conduct is for a given person's good, which should reduce to an empirical disagreement about that person's desires.

Desire theorists of the good for persons can now envisage the following possibility. They have an autonomous, rational desire for p, and so obtaining p is, other things being equal, for their good. But there are universal, ideal theorists who believe that p is bad for persons generally, and therefore bad in particular for the desire theorist to have p. With no empirical disagreement necessary between the two, it would be possible for ideal theorists, correctly applying their theory of the good for persons, to interfere on paternalistic grounds with desire theorists obtaining p, although the desire theorists are correct on their theory of the good for persons that p is for their good. This is no mere abstract possibility, but is just the sort of disagreement that often occurs between persons, for example, about whether it is good to participate in certain forms of sexual behavior such as homosexuality, to read pornography, to use pleasure-inducing drugs such as marijuana or cocaine, or to be lazy and waste one's talents and potential.

Such interference would be paternalism that desire theorists would correctly regard, on their theory of the good for persons, as unjustified, and that they would have good reason to want to erect barriers against. Rights to noninterference in those areas of conduct where universal ideals are present, and likely otherwise to serve as warrant for paternalistic interference, are one obvious form of barrier that might be erected. Desire theorists might well plausibly reason that their good would be more effectively protected and promoted over the long run by the adoption of legal rights to certain specific liberties, which make impermissible some paternalism they consider justified. The sacrifice of their good from paternalistic interference now prohibited that would truly have served their good, on their *own* theory of the good for persons, is outweighed by the prevention of paternalistic interference that would have been contrary to their good on their theory of the good for persons, although it might have promoted their good on the theories of the good held by others like the ideal theorists. This, I believe, is a perfectly sound form of argument for the establishment of particular sorts of rights at an institutional, political, or legal level, although not as basic moral principles.[27]

The argument for these rights or other limitations on paternalistic interference that has been made from the standpoint of a proponent of a desire theory of the good for persons. Some form of desire theory is commonly an important component of political liberalism, and an argument of this form is often an important basis for liberal support of constitutional or other legal rights restricting paternalism. It is worth noting, however, that the same kind of argument for rights limiting paternalism can be made from the standpoint of an ideal theorist considering the implications of other persons holding different and conflicting universal ideals. And so a universal ideal theorist, as well as a desire theorist, could in this way come to support rights restricting paternalistic interference.

We can extend this type of argument in its relevance for paternalism in a familiar way. Suppose specific persons, say government officials, are to be given legal authorization to interfere with other persons' conduct on paternalistic grounds, or individuals are to be taught in contexts of moral education that it is permissible to do so. These authorizations will be either for general categories of interference, or for general application of a paternalistic principle requiring maximization of the subject's good. General categories of authorized interference will cover particular instances that are relevantly dissimilar in complex and not entirely predictable ways. Considerable interpretation and judgment will commonly be necessary in the applications of such authorizations, and action will often have to be taken under a high degree of uncertainty. Moreover, such judgments and interpretations must, of course, be made by real persons whose intelligence and capacities for judgments are imperfect, and whose good will in the exercise of paternalistic interference will often be imperfect as well. (Considerations of these sorts would certainly be relevant to case 2 above.) In general, there is significant potential for abuse of paternalistic authorizations that persons will reasonably want to protect against in determining the kind and extent of the authorizations that are to be given. This is not to say that the potential for abuse means that no such authorizations would be given, but only that some may be withheld that include particular cases in which the paternalism would have been justified. The so-called slippery slope form of argument introduces related sorts of considerations: We had best be careful in permitting any interference on paternalistic grounds, even in cases of a clearly justified sort, because once the door is opened to paternalism at all, we will soon find ourselves saddled with additional interference of an unjustified sort.

Gerald Dworkin has suggested to me in discussion that such social policy considerations may show, contrary to what I suggested at the end of section I of this chapter, that my consequentialist treatment of paternalism in not neutral between consequentialist and nonconsequentialist treatments of distributive issues. For example, in case 1 above concerning smoking, suppose, not implausibly, that cigarette-smoking is contrary to most smokers' good, but in a minority of cases smoking is, all things considered, compatible with the smoker's good. No social policy, however, could discriminate effectively between these two classes of persons, and so a general prohibition of the sort envisaged in case 1 is the only policy option. Should such a prohibition be adopted? The policy of prohibition could be supported on the grounds that, since there are more persons whose good it would promote than there are persons whose good it would be contrary to, it is reasonable to suppose that the policy of prohibition will maximize good consequences overall. *This* treatment of the policy issue, however, is not neutral between consequentialist and nonconsequentialist views on distributive questions; it explicitly employs consequentialist reasoning. However, if nonconsequentialist principles of distributive justice (or moral rights) have been shown to be more acceptable than consequentialist ones, I believe they could be employed for questions such as the policy on smoking that concern distributions between different persons, consistent with a consequentialist treatment of paternalism in the case of a single individual. In general, a moral theory need not employ the same principle for cases in which only a single person's interests are affected, as for cases in which more than one person's interests are affected. A consequentialist treatment of the one-person case combined with a nonconsequentialist treatment of the many-person case may not yield a coherent moral theory. But if it does not, that is because the reasoning supporting the treatment of one sort of case is incompatible with the different treatment of the other. Whether that turns out to be the case depends on the particular nonconsequentialist distributive theory, but I do not believe that it must be the case.

In general, the kinds of arguments for limiting paternalism that I have been considering in this section rest on extensive empirical premises that I have only briefly indicated the general form of, but for which I have not attempted to marshal any of the needed evidence. Without that evidence, their force and scope in restricting paternalism is unclear. I do want to suggest, though, that restrictions on paternalism based on empirical considerations of these sorts, which might not too misleadingly be lumped under a general "potential for abuse" rubric, are especially important for the issue of paternalism, and are especially significant considerations in the formation of most persons' considered moral judgments regarding paternalism. It is a common form of criticism of consequentialist reasoning that it makes moral questions generally turn too heavily and in the wrong places on empirical considerations. The criticism is sometimes sound, but I believe that with regard to paternalism it has little force.

Important as well to assessments of when paternalism is justified in the consequentialist framework I have been exploring here are the familiar sorts of instrumental arguments for the value of individual liberty, and for the value of persons deliberating about and acting on their own conception of their good. These were ably stated by Mill and have been restated many times since, so I shall not rehearse them once more here.[28] But a few comments are in order.

First, one of the more important considerations cited by Mill and others is that our powers of judgment about our good are developed only by use; to be generally denied the right to exercise our own judgment, to be treated like young children, is to insure that we will remain like young children. We often learn best from our mistakes, but this means that to learn we must sometimes be permitted by others to act on our own judgment about our good even when those others rightly believe that we are mistaken. Good parents are well aware of this in raising their children. This too, I believe, is a considerstion of considerable practical significance limiting paternalistic interference.

Second, whenever paternalism interferes with liberty of action and involves the use of coercion, overall assessments of whether it promotes the good of the subject interfered with must always take into account the bad effect of the frustrations caused for the one interfered with. This frustration is sufficient to establish a significant presumption against the use of coercive paternalism. But not all paternalism involves the use of coercion, in particular, most paternalistic deception, as case 2 above illustrates. The presumption is therefore against the use of coercive paternalism, but not against paternalism generally. There may be an independent moral presumption against deception or lying, but it will not be based on the frustration from interference with liberty.

Third, a distinction between two kinds of activities has important implications for paternalism. In activities of the first sort, the end or goal sought in the activity is specifiable independently of the means employed to reach the end, and participants are indifferent about which means are employed, and about their own role in them, caring only about the efficacy of the means for attaining the end. Some patients have this attitude about medical treatment, saying to their physician something to the effect, "You do whatever you think best. Just get me well again." But in other activities, the end or purpose of engaging in the activity is, at least in part, the exercise of one's own judgment and abilities in the activity, defective or imperfect though they may be. It is not simply reaching some goal at which the activity aims. For example, a bridge or chess player does not want to be continually instructed throughout the game on the best next play or move by a more skillful player, even when that would increase the chances of winning; rather, the player wants to do the best possible, employing his or her own judgment and abilities. Many other activities, not just games, are, in different degrees, of this latter sort. To the extent that they are, paternalistic interference, for example, when the paternalist possesses superior judgment or skill in the activity in question, cannot be for the subject's good even though the "end," e.g., winning, might be more likely to be achieved.

There are two residual doubts about any consequentialist treatment of paternalism that I want to address very briefly now. The first concerns an aspect of the good for persons that has been stressed by Rawls and that seems particularly important for paternalism. Rawls suggests that besides the various ends and aims that fill out the content of our system of desires, and in turn our conception of the good at any point in time, we have a highest-order interest in our status as moral agents, able and free to form, revise, and rationally pursue our plans of life over time.[29] Can my treatment of paternalism give adequate recognition to this highest-order interest? Since I consider some claim of the sort Rawls makes to be sound (although just what the idea of a *highest*-order interest is, or should be, is unclear), I would hope that it can, but confess that I am not altogether certain about this. If consequentialists adopt some form of rational-desire theory of the good for persons, they can appeal to what I have labeled its strong subjective component, as well as to facts about how persons' desires change and develop over time, in support of this highest-order interest. A desire theory, the sort of theory Rawls himself supports, does appear to leave individuals sovereign over the content of their good in the manner this highest-order interest requires. The consequentialist account of when paternalism is justified that I have sketched in this section will seem to some to permit far too much paternalism but, even if that is so, it does not, so far as I can see, prevent the recognition of this highest-order interest. It is not whether paternalism is justified when it maximally promotes its subject's good, but rather the account of how a person's good is determined, and specifically whether the person is in the right ways sovereign in that determination, that is relevant for recognition of our interest in our status as autonomous, valuing agents.

Nevertheless, it may be that though a desire theory of the good for persons does not *prevent* recognition of this highest-order interest when the appropriate desire to be an autonomous, valuing agent in fact exists, it wrongly makes the existence of the interest for any person contingent on that person's having the appropriate desire, and so fails to *guarantee* this highest-order interest for all persons. This suggests one place at which the desire theorist may want to adopt a universal ideal, specifically the ideal of persons as autonomous agents, able to form, revise, and rationally pursue their conception of the good over time. As a universal ideal, this highest-order interest would not be dependent on the actual presence in a given person of the desire to be an autonomous agent. Consequentialists might then employ in their treatment of paternalism a desire theory of the good for persons constrained only by this one universal ideal. The adoption of this universal ideal ensures that this highest-order interest is taken into account in the consequentialist treatment of paternalism that I have been considering in this section. This is to be contrasted with a universal ideal theory that endorses other specific aims or ends as ideals, independently of whether those aims or ends have been adopted by a particular person; this would be roughly equivalent to what Rawls calls perfectionism, in contrast with his own view, and *would* be incompatible with recognition of this highest-order interest. A defense of this latter sort of universal ideal theory has, of course, been no part of my argument in this paper.

The second residual doubt concerns whether the consequentialist framework for paternalism suggested here in the end gives adequate recognition to what I believe probably remains for many the core intuition underlying resistance to paternalism. That intuition can be put as follows: "When my conduct harms no one else, and I bear its full consequences, why is it anyone's business but my own, and what gives anyone else a right to interfere?" If I am correct that a desire theory of the good for persons provides the right sort of personal sovereignty in each person's determination of the content of her or his own good, when this sovereignty is safeguarded by the sorts of considerations I have lumped together under the "potential for abuse" rubric, as well as by the instrumental considerations in support of noninterference, the response to this core intuition is: "What reason is there left to resist, rather than to welcome, this aid in promoting your good?" It now seems more reasonably and appropriately viewed as needed help to be welcomed, rather than misguided meddlesomeness to be resisted.

A concluding disclaimer. Since I have proposed here the position that paternalism is justified just in case it in fact maximally promotes the good of the subject of the paternalism, but have neither developed nor defended a full theory of the good for persons, it should be obvious that no full account of when paternalism is justified has been offered. Among other things, more work needs to be done concerning the causes and forms of incompetence, encumbrance, and involuntariness, and concerning the precise ways these are to be accommodated by a theory of the good for persons. But that is another paper. My main purpose here has been to suggest grounds for resisting the appeal to rights in favor of consequentialist reasoning on paternalism.[30]

Notes

1. Jeffrie G. Murphy, "Incompetence and Paternalism," *Archiv für Rechts and Sozialphilosophie* 60 (1974), pp. 465-86.

2. John Rawls, *A Theory of Justice* (Cambridge, MA: Harvard University Press, 1971), pp. 248-50.

3. Rosemary Carter, "Justifying Paternalism," *Canadian Journal of Philosophy* 7 (1977), pp. 133-45.

4. John Hodson, "The Principle of Paternalism," *American Philosophical Quarterly*, 14 (1977), p. 65.

5. This is not a precise definition of the concept of paternalism, but will do for my purposes in this paper. The issues I am concerned with here are raised by paradigm cases of paternalism that I believe would count as instances of paternalism on anyone's definition of the concept.

6. Hodson, p. 65.

7. Rawls, p. 248.

8. *Ibid.*, p. 249.

9. Daniel Wikler, "Paternalism and the Mildly Retarded," *Philosophy & Public Affairs* 8 (1979), pp. 377-92. (Reprinted in this volume; see chapter 5.)

10. *Ibid.*, p. 384.

11. *Ibid.*

12. Hodson, p. 65.

13. Joel Feinberg, "Legal Paternalism," *Canadian Journal of Philosophy* 1 (1971), pp. 105-24. (Reprinted in this volume; see chapter 1.)

14. *Ibid.*, pp. 110-11.

15. *Ibid.*, pp. 111.

16. In fairness to Feinberg, it should be pointed out that the incoherence I go on to develop in the text may not afflict his actual view. Feinberg is concerned with *legal* paternalism and, after noting that voluntariness is a matter of degree, suggests that paternalistic state interference is permissible only when the conduct interfered with is substantially nonvoluntary. His point may then be that running unreasonable risks, and so forth, is not substantially nonvoluntary, although it fails to be fully voluntary. If so, then the position contains no incoherence. Moreover, if his view is that permissible

legal paternalism requires substantial nonvoluntariness, rather than merely the absence of full voluntariness, for reasons of the sort I develop in section II of this paper, my own position here is essentially the same as his. I am interested in the use of a requirement of nonvoluntariness in a basic moral principle concerning paternalism, as well as the *necessity* for the sorts of considerations I cite in section II to justify restricting legal paternalism to cases of substantial nonvoluntariness, for example, by means of legal rights restricting paternalistic interference.

17. Harry Frankfurt, "Freedom of the Will and the Concept of a Person," *The Journal of Philosophy* 68 (1971), pp. 5-20.

18. This use of autonomy follows Frankfurt, "Freedom of the Will," and Gerald Dworkin, "Autonomy and Behavior Control," *The Hastings Center Report*, vol. 6, no. 1 (1976), pp. 23-8.

19. People's conception of their good is not to be construed narrowly here, so as to imply any form of egoism, or to imply that in pursuing our good we must be concerned only with our own welfare and not the welfare of others. Rather, I intend it in a broad sense in which promotion of the welfare of others about whom one cares, and action in accordance with moral principles to which one is committed, can both count as pursuit of one's good. Just how this latter can be the case requires explanation, but I shall not pursue it now as I do not believe it affects my argument here regarding paternalism.

20. This way of putting my argument, as a challenge to the moral-rights theorist regarding our conception of the person, I owe to Norman Dahl. In comments on an earlier version of this paper, Dahl undertook to meet this challenge by appeal to a noninstrumental account of rationality, suggesting that the crucial limitation in the conception of a person that I have appealed to is its merely instrumental account of rationality. His basic idea, which has both Aristotelian and Kantian orgins, was that reason can determine certain ends to be rational, and not merely what are the best means to our ends. With the proper use of practical reason, the ends one acquires will be rational ends, so that acting on one's own choices will be a rational end, and resistance to paternalistic interference with our acting on our choices will in turn be rationally intelligible.

Dahl's argument and the issues it raises are too complex for me to be able to do them any justice here. I shall only record my skepticism concerning a noninstrumental account of rationality that implies the ends one acquires in practical reasoning are rational ends. But even if a satisfactory noninstrumental account of practical reason can be given, it will still presumably be the case that reason in this noninstrumental sense can sometimes be improperly or mistakenly employed. A person's actual ends then will not be rational ends. In such cases, pursuing one's ends seems not to be rational, nor for one's good because rational. But then my challenge to the rights theorist regarding why it is rational to resist paternalistic interference when one is mistaken about one's good arises again and seems not to have been answered. Moreover, it is not clear to me how a noninstrumemtal account of rationality could establish the general rationality of acting on one's choices. When rationality has been improperly or mistakenly employed, the ends one acquires or chooses will not be rational ends. Why is it rational to act on those choices? But these instances of bad or foolish choices are just the cases in which the rights theorist needs to explain why it is rational to act on one's choices. So far as I can see, he will not have done so.

21. I would note that I am concerned here with a theory of the good for persons that is to be employed in a theory of paternalism. It may be that a theory of the good for persons employed for different purposes, for example, in a theory of distributive justice, should take a different form. For example, there may be good reason in a distributive theory to abstract from certain individual differences in the nature of persons and their circumstances that ought to be attended to in a theory of paternalism. Consider, for example, Rawls' argument, *op. cit.*, for assessing persons' levels of well-being in terms of an index of primary goods. This point is also suggested by T. M. Scanlon, "Preference and Urgency," *The Journal of Philosophy* 72 (1975), p. 562.

22. See Rawls, chapter 8.

23. The most detailed and subtle account with which I am familiar (though in my view mistaken on some important points) of the ways in which action, as well as desires and aversions, can be irrational is in Richard Brandt, *A Theory of the Good and the Right* (Oxford: Oxford University Press, 1979), Part I. While Brandt himself endorses a happiness theory of the good for persons, his discussion contains much that a desire theory could profitably incorporate as well.

24. The argument that follows is owed to Philippa Foot, "Moral Beliefs," *Proceedings of the Aristotelian Society* 59 (1958-59), pp. 83-104.

25. In fact, many personal ideals seem to have their basis in a desire to be a particular kind of person, and so are instances of what I have called desire theories. A more detailed account of the desire-ideal distinction is needed for it to be clear when, or even whether, there are personal ideal theories. I do not go into this because my interest here is in universal ideal theories.

26. This distinction between personal and universal ideal theories is similar to, but not the same as, Ronald Dworkin's distinction in *Taking Rights Seriously* (Cambridge, MA: Harvard University Press, 1977, chapter 12), between personal and external preferences, and the difference is important for paternalism. For Dworkin, roughly, personal preferences are for my doing or having something, while external preferences are for your doing or having something. His concern was with how policies based on external preferences can violate the right of each person to equal concern and respect. In a preference utilitarianism, if there are enough of you who want me to do x, although I prefer not to do x, your preferences for doing x may outweigh my preference for not doing x. But this can occur with no need for universal, ideal theories of the good for persons—only desire theory, preference utilitarianism is required. And the prospect that concerned Dworkin was not a case of unwarranted paternalism, as might be the interference by the universal, ideal theorist with the action of the desire theorist, because it was not paternalism at all. It was a case of the good of others conflicting with and outweighing my good, so that maximization of the good simpliciter favors their good over mine. That may be a problem for utilitarianism, and it may be an unwarranted interference with my doing as I want, but it is not unwarranted paternalism because it need not pretend to be for my good at all, and so is not paternalism of any sort.

27. This kind of argument from an act-utilitarian standpoint is more fully developed and generally applied in Rolf Sartorius, *Individual Conduct and Social Norms* (Encino, CA: Dickenson Publishing, 1975). On some forms of rule-consequentialist theories, rights justified in this way might still be moral rights. This line of reasoning is also similar to the two-tiered view suggested by T. M. Scanlon, "Rights, Goals and Fairness," in *Public and Private Morality*, ed. Stuart Hampshire (Cambridge: Cambridge University Press, 1978).

28. John Stuart Mill, *On Liberty*, many editions.

29. This conception of the good for persons is present many places in Rawls, *op. cit.*, and is discussed by T. M. Scanlon, "Rawls' Theory of Justice," in *Reading Rawls*, ed. Norman Daniels (New York: Basic Books, 1976). See also Rawls' Dewey Lectures on Kantian Constructivism in Moral Theory, in particular the first lecture, "Rational and Full Autonomy," *The Journal of Philosophy* 77 (1980), pp. 515-72.

30. This paper has benefited considerably from the discussions that followed presentations of an earlier version at the Liberty Fund Symposium on paternalism (and especially from Norman Dahl's very helpful and penetrating comments presented there) and at the Kennedy Institute of Ethics, Georgetown University. Norman Daniels also provided helpful criticisms of an earlier draft. My thinking on paternalism generally has benefited from numerous discussions of the topic with George Miller, as well as from reading his unpublished Ph.D. dissertation, "The Problems of Paternalism."

Chapter 14

Paternalism and Rational Desire

Norman O. Dahl

One of the areas in which rights-based moral theories appear to be in a position of strength is in their discussion of paternalism. Nothing seems more natural than to say that what is objectionable about paternalism is that it infringes on a right such as people's rights to determine what happens to them by means of their own choices. However, recently Dan Brock has raised an important challenge to the attempt to deal with questions surrounding paternalism by appealing to moral rights.[1] He argues that a consequentialist theory of paternalism is preferable to any theory that tries to restrict paternalism by appealing to a basic right like the right of self-determination. If Professor Brock is right, he will have changed what appears to be a stronghold for rights-based theories into an area of vulnerability. In what follows I shall try to see what might be said in response to the challenge raised by Professor Brock.

I

Any adequate treatment of paternalism would seem to have to account for two intuitions: that there are some cases in which paternalism is *not* permissible, and that there are some cases in which it is. Rights-based theories account for the first intuition by invoking a basic right that includes the right to act on one's own choices even when so acting turns out not to be beneficial. Rights-based theories have tried to account for the second intuition by invoking as a necessary condition for justified paternalism a condition such as the incompetence of the agent,[2] or the encumbrance,[3] or the involuntariness[4] of the agent's decisions. Brock begins his

---

In writing this paper I have benefited from discussions with Dan Brock, Allen Buchanan, and William Hanson.

261

assault on rights-based theories by criticizing their account of this second intuition. He points out that each of the above three conditions is open to an interpretation according to which it holds if and only if the agent's decisions, if carried through, would not maximize the agent's benefit. Brock focuses on why such conditions provide a basis for paternalistic interference and argues that there is no reason not to accept such an interpretation. This, however, leaves one with a consequentialist account of the second intuition. What underlies this criticism is the conception of a person who acts autonomously and rationally when acting to maximize his or her good. According to this conception, insistence on a right against interference even when that interference will be beneficial is paradoxical and irrational. Thus, the account of the first intuition is undermined.

A consequentialist theory, however, can account for both intuitions. It, of course, justifies paternalism on consequentialist grounds. If one accepts a certain kind of theory of a person's good, one will see how a consequentialist can also argue for important restrictions on paternalism. Theories of a person's good can be classified to the extent to which they are *desire* or *ideal* theories. A theory of a person's good is a desire theory to the extent to which a person's good consists in the satisfaction of desires that the person in fact has. It is ideal to the extent to which something's being a constituent of a person's good is independent of whether the person desires it or not. With a few qualifications,[5] Brock accepts a desire theory of the good. What is important, though, is that people can and do hold ideal theories of a person's good. In acting on these theories, they will engage in paternalistic interference that on a desire theory will not be justified. Given this, someone who holds a desire theory will have good consequentialist reasons for restricting paternalism in cases in which others might act on an ideal theory of a person's good.[6] If one adds to this the more familiar considerations about the possibility of abuse of an authorization to interfere with a person's decisions, and the fact that an important part of people's good may be their securing what they aim at by their own decisions, one can see how a consequentialist can argue for important restrictions on paternalism.

If, in addition, a consequentialist theory can explain why certain cases are hard cases,[7] a consequentialist approach to paternalism will indeed seem to be preferable to a rights-based approach.

I shall concentrate on Brock's criticisms of a rights-based approach to paternalism, for I think that here is where the central issues lie. I shall argue that, given Brock's assumptions, it is not at all surprising that he finds no room for a right against paternalistic interference when that interference will be beneficial; according to Brock's assumptions, freedom from interference is valuable only to the extent that it contributes to a person's benefit. I shall suggest that his conception of a person needs to be amplified. Its crucial limitation seems to be its failure to recognize anything other than an instrumental conception of rationality. With an expanded notion of rationality I think one can begin to see how a right that erects barriers against paternalistic interference can make sense.

II

Let us begin with Brock's criticism of rights-based theorists' use of the notions of incompetence, encumbrance, and involuntariness. Brock considers one conception of competence that might be used in connection with a rights-based theory competence as a minimal capacity to understand and avoid major harms. However, Brock points out that people undertake activities to obtain benefits as well as to avoid danger:

> They seek to promote their good quite as much by obtaining such benefits as by avoiding such harms, and the former is equally relevant *to their capacity or competence to promote their good effectively in an activity* [Italics mine].

In arguing for an expanded notion of incompetence, he says:

> And why shouldn't the necessary condition for paternalistic interference be incompetence in this expanded conception, since incompetence$_t$ is only . . . one way in which people's choices and resultant conduct may fail to be fully rational *and fail best to promote their good* [Italics mine]?

Brock's argument seems to assume that the relevance of competence or incompetence is the extent to which it allows or prevents people from failing to obtain their own good. It is not surprising, then, that what emerges is a notion of incompetence that allows paternalistic interference if it maximizes the person's good.

Brock also considers a conception of an encumbered decision as a decision made in circumstances known to affect decisions in ways that make people believe sometimes that the decisions are mistaken or unfortunte. He says:

> But then it would seem that *any* conditions, temporary or permanent, that lead Jones to make decisions that he comes to view as unfortunate or mistaken, *as failing best to promote his good* [Italics mine], are encumbrances of impairments. And, likewise, any decisions that in avoidable ways do not maximally promote his good are encumbered or impaired.

He says that the point can also be put in terms of rights:

> If rights to self-determination may be overridden on paternalistic grounds when one's decisions are impaired by a temporary encumbrance like unusual emotional stress, why should they not be overridden as well when they are impaired by permanent encumbrance like limited intelligence? Both create defective decisions *that prevent people from best promoting their good* [Italics mine].

His argument here seems to assume that decisions are defective or will come to be regarded as mistaken to the extent that they fail to promote the agent's good. It is not surprising, then, that adherence to a right to act on one's own choices even when doing so would not be beneficial appears puzzling. The very assumptions of Brock's arguments seem to remove the value, relevance, or reasonableness of insisting on making one's own choices when acting on them will not be beneficial.

These assumptions come out most clearly in Brock's conception of the person. According to Brock, persons are people who act to secure ends that they desire. But they are more than this. People are capable of reflecting on the desires and ends that they have, and on the basis of deliberation they are capable of forming second-order desires, desires to have or not have first-order desires. This reflection and deliberation provide people with their own conception of the good, and allows one to distinguish between the particular motivational structure people may have at a given time and their conception of the good. For Brock, the conception of rationality involved in such reflection and deliberation is an instrumental one, according to which it is rational to select the action that maximally promotes one's system of ends:

> In autonomous, rational action, then, we seek maximally to pursue and achieve our good as we perceive it—this is the ideal toward which purposive action is aimed.

The consequences for paternalism of this picture of a person are clear. Adherence to a right that allows one to act on one's own choices, even when this will not maximize one's benefit, appears to be irrational:

> In purposive, autonomous, and rational action, persons seek to promote their good. Why, then, when they are in fact failing to do so, and the interference of others would, in fact, better promote their good, is it rational for a purposive, autonomous agent to resist rather than to accept, indeed welcome, the interference? To so resist the interference would seem inconsistent with assumptions of rational agency.

Brock seems right when he says:

> Without giving up this conception of purposive, autonomous action, the resistance to paternalism and defense of this feature of moral rights appear to be irrational, or at least in need of further explanation.

Given Brock's conception of purposive, rational action, one will, of course, be puzzled by the assertion that there is something so valuable about acting on one's own choices that it merits the protection of a claim of right even when so acting is not beneficial. If one limits one's conception of rational action to action that benefits the agent, of course such a right will appear irrational.

In saying this, I am not claiming that Brock has begged the question against a rights-based theorist. The conception of rational, purposive action contained in Brock's conception of the person is certainly part of what is involved in rational, purposive action. Given just this part of rational, purposive action, the claims of a rights-based theorist do appear puzzling. Brock's arguments are best taken as raising a challenge to rights-based theorists. Unless they can indicate what more there is to rational, purposive action, something that does make their appeal to a right reasonable, their appeal will seem to be without foundation. If, further, a consequentialist theory can account for the main intuitions associated with paternalism, it appears that a consequentialist theory of paternalism will be preferable to a rights-based theory.

III

Is there anything a rights-based theorist can say to meet this challenge? What more can there be to the concept of the person than Brock has allowed? I think the answer lies in the area in which people form their conception of the good, in particular, in the kind of rationality involved in the reflection and deliberation that lead people to form the relevant second-order desires. If this conception of rationality is solely instrumental, as Brock maintains, I am inclined to think that Brock's defense of a consequentialist approach to paternalism is correct. If, however, reason can play a role in determining what ends people should have, I think an appeal to the kind of rights that rights-based theorists have invoked can be made intelligible.

But how can reason play a role in determining ends? There are two ways in which this might happen. The first is by providing people with specific ends. The second is by limiting or expanding already existing ends. There are at least two ways in which one might try to explain how reason could be involved in the first of these. One comes from John McDowell.[8] McDowell takes his stimulus from Aristotle, who says that ethics is an area that lacks the precision of the theoretical sciences and involves general principles whose content cannot be stated precisely. McDowell explains this in terms of the essential indeterminateness of the ends involved in moral behavior. For example, one may be able to give a rough, general characterization of what it is to be just, according to which actions in certain unproblematic cases can be seen to be just or unjust, but for every such specification there will be other cases in which the justice of the actions cannot be seen from the specification. The best one can do in these cases is to say that just actions are *like* those in the unproblematic cases. Exactly how they are alike, though, one cannot say. Whether such actions are just or not is something that has to be discovered by *perception*, but a perception based on *experience*. McDowell likens the task of providing such content to moral ends to what Wittgenstein says when he discusses how to specify the correct way of continuing a given series of numbers. If one says, for example, that the series is one that continues by increments of two because that's the way it has gone so far, there seems to be in principle no way of ruling out the possibility that instead it will change to increments of four when one reaches 1,000. The best general characterization one can give is to say that the rest of the series will be *like* what has gone before. To understand exactly what this is, one must learn from experience what our practice of counting such a series is. Similarly, one must learn from experience what our moral practice is, and this includes learning the content of moral ends. According to this suggestion, an "inductive" use of reason plays a role in determining what specific ends one should have.

A second way in which reason might determine specific ends is suggested in a forthcoming manuscript of my own.[9] It too takes its stimulus from Aristotle. I suggest that, according to Aristotle, there are ends that people aim at by nature in the sense that these ends are what people "really want," and that their conscious desires and dispositions can be seen as more or less successful attempts at securing these "natural" ends. By reflecting on their own actions and the actions of others, people can make an inductive inference to what it is that they are aiming at by nature, thus inferring the ends they should consciously be aiming at. Although such self-conscious determination of what ends one should aim at may be atypical, the more common modification of one's ends in the light of satisfaction or dissatisfaction obtained from them can be seen to be the unreflective analogue of this self-conscious determination of ends.

In both these suggestions, there is a kind of "inductive" use of reason, a learning from experience, that allows one to acquire certain specific ends. If one engages in this exercise of reason properly, the ends one acquires will be *rational ends*. Those contrary to such ends will be *irrational*. If one of these suggestions (or something else that does the same job) is at all plausible, and *if* the proper exercise of the kind of reason in question yields that acting on one's own choices is a rational end, one can begin to see how a rights-based theorist's appeal to a right against paternalism can seem to be reasonable. There will be something reasonable about simply acting on one's own choices.

One might think that Brock can easily accommodate such an account of the value of acting on one's own choices. His theory of a person's good is already a rational desire theory in that whether what a person desires is a constituent of his or her good depends on the constraints of instrumental rationality. Brock acknowledges that for some activities acting on our own choices is part of what these activities aim at, and he does acknowledge being an autonomous agent as an ideal component of a person's good.[10] Why can't he simply acknowledge that the rationality of the desire to act on one's own choices explains (at least in part) why being an autonomous agent is an ideal component of a person's good?

I doubt, however, that the value of acting on such a rational desire is adequately captured by simply taking it as an ideal component within Brock's theory of a person's good. Given the instrumental conception of rationality that dominates Brock's theory, it looks as if such an ideal component could easily be outweighed if it conflected with other things that the person in fact wanted. This seems to ignore the importance of this rational desire (I would say the importance of the rationality of this desire), for it treats it on a par with other desires that are no more rational to pursue than they are rational not to pursue. If, for example, reflecting on their own actions and the actions of others leads people to realize that what they "really want" is to act on their own choices even if doing so would not maximize the satisfaction of all their desires (i.e., to *prefer* acting on their own choices to maximizing the satisfaction of their desires), the rationality of this desire would seem to constrain its being traded off for the sake of maximizing the satisfaction of desires. The rationality of such a desire seems to limit what can be said to be rational simply on the basis of instrumental considerations.

It is not at all clear that such a rational desire should always be included as part of a person's good. Consider Thomas Hill's case of the Deferential Wife.[11] Much of the wife's happiness derives from the subservient role she plays. Changing this role and acting more on the basis of her own decisions may introduce a good deal of unhappiness into her life for at least a considerable length of time. To the extent that considerations of happiness parallel considerations of a person's good,[12] one may want to say that although it is *good* for the deferring wife to start acting on her own choices, nevertheless it may not be good *for her* to do so. That this is so becomes even more plausible if one turns to the second way in which I said reason might determine the ends of action. This coupled with what has already been said about the rationality of acting on one's own choices yields the result that there is a value to people acting on their own choices whether or not it benefits them.

Besides those views in which specific ends are rational, there are ones that set out formal principles of rationality limiting or extending the pursuit of individuals' ends, including their rational ends. They are *formal* principles because they require the existence of specific rational desires to serve as their *matter* in order for them to be applied. The best example of such a principle is Kant's categorical imperative.[13] As I interpret the categorical imperative, it attempts to set out what is rational independent of any particular ends a person might happen to have. It says that it is irrational to pursue a given end if the universalization of that pursuit cannot consistently be willed to be a universal law. As I interpret what it is to be able consistently to will something to be a universal law, it is for that universalization to be compatible with what one must want insofar as one is rational. This includes any ends that turn out to be rational ends.[14] That is, according to the categorical imperative, it is irrational to pursue even one's rational ends if that pursuit is incompatible with the rational ends of someone else, because the universalization of such pursuit will be incompatible with one's own rational ends.[15]

Thus, as I interpret the categorical imperative, *if* acting on one's own choices is a rational end, it will be irrational to secure the benefit of another at the expense of a third party's ability to act on his or her choices, for the universalization of that kind of action will be incompatible with the agent's own rational desire to act on her or his own choices. If this is correct, the same conclusion would seem to follow in a case in which the person benefited and the person whose ability to act on his or her own choices was sacrificed are the same.[16] Applying this formal principle on the basis of the rationality of acting on one's own choices yields just what the rights-based theorist needs, the rationality of resisting paternalistic interference even when this interference would be beneficial. Thus, if one enlarges the conception of rationality involved in people's capacity to acquire a conception of the good so that it includes the ability to recognize both material and formal principles of rationality, one develops a concept of the person according to which a right against paternalistic interference does seem reasonable. Here is at least one way in which one might try to meet the challenge raised by Brock's arguments.[17]

IV

Even if one grants everything I have suggested (and it certainly is a good deal to grant), Brock's challenge would not have been fully met. One still needs an explanation of when paternalism is justified, one involving some such condition as incompetence, encumbrance, or involuntariness that doesn't reduce to the inability to maximize one's benefit. I shall not take up this issue in any detail, but an initial direction seems clear. What should be contained in such a notion is the absence of or inability to exercise those capacities that make action on the basis of one's choices rational. This would seem to be the absence of or inability to exercise capacities involved in acquiring a conception of the good, since acting on one's choices is paradigmatically acting on the basis of a conception of the good. Since these are just the capacities involved in the enlarged concept of the person, they would not seem to be capacities that guarantee that one will maximize one's own benefit.

However, this suggestion raises another question about whether the enlarged concept of the person I have suggested can be used to meet Brock's challenge. If acting on one's choices is simply exercising those capacities involved in acquiring a conception of the good, there is no guarantee that in acting on one's choices one will exercise those capacities *well*. That is, there is no guarantee that one will end up pursuing what is rational to pursue. If, however, what people will end up doing will be irrational, why shouldn't one interfere with their acting on their choices? Indeed why shouldn't such interference be rational? If it would, and if it extends to cases in which what people will do will be irrational because it fails to maximize their own good, then it looks as if Brock's consequentialist justification of paternalism will still hold.[18]

It is true that on the kind of formal principles I have suggested, interference with people's ability to act on their choices when their action would be irrational will sometimes be justified. But it is important to note that it is not justified simply on the basis of the consequences of such interference, nor is it always justified when the action in question is irrational because it fails to maximize the agent's good. As I interpret it, the categorical imperative justifies interference with people's acting on their own choices if in so acting they would effectively eliminate their ability to act on their own choices in the future (for example, by selling themselves into slavery). Even though interference under these circumstances does inhibit people's pursuit of one of their rational ends, it does so in order to further that self-same end overall. However, the justification of such interference is not simply that overall it promotes a rational end of the people interfered with. The justification is that it would be *irrational* not to interfere, because the universalization of noninterference is incompatible with what anyone must want insofar as they are rational, namely, to be able to act on their own choices throughout their lives.[19]

Just as important, this justification does not extend to every case in which were people to act on their own choices they would act irrationally. In particular, it does not extend to every case in which what would be done would be irrational because it fails to maximize the agent's own good. If, as I suggested in section III, the exercise of whatever form of reason leads people to want certain ends would lead them to *prefer* acting on their own choices under certain circumstances even if doing so would not maximize their own good, then people will not be able to will interference with their acting on their own choices under such circumstances without their wills being in contradiction with themselves. Just as formal principles of rationality can limit the pursuit even of rational ends when this pursuit conflicts with the rational ends of others, so rational ends can limit the pursuit of what would be rational on instrumental grounds when this pursuit conflicts with rational ends. Even in situations in which if people were to act on their own choices it would be irrational of them not to maximize their own good, if they cannot both act on their own choices *and* maximize their own good, it may still be rational for them to act on their own choices rather than to have their good maximized for them. Thus, on the enlarged conception of the person I have suggested, it can be rational to allow people to act on their own choices even if their doing so won't maximize their good. It is just this that a rights-based theorist needs to make a right to self-determination reasonable.

The enlarged conception of the person I have suggested thus provides one way in which a rights-based theorist might meet the challenge raised by Brock's arguments for a consequentialist approach to paternalism.

Notes

1. Dan Brock, "Paternalism and Promoting the Good," this volume, chapter 13.
2. See, for example, Jeffrie G. Murphy, "Incompetence and Paternalism," *Archive für Rechts und Sozialphilosophie* 60:465-486 (1974) and Daniel Wikler, "Paternalism and the Mildly Retarded," *Philosophy and Public Affairs* 8:377-392 (1979).
3. See, for example, John Hodson, "The Principle of Paternalism," *American Philosophical Quarterly*, 14: 61-69 (1977).
4. See, for example, Joel Feinberg, "Legal Paternalism,"*Canadian Journal of Philosophy* 1: 105-124 (1971).
5. The qualifications are that what a person desires is subject to the constraints of instrumental rationality, and that being an autonomous, valuing agent may have to be taken as an ideal component of a person's good. The latter would be done to guarantee the importance of what Rawls has described as a highest order interest in our status as moral agents. (See John Rawls, "Kantian Constructivism in Moral Theory," *Journal of Philosophy* 87 (1980), pp. 525-6.)
6. Those holding an ideal theory of a person's good would have similar consequentialist reasons for restricting paternalism to guard against others acting on different ideal theories of a person's good.
7. Brock suggests as hard cases government prohibition of the production, sale, and use of cigarettes after widespread educational programs have failed to keep people from smoking, and a psychoanalyst's lying to a friend in order to break up a pending marriage which she is confident will end in suffering, even though the friend, knowing the analyst's misgivings, wants to go through with the marriage.
8. John McDowell, "Virtue and Reason," *The Monist* 62: 331-350 (1979). See also his "Are Moral Requirements Hypothetical Imperatives?" *Proceedings of the Aristotelian Society* 52: 13-29 (1978).
9. Norman O. Dahl, *Practical Reason, Aristotle, and Weakness of the Will*, forthcoming, University of Minnesota Press.
10. See note 5 above.

11. This is a woman who is utterly devoted to serving her husband. She buys clothes *he* prefers, invites the guests *he* wants to entertain, and makes love whenever *he* is in the mood. She willingly moves to a new city in order for him to have a more attractive job, counting her own friendships and geographical preferences insignificant by comparison. She loves her husband, but her conduct is not simply an expression of love. She is happy, but she does not subordinate herself as a means to happiness. She does not simply defer to her husband in certain spheres as a trade-off for his deference in other spheres. On the contrary, she tends not to form her own interests, values, and ideals; when she does, she counts them as less important than her husband's. She readily responds to appeals from Women's Liberation and she agrees that women are mentally and physically equal, if not superior, to men. She just believes that the proper role for a woman is to serve her family. As a matter of fact, much of her happiness derives from her belief that she fulfills this role very well. No one is trampling on her rights, she says, for she is quite glad, and proud, to serve her husband as she does. (Thomas E. Hill, Jr., "Servility and Self-Respect," *The Monist* 57 (1973) p. 87.)

12. Brock seems to think that there are some parallels.

13. Other examples of formal principles of rationality are Rawls' principles of justice viewed under the Kantian interpretation (John Rawls, *A Theory of Justice* [Cambridge: Belknap Press of Harvard University Press, 1971]), and Thomas Nagel's principle that if a person has a subjective reason to promote some end, anyone has an objective reason to promote that same end (*The Possibility of Altruism* [Oxford: Oxford University Press, 1970]).

14. Kant mentions three rational ends—freedom, happiness, and perfection—but to my knowledge he never provides any arguments for why they are rational ends. While Kant may not have approved of them, the two views mentioned above at least have the virtue of providing a basis for arguing for the rationality of certain ends.

15. One might ask why it is *rational* to limit the pursuit of one's own ends when they come in conflict with the rational ends of someone else. What exercise of reason is it that leads one to want to limit the pursuit even of one's own rational ends when they conflict with the rational ends of others? As a beginning one might adopt a suggestion of Thomas Nagel's. People have the capacity to step back and reflect on themselves as one rational being among others. To the extent to which from this perspective our own rational desires still matter (i.e., are still ones that we want ourselves to have), to that extent the rational desires of other rational beings must also matter. If my rational desires still matter from this perspective, then they must matter simply because they are the rational desires of a rational being. But then the recognition of others as rational beings must also make their rational desires matter. The exercise of my capacity to step back and view myself as one rational being among others will thus make me want not to interfere with the rational ends of others. This is not enough to make me want to limit the pursuit of my own rational ends when they interfere with the rational ends of others (for from the same perspective I will also want to pursue my rational ends), but it is at least a beginning.

16. Of course, it is arguable that it makes a difference whether the person benefited and the person whose ability to act on her or his choices is sacrificed are the same, but the burden of proof would seem to be on one who would argue that this does make a difference.

17. If I am right in this, Brock's argument for a consequentialist treatment of paternalism is not neutral on the question of the overall adequacy of consequentialist or rights-based moral theories in the way that Brock thinks it is. Brock thinks that his argument is neutral because he thinks that the conception of the person that he offers says nothing about whether or when a person's interests can be sacrificed for the greater well-being of others. It thus says nothing about whether a defense of a right against such sacrifice is possible. However, to the extent that his conception of a person rules out formal and material principles of rationality of the sort I have discussed, it rules out a prominent basis for a number of traditional rights-based theories. Indeed, if his concept of a person includes only an instrumental conception of rationality, according to which only action that will benefit a person can be seen to be reasonble, it is hard to see what kind of principle limiting or requiring sacrifices in the pursuit of people's well-being can be reasonable other than ones that in the long run will benefit everyone. If there are any such principles, they would seem to be consequentialist principles.

18. Brock raises essentially this objection in note 20.

19. This requires a qualification in the summary of what follows from the categorical imperative near the end of section III. It will sometimes be rational to interfere with the rational ends of someone else, provided (i) such interference overall promotes that person's rational ends and (ii) it does not overall interfere with the rational ends of some other person. It is for this reason that I said at the beginning of section III that formal principles can expand as well as restrict a person's rational ends. Under the kind of circumstances just discussed, they can lead one to want to promote the rational ends of others, as well as to want not to interfere with the rational ends of others.

Bibliography

Bibliography

Mary Ellen Waithe, Ph.D.

Agich, George J. "When Consent is Unbearable: An Alternative Case Analysis," *Journal of Medical Ethics*, vol. 5, (March, 1979) p. 26.

Allen, David F., and Allen, Victoria S. *Ethical Issues in Mental Retardation.* Nashville: Abingdon Press, 1979).

Annas, George F. "The Incompetents' Right to Die," *Hastings Center Report*, vol. 8 (February, 1978), p. 15.

————. "Medical Paternity and 'Wrongful Life,'" *Hastings Center Report*, vol. 9 (June, 1979), p. 15.

————. "Refusing Treatment for Incompetent Patients: Why Quinlan and Saikewicz Cases Agree on Roles of Guardians, Physicians, Judges, and Ethics Committees," *New York State Journal of Medicine* (April, 1980), p. 816.

————. "Refusing Medication in Mental Hospitals," *Hastings Center Report*, vol. 10 (Fall, 1980), pp. 21-22.

Arneson, Richard J. "Mill versus Paternalism," *Philosophy Research Archives*, vol. 5, no. 1302 (1979).

Battin, M. Pabst. *Ethical Issues in Suicide.* Englewood Cliffts, NJ: Prentice-Hall, Inc., 1982.

Bayles, Michael D. "Criminal Paternalism," in *The Limits of Law, Nomos*, vol. 15 (New York: Lieber-Atherton, 1974), p. 174.

Beauchamp, Tom L. "Paternalism and Biobehavioral Control," *Monist*, vol. 60 (January, 1977), p. 62.

Beauchamp, Tom L., and Faden, Ruth R. "Decision-Making and Informed Consent: A Study of the Impact of Disclosed Information," *Social Indicators Research*, vol. 7 (January, 1980), pp. 313-36.

Blustein, J. "On Children and Proxy Consent," *Journal of Medical Ethics*, vol. 4 (Spring, 1978), pp. 138-40.

Bok, Sissela. *Lying: Moral Choice in Public and Private Life.* New York: Vintage, 1979.

Brock, Dan W. "Involuntary Civil Commitment: The Moral Issues," in Brody, B. A., and Engelhardt, H. Tristram, Jr. (eds.), *Mental Illness: Law and Public Policy.* (Hingham, Ma: D. Reidel, 1980).

Brown, Robert. "Physical Illness and Mental Health," *Philosophy & Public Affairs*, vol. 7, no. 1 (Fall, 1977).

Buchanan, Allen. "Medical Paternalism," *Philosophy & Public Affairs*, vol. 7, no. 4 (Summer, 1978), p. 370.

————. "Medical Paternalism or Legal Imperialism: Not the Only Alternatives for Handling *Saikewicz*-type Cases," *American Journal of Law and Medicine*, vol. 5 (Summer, 1979), pp. 97-117.

Carr, Charles. "Children, Medical Research and Informed Consent," *Journal of Social Philosophy*, vol. 9 (Spring, 1978), p. 14.

Carter, Rosemary. "Justifying Paternalism," *Canadian Journal of Philosophy*, vol. 7, no. 1 (March, 1977), p. 133.

Dershowitz, A. "Toward A Jurisprudence of 'Harm' Prevention," in Pennock, J.R., and Chapman, J.W. (eds.), *The Limits of Law, Nomos*, vol. 15 (New York: Lieber-Atherton, 1974), p. 135.

Donagen, Alan. "Informed Consent in Therapy and Experimentation," *Journal of Medicine and Philosophy* (December, 1977).

Douglas, Jack D. *Creative Deviance and Social Change*, forthcoming.

Drinkwater, C.K. "Officiously to Keep Alive," *Journal of Medical Ethics*, vol. 3 (December, 1977), p. 189.

Dundon, Stanislus J. "Karen Quinlan and the Freedom of the Dying," *Journal of Value Inquiry*, vol. 12 (Winter, 1978), p. 280.

Dworkin, Gerald. "Paternalism," *Monist*, vol. 56, no. 1 (January, 1972).

————. "Autonomy and Behavior Control," *The Hastings Center Report*, vol. 6, no. 1 (1976), pp. 23-28.

Dworkin, Ronald. *Taking Rights Seriously*. Cambridge: Harvard University Press, 1977.

Engelhardt, H. Tristram, Jr., and Spicker, Stuart F. *Philosophy and Medicine—Mental Health: Philosophical Perspectives*. Hingham, MA: D. Reidel, 1977.

Faden, Ruth, and Faden, Alan. "False Belief and Refusal of Medical Treatment," *Journal of Medical Ethics*, vol. 3 (December, 1977), p. 133.

Feinberg, Joel. "Legal Paternalism," *Canadian Journal of Philosophy*, vol. 1, no. 1 (September, 1971), p. 105.

————. *Reason and Responsibility*. Encino, CA: Dickenson, 1975.

————. "The Nature and Value of Rights," in Gorovitz et al., *Moral Problems in Medicine*. Englewood Cliffs, NJ: Prentice-Hall, 1976.

————. "Voluntary Euthanasia and the Inalienable Right to Life," *Philosophy & Public Affairs*, vol. 7 (Winter, 1978), p. 93.

————. "Liberty-Limiting Principles," in Beauchamp, Tom, and Walters, LeRoy, *Contemporary Issues in Bioethics*. Encino, CA: Dickenson, 1978.

————. "Legal Moralism and Freefloating Evils," *Pacific Philosophical Quarterly*, vol. 61 (January/April, 1980), p. 122.

Fotion, N. "Paternalism," *Ethics*, vol. 89 (January, 1979), p. 191.

Gert, Bernard, and Culver, Charles M. "Paternalistic Behavior," *Philosophy & Public Affairs*, vol. 6 (Fall, 1976), p. 45.

————. "The Justification of Paternalism," *Ethics*, vol. 89 (January, 1979), p. 199.

Golding, Martin P. "Is Civil Commitment a Mistake?" in *The Limits of Law, Nomos*, vol. 15 (New York: Lieber-Atherton, 1974), p. 168.

Harris, C. Edwin, Jr. "Paternalism and the Enforcement of Morality," *Southwestern Journal of Philosophy*, vol. 8 (Summer, 1977), p. 85.

Hart, H.L.A. "Are There any Natural Rights?" *Philosophical Review*, vol. 64, no. 2 (1955), p. 175.

Hodson, John D. "The Principle of Paternalism," *American Philosophical Quarterly*, vol. 14, no. 1 (January, 1977), p. 61.

Husak, Douglas N. "Paternalism and Autonomy," *Philosophy & Public Affairs*, vol. 10, no. 1 (Winter, 1981), p. 27.

Kaplan, Leonard V. "The Mad and The Bad: An Inquiry into the Disposition of the Criminally Insane," *Journal of Medicine and Philosophy*, vol. 2, no. 3 (September, 1977), pp. 244-304.

Kenny, Michael. "Patterns of Patronage in Spain," *Anthropological Quarterly*, vol. 33, no. 1 (January, 1960), pp. 14-23.

Kindregan, Charles P. "The Court as Forum for Life and Death Decisions: Reflections on Procedures for Substituted Consent," *Suffolk University Law Review*, vol. 11, no. 4 (Spring, 1977).

Kottrow, M. "When Consent is Unbearable: A Case Report," *Journal of Medicine Ethics*, vol. 4 (June, 1978), p. 78.

Langham, Paul. "Parental Consent: Its Justification and Limitations," *Clinical Research*, vol. 27 (December, 1979), p. 349.

Levine, Andrew. "Foundations of Unfreedom," *Ethics*, vol. 88, no. 2 (January, 1978), p. 162.

Livermore, Joseph, Malmquist, Carl, and Meehl, Paul. "On the Justifications for Civil Commitment," *University of Pennsylvania Law Review*, vol. 117 (November, 1968), p. 75.

Livermore, Joseph, and Meehl, Paul. "The Virtues of M'Naghten," *Minnesota Law Review*, vol. 51 (1967), p. 789.

Lomasky, Loren E. "Medical Progress and National Health Care," *Philosophy & Public Affairs*, vol. 10, no. 1 (Winter, 1981), p. 65.

Lomasky, Loren E., and Detlefsen, Michael. "Medical Paternalism Reconsidered," *Pacific Philosophical Quarterly*, vol. 62, no. 1 (January, 1981), pp. 95-98.

McDonald, Michael F. "Autarchy and Interest," *Australasian Journal of Philosophy*, vol. 56, no. 2 (August, 1978), p. 109.

Michels, Robert. "Commentary on 'Forced Transfer to Custodial Care,'" *Hastings Center Report*, vol. 9 (June, 1979), p. 19.

Mill, John Stuart. *On Liberty*. Edited by Gertrude Himmelfarb. New York: Penguin Books, 1975.

Miller, George. *The Problems of Paternalism*. Ph.D. dissertation, Brown University.

Morris, Herbert. *Freedom and Responsibility: Readings in Philosophy and Law*. Stanford: Stanford University Press, 1961.

————. *On Guilt and Innocence*. Berkeley: University of California Press, 1976.

Murphy, Jeffrie G. "Incompetence and Paternalism," *Archiv für Rechts und Sozialphilosophie*, vol. 60, no. 4 (1974), pp. 465-86.

Pierce, C. "Hart on Paternalism," *Analysis* (1975), pp. 205-7.

Rawls, John. *A Theory of Justice*. Cambridge, MA: Belknap Press of Harvard University Press, 1971.

Reed, T.M., and Johnson, Patricia. "Children's Liberation," *Philosophy*, vol. 55 (1980), p. 263.

Regan, Donald. "Justifications for Paternalism," in *The Limits of Law, Nomos*, vol. 15 (New York: Lieber-Atherton, 1974), p. 189.

Relman, A. "The Saikewicz Decision: A Medical Viewpoint," *American Journal of Law and Medicine*, vol. 4 (1978), p. 236.

————. "A Response to Allen Buchanan's views on decision-making for terminally ill incompetents," letter to editor, *American Journal of Law and Medicine*, vol. 5 (Summer, 1979), pp. 119-23.

Rothman, Marcus et al. *Doing Good*. New York: American Civil Liberties Union, 1978.

Sartorius, Rolf. *Individual Conduct and Social Norms*. Encino, CA: Dickenson, 1975.

————. "The Enforcement of Morality," *Yale Law Journal*, vol. 81, no. 5 (1972), p. 891.

————. "Paternalistic Grounds for Involuntary Civil Commitment: A Utilitarian Perspective," in Brody B.A., and Englehardt, H. Tristram, Jr. (eds.), *Mental Illness: Law and Public Policy*, (Hingham, MA: D. Reidel, 1980), pp. 137-45.

————. "Coercive Suicide Prevention: A Libertarian Perspective," forthcoming in *Suicide and Life-Threatening Behavior: Special Issue on "Suicide and Contemporary Moral Theory:"* 13:3 (1983).

————. "Paternalism and Restrictions on Liberty," in Regan, Tom and VanDeVeer, Donald, eds. *And Justice For All*. (Totowa, NJ: Rowman and Littlefield, 1982).

Scarre, Geoffrey. "Children and Paternalism," *Philosophy*, vol. 55 (1980), p. 117.

Schrag, Francis. "The Child in the Moral Order," *Philosophy*, vol. 52 (1977), p. 167.

Siegler, Mark. "Ethical Problems in Clinical Practice: The Limits of Autonomy," *Hastings Center Report*, vol. 7 (October, 1977), p. 12.

Sieverts, Steven. "Commentary on 'Forced Transfer to Custodial Care,'" *Hastings Center Report*, vol. 9 (June 1979), p. 20.

Struhl, Paula Rothenberg. "Mill's Notion of Social Responsibility," *Journal of the History of Ideas*, vol. 37 (January/March, 1976), p. 155.

Szasz, Thomas. "Hospital Refusal to Release Mental Patient," *Cleveland-Marshall Law Review*, vol. 9 (1960), p. 220.

————. "Civil Liberties and the Mentally Ill," *Cleveland-Marshall Law Review*, vol. 9 (1960), p. 399.

Taylor, Gwenneth. "On Doing What One Wants To Do," *Canadian Journal of Philosophy*, vol. 5 (November, 1975), p. 435.

Ten, C.L. "Mill on Self-Regarding Actions," *Philosophy*, vol. 43 (1968), p. 29.

————. "Self-Regarding Conduct and Utilitarianism," *Australasian Journal of Philosophy*, vol. 55 (August, 1977), p. 105.

————. *Mill On Liberty*. Oxford: Clarendon Press, 1980.

Trivers, R.L. "The Evolution of Reciprocal Altruism," *Quarterly Review of Biology*, vol. 46, no. 4 (1971), pp. 35-57.

VanDeVeer, Donald. "Paternalism and Subsequent Consent," *Canadian Journal of Philosophy*, vol. 9, no. 4 (December, 1979), p. 631.

————. "The Contractual Argument for Withholding Medical Information," *Philosophy & Public Affairs*, vol. 9 (Winter, 1980), pp. 198-205.

Wasby, Stephen L. "Beyond Dershowitz: Limits in Attempting to Secure Change," in *The Limits of Law, Nomos*, vol. 15 (New York: Lieber-Artherton, 1974), p. 159.

Wikler, Daniel. "Persuasion and Coercion for Health: Ethical Issues in Government Efforts to Change Life-Styles," *Millbank Memorial Fund Quarterly/Health and Society*, vol. 56, no. 3 (1978).

————. "Paternalism and the Mildly Retarded," *Philosophy & Public Affairs*, vol. 8, no. 4 (Summer, 1979), p. 377.

Wikler, Daniel, and Green, Michael B. "Brain Death and Personal Identity," *Philosophy & Public Affairs*, vol. 9 (Winter, 1980), pp. 105-33.

Young, Robert. "Autonomy and the 'Inner Self,'" *American Philosophical Quarterly*, vol. 17, no. 1 (January, 1980), p. 35.

Contributors

Dan Brock, Dept. of Philosophy, Brown University, Providence, RI, 02912.

Allen Buchanan, Dept. of Philosophy, University of Arizona, Tucson, AZ, 85721.

Norman Dahl, Dept. of Philosophy, University of Minnesota, Minneapolis, MN, 55455.

Jack Douglas, Dept. of Sociology, University of California, San Diego, La Jolla, CA, 92093.

Gerald Dworkin, Dept. of Philosophy, University of Illinois at Chicago Circle, Chicago, IL, 60680.

Joel Feinberg, Dept. of Philosophy, University of Arizona, Tucson, AZ, 85721.

Hebert Morris, The Law School, University of California-Los Angeles, Los Angeles, CA, 90024.

Donald Regan, The Law School, University of Michigan, Ann Arbor, MI, 48109.

Rolf Sartorius, Dept. of Philosophy, University of Minnesota, Minneapolis, MN, 55455.

Mary Ellen Waithe, Dept. of Philosophy, University of Minnesota, Minneapolis, MN, 55455.

Daniel Wikler, Dept. of Philosophy, University of Wisconsin, Madison, WI, 53706.

Index

Index

Abegglen, James C., 193
Act-utilitarian, 98, 100
Altruism: reciprocal, 175-77, 180, 189; as human nature, 178-80; Christian, 179-80
American Psychiatric Association, 95-97
Amigocracy, 187
Aristotle, 7, 265-66
Autonomy, 38-40, 98-99, 107, 111, 203-5, 237-38, 241, 264, 266

Beardsley, Richard K., 190
Behavior: self-destructive, 42-44, 46-48, 50; paternalistic, 172, 176; altruistic, 176-77; reckless, 246; moral, 265-66
Beidelman, Thomas O., 183-84
Bernard, Saint, 180
Best interest: standard of, for incompetents, 159, 166; of children, 173-75; as motivation for genetic paternalism, 175
Blechertown State Schools, Superintendent of, vs. Saikewicz, 154-65 *passim*
Bloch, Marc, 180
Brain death, 153. *See also* Harvard Criteria, for brain death
Brock, Dan, 261-69
Buchanan, Allen, 106

Cancer patients. *See* Medical paternalism
Carter, Rosemary, 238
Caste system, 184-85
Categorical imperative, Kant's, 267-68
Change of mind, 128-34
Cheating, as exploitation, 223

Child-parent relations, 171-80
Children: medical paternalism in treatment of, 64-65, 67-68, 72-73; best interest of, 139, 173-75; reaction of, to punishment, 144-45
Choice: deliberate, 7; voluntary and involuntary, 8; freedom of, 115-16. *See also* Freedom, of choice
Civil liberties, for the retarded, 83-85, 91-92
Coercion: justification for, 5, 23, 53-54, 99, 114-15; and paternalism, 23-25, 113, 115, 256; of health-behavior-change programs, 52-53; by regulative measures, 55; by the state, 55, 105; within the family, 144; definition of, 201-3; and exploitation, 202-3, 222
"Coercive offers," 208-9
Collective decisions: and paternalism, 108-10; majority and minority rights in, 110
Commitment. *See* Involuntariness
Competence; setting standards of, 85-91; mental, 87-89, 92; physical, 90; conceptions of, 241-42, 263; and paternalism, 241, 242; definition of, 243. *See also* Competent persons; Incompetence
Competent persons: rights of, 154-55, 161-62; medical treatment for, 154-55. *See also* Competence
Conflictful paternalism, 174-75, 185, 193, 196-98
Confucius, 178, 198